MW01252819

Palgrave Macmillan Studies in Banking and Financial Institutions

Series Editor: **Professor Philip Molyneux**

The Palgrave Macmillan Studies in Banking and Financial Institutions are international in orientation and include studies of banking within particular countries or regions, and studies of particular themes such as Corporate Banking, Risk Management, Mergers and Acquisitions, etc. The books' focus is on research and practice, and they include up-to-date and innovative studies on contemporary topics in banking that will have global impact and influence.

Titles include:

Steffen E. Andersen
THE EVOLUTION OF NORDIC FINANCE

Mario Anolli, Elena Beccalli and Tommaso Giordani (*editors*)
RETAIL CREDIT RISK MANAGEMENT

Seth Apati
THE NIGERIAN BANKING SECTOR REFORMS
Power and Politics

Caner Bakir
BANK BEHAVIOUR AND RESILIENCE
The Effect of Structures, Institutions and Agents

Dimitris N. Chorafas
BASEL III, THE DEVIL AND GLOBAL BANKING

Dimitris N. Chorafas
SOVEREIGN DEBT CRISIS
The New Normal and the Newly Poor

Stefano Cosma and Elisabetta Gualandri (*editors*)
THE ITALIAN BANKING SYSTEM
Impact of the Crisis and Future Perspectives

Violaine Cousin
BANKING IN CHINA

Peter Falush and Robert L. Carter OBE
THE BRITISH INSURANCE INDUSTRY SINCE 1900
The Era of Transformation

Juan Fernández de Guevara Radoselovics and José Pastor Monsálvez (*editors*)
CRISIS, RISK AND STABILITY IN FINANCIAL MARKETS

Juan Fernández de Guevara Radoselovics and José Pastor Monsálvez (*editors*)
MODERN BANK BEHAVIOUR

Franco Fiordelisi and Ornella Ricci (*editors*)
BANCASSURANCE IN EUROPE
Past, Present and Future

Franco Fiordelisi, Philip Molyneux and Daniele Previati (*editors*)
NEW ISSUES IN FINANCIAL AND CREDIT MARKETS

Franco Fiordelisi, Philip Molyneux and Daniele Previati (*editors*)
NEW ISSUES IN FINANCIAL INSTITUTIONS MANAGEMENT

Kim Hawtrey
AFFORDABLE HOUSING FINANCE

Jill M. Hendrickson
FINANCIAL CRISIS
The United States in the Early Twenty-First Century

Jill M. Hendrickson
REGULATION AND INSTABILITY IN U.S. COMMERCIAL BANKING
A History of Crises

Paola Leone and Gianfranco A. Vento (*editors*)
CREDIT GUARANTEE INSTITUTIONS AND SME FINANCE

The full list of titles available is on the website:
www.palgrave.com/finance/sbfi.asp

Palgrave Macmillan Studies in Banking and Financial Institutions
Series Standing Order ISBN 978–1–4039–4872–4

You can receive future titles in this series as they are published by placing a standing order. Please contact your bookseller or, in case of difficulty, write to us at the address below with your name and address, the title of the series and the ISBN quoted above.

Customer Services Department, Macmillan Distribution Ltd, Houndmills, Basingstoke, Hampshire RG21 6XS, England

---

International Debt
Economic, Financial, Monetary, Political and Regulatory Aspects

Edited by

Otto Hieronymi
Professor of International Relations, Webster University, Geneva, Switzerland

and

Constantine A. Stephanou
Professor and Director, European Center of Economic and Financial Law,
Panteion University, Athens, Greece

First published 2013 by
PALGRAVE MACMILLAN

Palgrave Macmillan in the UK is an imprint of Macmillan Publishers Limited,
registered in England, company number 785998, of Houndmills, Basingstoke,
Hampshire RG21 6XS.

Palgrave Macmillan in the US is a division of St Martin's Press LLC,
175 Fifth Avenue, New York, NY 10010.

Palgrave Macmillan is the global academic imprint of the above companies
and has companies and representatives throughout the world.

Palgrave® and Macmillan® are registered trademarks in the United States,
the United Kingdom, Europe and other countries.

ISBN 978–1–137–03056–6

This book is printed on paper suitable for recycling and made from fully
managed and sustained forest sources. Logging, pulping and manufacturing
processes are expected to conform to the environmental regulations of the
country of origin.

A catalogue record for this book is available from the British Library.

A catalog record for this book is available from the Library of Congress.

10   9   8   7   6   5   4   3   2   1
22 21 20 19 18 17 16 15 14 13

Printed and bound in the United States of America

Contents

List of Figures and Tables

Figures

Tables

Notes on Contributors

André Baladi is a Geneva-based international financial expert and a long-standing corporate governance-driven shareholder value advocate. He is co-founder, former co-chairman and an active member of the International Corporate Governance Network (ICGN), which assembles investors' holding equity assets of US$15 trillion. He was awarded the 2001 ICGN Appreciation Certificate for Outstanding Services and the 2007 ICGN Award for Excellence in Corporate Governance. He is a Member of the Consultative Team of the Intergovernmental Working Group of Experts on International Standards of Accounting and Reporting (ISAR) of UNCTAD in Geneva, of the OECD Consultative Corporate Governance Group in Paris, and of the International Advisory Board of the NYSE Euronext Stock Exchange. He chairs Geneva's International Arbitration Organization, which founded the CARICI Arbitration Court. He is also Honorary Participant of the Council of Institutional Investors (CII) in Washington, DC. After majoring in economics at Geneva's Graduate Institute of International Studies, he managed for 15 years several Nestlé projects in France, Italy, Japan, South East Asia, Switzerland and the USA. He was then associated for five years, as an international M&A expert, with the corporate finance group of the consortium set up by Banque Nationale de Paris (BNP), Smith Barney and Société Financière Européenne (founded by Algemene Bank Nederland, Banca Nationale del Lavoro, Bank of America, Banque Bruxelles Lambert, BNP, Barclays, Dresdner, Sumitomo Bank and UBS). In 1981, he founded his international financial advisory firm in Geneva. He has also developed an algorithm for enhancing index-tracking equity funds with corporate governance inputs.

Péter Ákos Bod is Professor of Economics and Head of Department, Corvinus University (of Economics), Budapest. He was Minister of Industry from 1990 to 1991, President of the Hungarian National Bank from 1991 to 1995 and Director of European Bank for Reconstruction and Development (London) from 1995 to 1997. His numerous publications on monetary and economic policy issues include a textbook on monetary economics, books and articles on the domestic and international dimension of monetary and economic integration, deregulation and institution building, monetary and exchange rate policy, banking and finance in Central Eastern Europe.

Christos Gortsos is Associate Professor of International Economic Law at the Panteion University of Athens and visiting Professor at the Europa Institute of the University of Saarland. He teaches international, European and Hellenic monetary and financial law, as well as economic analysis of law, fields in which he has also published extensively, in Greece and internationally. Since 2010 he has been a member of the Management Committee of the European Center of Economic and Financial Law (ECEFIL). Apart from his academic career, Professor Gortsos, a member of the Athens Bar been the Secretary General of the Hellenic Association, has since July 2000 Bank Association. He studied law, economics and finance at the Universities of Athens and Zürich, at the Wharton Business School (University of Pennsylvania), and at the Graduate Institute of International Studies of the University of Geneva, where he was awarded his Ph.D. on international banking regulation (1996). During the period 1996–8 he worked as a research assistant at the International Center for Monetary and Banking Studies of the University of Geneva. Since 2005 he has been a member of the Monetary Committee of the International Law Association (MoComILA).

Nikolas G. Haritakis is Assistant Professor in Economics in the University of Athens. In the past, he has served as Secretary General on Privatization of the Ministry of Industry, Energy and Technology and lately as CEO of the Greek Tourism Development S.A. He has also served as an advisor at many private companies. He holds a Ph.D. and an MA in Economics from Clark University, Massachusetts. Besides his academic position he is also Vice Chairman and CEO of TANEO, the first and only "fund of funds" in Greece, with Euro 150 million under management, which fosters the competitive development of venture capital funds oriented toward supporting SMEs. Through the 11 TANEO funds, more than Euro 280 million has been directed to Greek SMEs.

Otto Hieronymi is Professor of International Relations at Webster University, Geneva and the former Head of its International Relations Program (1995–2006). He earned his doctorate in International Economics and Politics at the Graduate Institute of International Studies in Geneva. Prior to joining Webster, he was Senior Economist, responsible for economic analysis and forecasting, at Battelle's Geneva Research Center from 1970 to the end of 1994 and an International Economist with Morgan Guaranty Trust in New York between 1966 and 1970. Between 1990 and 1994, while still on the Battelle staff, he was Personal Economic Advisor to the Hungarian Prime Minister Jozsef Antall and Senior International Economic Advisor to the Hungarian Government. He was the Secretary of the Hungarian Bank Reform Commission and a Founding Member of the Board of Directors, Hungarian Investment and Development Bank. He was also in charge of developing the Antall Government's concept of "loan consolidation" (dealing with the banks' bad debts) and the initial Hungarian program of bank privatization. International monetary and financial issues have been among his principal areas of research and forecasting work since the 1960s. He has published extensively on economic, monetary, political and humanitarian issues. His publications include *Globalization and the Reform of the International Banking* *and Monetary System* (ed. 2009), "Agenda for a New Monetary Reform" (1998), *The Spirit of Geneva in a Globalized World* (ed. 2007), "Rebuilding the International Monetary Order: The Responsibility of Europe, Japan and the United States" (2009), "The Responsibilities of Business and Governments in the Age of Global Finance" (2008), *Hungarian Economic, Financial and Monetary Policies: Proposals for a Coherent Approach* (1990), *Global Challenges, the Atlantic Community and the Outlook for International Order* (ed. 2004), *Wilhelm Röpke: The Relevance of his Teaching Today—Globalization and the Social Market Economy* (ed. 2002), *The New Economic Nationalism* (ed. 1980) and *Renewing the Western Community: The Challenge for the US, Europe and Japan* (will be published in 2013).

Daniel Kaeser was from 1992 to 1997 Permanent Representative of Switzerland to the International Monetary Fund in Washington, DC and an Executive Director of the IMF. He obtained degrees in economics and law at the University of Lausanne. From 1977 to 1992 he was Deputy Director of the Swiss Federal Finance Administration in charge of the Treasury and of Economic and Monetary Affairs. Before 1977 he occupied other senior positions in the Ministry of Finance as well as in the Swiss National Bank and the Swiss Permanent Mission to the OECD. His publications include *La Longue Marche Vers Bretton Woods* [The Long Road Towards Bretton Woods].

Michael Sakbani has been Adjunct Professor of Finance and Economics at Webster University, Geneva since 1981. He obtained his Ph.D. at New York University. Before joining UNCTAD in Geneva he was Senior Economist with the Federal Reserve Bank of New York. At UNCTAD he was responsible for many years for monetary and financial cooperation, and Director of the Division of Cooperation among Developing Countries. One of his principal areas of interest is monetary policy and the international monetary system. His numerous publications include *A Re-Examination of the Architecture of the International Economic System in a Global Setting: Issues and Proposals* (2006), *The Global Economic System: Asymmetries and Inconsistencies* (2005), *The Euro on Schedule: Analysis of its European and International Implications* (1998) and *International Monetary Reform: Issues and Proposals* (1985).

Constantine A. Stephanou is Professor and Director of ECEFIL, Panteion University, Athens, Greece. He studied law and international relations at the University of Geneva and the Graduate Institute of International Studies in Geneva. In 1980 he earned a Doctoral Degree in Law with distinction from the Aristotle University of Thessaloniki. Since 1999 he has been Full Professor at the Department of International and European Studies of Panteion University, holder of the first Jean Monnet Chair in European Law and Institutions. From 1999 to 2007 he served as Director of the Master's Program in International and European Studies in the same department and from 2007 to 2009 as Director of the Institute of International Relations, affiliated with Panteion University. He is the founding Director of the ECEFIL, established in 2010. He has also served as visiting professor/teaching associate at French universities (Nice, Grenoble, Bordeaux, Paris II), as well as the Universities of Utah and Madrid (Alcala de Henares), the Hebrew University of Jerusalem and currently at the European Institute of the University of Geneva (IEUG). He has participated as external referee for the assessment of numerous theses in foreign universities and for the appointment of a Professor of European Law at EUI, Florence. As a practicing lawyer he has served with SIFIDA in Geneva (1973–4) and the Bank of Crete (1975–81). He has also served as Vice-President of the Commercial Bank of Greece (1996–2000) and since 2001 in various positions at the Hellenic Banks Association (HBA), and is currently a member of its legal council. He has also acted as advisor to the Greek Ministry of Foreign Affairs during the four Greek presidencies of the Council and the five Intergovernmental Conferences (IGCs) for the revision of the founding treaties. His main research areas include economic regulation, European Union governance and policies.

Alexandre J. Vautravers has been Professor of International Relations and the Head of the International Relations Department, Migration and Refugees Program, Webster University, Geneva since 2006. He is also a Lieutenant-Colonel in the Swiss Army, Editor-in-Chief of the *Revue militaire suisse* and President of the Research Center on Security and Development in the Middle East, Geneva. His academic degrees include a Ph.D. in Social and Economic Sciences, University of Geneva, and in Contemporary History, University of Lyon 2. He has a wide-ranging teaching and research experience in Switzerland and abroad, including China. He is the author of numerous publications, including *Le futur de la Guerre. La technologie est-elle une solution?* (ed. 2004) *Identity and Conflict* (ed. 2010) *Humanitarian Space* (ed. 2010) *Children at Risk* (ed. 2009).

Acknowledgments

The idea of the present book was developed in a discussion between the two editors with the objective of developing cooperation in the area of international monetary and financial issues between the International Relations Program of Webster University in Geneva and the European Center of Economic and Financial Law of Panteion University, Athens. This discussion in June 2011 in Geneva led to the joint organization of a conference on the international debt issue in November 2011 held at the Webster University Campus in Bellevue, Geneva and to the preparation of the manuscript of the present volume. From the start we aimed to bring together a group of academic and other experts to discuss the current situation and the outlook of the international debt issue from multiple perspectives and to address the economic, monetary, financial, political and regulatory aspects of this complex topic. The concept of this book and the conference was a follow-up to a volume, published by Palgrave Macmillan, in 2009 on *Globalization and the Reform of the International Banking and Monetary System*. Thus, we are particularly pleased that this volume on *International Debt* is also coming out under the Palgrave imprint and as part of the Palgrave Macmillan Studies in Banking and Financial Institutions. We take this opportunity to express our deep appreciation for the quality of the cooperation with the staff of Palgrave Macmillan. Their encouragement and unique professional qualifications have made this project possible.

The credit for the success of the November 2011 conference, as of numerous similar events organized on the Webster campus, belongs to a significant extent to the Student Organizing Committee. Among the members of this committee the following students should be mentioned—without forgetting or belittling the contribution of those who remain unnamed here—Antonia Chapman Nyaho, Aline Duperrex, Yvita Fox, Shea Holland, Allison Ralston, Vasiliki Sarafi, Mikaelah Stark, Johan Verbeek Wolthuys and Delina Wejdeby. Among the Webster staff and faculty the help and support of Hilary Hofmans, Liz Torrente, Maureen Gisiger, Ron Daniel and Robert Spencer should be mentioned. In Greece special thanks are due for the work of Sophia Ziakou and for the support of the Hellenic Bank Association. We also would like to thank our fellow speakers and authors for their work and support throughout the planning and realization of both the conference and this book. The editors are also grateful to Catherine Hieronymi for contributing to the editing of the manuscript. We also would like to thank Webster University for its financial contribution to the organization of the November 2011 conference and to some of the research involved in the preparation of this book. Finally, we would like to thank the staff of the numerous organizations—in particular the OECD and the IMF—who have been helpful in providing access to their statistics and other resources.

Otto Hieronymi, Geneva
Constantine A. Stephanou, Athens

Introduction

Otto Hieronymi and Constantine A. Stephanou

The issue of debt has moved to the center of economic, political and social concern throughout the OECD countries. Finding a solution to the debt problem has become a major challenge for the richest and most highly developed economies in the world. The trends that have led to the current debt crisis started well before the outbreak of the so-called subprime crisis in 2008. The worldwide monetary crisis amplified these trends both in large and small economies, leading to the outbreak of a "sovereign-debt crisis" in early 2010. While Greece has become the symbol or the catalyst of the "debt crisis," it is far from an isolated case, and it would be an error to say that Greece or earlier Iceland or Ireland have been exceptions in an otherwise healthy financial and fiscal environment, and the primary challenge was to keep these countries from "contaminating" the sound fiscal and economic position of their European and world-wide partners. The positive feature of the period since the outbreak of the debt crisis has been the determination of the Members of the European Union and in particular of the Euro Zone not to let the current crisis destroy the extraordinary achievements of 60 years of political and economic integration in Europe. Whatever the merits or shortcomings of specific measures proposed or adopted such as the "fiscal pact" or the "banking union" there is no question that a breakddown of solidarity between "strong" and "weak" countries in the European Union would be a severe blow to the stability of Europe but also of the Western Community as a whole and of international order in general. So far there seems to have been sufficient political determinatto to prevent this from happening. That this must not be allowed to happen in the future either is the central message of this book.

The debt crisis: Stage II of the crisis of the international monetary and banking system

The global systemic crisis that began in the American economy with the collapse of Lehman Brothers did not really come to an end in ensuing years. It is true that the massive and more or less coordinated action of the central

1

banks and the national treasuries helped prevent a financial meltdown and the collapse of the leading international banks and other financial institutions. It also kept the recession from turning into a true depression on the model of the 1930s. The "debt crisis" has been a seamless follow-up, a Stage II of the global crisis of the international monetary and financial system. A conclusion of the present book is that unless a series of major problems are successfully addressed, including the legacy of Stages I and II as well as the long-term shortcomings of the international monetary system, the outbreak of Stages III and IV of the crisis of the international monetary and financial system may become increasingly imminent.

In the last 20 years, the world economy has become the victim of global finance. It seemed that inflation, the scourge of earlier times, had been conquered. Only prices of financial and other assets rose systematically. The combination of low consumer price inflation and high asset price inflation appeared to be the miracle recipe, the straight road to current prosperity and future wealth. Financial engineers, investment bankers and fund managers as well as central bankers seemed to deserve all the praise that they could get. With both nominal and "real" interest rates relatively low—and credit easily available to all comers—who could have blamed the fiscal authorities, who began also to believe that cutting taxes was the surest way for reducing or even eliminating future government deficits and debt?

To talk about a (traditional) bubble was and is dangerous since it tends to underestimate the complexity of the phenomenon and conjures the possibility of relatively simple even if drastic solutions. A widely read and quoted recent book on the debt problem by two outstanding authors conveys the impression that the current crisis is not that different from sovereign debt crises in the past.[1] The differences, however, are as important as the similarities, even when one considers the relatively recent international financial crises of the 1980s and 1990s. These differences are due to the sheer magnitude of the current crises and the importance that global finance has gained even when compared with its role during the last decade of the twentieth century. In a globalized world, finance has become by far the most global factor at the same time that it became an increasingly decisive element in all economic decisions at the expense of the so-called real economy.

The origins of the financial crisis of this decade are rooted in the nature and workings of the current international monetary system (or "non-system," as it is often described). This had been the case also with virtually all the other major international debt crises since the 1970s. Rather surprisingly, this dimension of the "subprime crisis" received little attention. The most frequently mentioned issue regarding the reform of the International Monetary Fund (IMF), also in the context of the deliberations of the G20 and other international bodies, was the idea of redistributing the voting rights within the Fund in favor of the large "emerging" countries. Since the outbreak of Stage II of the crisis, the issue of the international monetary system has been receiving more and more attention even if most of time still only implicitly. By late 2011 and early 2012 there had been a growing amalgam both by the "markets" and the national and international authorities between the "debt issue" and the working, and the very survival of, the Euro zone itself. What had been designed 20 years ago, and implemented a decade later, to counter at least at the European level, the volatility and irrationality of post-Bretton Woods international monetary relations has become the biggest scapegoat for the outbreak of the debt crisis and the alleged inability of the richest countries in the world to deal with it and its consequences.

Once again, even more than after September 2008, there has been growing agitation, calls for action and reform, summit and expert meetings, official declarations and rating downgrades, mobilization of unprecedented amounts of money, negotiations and threats to stop the vicious circle in which the loss of confidence in governments is amplified through the troubles of the Euro zone as an institution. At the same time, the growing distrust of the "markets" has been depressing economic activity and increasing the burden of the debt and further undermining the Euro zone as a common area of stability and growth.

Through the countless declarations, new agreements and commitments, it is difficult to distinguish the risks and threats, the priorities, and those who bear one or another part of the burden. Repeatedly, the victory statements tend to sound as if they were explanations for why the previous measures did not work or were insufficient.

Is the principal objective to avoid a further splitting of the international bond market and the ultimate threat of a chain reaction of defaults on sovereign debt? This would have incalculable consequences for the European and world economy, for households, and young and old people whether working, unemployed or retired.[2]

International debt has become a highly explosive short-term issue. This short-term dimension has become all the more important as one of the most visible consequences of globalization and in particular of "global finance" has been the drastic shortening of the time horizon of economic and financial decisions throughout the world. The world and especially the financial markets function in "real time" only—with little if any depth of the past or perspective on the future. However, much of the short-term preoccupation is due to concern about the long-term consequences of the current situation and trends for the future and to doubts about the ability and/or willingness to reverse these trends and avoid a devastating impact on the general economic situation and the income and savings—the essential determinants of living standards—of the vast majority of the population of the OECD countries.

Multiple dimensions of the debt issue

Complexity and interdependence are among the hallmarks of the present globalized world economy. The international debt issue has multiple dimensions: economic, financial, monetary, political and regulatory. These various aspects and their ramifications are discussed in greater or lesser detail by the authors of the present volume. While all debt in one form or another has a "national origin and identity," the international dimension is currently more immediately evident to all observers and decisions makers than in any other previous crisis, including the 1930s and the 1970s. Thus, this book addresses primarily the international aspect of the debt issue, without, however, ignoring the national dimension.

The spreading of global finance up until 2007–8—and the apparent success in finding solutions for the major crises that erupted at regular intervals since the 1970s—stifled much of the debate about the reforms and safeguards necessary for a more balanced system. Thus, as in most political, economic and social crises, the "intellectual sins of omissions and commissions" are as important as the "objective" or "material" factors. Many of the issues that have to be addressed urgently today, in the midst of some of the most turbulent conditions in recent economic history, have been systematically struck from the agenda at national and international levels, at least since the 1980s, in the political debate, among corporate leaders and much of the academic community.

The issue of adequacy of the regulatory and supervisory frameworks

There seems to be new and broad agreement that markets cannot properly function without rules and authorities to enforce them. When it comes to specifics, however, the agreement becomes much more elusive. In the highly integrated European economy, the EU context seems to be a more appropriate framework than the individual member states for regulating financial markets. Yet, the EU legislative process has been slow in responding to the financial crisis. At the time of writing, the amendment of the capital adequacy directive and of the regulation on credit rating agencies were still pending; the directives on alternative investment funds and derivatives had reached the final stage of the legislative process. Nevertheless, important concessions had been made to allow for the adoption of these texts; thus, for example, in the proposed amendment of the credit rating agencies regulation, the conflict of interests provision had been removed. On the positive side, however, it should be noted that the bailout instruments had been adopted in record time, although market players challenged their effectiveness.

Who pays for the crisis?

The competition between States and markets since the beginning of the financial crisis raises the question of who pays for the crisis. In past crises, irresponsible creditors and investors were punished for their behavior but the crisis did not affect taxpayers. This is not true any more. The United States appears to have overcome the worst consequences of the subprime crisis, and the EU will most likely overcome the sovereign debt crisis without a meltdown or an EU-wide "domino-collapse." Taxpayers, however, are clearly the losers, in the sense that governments are obliged to intervene by creating public debt in order to rescue the victims of market behavior and safeguard the system. Also there has been a sharp decline in the wealth (value of assets) of households on both sides of the Atlantic—although it has not reached the extent of the asset deflation experienced in Japan in the early 1990s.

In the EU context, fiscal discipline has been a *quid pro quo* for fiscal solidarity. The way it was conceived, however, may backfire by eliminating the growth prospects of the Euro zone economies. There is therefore a pressing need for a new "grand bargain" in the Euro zone that could generate positive spill-over effects on the world economy.

Overview of the main themes of the book

Chapter 1 discusses the close link between the debt crisis and the characteristics of the current international monetary system. The main role of the international monetary order is to prevent distortions in the "real economy" (in trade flows, employment and investments) and monetary and financial excesses, and the transmission and amplification of monetary shocks across the world economy. The fragmented international monetary system that has prevailed since the 1970s has been a source of instability, rather than a balancing influence, and a major source of the successive international financial crises of the last 40 years. This was also true for the crisis that broke into the open in 2008 and which brought the world to the brink of a global financial meltdown, and the "debt crisis," which followed seamlessly on the "subprime crisis" and which threatens to stifle the growth of the most advanced economies in the world for decades to come. The main conclusion of *Chapter 1* is that without a concerted effort by the United States, the European Union and Japan, the leading liberal market economies in the world, to create a stable rule-based international monetary system, the search for a long-term solution to the debt problem is bound to fail. Also, the future monetary and financial crises that are looming on the horizon will be all the more difficult to manage.

In *Chapter 2*, Michael Sakbani, Professor of Finance and Economics at Webster University and a Former Director at UNCTAD, addresses the issue of the "dual debt" problem in Europe and the United States, that is, the link between the current account deficit and the fiscal deficit that led to the need to borrow from domestic and external sources. In both the United States and Europe fiscal deficits are the result of cyclical slowdowns—slow recovery from the recession brought about by the "subprime crisis"—and structural factors. Both Europe and the United States have to address these factors in the right order: dealing with the recession first and then correcting the structural causes of the deficits. Otherwise there is a major risk of a lasting deceleration of the world's leading economies and further aggravation of the debt situation. In the case of the United States, it is important to assure adequate government revenues through higher tax income in order to finance programs in education research and other areas that are essential for securing the long-term dynamics of the American economy. In Europe, it is important to avoid a process in which the debt problems of relatively small countries lead to a downward cycle and threaten the entire "European project."

Chapter 3 deals with the question of "monetary sovereignty." Its author, Péter Akos Bod, Professor of Economics and Former Governor of the Hungarian National Bank, puts forward the thesis that under globalization, in modern, open economies, monetary sovereignty has become largely an "illusion." This is the case not only for relatively small economies, but also for the largest economy in the world—the United States. He argues that "globalization is, in fact, *institutionalized economic openness*: policy options of nation states are shaped and constrained by international rules." During crises, however, rules tend to change and lead to greater diversity and "trial and error" approaches by national authorities to deal with the specific situation of their economies. The greater fragility of so-called peripheral countries becomes evident, partly because of the greater distrust of markets and international organizations, such as the IMF. Thus it is not certain that the hasty recourse to an IMF loan in 2008 with its attendant rigid conditionality eased or aggravated Hungary's economic, financial and social crisis.

Constantine A. Stephanou, Professor and Director, European Center of Economic and Financial Law, Panteion University, evaluates in *Chapter 4* the European responses to the sovereign debt crisis and the attempts to build "fire walls." He argues that the crisis constitutes a "novelty" because it involves members of a monetary union. The Maastricht consensus on Economic and Monetary Union was difficult to implement from the beginning, with France and Germany exceeding the deficit target and profligate borrowers such as Greece being immune from market pressure until very late in time. The Euro zone responded to the crisis by setting up bailout mechanisms and enhancing fiscal discipline. The common feature of the bailout mechanisms, inspired by IMF practice, was policy conditionality. Its expediency and effectiveness have been questioned. In the case of Greece it was soon realized that policy conditionality was not sufficient to ensure debt sustainability. The idea of combining financial assistance with debt restructuring through private sector involvement (PSI) became a crucial element of the second Greek bailout and the permanent bailout mechanism, the ESM, designed to replace the provisional mechanisms. The author assesses the basic premises of bailouts, the moral hazard argument and the risks of contagion. He then argues that, since the beginning of the crisis, fiscal solidarity was related to fiscal discipline—initially in the context of the financial support programs and subsequently in the context of the revision of SGP and the Fiscal Compact Treaty. Finally, Stephanou reviews the implementation and enforcement mechanisms, while also examining possible amendments to the treaties that would allow greater emphasis on growth. Stephanou argues that although the crisis has been contained by means of bailout mechanisms that reflect the Euro area's acceptance of the solidarity principle, the determining factors in the setting up of these mechanisms were self-preservation and the risks of contagion. Moreover, private sector involvement in debt restructuring reflected a new approach to state insolvency, involving a delicate balancing of moral hazard and risks of contagion. The bailout programs, as well as the ECB's role as a "hidden" lender of last resort, departed from the Maastricht consensus. Among the various formulas and ideas that were recently submitted for the purpose of alleviating the sovereign debt problem, perhaps the most feasible would be the issuance of the so-called project bonds, which are foreseen in Europe's 2020 Strategy. Stephanou also considers that fiscal sovereignty, in the sense of decision-making autonomy, has been curtailed to a point where national budgets now have to be approved by the Commission prior to being approved by national parliaments, thereby putting at risk the political consensus on participation in the Euro area. He also observes that although weak economies benefit the most from international regimes, strong economies may benefit too. In the European context, Germany chose to participate in the Euro area but there are signs of German ambivalence on the issue. Under German guidance, however, fiscal discipline was drastically enhanced by means of the revised SGP and the Fiscal Compact Treaty. This policy orientation has been challenged, to the extent that debt sustainability, especially in the peripheral members of the Euro area, very much depends on these countries' growth prospects. The adoption of a clear commitment to growth, entailing treaty changes and additional funding capabilities, is gradually emerging as a policy priority. Stephanou concludes that the sovereign debt crisis has demonstrated that European integration is a market-driven and reactive, rather than proactive, process. Moreover, the bailout and austerity programs have raised sensitive redistribution issues, which make a new "grand bargain" necessary for the survival of the Euro area.

Daniel Kaeser, formerly chief official in charge of International Financial and Monetary Issues at the Swiss Ministry of Finance, presents in *Chapter 5* the "Case for a Bankruptcy Procedure for Sovereign States." In this context, he reminds readers of the focused discussions that took place within the IMF on a sovereign bankruptcy procedure and the proposals that had been prepared between 2001 and 2004 to deal with this issue in the light of extensive historical experience. Unfortunately, the members of the IMF decided not to follow the recommendations that had been prepared by senior officials within the Fund. The author introduces the subject by noting the fundamental differences between a private enterprise and a sovereign borrower. He reviews the achievements of the Paris and London Clubs of private and sovereign creditors respectively and draws the attention to the problem of "rogue creditors" or "free riders." The author then looks at the means to give legal force to a sovereign bankruptcy procedure and relevant implementation issues. Kaeser argues that the mechanisms of the Paris and London Clubs of creditors for dealing with sovereign debt problems have shown their limits, and it is now time to adopt a sovereign bankruptcy procedure at the intergovernmental level, based on an amendment of the Articles of Agreement of the IMF or the World Bank, or a new international agreement. The agency entrusted with its implementation would have to cooperate with existing bodies, like the Paris and the London Clubs. He concludes that the deregulating mood, which prevailed before the financial crisis, and led to it, has lost momentum.

The subject of *Chapter 6*, the "impact of the Euro zone fiscal crisis on the Greek banking sector and the measures adopted to preserve its stability" is at the heart of the debate on the European and world-wide debt issue. Its author, Professor Christos Gortsos, is Deputy Director of the European Center of Economic and Financial Law and Secretary General of the Greek Bankers' Association. He provides a systematic review and in-depth analysis of the impact of the two phases of the crisis that began in 2008—the financial crisis of 2008–9 and the fiscal crisis of 2010–12—on the Greek banking system and of the evolution of the regulatory framework at the European and the Greek national level. The author points out that during the first phase of the crisis the Greek banking system was relatively less affected because of its lesser exposure to toxic assets. During the second phase—the fiscal crisis—Greek banks, given their large holdings of Greek government bonds, were much more directly affected through the "private sector involvement" (PSI) in the international efforts to deal with the Greek sovereign debt issue. Gortsos observes that during the global financial crisis the Greek banking sector remained healthy, adequately capitalized and highly profitable. It was negatively affected by the Euro zone fiscal crisis when all the channels for the transmission of the problems from the government to the banking sector were activated. Thus, the downgrading of Greek sovereign debt was followed by the downgrading of Greek banks, a significant flight of capital and banks' inability to finance themselves from the interbank market. He then assesses the measures that are envisaged in order to safeguard the solvency and liquidity of Greek banks and underlines the need to prepare the adjustment to the new capital adequacy directive. The author identifies three main challenges for the Greek banking system: (1) maintaining solvency and a recapitalization preferably from the private sector; (2) maintaining liquidity and regaining independence from European Central Bank and Bank of Greece financing; and (3) providing credit to the Greek economy to stimulate growth. The author concludes: "In the medium term, however, the Greek banking sector will also have to adapt to the European regulatory 'tsunami' underway ... it can be rightly argued that the current business model of EU credit institutions is in the process of a radical review."

In *Chapter 7*, Professor Nikolas G. Haritakis discusses the complexity of the measures to be adopted to restore financial stability "under extreme conditions," using the example of the Greek sovereign debt. The Greek economy has experienced for a number of years a classic "dual deficit" pattern: large government fiscal deficits and balance-of-payments current account deficits. The accumulated fiscal deficits led to the excessive debt problem creating a solvency issue for the Greek state. This structural problem appeared to be manageable while sufficient liquidity was available given the financial conditions in Europe and in the world economy. The Greek debt crisis was the result of the worsening of the fiscal situation simultaneously with the international financial crisis. Haritakis raises some essential questions before analyzing the Greek case and focusing on remedies; he asks, for example, whether we should remove the risk-free sovereign tag in relation to reserves or counterparty risks and, further on, what does actually risk-free mean in a monetary union framework. He notes that by early 2008 the financial crisis forced all players to make a real paradigm shift. By 2010 woes had mounted for most Euro zone countries, and sovereign debt among them was no longer considered a risk-free asset. The Greek situation and the international rescue efforts have shown the difficulties encountered when dealing with large deficit and debt accumulation at a time of global crisis, and the lesson has been that monetary and fiscal rescue present different challenges.

In *Chapter 8* André Baladi, a leading expert on corporate governance issues, discusses the importance of corporate governance principles in times of crises and the relevance of these principles for the broader context of "national financial management." Promoting good corporate governance aims at protecting savers and investors. The history of the corporate governance movement shows the need for a broad debate among stakeholders at the international level on key issues and common objectives and standards. The author raises the question whether, in light of the lessons of the current fiscal and debt crisis, the work of the national economic administrations should not mirror the constraints of corporate management.

In *Chapter 9*, on "International Public Debt as a Factor of Globalization," Professor Alexander Vautravers, Director of the International Relations Program of Webster University Geneva, places the international debt problem in a historical perspective. In the past, unilateral solutions by sovereign borrowers or opaque agreements with their creditors dealt more or less effectively with sovereign debt problems. Under the current conditions of financial globalization, these problems are difficult to contain and the proposed solutions to overcome them actually lead to debt creation. Vautravers underlines the growing dependency of the United States on emerging countries and examines alternative scenarios for dealing in particular with the US debt problem. Vautravers notes that today the powerful and wealthy countries seem to be the developing nations and that "the poor are paying for the rich." Reducing debt can only be achieved through economic growth and positive balance of payments. Although, as is the case with many historians, the author does not sound unduly optimistic, he concludes that in a world of growing economic and financial interdependence it is in the interests of both debtors and creditors to help manage the relationship and avoid a new, more profound crisis.

In *Chapter 10*, the volume editors, Otto Hieronymi and Constantine Stephanou, present a brief conclusion, drawing on the analysis and principal arguments of the authors of the different chapters. The following three key points should be mentioned here. The first and most important conclusion is that despite the magnitude and complexity of the short- and long-term debt problem, the OECD economies have the resources and are sufficiently strong and resilient to overcome the current crisis. The second point is that there is no either/or solution. The way out of the debt crisis requires both strong economic growth and fiscal correction and discipline. The third concluding point is that there is continued need for close cooperation and innovation among the leading OECD countries both in managing the crisis and in bringing about a more fundamental reform of the international monetary and financial system.

Notes

1. Carmen M. Reinhart and Kenneth S. Rogoff (2009) *This Time is Different: Eight Centuries of Financial Folly*, Princeton: Princeton University Press.
2. In the America of the early 1960s the memory of the Great Crash and of the Great Depression was still extremely vivid in middle-class families, many of whom, despite the prosperous Truman and Eisenhower years, could not fully overcome the material losses and the emotional wounds that they had suffered 30 years earlier.

1

The International Monetary System and the Debt Issue

Otto Hieronymi

Introduction

The crisis of "global finance" that broke into the open in 2008 has not been resolved so far. There is a broad consensus that it is in the interest of all countries to find a solution that will prevent a drastic erosion of the value of financial assets—people's savings—and will allow a return to sustained growth. This solution will have to be based on reliable theoretical concepts and up-to-date data and analyses. Above all, it will need political cooperation, innovation and reforms. A key task in this context is the rebuilding of a stable international monetary system.

The present chapter is divided into six sections:

1. The debt crisis as "Stage II" of the crisis of the international monetary and financial order
2. The international monetary system as a "balancing" or a "destabilizing" factor
3. The "40-year crisis," a period of recurring international debt crises
4. The current debt crisis and the crisis of the Euro zone
5. The role of economic theories and societal models and the future of the model of the "social market economy"
6. The necessary conditions for finding "the way out."

1.1 The debt crisis: "Stage II" of the crisis of the international monetary and financial order

The circumstances, the mood in the world economy, the financial, monetary, economic and political uncertainty, and the fear of a global collapse in the autumn of 2008 eerily resemble the situation prevailing in the spring of 2012. The "international debt crisis," which began to capture the attention of both markets and policy makers in the spring of 2010, represents "Stage II" of the crisis of the international monetary and financial system that broke

11

fully into the open with the demise of the investment bank Lehman Brothers in September 2008. The extent and suddenness of Stage I—the so-called sub-prime crisis—had caught the markets, the authorities and the general public off-guard and induced widespread fear of a meltdown of the international banking system with unprecedented consequences for the world economy. Stage II—the debt crisis—should have been less "unexpected." Its emergence had some common causes with the "subprime crisis" (which obviously was also a "debt crisis"). At the same time, it was and remains the logical sequence and consequence of (1) the subprime crisis itself and (2) the pano-ply of emergency measures adopted to avoid a free fall of economic activity and the unraveling of the entire "global finance" system.

At the time of writing, it seems that the crisis of the international mon-etary and financial system is far from over. For one, despite the important and courageous efforts undertaken, and the remarkable degree of coopera-tion between national and international authorities and the private sector, no fully reliable and acceptable solution of the short- and the long-term debt problem has been found so far. It is also clear that a real threat of "Stage III" and "Stage IV" of the global crisis is looming on the horizon.

These new potential stages can best be highlighted with two sets of questions:

1. How and when will the main Organization of Economic Cooperation and Development (OECD) economies return to "real interest rates"? Will or can there be a "soft-landing"? What will be the consequences for sav-ers, borrowers and for economic activity? Who will be the winners and the losers? Will there be equitable burden sharing?
2. What happens if the financial and monetary crisis and in particular the debt crisis and the solutions being adopted to deal with it lead to a signif-icant and lasting reduction of the growth rate of the OECD economies? How will this affect the individual countries (the "weak ones" and the "strong ones"), and what will be the impact on the already excessive gap between a well-off minority and a struggling majority? Will the loss of momentum in the "real economy" aggravate the financial and monetary crisis and jeopardize the solution of the debt problem?

Stages III and IV are not part of this chapter nor of the book as a whole. They are mentioned here essentially because they will have to be dealt with sooner or later if the threat of "Stage III" and "Stage IV" is to be avoided. One of the factors responsible for the gravity of the "debt crisis" was the "short-termist view" that prevailed before and after the Lehman Brothers explosion. A second reason, closely connected to the first one, is that a principal cause of the "subprime crisis," the "debt crisis" and the fragility of the global financial system is the absence of a properly working international monetary order. This is the topic of the present chapter.

The first and most important issue here—and in fact in the entire book—is the extent to which "international monetary systems" are a "balancing factor" or a "factor of destabilization." The common view is that they can be both, depending on the international monetary system and national monetary orders and policies. The conclusion of the authors of this book is that the current fragmented international monetary system is responsible for the present and previous financial and debt crises, and the main source of concern about the future. The connection between the debt problem and the defects of the international monetary system can be illustrated by the facts that (1) the United States, the largest and richest economy, is facing considerable difficulty to reduce its large balance-of-payments deficits and halt its growing external indebtedness; and (2) the debt problems of Greece, one of the smaller member countries of the European Union and the Euro zone, are threatening the very survival of the Monetary Union and the European project itself.

This book is a follow-up to an earlier volume also published by Palgrave Macmillan in 2009, under the title *Globalization and the Reform of the International Banking and Monetary System*. Unfortunately, some of the conclusions and warnings that were raised in that earlier book seem to have been proved correct. The announcement of Webster University's November 2011 conference (which led to the preparation of the present volume) stated:

> One of the conclusions of the 2008 Webster conference and of the 2009 book was that the crisis of global finance threatens to become the crisis of globalization itself. It was also clear that correcting the root causes of the 2007 and 2008 crisis and overcoming its consequences will be a long-term process that will require both political consensus and national and international solidarity. Four years after the outbreak of the "subprime" mortgage debt crisis and three years after the collapse of the investment bank Lehman Brothers, the debt issue remains today at the center of national and international political and economic preoccupations. The massive injections into the world economy of central bank liquidity and of government funds helped prevent a collapse of the international banking system, but as expected, they have aggravated rather than eased the issue of excessive indebtedness.

1.1.1   Why "Stage II" of the crisis?

The following related groups of factors have been responsible for the nature and the magnitude of the "second wave" of the crisis: (1) structural shortcomings of the Euro zone system; (2) reckless policies in some of the member countries and policy divergences throughout the Union; and (3) the exorbitant cost of dealing with the impact of the "first wave" of the crisis and in particular the solutions chosen to prevent bankruptcies in the banking and financial system. Considering the magnitude of these challenges and

Table 1.1 Government debt of the OECD countries, 2007–13: General government gross financial liabilities as a percentage of GDP

	2006	2007	2008	2009	2010	2011	2012	2013
Australia	15.5	14.4	13.7	19.4	23.6	26.8	27.9	27.9
Austria	66.4	63.4	68.4	74.4	78.2	79.9	81.9	83.2
Belgium	91.6	88.0	93.0	100.0	100.2	100.3	101.5	101.0
Canada	70.3	66.5	71.1	83.4	85.1	87.8	92.8	96.6
Czech Republic	32.6	31.0	34.4	41.1	44.5	47.1	48.7	49.7
Denmark	41.2	34.3	42.6	52.4	55.6	56.1	58.0	58.2
Estonia	8.0	7.3	8.5	12.7	12.5	12.3	13.1	13.0
Finland	45.6	41.4	40.4	51.6	57.6	61.2	65.5	68.5
France	71.2	73.0	79.3	90.8	95.2	98.6	102.4	104.1
Germany	69.8	65.6	69.7	77.4	87.1	86.9	87.3	86.4
Greece	116.9	115.0	118.1	133.5	149.1	165.1	181.2	183.9
Hungary	72.4	73.4	77.0	86.7	86.9	89.8	90.8	91.5
Iceland	57.4	53.3	102.1	119.8	125.0	127.3	127.4	126.2
Ireland	29.2	28.7	49.6	71.1	98.5	112.6	118.8	122.4
Israel	84.7	78.1	77.0	79.4	76.0	74.6	73.8	72.4
Italy	116.9	112.1	114.7	127.1	126.1	127.7	128.1	126.6
Japan	172.1	167.0	174.1	194.1	200.0	211.7	219.1	226.8
Korea	28.5	28.7	30.4	33.5	34.6	35.5	36.3	36.8
Luxembourg	11.5	11.3	18.3	18.0	24.5	28.2	30.9	34.6
Netherlands	54.5	51.5	64.8	67.4	70.6	72.5	75.3	76.9
New Zealand	26.6	25.7	28.9	34.4	37.8	44.1	47.6	50.2
Norway	59.4	57.4	55.0	49.1	49.7	56.5	51.3	48.6
Poland	55.2	51.7	54.4	58.5	62.4	64.9	65.4	64.7
Portugal	77.6	75.4	80.7	93.3	103.6	111.9	121.9	123.7
Slovak Republic	34.1	32.9	31.8	40.0	44.8	49.8	53.4	55.3
Slovenia	33.8	30.7	30.4	44.3	48.4	53.7	58.1	61.0
Spain	46.2	42.3	47.7	62.9	67.1	74.1	77.2	79.0
Sweden	53.9	49.3	49.6	52.0	49.1	46.2	45.3	43.1
Switzerland	50.2	46.8	43.6	43.7	42.6	42.0	41.2	40.7
United Kingdom	46.0	47.2	57.4	72.4	82.2	90.0	97.2	102.3
United States	60.9	62.1	71.4	85.0	94.2	97.6	103.6	108.5
Euro area (14 countries)	–	–	–	–	–	–	–	–
OECD–Total	74.6	73.3	79.7	91.4	97.9	101.6	105.7	108.4

Last updated: 5 December 2011.
Source: OECD Economic Outlook No. 90, OECD Economic Outlook: Statistics and Projections (database).

the risks involved in both action and inaction, European governments and institutions have done quite well in stemming the crisis and finding common solutions and compromises under great time pressure. Compared with the brinkmanship that has prevailed in the United States—especially on the side of the Republicans—since September 2008 in fiscal, monetary and regulatory respects, the performance of European leaders and institutions has been quite remarkable.

In contrast to the financial and monetary crises of the 1980s and the 1990s (the post-oil shock international debt crisis, the second Mexican debt crisis, the Asian and Russian financial crises), the current crisis is centered on the OECD economies: the United States, the small and large Western European countries (and the Euro area as a whole) (Table 1.1). The countries directly concerned also include Japan, where, faced with a debt to GDP ratio of 200%, the authorities, the banks and the corporations remain clueless in trying to bring their economy back to the path of its impressive past performance. The crisis also reached Switzerland where the authorities had to resort to extraordinary measures to ward off speculative currency inflows and the resulting overvaluation of the Swiss currency.

1.1.2   Principal conclusions

The conclusions of this chapter[1] can be summed up in the following points:

The breakup of the Monetary Union has to be prevented: Preventing the breakup of the Monetary Union has to remain the first priority not only of the European Union but also of the other leading OECD countries—the United States and Japan (Table 1.2). The rules of the Euro zone are far from perfect. In particular, the lack of explicit rights and duties of the European Central Bank (ECB) to show concern for the external value of the common currency and for the level of economic activity represent serious shortcomings in the initial design and in the actual record of the ECB. However, without the Euro zone the international monetary and financial crisis would have been even more difficult to manage than was the case in the period since 2008. The *de facto* exclusion of the country that looks like the "weakest link" at present (which happens to be Greece) could sooner or later have a domino effect. Moreover, the negative impact on the so-called strong economies (in particular Germany) would be much larger than expected by those—within the European Union and outside—who are not only predicting but also advocating the end of the "experiment with the common currency." The international consequences could be comparable to the aftermath of the Camp David decisions of August 1971 or following the collapse of the Austrian Creditanstalt in the early 1930s.

Table 1.2 Government deficit of the OECD countries, 2006–13: Net lending/net borrowing as a percentage of GDP, surplus (+), deficit (–)

	2006	2007	2008	2009	2010	2011	2012	2013
Australia	2.1	2.1	0.5	–4.1	–4.8	–3.3	–1.5	–0.3
Austria	–1.7	–1.0	–1.0	–4.1	–4.4	–3.4	–3.2	–3.1
Belgium	0.1	–0.3	–1.3	–5.9	–4.2	–3.5	–3.2	–2.2
Canada	1.6	1.4	–0.4	–4.9	–5.6	–5.0	–4.1	–3.0
Czech Republic	–2.4	–0.7	–2.2	–5.8	–4.8	–3.7	–3.4	–3.4
Denmark	5.0	4.8	3.3	–2.8	–2.8	–3.7	–5.1	–3.0
Estonia	2.5	2.4	–2.9	–2.0	0.3	0.1	–1.9	0.0
Finland	4.0	5.3	4.2	–2.7	–2.8	–2.0	–1.4	–1.1
France	–2.4	–2.7	–3.3	–7.6	–7.1	–5.7	–4.5	–3.0
Germany	–1.7	0.2	–0.1	–3.2	–4.3	–1.2	–1.1	–0.6
Greece	–6.0	–6.8	–9.9	–15.8	–10.8	–9.0	–7.0	–5.3
Hungary	–9.4	–5.1	–3.7	–4.5	–4.3	4.0	–3.4	–3.3
Iceland	6.3	5.4	–13.5	–10.0	–10.1	–5.4	–3.3	–1.4
Ireland	2.9	0.1	–7.3	–14.2	–31.3	–10.3	–8.7	–7.6
Israel	–2.5	–1.5	–3.8	–6.4	–5.0	–4.0	–3.8	–3.5
Italy	–3.4	–1.6	–2.7	–5.4	–4.5	–3.6	–1.6	–0.1
Japan	–1.6	–2.4	–2.2	–8.7	–7.8	–8.9	–8.9	–9.5
Korea	3.9	4.7	3.0	–1.1	0.0	0.8	1.3	1.9
Luxembourg	1.4	3.7	3.0	–0.9	–1.1	–1.2	–2.0	–1.8
Netherlands	0.5	0.2	0.5	–5.5	–5.0	–4.2	–3.2	–2.8
New Zealand	5.3	4.5	0.4	–2.6	–4.0	–8.0	–4.0	–3.3
Norway	18.4	17.5	19.1	10.7	10.6	12.5	11.5	10.7
Poland	–3.6	–1.9	–3.7	–7.4	–7.9	–5.4	–2.9	–2.0
Portugal	–4.1	–3.2	–3.7	–10.2	–9.8	–5.9	–4.5	–3.0
Slovak Republic	–3.2	–1.8	–2.1	–8.0	–7.7	–5.9	–4.6	–3.5
Slovenia	–1.4	0.0	–1.9	–6.1	–5.8	–5.3	–4.5	–3.3
Spain	2.4	1.9	–4.5	–11.2	–9.3	–6.2	–4.4	–3.0
Sweden	2.2	3.6	2.2	–0.9	–0.1	0.1	0.0	0.7
Switzerland	0.8	1.7	2.3	1.0	0.6	0.8	0.5	0.6
United Kingdom	–2.7	–2.8	–5.0	–11.0	–10.4	–9.4	–8.7	–7.3
United States	–2.2	–2.9	–6.6	–11.6	–10.7	–10.0	–9.3	–8.3
Euro area (14 countries)	–	–	–	–	–	–	–	–
OECD–Total	–1.2	–1.3	–3.4	–8.3	–7.7	–6.6	–5.9	–5.1

Last updated: 5 December 2011.
Source: OECD Economic Outlook No. 90, OECD Economic Outlook: Statistics and Projections (database).

Table 1.3 Real gross domestic product of the OECD countries, 2006–13: Percentage change over previous period

	2006	2007	2008	2009	2010	2011	2012	2013
Australia	2.5	4.7	2.4	1.5	2.5	1.8	4.0	3.2
Austria	3.6	3.7	1.2	–3.7	2.4	3.2	0.6	1.8
Belgium	2.7	2.8	0.9	–2.7	2.3	2.0	0.5	1.6
Canada	2.8	2.2	0.7	–2.8	3.2	2.2	1.9	2.5
Chile	4.9	4.9	3.2	–1.5	5.1	6.6	4.0	4.7
Czech Republic	7.0	5.7	3.1	–4.7	2.7	2.1	1.6	3.0
Denmark	3.4	1.6	–1.1	–5.2	1.7	1.1	0.7	1.4
Estonia	10.1	7.5	–3.7	–14.3	2.3	8.0	3.2	4.4
Finland	4.4	5.3	1.0	–8.2	3.6	3.0	1.4	2.0
France	2.7	2.2	–0.2	–2.6	1.4	1.6	0.3	1.4
Germany	3.9	3.4	0.8	–5.1	3.6	3.0	0.6	1.9
Greece	5.5	3.0	–0.2	–3.2	–3.5	–6.1	–3.0	0.5
Hungary	3.9	0.1	0.9	–6.8	1.3	1.5	–0.6	1.1
Iceland	4.7	6.0	1.3	–6.7	–4.0	2.9	2.4	2.4
Ireland	5.3	5.2	–3.0	–7.0	–0.4	1.2	1.0	2.4
Israel	5.6	5.5	4.0	0.8	4.8	4.7	2.9	3.9
Italy	2.2	1.7	–1.2	–5.1	1.5	0.7	–0.5	0.5
Japan	2.0	2.4	–1.2	–6.3	4.1	–0.3	2.0	1.6
Korea	5.2	5.1	2.3	0.3	6.2	3.7	3.8	4.3
Luxembourg	5.0	6.6	0.8	–5.3	2.7	2.0	0.4	2.2
Mexico	5.1	3.2	1.2	–6.2	5.4	4.0	3.3	3.6
Netherlands	3.5	3.9	1.8	–3.5	1.6	1.4	0.3	1.5
New Zealand	2.0	3.4	–0.7	0.1	2.3	1.4	2.5	3.0
Norway	2.3	2.7	0.7	–1.7	0.3	1.5	2.0	2.7
Poland	6.2	6.8	5.0	1.6	3.8	4.2	2.5	2.5
Portugal	1.4	2.4	0.0	–2.5	1.4	–1.6	–3.2	0.5
Slovak Republic	8.3	10.5	5.9	–4.9	4.2	3.0	1.8	3.6
Slovenia	5.8	6.9	3.6	–8.0	1.4	1.0	0.3	1.8
Spain	4.1	3.5	0.9	–3.7	–0.1	0.7	0.3	1.3
Sweden	4.6	3.4	–0.8	–5.1	5.4	4.1	1.3	2.3
Switzerland	3.6	3.6	2.1	–1.9	2.7	1.8	0.8	1.9
Turkey	6.9	4.7	0.7	–4.8	9.0	7.4	3.0	4.5
United Kingdom	2.6	3.5	–1.1	–4.4	1.8	0.9	0.5	1.8
United States	2.7	1.9	–0.3	–3.5	3.0	1.7	2.0	2.5
Euro area (14 countries)	–	–	–	–	–	–	–	–
OECD–Total	3.2	2.8	0.1	–3.8	3.1	1.9	1.6	2.3

Last updated: 5 December 2011.
Source: OECD Economic Outlook No. 90, OECD Economic Outlook: Statistics and Projections (database).

Absence of international monetary order: The so-called subprime crisis that threatened a global financial meltdown was not just an overblown, unexpected bubble due to real-estate mortgage debt manipulation and speculation. It was likely to happen and should have been expected. It was the latest and most dangerous in the long series of avoidable crises that the world has known since August 1971—that is, ever since a common or global international monetary order has been lacking.

Monetary nationalism vs financial and economic globalization: There has been a dichotomy between financial and economic liberalization, marketization and globalization, on the one hand, and the prevailing monetary nationalism and refusal of central banks and governments to recognize the importance of a stable, flexible and rule-based international monetary order, on the other. This and the refusal to assume the responsibility to design, negotiate and implement such an order would remain the main obstacles to rebuilding an equitable and liberal financial system.

Short-term agitation and the unbalanced reform-agenda: Although there was massive response to the "subprime" and "Lehman Brothers" crises, this response and the "reform agenda" were dangerously unbalanced. They were reactive and marked by short-termism. They focused almost exclusively on "banks" (according to their definition of "banks") and neglected domestic as well as international monetary issues. Especially there was no attention paid to the reform of the international monetary system and scant attention to the consequences of massive short-term rescue spending and liquidity creation. Today's "debt crisis" and "Euro zone crisis" are reminders of yesterday's short-sightedness.

The need for close cooperation between the US, Europe and Japan on the reform of the international monetary system: In order to manage both Stage II (the debt crisis) and the possible Stages III and IV mentioned previously, a closer cooperation between the three pillars of the liberal international economic system—the United States, Europe and Japan—is indispensable not only in short-term crisis management, but also on the important longer-term task of creating a rule-based international monetary system (Table 1.3). The architects of this new system should learn from the shortcomings both of the gold exchange system and of the instability and excesses of the "non-system" that has prevailed for the last 40 years.[2]

1.2   The international monetary system: Balancing or destabilizing?

1.2.1   The functions of an international monetary system

One of the simplest definitions of an international monetary system is that it is the virtual space where transactions in different currencies are carried out by public and private actors, as well as the national and international, private and public set of national and international rules and institutions that shape, regulate and facilitate these transactions. The international monetary system can also be defined as the way different national monetary systems interact.

As usual, an international system or order is something different from the simple sum of national systems. The functions of an international monetary system include the following:

- Similarly to a domestic currency and monetary system, it provides the tools and framework for the stable, efficient and equitable development of the national economy (to stimulate "commerce and industry" to quote the old expression, also used by Kant). The primary goal of an international monetary system has to be to allow international economic cooperation (trade and investment) and integration on a stable basis.
- It should help preserve the value of legitimately earned and saved assets and to avoid "unjustified or unearned" gains at the expense of "legitimate" asset holders (speculation for the sake of speculative gains) as well as through inflation or deflation.
- It acts as a transmission mechanism or a barrier to monetary or real sector shocks and crises, from and to national economies.
- It ought to help achieve equilibrium in the external accounts of national economies with the rest of the world.[3]

There are a number of questions that have kept recurring during the last 100 years with respect to the functions of international monetary order:

- Should the international monetary system promote or hamper the integration and development of the world economy as a whole and of the individual national economies? And how should this happen?
- Should the international monetary system help isolate and protect the national economies from outside developments (the issue of national policy autonomy)? And how should it do so?
- Should the international monetary system be protected and isolated from shocks emanating from national economies? And how should this be done?

National currencies and the quality of money

The classic definition of the tripartite role of money is: means of exchange, measure of value and store of value. "Good money" fulfills all three tasks in a "satisfactory" manner. What is satisfactory, however, depends on economic conditions and structures, and political preferences as well as prevailing economic and monetary theories. A central issue in the debate in monetary theory is whether money also has other important economic and social functions, such as affecting the level of employment and unemployment, investments and productivity, and thus long-term growth (or stagnation) as well as the distribution of income and as such the social cohesion or tensions in a political community. Thus, there are arguments about the hierarchy of the objectives of money and monetary policy with regard to a national currency. But there is broad agreement that national currencies serve primarily national goals. According to this view, "monetary nationalism" is neither good nor bad, it is a given.[4]

The monetary history (and much of political and economic history), at least of the last 100 years, has been marked by the competition of currencies, between strong and weak, stable and unstable national moneys, trustworthy and untrustworthy currencies. The quality of money depends on a combination of various actors and factors. The actors include: central banks, governments and "markets" or "market participants." The factors include: rules, policies, possibly even commodities, such as gold, as well as the economic and political environment—within and outside a national economy. The quality of money, of a national currency, is a reflection of the quality of an economy. There is broad agreement about this statement, and probably there is much truth in it as well.

For most of history, or at least economic history, "national currencies"—the coins or paper money issued by the absolute monopolist, that is, the king or the government—coexisted with a globally valued commodity that could equally serve as money, most frequently gold. Even under the so-called classic gold standard, which many people consider as the best international monetary system that the world has ever known, national currencies thrived and played a useful role. Today, the monetary role of gold has almost completely disappeared, and national or "regional" currencies have all lost any links with physical commodities of relatively short supply.

The denationalization of money?

The quality of money is traditionally measured in terms of its stability or loss of domestic value (price index) and stability or depreciation of its external value (exchange rate). To the question "who is responsible for the quality of money (good or bad)?" the traditional answer is: "the government." This led Friedrich Hayek—a life-long advocate of monetary stability and an early critic of flexible exchange rates—to suggest, as a desperate reaction to the monetary disorders in the 1970s and 1980s, the "denationalization of money," that is, the abolition of the government monopoly of money.[5] Hayek, who was known for his systematic distrust of governments and often showed less critical judgment when it came to the behavior of banks and other corporations and to the functioning of markets, argued that private markets would be better custodians of monetary stability than governments and central banks. Unfortunately, the experience with the *de facto* partial "denationalization" of money and the "free banking" that actually occurred since the 1980s showed that Hayek's optimism on this account had been largely unjustified.

1.2.2   Today's fragmented international monetary system

The "world" has never known a truly universal, common monetary system. This was true for the age of the "classic gold standard," as well as for the two decades before the "collapse of the Bretton Woods system." At a conference organized at Battelle-Geneva in 1978 on the "New Economic Nationalism," Robert Mundell said that we and our contemporaries have seen more "international monetary systems" in our lifetime than there had been in existence in the preceding history of mankind:

> Since 1971, we have moved through three or four different international economic systems. In eight years we have had more experience with international monetary systems than Alfred Marshall had in his whole lifetime. ... In the twentieth century we have had such confusion in the monetary system that everybody seems to be a monetary expert. In fact we are faced with so many monetary experts and so many explanations for each problem that it is difficult to judge who is right and who is wrong. We have champions of both fixed and flexible exchange rates, advocates of the gold standard, the dollar standard and the SDR standards; monetarists and fiscalists, optimum currency area specialists, integrationists and so on. Those of us who grew up on the gold exchange standard, when the world was stable, used to be able to call ourselves monetary experts; today the public might be forgiven for doubting whether we are monetary experts anymore.[6]

In the almost 35 years since that meeting, Professor Mundell must have added to his list a large number of new variations of international monetary systems.

Since the 1970s the concept of an "international monetary system" has undergone profound changes:

1. Passage from a system of fixed (but adjustable) exchange rates to a wide range of exchange-rate systems, from permanently fixed (common currency) to different degrees of floating and flexibility.
2. Passage of different degrees of convertibility according to the nature of the underlying transactions, and in particular a fairly wide range of controls on short-term capital transactions to full convertibility, and the abolition of all distinctions according to the nature of transactions.
3. From a fairly stable exchange-rate structure to wide, frequent and erratic fluctuations in exchange rates, with virtually no connection to relative prices and current account surpluses and deficits, and with overshooting above and below theoretical "equilibrium exchange rates."
4. An enormous growth of the volume of cross-border transactions in the same currency and between currencies.

5. Instead of reducing the need for reserves, despite the elimination of the official reserve role of gold, there has been an expansion of the volume of international reserves held primarily in a small number of currencies.

A characteristic of the present situation is the absence of common rules and in many respects the complete absence of rules. The current fragmented situation represents a unique situation in the long history of money and finance. In today's world we have, for the first time ever, truly "global finance"—in fact, "global finance" is the single most important dimension of our globalized economy. At the same time, in contrast to the globalization of financial markets, there are three major and contrasting international regimes in the international arena (and countless "sub-regimes").

1. The first is the one centered on the US dollar and American policy makers. Professed lack of interest in the external value of the dollar (prohibition by law to worry about the exchange rate of the dollar) and *de facto* lack of interest in the balance of payments and consequences of the size of American international indebtedness.
2. The second is the "Euro zone." Abolition of the exchange rate among the member countries, combined with a legal prohibition to think, talk or do something about the exchange rate of the Euro.
3. The third is the one that prevails between the United States and the Euro zone and the other "major players" in the world economy. The two most important to be mentioned here are Japan and China.

1.2.3   The role of the international monetary system in a globalized economy

Today, there is considerable confusion about the very nature of the international monetary system, about the objectives and desirable features and the functioning of the international monetary system. This confusion exists at the level of theory and the theoretical debate, among policy makers (including central bankers) and among bankers and corporate leaders. This is also true for the high officials and of the expert staff of the leading international monetary institutions: the International Monetary Fund (IMF) and the Bank of International Settlements (BIS).

The role of international monetary order is similar to that of domestic or national monetary order. Yet, since the 1970s there has been a growing contrast, on the one hand, between the increasingly fragmented nature of the international monetary system (in an understatement, qualified as a "non-system" among others by Professor Charles Wyplosz) and, on the other hand, the emergence and dominant position of "global finance" and the increasing globalization of trade in goods and services.

Some of the traditional key issues and controversies include:

- The freedom and conditions of exchanging currencies into other currencies
- The right or the duty of national authorities (government, central banks) to set conditions or to intervene on the currency market
- The use of certain currencies to denominate international transactions
- The use of certain assets as "international reserves" (gold or national or common currencies)
- The conditions of price formation
- The stability or instability of exchange rates.

Who is in charge?

Who is in charge, who is the driver when it comes to "international monetary systems"? Essentially we can distinguish three main actors: (1) governments, (2) central banks and (3) markets. International organizations like the IMF and the BIS are essentially auxiliaries of the first (IMF) or the second (BIS). Under the various systems one or two may be the dominant actors, with the second and third usually silent partners.

1.2.4   A shift in roles—an increasingly "market-driven system"

Major crises tend to lead to a shift of roles. Thus, for example, the collapse or the destruction of Bretton Woods can rightly be blamed on the inflexibility and inability to cooperate effectively of the Western governments and central banks. Thus, following August 1971, the international monetary system(s) became increasingly "market-dominated." Central banks withdrew to "domestic monetary policy" and governments were discharged of all responsibilities ("there is no more balance of payments under globalization") and were even forbidden to care or acknowledge that exchange rates could matter. Today, of course, we see the consequences of an all-market-driven international monetary system and in particular what it has done to asset price distortions, international relative prices and competitive positions. Also, the two essential features of a domestic and international monetary system—two apparently irreconcilable features—stability, transparency and predictability, on the one hand, and flexibility and absence of constraining rules, on the other, are present to varying degrees in the different models of international monetary systems that we have known.

The current exchange-rate regimes

The IMF's *Annual Report on Exchange Arrangements and Exchange Restrictions 2010* shows the complex system of "exchange rate regimes and monetary policy frameworks." The report presents the IMF "members' exchange rate arrangements against alternative monetary policy frameworks in order to highlight the role of the exchange rate in a broad economic policy (perspective) and illustrate that different exchange-rate regimes can be consistent with similar monetary frameworks." The categories of "monetary frameworks" distinguished by the IMF are: (1) exchange rate anchor, (2) monetary aggregate target and (3) inflation-targeting framework.[7] Interestingly, the IMF did not find among the member countries a "balance-of-payments targeting" monetary framework. According to this report the membership of the Fund can be divided into categories according to their exchange-rate arrangements:[8]

Hard peg	13.2%
Soft peg	50.8%
Floating	36.0%

In fact these unweighted percentages underestimate the share of floating and free floating in particular as the United States, the Euro zone and Japan all list their exchange-rate regimes as freely floating.

1.2.5   The objectives of the post-war international monetary system ("Bretton Woods")

The objective of the architects[9] of the post-war international monetary system was to build a system that would help avoid the kind of breakdown of the international monetary order that occurred during the 1930s and its consequences. The "Bretton Woods" system was based on the acceptance and respect by national governments of certain common well-defined rules. The system was built around the US dollar, the currency of the strongest and largest economy. The rules were strict for both the United States and for the other economies. They differed in some respects but in fact they were (or at least seemed to be) stricter for the United States than for the other countries. International bank lending and other forms of short-term capital flows were viewed as a source of potential problems rather than as an effective mechanism for the movement of savings from countries where capital was abundant to countries where it was scarce.

The following features of the international monetary system devised at Bretton Woods should be mentioned here:

- Price and exchange-rate stability were key objectives of the system. They were meant to be mutually reinforcing. Exchange-rate changes were acceptable only as exceptional measures and not as regular policy instruments.
- Each country was to aim at balance-of-payments equilibrium, that is, current-account plus long-term capital movements.
- Official international reserves (gold and convertible currencies) were destined to deal with short-term balance-of-payments deficits.
- The role of the IMF was threefold: (1) monitor the balance-of-payments situation of the member countries, (2) provide short-term loans of

reserves as a complement to a country's reserves in case of deficits and (3) monitor the domestic policies of the members to assure the preventing respectively the correcting of balance-of-payments deficits.

- Currency convertibility meant first "current-account convertibility," to be complemented by "long-term capital convertibility." Short-term private capital movements were to remain under control and discouraged. (For the United States convertibility meant the obligation to exchange dollars—the key currency—against dollars at a fixed price on request by foreign central banks.)
- The principal rule concerning the "surplus countries" was the so-called scarce-currency clause, which permitted the introduction of trade restrictions *vis-à-vis* a country whose currency became "scarce," that is, one that was consistently running large balance-of-payments surpluses.

The principal variable was the "current-account balance" of all the countries that were part of the system, followed by the "par value" of the national currency expressed in terms of gold, but in fact in terms of the US dollar. The theoretical objective was a "balanced" current account—or a current account in "equilibrium" for all countries. Economic policies—monetary, fiscal and wage and price policies—in each country were to aim at achieving a balanced current account, while maintaining a liberal external trade position (no quantitative trade restrictions and exchange controls). The objective of a "current-account equilibrium" was viewed in an asymmetrical perspective. The problems were caused by the deficits, and more specifically by the lack of discipline, the inflationary or reckless fiscal, monetary or wage policies of the deficit countries. The "return" to balance, thus, was seen as first and foremost the task of the deficit countries.

Balance-of-payments surpluses (the mirror image of the deficits) were the result of the "virtuous" or non-inflationary policies of the surplus countries and the carelessness of the deficit countries. Balance-of-payments surpluses were truly or allegedly unwanted by the surplus countries and in particular by their monetary authorities (and especially by the German Bundesbank) because they were seen as a major threat of "imported inflation." At the same time, throughout the years and decades since the German monetary reform in 1948, they have consistently been more concerned by the (rare) threat of a current-account deficit than by the substantial current account surpluses achieved by Germany, before and since the creation of the Euro. For the German authorities, the general public and business leaders the current-account surplus remains a key indicator of the "health of the German economy."

Optimum currency areas or a fragmented international system?

The "Bretton Woods system" became fully operational only at the end of 1958, when "regional discrimination" of the members of the OEEC countries was finally terminated in favor of the IMF's convertibility clause.[10]

Were the war-torn European countries in the late 1940s an "optimum currency area"? Has this been the case since the temporary trade and payments discrimination against the United States gave way to the more permanent and much more far-reaching economic integration of Europe?

The first "regional" (temporary) international monetary system was the European Payments Union created during the Marshall Plan period. It ceased its operations with the adoption at the end of 1958 by all its important members (in particular France) of the current-account convertibility obligations of the IMF Articles of Agreement.

The differences in "balance-of-payments performance"—deficits vs surpluses—among its members turned out to be as important as the differences between the European countries and the United States. In fact, the European Payments Union (EPU) was based on a misunderstanding (though a fortunate one). This was the confusion between a "resource shortage" and a "means of payments" shortage (i.e., the alleged "dollar shortage").

Professor Robert Mundell was awarded the Nobel Prize in economics primarily in recognition of his contribution to the theory of "optimum currency areas." The concept of "optimum currency areas" has had a major impact on the thinking of both academic economists and policy makers. Mundell himself, however, moved on from the narrow interpretation of his original theory. He became not only an early advocate of a common currency in Europe but has been also a consistent and vocal critic of the system of unstable exchange rates and the absence of a global or universal international monetary order worthy of its name.

1.2.6   Why did Bretton Woods fail?[11]

It is true that the Bretton Woods system was far from perfect. At the same time the so-called reform debate of the 1960s showed a broad range of views about the strengths and weaknesses of the system and of proposals to reform or replace the Bretton Woods rules. These ranged from a return to a pure gold standard to free floating of exchange rates and the complete replacement of the US dollar by Special Drawing Rights (SDR) for official international reserve holdings.[12]

It was also evident that beyond the basic architecture it also required extensive cooperation and consultation among central banks and national treasury officials.[13] Some people considered the need for extensive policy cooperation as one of the shortcomings of the system, while others saw this as one of the most useful features. The end of Bretton Woods was brought about by the inherent shortcomings of the system, "tensions in the real economy" (including commodity price developments), and the policies of the principal industrialized countries and their lack of willingness to cooperate on international monetary matters. The opposition among the leading Western countries was between "soft" and "hard" currency countries, the "rigorous" and the "lax," and also the "deficit" and the "surplus" countries.

The debate was usually defined in terms of current-account balances and domestic and export price competitiveness.

There is still an open debate about whether the collapse of the fixed-exchange rate system or the "par-value system" was the result of (1) inevitable structural and material factors, (2) policy errors respectively policy conflicts, (3) commodity price inflation, or (4) the growth of international capital movements and exchange-rate speculation. Probably all these factors played a role. It is also certain that once "Bretton Woods" collapsed or was destroyed there was a lack of sufficient common political will, not to restore the system as it had existed before August 1971, but to try to rebuild an international monetary system that would have included the best features of Bretton Wood while attempting to correct its shortcomings.

Pressures on the par-value system came from a number of directions:

- The growing pressure (both on the demand and the supply side) for freer international capital movements was probably the most important factor. Switzerland was virtually the only country that allowed full convertibility for its residents, but capital inflows were also subject to some control.
- The development of the eurodollar market contributed to the pressure for liberalizing banking regulations.
- Differences in economic policies and in particular the consequences of US fiscal policies under both the Johnson and Nixon Administrations. The simultaneous fiscal burden of the "Great Society" programs and of the Vietnam War was a key factor responsible for the loss of confidence in the dollar.[14]
- The slow adjustment in exchange rates (especially upward adjustments).
- The sensation of loss of control by both deficit and surplus countries.

The Bretton Woods system was considered imperfect, rightly or wrongly, both by "strong currency countries" and "weak currency countries"—thus floating was espoused with enthusiasm both by surplus and deficit countries. However, when currency speculation threatened to destroy economic and political integration in Europe, a single currency was introduced (no flexibility possible). This in turn became increasingly difficult to manage when the ECB (and the European governments) paid insufficient attention to the exchange rate of the Euro or the level of economic activity and price and wage developments in various parts of the European Union.

1.2.7 Fixed vs flexible exchange rates

The objective of "fixed exchange rates," at the heart of the original IMF order, was to secure both domestic and international price and monetary and balance-of-payments stability. A central objective of the system, which allowed for only limited upward and downward fluctuations around the official par values (similar to the "gold points" under the gold standard), was to discourage currency speculation that would lead to inflation or deflation—and to protectionism and recession. Upward or downward adjustments in exchange rates were supposed to be made—with prior consultation with the IMF—only as a last resort, in the case of "fundamental balance-of-payments disequilibria."[15] The main burden rested once more primarily on the deficit countries. Devaluations would generally result in a deterioration of the countries' terms of trade. At the same time, currency devaluations were to be accompanied by monetary and fiscal restrictions in order not to lose the competitive advantage gained at the price level and not to "liberate resources" for exports.

According to the German Government in 1964:

> Fixed exchange rates are an indispensable element in a world committed to integration; with a system of flexible rates the existing readiness to cooperate and integrate might be destroyed at the first appearance of serious difficulties since flexible rates would offer such an easy opportunity for isolated action.[16]

The main reservation about the so-called gold-exchange standard was that allegedly it did not allow sufficient national autonomy for domestic policies (anti-inflationary or expansionary) and was an imperfect system to correct major balance-of-payments disequilibria. Opponents of flexible exchange rates argued that they were an expression, just like trade protectionism, of economic nationalism. This line of thought had been developed by Hayek as early as 1939,[17] and was unwittingly confirmed by the late Harry Johnson, a fervent advocate of flexible exchange rates:

> The fundamental arguments for flexible exchange rates is that they would allow countries autonomy with respect to their use of monetary, fiscal and other policy instruments. ... The argument for flexible exchange rates can be put more strongly still: flexible exchange rates are essential to the preservation of national autonomy and independence consistent with efficient organization and development of the world economy.[18]

Yet, the system of floating exchange rates and the growing volume of short-term financial movements proved to be much less effective in eliminating balance-of-payments imbalances and ultimately greatly reduced national policy autonomy. In the same context, there were sharp fluctuations in bilateral exchange rates and the pattern of exchange rates. Exchange-rate flexibility did not lead to "equilibrium rates," or to a "balancing of current accounts." Exchange-rate flexibility led to instability in foreign exchange markets. Overshooting beyond or below what would have been theoretical "trade-and-price-adjusted equilibrium exchange rates" became the rule, not the exception, not only in the 1970s but also throughout the following decades. Relative inflation rate differences between "virtuous" and "undisci- plined" countries were exacerbated. The floating rate system has had a defla- tionary bias for countries that had a reputation for "weak currencies" and "lax" domestic policies. The system clearly "favored" countries with "strong currencies" in fighting inflation. The end of the obligation to maintain fixed exchange rates eliminated an important outside constraint. This made the adoption of prudent fiscal and monetary policies politically more difficult, if not impossible. Credibility had now a higher price.

One of the myths that had preceded the collapse of the par-value system was that exchange-rate flexibility would facilitate balance-of-payments adjustments (corrections) both for deficit and surplus countries. In fact, the exact opposite happened. Carol M. Connell quotes Fritz Machlup:

> I started out as a less critical advocate of free and unlimitedly flexibility of exchange rates than I find myself to be at the end of the discussions. After all the assumptions for the success of such a system had been brought out, I realized that a stronger case could be made for a system of limited flexibility.[19]

According to Rudiger Dornbusch, also an advocate of flexible exchange rates, the tendency of overshooting of foreign exchange markets carried a high cost:

> There are also short-run costs, which may be quite high, that are brought about by the very fact that the exchange rate is too flexible. These short-term costs, in turn, are higher, the more fervently policymakers (mistakenly) believe that the use of flexible rates is tantamount to macroeconomic independence. If many policymakers hold this erroneous view, the use of flexible rates may well have a destabilizing effect on the world economy.[20]

1.2.8 The role of international reserves

What is the correct amount of international reserves at the national level and for the international economy as a whole: the right amount that will not be inflationary, nor will it keep trade and employment below its potential?

This was a central issue under the "pure" gold standard, and it was even more so under the "gold-exchange standard" devised in the wake of the First World War in order to cope with the insufficient supply of gold. The fear of a permanent "dollar shortage" during the decade following the end of the Second World War reflected a concern about a lack of international reserves or means of payment, and its impact on trade and economic growth. Highly topical issues also today, in the context of the international debt crises, are the accumulation of vast international reserves by China (which represent highly liquid claims on the United States in particular) and the national and international funds required and/or available to help deal with debt and balance-of-payments crises of individual countries or group of countries. The central objective of the International Monetary Fund was to help deal with temporary shortages of reserves by individual member countries. This help is provided and to help under conditions that should allow the borrowing countries to repay these temporary debts quite rapidly, and before they would repay any other of their official or non-official debts.

The question of international reserves, their composition (gold, national currencies like the dollar, even other commodities than gold) was also at the center of the debate about the reform of the international monetary system during the decade that preceded the collapse of Bretton Woods. Under the powerful reasoning (and advocacy) of Professor Robert Triffin of Yale, the risk and the likelihood of a potential major shortage of international liquidity (i.e., of reserves or ultimate means of payments) occurring under the "dollar-exchange standard" became a major subject in the reform debate. The creation of the SDRs through the First Reform of the Articles of Agreement of the IMF was a testimony to the energy and persuasiveness of Professor Triffin.[21]

The role of official international reserves under the par-value system was essentially two-fold. Their first role was to cope with shortfalls of foreign currency resulting from temporary balance-of-payments deficits. The advocates of flexible exchange rates used to argue that under the system of floating rates the need for foreign-exchange reserves would diminish. This would be due to an automatic balance between supply and demand in the foreign exchange markets. In fact, the volume of reserves held or needed has greatly increased in the last 40 years because of the tendency to overshoot in the foreign exchange markets.

The second major role of foreign exchange reserves (and especially of changes in reserves) under the Bretton Woods system was as a guide for monetary policy and a factor in helping achieve domestic monetary stability. The sale to banks or the purchase of foreign currencies (primarily dollars) from banks by the Central Bank against national currency had a direct impact on the liquidity position of the banking system and the ability of banks to lend. This second role was particularly resented by both the deficit and the surplus countries. The first ones saw this as a deflationary or recessionary constraint on employment and growth. The second ones considered it to be the conduit for imported inflation, hence their attempt to "sterilize" the domestic liquidity impact of the rise in foreign currency reserves. The deficit countries argued that the shortage of foreign reserves led to a loss of output (growth below the potential rate), while surplus countries saw the rise of their foreign exchange holdings as a form of forced savings (Table 1.4).

Table 1.4 World total reserves (million US dollars)

	2008	2009	2010	2011	2012 Jan.
World	4,843,975	5,482,431	6,297,405	6,968,131	6,926,605
Advanced Economies	1,674,769	1,954,435	2,196,889	2,438,805	2,427,660
Emerging and Developing Countries	3,165,445	3,524,440	4,096,786	4,525,614	4,495,235
Developing Asia	1,654,908	1,973,767	2,370,440	2,636,841	2,611,780
Europe	480,693	501,070	550,677	567,314	564,191
Middle East and North Africa	603,687	597,336	661,313	727,232	727,683
Sub-Saharan Africa	102,270	101,816	102,731	113,653	112,827
Western Hemisphere	323,888	350,452	411,624	480,986	478,961

Source: International Financial Statistics (IFS).

Under the original Articles of Agreement the IMF was to monitor the balance-of-payments evolution of the member countries and provide short-term financing to help overcome their temporary foreign-exchange shortages. The real power of the IMF was over the countries that had to have recourse to its resources. The conditions of access to IMF resources and of repayment represented a major source of influence over the economic policies of the borrowing countries. Following the end of the par-value system and the adoption of a completely new version of Article IV with the Second Reform of the IMF (the "Jamaica Agreement"), the industrialized countries *de facto* ceased to have recourse to borrowing from the IMF.[22] One of the consequences of the international financial crisis has been to give a new lease of life to the IMF lending capacity in fighting the consequences of financial and debt crises no longer only at the "periphery" of the world economy, but once more also in the center of the OECD countries.

1.2.9 International capital movements and the issue of "resource transfers"

John Maynard Keynes first achieved international fame through his powerful plea for not overburdening defeated Germany with excessive reparation payments after the First World War. In what was one of his most farsighted and politically important books he warned—in vain—against the economic and political consequences of an excessive resource transfer from the already weak German economy. Keynes was also an active participant in the debate a decade later on the so-called transfer issue still related to German reparations.[23] During the planning and negotiations for post-Second World War international economic order, Keynes had originally hoped that one of the main functions of the international monetary rules and institutions would be to facilitate a massive resource transfer from the United States to the capital-starved rest of the world, and in particular to Britain and the British Empire.[24] However, by the time the Articles of Agreement of the International Monetary Fund were drafted and adopted there was not much left of this idea.[25] The main interest of the United States was to assure that there would be no systematic restrictions on trade (and in particular no discrimination against American exports). The principal role of currency convertibility was to allow the liberalization of the flow of trade.

The transfer of resources ultimately did take place—but outside the framework of the Bretton Woods institutions. Paradoxically, the instrument of this massive resources transfer, the European Recovery Program or, as it is generally known, the Marshall Plan, was not conditional on liberalizing imports from the United States and eliminating discrimination against American products by the recipients of aid. Rather one of the conditions was the organizing of effective, temporary discrimination against the United States in Europe.[26] The Marshall Plan represented, however, a unique example of a massive transfer, which came to be repeated only once in modern history: the resource transfer following German reunification in 1990 from the original member states of the Federal Republic of Germany to the new member states that used to constitute Communist East Germany.

The Marshall Plan served as an inspiration for "foreign aid" to the "underdeveloped countries." International economic aid has been a useful innovation in trying to stimulate economic development. However, the volume of foreign aid has been constrained by political factors virtually from the start. At the same time its efficiency has been limited by bureaucratic practices and unrealistic expectations and conditions on both the donor and receiving side. A frequently heard argument in favor of unrestricted international capital movements (combined with arguments to further slow the growth or even reduce the volume of foreign aid) is that private capital flows have made a spectacular contribution to the growth of some of the most successful economies in the last 20 years, with China being at the top of the list.

The debt crisis and the resource shortage after the end of Communism in Eastern Europe: The lack of Western solidarity

The international debt crisis of the 1980s also had an impact on the economies of Communist countries in Europe. Several of these countries had taken advantage of the availability and the relatively favorable conditions of borrowing from Western banks and other sources, including exporters, during the 1970s. The increased weight of the debt (the size of which was traded as a major state secret) resulting from the reversal in financial markets and the world economy in the early 1980s created significant debt servicing problems and had a negative impact on consumption and investments. The external debt problems also highlighted the inherent rigidities and inefficiencies of the Communist economic system and thus contributed to the collapse of the system and the political and economic regime change at the end of the 1980s.

This was particularly true for Hungary, which had the highest external debt/GDP ratio among the Communist countries. Following the change from Communism to parliamentary democracy and from a state-owned and state-controlled economy to a market economy based on private initiative and private ownership, the size of the external debt and the debt service proved to be a constraint on the Hungarian economy. The new, freely elected government chose not to default on the debt, not to ask for a moratorium on the service of the debt—despite more or less direct suggestions from the US Treasury. The rationale of the Hungarian government was the legitimate fear that a debt default would have negative consequences for Hungary's international position and standing both on financial markets and potential direct investors. This "confidence-building" policy did have positive results, as shown by the large volume of foreign direct investments in Hungary between 1990 and 1994.

The repeated attempts of Prime Minister Joseph Antall's government to bring to the attention of the leaders of the OECD countries the severe resource shortage (the debt problem was one of the principal causes) in the Hungarian economy in the wake of the regime change met with no interest in the United States, the United Kingdom, France, Germany or Japan. This created considerable disappointment in the Hungarian public, which had expected some material aid for the reconstruction of the Hungarian economy. The refusal to recognize this problem, during the crucial initial period following the end of the Communist regime, by the Bretton Woods institutions and the newly created European Bank of Reconstruction and Development (EBRD), is one of the reasons Hungarians have a negative view of the IMF, the World Bank and the EBRD.[27] The absence of effective reconstruction aid was all the more difficult to understand for Hungarian (and other East European) citizens in the light of the very large resource transfer from West to East Germany following reunification. The total official resource transfer from the "old Federal Republic" to the new Eastern provinces was estimated at around DM 1.5 trillion during the 15 years following German reunification. Even a decade and a half after reunification, the transfers from West to East Germany amounted to about 4% of German GDP.[28] The amount of direct regional aid by the European Community to the new German Länder (which automatically became members of the Community) was larger than the total aid to all the former Communist economies taken together.

1.2.10   Capital movements and the end of Bretton Woods

Freeing up international capital movements was both the consequence of the breakdown of the Bretton Woods system and the explicit or implicit objective of the decision not to return to a fixed or stable exchange-rate system.[29] It was clear also in the 1950s and 1960s that private capital movements had an important potential role in a world economy where trade was increasingly liberalized, and international competition and economic integration proved to be a powerful engine of economic growth. There was an economic justification for both short-term and long-term international capital movements. They could benefit both capital importers and exporters. This was true also under the Bretton Woods system—which, however, was clearly ill-adapted for full liberalization of international capital movements. There is no doubt that one of the factors that brought down the system was the upsurge of primarily short-term capital movements for which it had not been created or adjusted.

Capital movements have always been an important component of international economic relations. They are a major factor stimulating economic progress, both through "technology diffusion" and through providing capital where it was scarce, and income for savers who could not (or not longer) earn through "productive activities." International capital movements play an important positive role in the growth of the world economy and in reducing poverty, creating jobs and raising living standards throughout the world economy. However, capital movements, like other aspects of economic activity and economic decisions, often failed to achieve the expected results. Earnings and security—return and risk—are supposed to be the key factors influencing the decisions of savers and money managers with respect to international capital flows.

The breakdown of the fixed exchange-rate system did not eliminate excessive imbalances—in fact it amplified them. Nor did it bring about a more equitable adjustment. It made it more difficult to correct excessive deficits or surpluses. It stimulated short-term, speculative cross-border capital movements and gradually created an entirely new world of financial asset creating and trading. At the end of the 1960s, shortly before the end of the fixed-exchange rate system, Egon Sohmen, a prominent advocate of floating exchange rates, argued:

> It is taken for granted that capital flows are liable to be unpredictable and erratic when exchange rates are not pegged. Neither theoretical considerations, nor practical experience lend support to this view.[30]

The following 40 years provided ample evidence contrary to his views. There is no doubt that the volume, the composition, the herd-like behavior, the growing distance between "real transaction" and the volume of funds moving through capital markets have all contributed to the instability of financial and monetary conditions, and often have dampened rather than stimulated economic growth.

The virtual disappearance of the distinction between "short-term" and "long-term" capital movements, the growing "anonymity" of financial assets, the growing distance between actual savers and the ultimate users of the savings have greatly contributed to the series of spectacular international financial crises that have marked the last 40 years. The illusion that trading by itself could create value and returns that were well above rates that could be sustained by technological innovation, productivity growth and rationalization have led to risk taking well beyond the point of rational entrepreneurial decisions and projections.

The excessive volume of international capital movements has also been a factor in severe crises in the real economy. The bulk of the burden of the losses incurred in these crises was not carried by those most directly responsible for imprudent money management and risk taking. In most cases the international monetary system or arrangements acted as "amplifiers" rather than "brakes" on these excesses. These observations with respect to the "burden-sharing" and the role of the international monetary system hold true across most of the international financial crises since the early 1970s.

1.2.11 The link between the international trade and monetary orders

The most visible material links between "national economies" are those of trade and the cross-border ownership of production facilities and other assets. However, these links are made possible and conditioned by the international monetary system. The international monetary system has always provided the key mechanism in linking what happens inside national economies and the rest of the world. This was true even at the time when international monetary and financial transactions were even more tightly controlled and restricted than trade in goods and services. The breakdown of the international economic order in the 1930s was as much a breakdown of the monetary and financial system as of the world trading system. The situation was similar in the immediate post-war period. The system of trade restrictions (especially through quantitative restrictions) was tightly intertwined with strict, paralyzing exchange controls. The liberalization of trade during the 1950s and 1960s, primarily among Western democracies, and the revival of large-scale direct investments (especially by American companies) were key elements in the rapid reconstruction of war-torn economies, and also in the remarkable growth and "upward convergence" of economies that participated in the process of regional (European) and worldwide economic integration.

The growth of trade and direct investments could not have been possible without the restoration of a functioning and stable international monetary system. Progress of *de facto* and *de jure* convertibility was the key element of a temporary regional system achieved through the mechanism of the European Payments Union (EPU), the sister organization of the Organization of European Economic Cooperation (OEEC). Convertibility was extended increasingly also on a universal scale (i.e., among the market economies) through the implementation of the rules laid down at Bretton Woods and through the principal Bretton Woods institution, the International Monetary Fund (the counterpart of the forum for trade liberalization, the General Agreement on Tariffs and Trade, or (GATT). During the two decades preceding the breakdown of the Bretton Woods system in 1971–3, trade liberalization and integration through trade and direct investments (including the massive technology transfers and the new economies of scale achieved in both Western Europe and Japan on the American model) clearly outpaced the progress of international monetary and financial liberalization and integration. The progress of currency convertibility, however, was undeniable, and on the whole exchange rates were fairly stable and inflation remained modest. Inflation differences were relatively limited—especially when compared with what was to come after the "end of Bretton Woods."

The threat that the shortcomings of the international monetary system represent for the liberal trading system can be illustrated by a quote from a leading "free trade economist" and the author of a book *In Defense of Globalization*. According to Professor Jagdish Bhagwati:

> [The critics of globalization] argue as if the case for free trade had been exposed as illusory by the financial crisis ... [that devastated East Asia in the latter half of the 1900s]. But openness to trade had been at the heart of the East Asian "miracle," whereas imprudent and hasty freeing of financial flows was at the heart of the brutal interruption of this miracle. ... The case for free trade and the case for free capital flows have important parallels. But the differences are yet more pointed. The freeing of capital flows in haste, without putting in place monitoring and regulatory mechanisms and banking reforms, amount to a rash, gung-ho financial capitalism. It can put nation-states at serious risk of experiencing massive, panic-led outflows of short-term funds, which would drive the economies into a tailspin.[31]

During the years since the end of Bretton Woods, time and again there were economists and policy makers who tended to belittle or even deny the relevance of the "current account" and hence also of the "trade account" of the balance of payments. This was the case in the United States[32] and also at times in the Euro zone. The current international financial and debt crisis, however, has focused the policy debate once more on the issue of the current account in a dramatic manner, both for the United States, the bastion of the "non-system" in the international monetary area, and in the common currency union of the EMU. It seems to be clear that if the lack of rules in the international monetary area will continue, this would represent a growing danger also for the rule-based liberal international trading order.

1.3 The 40-year crisis: The absence of international monetary order and the recurring international debt crises (1971–2012)

It is no exaggeration to speak of a "40-year crisis" in the world financial and monetary system. This period witnessed widespread financial excesses and disequilibria and growing systemic fragility, not only in the financial system but also in the real economy.

The financial crises of the last 40 years have been characterized by:

- Loss of effective control by the monetary authorities (governments and central banks) over domestic and international monetary developments.
- Hedging, which was meant to reduce uncertainty, becoming increasingly destabilizing and a source of uncertainty and bad decisions.
- Financial assets (in particular government debt) becoming the "riskiest" instead of the "safest" stores of value.

The four decades of crises started at the heart of the world economy, with the devaluation and the floating of the dollar, and then moved to the developing world or the "second tier" of the OECD countries.

The present crisis started again with the US economy and the debt problem exported from the US monetary and financial system, and it now encompasses virtually the entire OECD area. When most of the world's wealthiest economies are "condemned to grow," not only to avoid increasing polarization between the affluent and the struggling elements in the societies, but also to avoid outright bankruptcy in the long run, something must be wrong with the system. That the rich are being crushed by their debts, that their debts seem to be the principal legacy to bequeath to future generations, is certainly not a sign of prudence or of a well-functioning monetary system.

1.3.1 Financial and monetary crises and debt crises

Each major international financial and monetary crisis has its own characteristics: the time sequence and the build-up, the factors that trigger the explosion, and the magnitude, geographic scope and duration of the consequences. However, all international financial and monetary crises are in their origins and in their consequences essentially debt crises. One of the roles of a properly functioning international monetary system is to help prevent international financial and in particular debt crises. Systemic defects or the malfunctioning of the international monetary mechanisms may allow or even facilitate the buildup of excesses and disequilibria that lead to debt crises. The nature of the international monetary system also plays a major role in easing or aggravating the long-term consequences of debt crises, as well as the sharing of the long-term consequences among the various actors. The close connection between international debt crises and the absence of a properly working international monetary system is apparent once more in what is considered to be the most complex and volatile situation in the international monetary system since the late 1940s.

Borrowing and lending—credit and the creation of debts

Borrowing and lending are essential elements of modern economies. Jean Calvin contributed to the "rise of capitalism" by lifting the Christian ban on lending (for "legitimate purposes") against reasonable payment of interest by borrowers (but no "usury" rates, which remained subject to punishment).[33] One of the aims of a "monetary system," either a "national system" organized around a "national economy" and a "national currency," or an "international monetary system," is to facilitate and regulate the working of credit systems. Where there are credits, there are also debts. As the saying goes: "no deficit (or debt) can come into being without its being financed." Borrowers and lenders thus jointly bear the responsibility for the creation of domestic and international debt.

Prudence—the short- and long-term condition of success

All theorists and practitioners hold prudence to be an important quality of both borrowers and lenders, and excess as the main source of trouble, even if it is disguised behind sophisticated-sounding names such as "financial engineering," "product innovation," "securitization" or "high-speed trading." Another practice called "passing on the risk," resulting from shady transactions by lenders or borrowers or both, to unsuspecting third parties is not only morally wrong, but is a threat in the long run to a sound credit system.

1.3.2   The crises of the 1970s, 1980s and 1990s

The 1970s to the 1990s was a period in which the close connection between the (mal)functioning of the international monetary system, on the one hand, and a global debt crisis, on the other, was dramatically demonstrated. Some of the key features of the "debt crisis" of the 1970s and 1980s and those of the "Asian financial crisis" of the 1990s illustrate these observations.

The following is a list of some of the causes and consequences related to the monetary and financial crises:

- Terms of trade (weak currency countries losers, strong currency countries winners)
- Structural or policy changes
- Excess spending

- Excess borrowing and lending
- Monetary and financial tensions and crisis
- Debt crisis
- Recession
- Aggravation of monetary and financial crisis.

The devaluation of the dollar in August 1971 and its subsequent further decline throughout the 1970s represented a *de facto* bankruptcy, as the dollar-denominated official US obligations (whether held by foreign official agencies or other foreign holders) became worth less and less in terms of gold, and in terms of other major currencies, such as the German mark, the Swiss franc and the Japanese yen. The end of the Bretton Woods system also contributed to upward pressure on commodity prices, which had been denominated primarily in US dollars by then, and has been a cause of excessive commodity price fluctuations ever since. Particularly dramatic was the impact on the price of oil. The four-fold increase in the price of oil (some of this increase had been undoubtedly overdue) represented a sudden and huge income transfer from the oil-importing to the oil-exporting countries. The terms-of-trade effect (the principal numerical indicator of this transfer), however, was alleviated for the countries with currencies that were "revalued" against the US dollar, compared with the countries with currencies that were devalued in terms even of the dollar. This brought about a further widening in the inflation performance between countries in Europe (as well as in their real income situation). Germany and Switzerland weathered much better the oil crisis in real income terms than, for example, Italy, to mention only some of the most extreme cases.

The oil crisis also created overnight enormous new savings (by the oil-exporting countries), and enormous financing needs (in the oil-importing countries). The "low-population" major oil-exporting countries especially (essentially the Gulf countries) accumulated very large amounts of liquid assets, which were entrusted for the most part to major international banks. At the same time, the oil-importing economies (especially the developing countries) had to find funds to finance the increased costs of energy imports.

The resulting recycling of "petrodollars" seemed to be in the interests of all. For the owners of the assets (OPEC countries) entrusting their new wealth to reputable international banks ("first addresses") was a safe temporary, or even permanent, solution. For the banks, it was also a welcome solution because it provided them with new lending opportunities at a time when the recession, partly caused by the oil crisis, curtailed their traditional outlets, and they had plentiful resources to lend. Lending to developing countries provided good margins, and, although borrowers often fell in the category of "third addresses," the risks were as a rule tempered by government guaranties. As for the borrowing countries, the opportunity to deal with their balance-of-payments problems through private bank financing looked like an attractive solution, especially if compared with the alternative of trying to get short-term official (IMF) financing. The leading Western governments and the international economic and monetary and financial organizations (IMF, OECD, World Bank, etc.) were also delighted. The "recycling of petrodollars" appeared to be an ideal solution to two problems. It helped avert a worsening of the economic outlook in the world economy, and it eased the political pressure on the OECD countries to provide more official aid to the developing countries. This came at a time of rising unemployment in the industrialized countries, and when there was a growing disaffection for the "Third World" among voters in the industrialized countries as a result of the OPEC action and the growing militancy of the developing countries in favor of a new "world economic order."

Beside the "macro-economic" and "macro-political" arguments in favor of massive recycling of petrodollars, dollar-denominated borrowing (the bulk of the recycling operations) made good business sense for borrowers: US inflation was high, and was expected to remain so, and compared to the rate of inflation interest rates were not very high. In fact, "real interest rates" were often negative. Finally, the value of the dollar was declining and was expected to continue to do so through the foreseeable future. Not to borrow under these conditions was not the prudent decision—as was also explained by the countless executives of international banks whose brief was to "sell loans" in the developing countries and convince both government officials and the private sector that there were no real risks in the expanding volume of international debt. (At a different, less lofty level, these arguments were rephrased by some of the very same banks 30 years later when "selling mortgages"—that whatever your income, you "cannot afford not to invest in real estate.")

According to the IMF's historian Margaret Garritsen de Vries:

> Many non-oil developing countries had been borrowing heavily after 1973, especially from commercial banks, to finance their balance-of-payments deficits. By mid-1982, their aggregate external debt was over $600 billion, over half of which was on commercial terms. Readily available credit from private sources—at favorable interest rates for that period—had helped induce countries to borrow. And steadily rising deposits, particularly as oil exporting countries banked their vastly enlarged oil reserves, had induced creditors, especially commercial banks, to lend.[34]

The reversal was as dramatic as it was unexpected by the banks as well as by the leading national and international financial and monetary experts and officials. It is true that Paul Volcker, the new Chairman of the US Federal Reserve, sought both the surprise and the shock effect to deal with the combined problems of US inflation and the downward spiral of the dollar.[35]

The action did come as a surprise, despite the fact that for months and years there had been virtually unanimous calls, in the United States and abroad, to halt the domestic and external loss of the value of the dollar. What happened is a well-known and oft-told story: halt to inflation, a sharp rise of nominal and real interest rates, a recession that was said to be "the worst since the 1930s" and the beginning of an upward climb of the dollar. There was also a major dampening of commodity prices. Most unexpectedly, even for the sophisticated forecasting groups in the major oil companies, the second oil-price shock was rapidly followed by a downward turn in oil prices. It should be mentioned here that the experts of some of the "majors" in the early1980s in their oil-price scenarios used $100 per barrel (in constant prices) for 1990 for their "conservative" or favorable projections. The worst-case scenarios assumed a significantly higher oil-price level.

The "international debt problem," which had been in the making for years, represented a major challenge for individual lenders and borrowers, for small and large national economies, and for the world economy as a whole. It was a major short-term and long-term problem for the borrowing countries. In the short term they were facing a liquidity problem, that is, finding funds to "service their debts"—to meet their interest payments and to "roll over" the principal. The long-term problem, however, was more dramatic: it was the increase in the "weight of the debt," as a result of higher real interest rates, and the rise in the value of the dollar-denominated loans and bonds. The banks and the international banking system faced the real possibility of a payments default—first by Mexico, and then a cascading series of countries unable to find funds to finance their payment obligations both in the short run and possibly also in the long term. The debt crisis of the 1980s was essentially a "foreign-debt crisis." For debtors, it was the burden of their foreign payment obligations, which turned out to be quite suddenly too heavy, beyond their means to service their financial obligations in foreign currencies. For creditors—primarily the large banks in the leading OECD countries—the danger was the equally sudden deterioration of their international (developing or Communist country) loan portfolio.

The debt crisis of the 1980s was seen largely at the time, and also subsequently, as pitting against each other: developing country (and Communist country) borrowers (either sovereign borrowers or private borrowers with government guaranties) and OECD country international banks.

1.3.3 The consequences of floating exchange rates

Today there is still an open debate about the question whether the crises that followed its end were the result of the collapse of Bretton Woods, or delayed consequences of its working and the growing imbalances ("pent-up imbalances") in the world economy that resulted from its shortcomings. However, ever since the 1970s it has become clear that it had been an illusion to think that free floating brings about equilibrium between supply and demand in the foreign exchange markets. Exchange rates came to be more and more determined by (primarily short-term) capital movements and differences in interest rates and "risk assessments," rather than trade in goods and services and relative price levels (price competitiveness). As a result foreign exchange markets have been shaped by the "herd instinct" leading to systematic over- and under-valuation of currencies. The manifestations of this phenomenon were the excessive decline of the value of the "weak currencies" and the excessive rise of the value of the "strong currencies." The US dollar was leading the pack of "weak currencies" in the 1970s, whereas in the first half of the 1980s it underwent a spectacular strengthening and overvaluation. Ever since then, it has continued to ride a roller coaster in the global foreign exchange markets. Whatever the theory espoused by the US Congress with respect to the superiority of "non-intervention" over different types of fixed or managed exchange-rate systems, one of the most pronounced and most systematic "market failures" during last 40 years of financial liberalization and deregulation could be observed in the foreign exchange markets.

The floating exchange-rate system has represented a major factor of disequilibrium both during "expansionary" phases and during the "correction" process. In the expansionary phase, the herd behavior stimulates an inflated rise in the exchange rate as well as the trend toward excess borrowing (the two being closely connected) and general asset price inflation. The rise in the market value of financial assets encourages further borrowing by both financial and non-financial actors. (The well-known practice of "pricing to market" is one of the important pro-cyclical factors in this process.) In the downward phase, the "correction" of the exchange-rate overvaluation and of the excess borrowing and lending is also subject to the same herd behavior and pro-cyclical developments. Monetary tightening aimed at avoiding an exchange-rate collapse constrains economic activity, employment and profits. The slowdown in its turn contributes to the downward pressure of asset prices. Due to the combined effect of higher interest rates and the downward shift in exchange rates, the real weight of debt—especially of debt to external creditors—tends to rise sharply. This occurs when credit becomes scarce and the rollover or refinancing of debts becomes more difficult and costly. When borrowers have difficulty in servicing the debt and interests are added to the principal, the debt and its weight become less and less easy to deal with. Thus, through this "snow-balling effect," the total accumulated debt tends to become much larger and less manageable than originally expected—or what the sophisticated calculations and models of the financial salesmen had promised and predicted.

Relative inflation rate differences between "virtuous" and "undisciplined" countries were exacerbated. The floating-rate system has had a deflationary bias for countries that had a reputation for "weak currencies" and "lax" domestic policies. The system clearly "favored" countries with "strong currencies" in fighting inflation. The end of the obligation to maintain fixed exchange rates eliminated an important outside constraint. This made the adoption of prudent fiscal and monetary policies politically more difficult, if not impossible. Credibility had a higher price.

One of the myths that had preceded the collapse of the par-value system was that exchange-rate flexibility would facilitate balance-of-payments adjustments (corrections) both for deficit and surplus countries. In fact, the exact opposite happened. This classic "vicious circle" also includes systematic "asset destruction," which often goes beyond artificial "asset creation" during the upward phase. Savings are lost and material assets are either closed down for good or change ownership at bargain prices or at zero valuation. Sometimes this means "nationalization," sometimes "privatization." For countries with large foreign debts, this may lead to a large shift from domestic to foreign ownership of a significant portion of the indebted country's productive assets and natural resources (including land). When there is an oversupply of assets, this can take place only at deflated prices or even symbolic prices. This was certainly the case in Eastern Europe after the collapse of the Communist system and in the wake of the successive Latin American financial and debt crises of the 1980s and 1990s as well as in many African countries going through a "structural adjustment process" as part of dealing with their debt crisis.

The jury is still out on the question whether the new owners who acquired or grabbed up these assets during the last several major financial crises turned out to be better owners, whether they husbanded the country's assets more carefully than the financial wizards who had been responsible for the collapse and the asset destruction in the first place. The record of Eastern Europe and Latin America suggests that the answer to this question is far from a clear "yes." To add insult to injury, the cycle of over-borrowing, excess contraction and asset destruction is often followed by a new wave of over-borrowing—to make up for the loss of saving and income and assets, despite the earlier experience with the burden of debt. This happened in Latin America—without warning from international financial leaders—and this happened in Hungary because of the opportunism of the new foreign owners of a large portion of the Hungarian banking system and the indifference of European Union officials.[36]

1.3.4 Globalization and financial instability

A recent BIS report sums up the close links between globalization and the amplification of financial and economic instability:

> By widening the scope for economic activity, globalisation also widens the potential exposure to instability. The same international links that increase welfare and efficiency ... serve as a powerful propagation channel for financial and economic shocks. ... In the early stages, rapidly falling asset

prices wreak havoc on the balance sheets of international investors; in the later stages, a collapse in world trade (may) punish many export-oriented economies. ... Gross financial inflows and outflows are substantially larger than the net flows associated with the current account and are often large even where current account balances are negligible. It is these gross flows, not the net, that must be accommodated by the receiving financial sector; and a sudden stop of gross flows risks economic crisis in the receiving economy. Gross flows also pose a threat to the extent that they contribute to vulnerabilities in the interconnected balance sheets of financial institutions, firms and households around the world. They can result in currency, liquidity and credit risk mismatches because the attributes of assets acquired through outflows are unlikely to exactly match those of the liabilities acquired through inflows—both at the level of individual market participants and in the aggregate. Furthermore, even if balance sheet positions are perfectly matched, they still give rise to counterparty risks. During the financial crisis, a sudden deterioration in balance sheets caused a large decline in economic activity, demonstrating that even seemingly small differences between the attributes of assets and liabilities—along with counterparty risks—can form a powerful propagation channel for shocks.[37]

1.3.5   Excessive borrowing and lending: whose fault was it?

As all debt crises, the crises of the last 40 years were all due to what turned out to be in the light of subsequent developments "excessive lending and borrowing." According to Alexandre Lamfalussy, in most cases the responsibility was clearly shared between lenders and borrowers:

> If I am right in singling out excessive debt accumulation as the most striking common feature of the four crisis experiences, the question arises as to what similarities can be detected in the process of debt accumulation. The first, not very original observation is that excessive debt accumulation could not have taken place without the demand for the funds meeting the supply, or vice versa. There could not have been "overborrowing" without "overlending."[38] ...

> But which of the two—supply or demand—was the driving force behind the process of debt accumulation varied from case to case, and even over time within the same episode. In some instances it is just not possible to allocate primary responsibility to one or the other side. Who can say that the apparently demand-led "overborrowing" was not initiated, or at least encouraged, by the lenders?[39] ...

> With the exception of the 1982–83 crisis, the disastrous working of the domestic banking systems played a major role in the build up of the crises and in aggravating their impact in the real economy."[40] ...

> To sum up, four conclusions emerge. ... First, that the build up of excessive short-term indebtedness and the accompanying asset price bubbles

were at the heart of the four crises. Second, the exuberant behaviour of the lenders and investors from the developed world played a major role in raising leverage and asset prices to levels that eventually became unsustainable, often under the influence of specific factors. Third, that the process of financial globalization aggravated all four cases and, if left unattended, would be likely to contribute to the eruption of new crises in emerging economies. Fourth, the jury is still out on the question whether the process of globalization has made the financial systems of the developed world more or less prone to fragility.[41]

There has been no real burden-sharing

Who has carried the burden for the financial excesses and consequences of the defective international monetary system? In most of the financial crises, there has been no real burden-sharing between borrowers and lenders. Essentially, borrowers had to bear responsibility for excess lending and the highly increased weight of the debt. In fact, the preferred short-term solution of providing liquidity and rolling over the debt, and adding the interests owed to the principal, increased rather than reduced the long-term weight of the debt.

For the decision makers in international organizations and in the OECD countries "moratorium" for the developing countries or a *de facto* bankruptcy of sovereign debtors (both as a result of direct government borrowing and due to government guaranties to private borrowers) represented the absolute economic and monetary nightmare scenario. Such an event would have wrecked havoc on the banks and the banking system—not only at the level of their international activity but also on the national banking systems of the OECD countries. A world-wide banking crisis would have inevitably further depressed the world economy and reversed the process of liberalization and integration that had been the prime source of prosperity since the late 1940s. The memory of the bankruptcy of the Austrian Creditanstalt and its ripple effect through the global financial system was even more vivid in the early 1980s than in September 2008 at the time of the collapse of Lehman Brothers.

The "long-term solutions" consisted of the so-called structural adjustment programs. The structural reforms which were advocated included marketization, liberalization, privatization (increased foreign ownership), asset destruction, cutback of social programs, export drives and floating-exchange rates. Many of these reform measures made sense and many were, in fact, overdue. They were, however, implemented (in fact, imposed) under highly unfavorable political, social and economic circumstances. Both the countries that had to adopt them and the international bureaucrats who had devised them saw these reforms more as a "punishment" than a "liberation" and as the road toward greater prosperity and social progress. There was no trace in them of the Erhardian optimism—"prosperity for all"—and the spirit of the post-war social market economy. In country after country they succeeded in giving a bad name to the "market economy."[42]

The costs of financial deregulation: The case of Japan

A major problem in recent years and decades has been that national monetary authorities have lost or given up much of their power—and this at a time when the monetary and financial dimension of the economy has become more important and complex than ever before. Japan serves as one of the best illustrations of this. Throughout the 1980s Japanese authorities were under constant pressure to "modernize" and to "liberalize" the financial and banking sector. This was also seen by American economists and policy makers as a way to deal with bilateral balance-of-payments imbalances between the United States and Japan.[43] In the case of Japan financial deregulation has exacted an enormous price. In the post-war period Japan was the first major industrialized country to have undergone asset inflation and asset destruction on such a vast scale and with such lasting recessionary consequences.

According to Richard Koo:

> Falling land and stock prices starting in 1990 ... accounted for the unprecedented loss of ¥ 1500 trillion in wealth, a figure equal to the entire nation's stock of personal financial assets. This figure is also equivalent to three years of Japanese GDP. In effect, falling asset prices wiped out three years of national output. To the best of my knowledge, this is the greatest economic loss ever experienced by a nation in peacetime.[44]

This massive collapse of asset prices has continued to depress the actual and potential growth rate of the Japanese economy ever since. Clearly, Joseph Schumpeter's concept of "creative destruction,"[45] a theory particularly favored by the advocates of "de-industrialization" in the OECD countries, did not work in Japan—one of the most dynamic and creative economies in the world, prior to financial deregulation and financial collapse.

1.3.6 The United States and the dollar

Ever since the 1970s American administrations have been hostile to a reform of the international monetary system. The attitude of American officials toward European efforts to remedy the absence of a global international monetary order through regional solutions ranged from skepticism to "benign" indifference. These views can be illustrated by the comments made at a Brookings Conference at the time of the creation of the European Monetary System (EMS) in 1979 by Robert Solomon, a leading US official and expert on international monetary issues, and by Larry Summers, a high official of the Clinton administration almost 20 years later.

> Solomon on the EMS: I am quite willing to accept the characterization (that the European Monetary System is simply not a regional Bretton Woods

system). *I also welcome the statement that protecting Europe against the vagaries of the dollar is not one of the purposes of the EMS.*[46] (emphasis added)

Summers on the EMU: The administration has never thought it fitting to enter the debate over whether economic and monetary union is right for Europe, nor over the details of how it should be structured.[47]

There is no question that US policies and the US approach to the international monetary system have had a destabilizing effect in the first decade of the twenty-first century. This has been the cumulative effect, prior to the outbreak of the crisis, of the lax fiscal policies of the George W. Bush administration, of the Federal Reserve's expansionary policies and the resulting asset price inflation, the low savings rate and the widening current-account deficit. The effect of the combination of these factors was aggravated by the business strategies of the leading financial institutions and the lack of effective supervisory policies of the American authorities. The resulting acute worldwide crisis had a major negative short-term and long-term impact on the financial system, on the fiscal position and the real economy of most of the OECD countries. It was also a major factor in the widening of the government budget deficits and the debt/GDP ratio across the OECD area. The international monetary system did not help to prevent or at least moderate the crisis: it was a major factor for its happening and its scale. It clearly acted as a crisis transmission mechanism.

What is the link between the issue of debt and the American position on the international monetary system?

The dominant view, held on the American left and right, among Keynesians and among libertarians is that (1) there is no alternative to the freely floating exchange-rate system and (2) the United States must not accept any binding rules that would limit in any way its freedom to pursue its economic, monetary, fiscal and other policies according to its own interests and its own "lights." The idea that common rules, even if relatively flexible, could be also in the interests of the United States, and that external constraints might have helped prevent some of the erratic policies and systemic near-disasters of recent years, meets with collective rejection by both liberals and conservatives.

When Tamar Frankel, Professor of Law at Boston University and a well-known American specialist of financial law, was asked recently whether she saw "a distinction between money (and the monetary system) and finance (and the financial system)" her straightforward answer was "no, I do not see any difference."[48] This statement, although surprising for economists especially from an international perspective, sums up the views prevailing not only on Wall Street but throughout the United States among bankers and other specialists of finance. This confusion between "money" and "finance" is paralleled by the equally widespread confusion between the American currency (and financial system) and the international monetary system. The much-quoted saying: "the dollar is our currency and their problem" (meaning the rest of the world) is a fairly accurate summary of the conventional wisdom not only of the American public but also of policy makers and other experts.

In the United States there is a lively and well-publicized debate about the banks, the practices in the financial markets, the responsibilities of the federal government and of the Federal Reserve, and the regulatory changes that should or should not have been adopted in the wake of the near-meltdown of the American and of the entire international financial system. There is a long list of books with a surprising wealth of detail about what the leaders of American finance did, or even thought, during the crucial weeks and months leading up to and immediately following September 2008—as well as during the preceding "do-nothing" years. In all this detailed information and in the articles and books about the lessons to be learned for the future there is very little mention of the international monetary system, even less about the need to reform it and virtually nothing about what such a reform ought to be like.

It is symptomatic that such a seasoned, widely respected monetary statesman as Alexandre Lamfalussy, who was one of the architects of the Euro and of the European Central Bank, in his public speeches tends to focus his analysis and advice on future central bank policies, without explicitly calling for a reform of the international monetary system as such and spelling out what such a reform should aim at. It is also interesting to note that Barry Eichengreen, one of the currently best known and most prolific authors writing about the international monetary system (and how it worked in the past), is extremely reserved about the likely or necessary changes in the international monetary system as such. In his recent *Exorbitant Privilege: the Rise and Fall of the Dollar and the Future of the International Monetary System,* Eichengreen does raise the question in the last chapter of what would happen if foreigners fled from the dollar: "What if the dollar does crash? What if foreigners dump their holdings and abandon the currency? What if anything could US policymakers do about it?"[49] without attempting to define a convincing long-term solution.

1.4   The current "debt crisis" and the "Euro-zone crisis"

The general government debt as a percentage of the GDP of the leading OECD countries increased 20–30 percentage points between 2007 and 2012. Economists agree that this was the "lesser evil": without the "pro-cyclical" behavior of public finances, the decline in the "real economy" would have been much greater, involving also a severe drop in the long-term potential growth rate of most of the Western market economies.[50]

The worldwide international financial crisis that broke out in the fall of 2008—the so-called subprime crisis—had been largely the result of a lack of effective safeguard mechanisms in the international monetary sphere. It was only a massive reversal of central bank and government policies—an overnight switch from careless passivity to feverish activity—that prevented the melt-down of the international financial system. While much was done (and improvised) to "save the banks" and sustain economic activity, not much thought was given to start correcting the international system, or rather to start creating an international monetary system required by a global, open, dynamic world economy. Moving from the "subprime crisis"—a debt problem of the private sector—to the current "sovereign debt crisis" was a logical sequence that could be predicted already in late 2008 and early 2009. The close connection between the "sovereign debt crisis" and the "Euro-zone crisis" is clearly not the "fault of the periphery" or of the "weakest links," but of the malfunctioning at the center, that is, of the recurring instability generated by the international monetary system itself. The "efforts to save Greece," bolster the Euro zone and impose fiscal discipline, not only in the short but also in the long run, created a second round of working-in-crisis mode, both in governments and international organizations and among "market participants."

In the first phase of the current world-wide crisis, the United States started and was at the center of the storm. In the second phase, European countries and in particular the Euro zone has captured much of the attention and the pressure of the markets. In the headlines and also at the highest policy discussions the current so-called sovereign-debt crisis has come to be associated primarily with the European economies and especially with the Euro area. This is partly due to the highly publicized complexities of the decision-making process. It is also due to the need to deal both with a short-term emergency—the magnitude of which was largely underestimated—and the effort to devise and negotiate long-term changes in rules at the national and European levels as well as to develop new tools and institutions to increase fiscal discipline and fiscal convergence among the members of the European Union and the European Monetary Union.

1.4.1 The mainsprings of the current debt crisis

The central questions related to the title of the present chapter are: has the absence of a properly functioning international monetary system contributed to the debt crisis of the private sector and the sovereign-debt crisis? Do debt crises contribute to the malfunctioning of the international monetary system or not?

The current debt crisis is not an unexpected development—nor can it be separated from the systemic causes that had been responsible for the preceding crises of the 1970s, 1980s, 1990s and of the mega-crisis that broke into the open in 2008. In principle, "debts" and "assets" are two sides of the same coin. In reality, there is often a long and complicated path between these two opposite poles—that is, of a financial obligation or liability and the ownership of a financial asset. During this long and often tortuous road, the volume, the quality, the security and the very nature of both debts and assets may change beyond recognition.

The following are the principal interconnected aspects of the "debt crisis" or more correctly of the "debt crises" that broke into the open since 2007–8:

- The excessive volume and poor quality of a large proportion of household debt ("subprime").
- The low level of private savings in many OECD countries, including some of the most prosperous ones—with lack of savings being often compensated by "asset prices inflation" (both for material assets—primarily real estate—and for financial assets). Nevertheless, in particular in the United States, many economists and policy makers began to speak again about a "savings glut," this time referring primarily, but not exclusively, to China.
- The excessive volume of short-term borrowing by banks and the high level of "leveraging."
- Asset price inflation and the subsequent asset price deflation.
- The lax fiscal policies of both large and small OECD countries, at least since the late 1990s—during both periods of economic slowdown and years of relatively satisfactory growth—and the accumulation of public debt and the narrowing of the scope for "discretionary fiscal policies."
- The enormous "rescue operations," financed by governments to save the national and international banking and financial system from collapse, the fiscal stimuli to sustain demand and employment and avert an even sharper recession, and finally the slowdown or drop in fiscal revenues due to the combined result of earlier tax cuts and of lower tax receipts due to the recession.

At a BIS seminar for high-level central bankers held in Lucerne in the summer of 2011, Stephen Ceccehetti, the Economic Adviser of the BIS, compared the current situation to the First World War reparations and debt problem:

> We are seeing signs that the international adjustment mechanism intrinsic to the current monetary regime is being put under strain by cross-country payment imbalances. And again, we are seeing signs of crippling debt burdens.

Then he continued: "As many of you know ... not enough attention is being devoted to the ominous trajectory of public debt in a number of advanced economies." And then, speaking of the "debt projections for the next thirty years for 12 OECD countries" that he and the BIS services had prepared earlier in 2011, he called them

> the most frightening picture I have seen for some time. ... (We) need to understand the long-term implications of the events we live through. This is a towering challenge. ... May I say that I have become much more humble than I was three years ago. And realizing the limitations of my earlier thinking, I must accept that, even now, I may be as oblivious to the implications of the events going on around us as were those giants of history [i.e., the "legendary central bankers" of the 1920s] to the events of their time.[51]

In his conclusions in his keynote speech at the Lucerne Seminar, Alexandre Lamfalussy said:

> All the actors—central banks, governments, international organizations and, naturally, market participants—are navigating in waters uncharted by reliable historic experience. The complexity of the current situation is without precedent. But there is no way of "opting out" of this complex world. Wishing that we could go back to the professional and intellectual comfort of the pre-crisis years is a pipe dream. This does not make me a pessimist. At a time when euro-pessimism is fashionable, I derive quite some hope from the progress being made towards setting up a European Systemic Risk Board, under the auspices of the ECB, which, if properly implemented, will respond to many of my queries.[52]

1.4.2 The economic and political rational of the EMS and of the Euro

The creation in 1979 of the European Monetary System was an important step in consolidating the progress achieved in European integration and in reversing the monetary and inflation contrasts between "strong" and "weak" currency countries, contrasts that threatened to tear the European Community apart within a not too distant future. It was a rare coincidence that both the German leader and the French President were trained economists. The creation of the EMS, on the insistence of Chancellor Helmut Schmidt and President Giscard d'Estaing, was a highly political decision. It was essential for the future survival of the European project to stop the *de facto* separation of the members into two categories: "virtuous," low-inflation, strong-currency economies and "crisis-prone," high-inflation, weak currency countries.

The economic objectives were equally clear:

- To achieve more stable economic and monetary conditions through-out the European Community and assure the conditions of sustained growth.

- To allow further progress in the integration of the members of the European Community.
- To assure the continued upward convergence of economic conditions (productivity and per capita income) among the members of the European Community.
- To improve the international competitive position of the European Community.

It is generally agreed that the EMS fulfilled the expectations of its promoters with respect to the aforementioned objectives. Success during the early years was facilitated by the determined anti-inflationary policies of the United States and the strong (and excessive) rise of the value of the dollar until the Plaza Meeting in 1985. There is also agreement that without the EMS the Single European Act and the ambitious Internal Market project could never have been adopted and implemented. The aim of creating a true "internal market" was to deepen the integration of the economies of the European Community members. It was also an expression of the renewed emphasis on the role of markets and competition. In this context the UK played a significant role—somewhat in contrast with the pronounced and well-advertised "euro-skepticism" of the then British Prime Minister. According to the German Council of Economic Experts (*Sachverständigenrat*):

> The European Monetary System ... of fixed, but adjustable exchange rates, to which ... the then European Community member states belonged, functioned very well, until it was subjected to fierce speculative attacks in 1992 and 1993. The related revaluation of the deutschmark reinforced the competitive difficulties diagnosed for Germany in the mid-1990s. The experiences other export-aligned countries have had do not necessarily allow us to assume that life with a national currency is without its problems. The example of the revaluation of the Swiss franc in 2010 and 2011 shows the momentum speculation on revaluation can have and what severe distortions to the real economy this can entail.[53]

By the time the EMS broke down or exploded it was clear that it had done its job and it had done it fairly well. Every time the history of the causes and conditions of the end of the EMS is told, the center of the story is the American financier George Soros and his determined strategy of "one-way speculation." This strategy was highly successful for Mr Soros. At the same time it seemed to demonstrate that speculation based on the markets' perception of which country (and currency) is weak (and a candidate for devaluation) and which country (and currency) is strong (and a candidate for revaluation) becomes a self-fulfilling prophesy. Governments and central banks would not be able or willing to counter this strategy with sufficient cohesion, determination and resources. In fact, part of the assumption of the market attacks against the EMS was that half-hearted and uncoordinated measures by governments and monetary authorities would add to, rather than diminish, the thrust of speculators and achieve the predicted exchange-rate movements. The legendary victory of George Soros was seen at the time as proof that no system of stable exchange-rate relations could withstand the overwhelming force of "market corrections."

The decision to create the European Monetary Union (EMU) and the common currency followed a similar logic. The political and economic argument was that European integration was the main source of the unprecedented prosperity and social progress in Europe since the late 1940s. The recurrence of monetary instability and the differences among the member countries concerning prices and exchange rates would threaten the very survival of the project. It was also clear to all the important decision makers that the peaceful success at the end of the 1980s of the "Western model" as opposed to the Soviet model—a success that led to the end of the Cold War—was closely linked to the success of European integration.

It also became clear, both to experts and the political leadership, that the trend toward more market freedom—and in particular more dynamic, open and internationally integrated financial markets (and international capital flows)—would gain further momentum. "Market-based" rather than "relationship-based" banking and finance was the "wave of the future." These trends implied simultaneous shrinking of the ability and the willingness of governments and central banks to intervene in financial markets and in particular to "fine-tune" exchange-rate developments. The lack of effectiveness of "fiscal fine-tuning"—a specialty in particular of British post-war Keynesian economic policies—had become evident by the 1970s. Hence, its replacement by "monetarism"—a new equally powerful theoretical and policy fashion—the limitations of which, however, were to become evident even more rapidly.

Thus, the only truly radical alternative to a system of floating or flexible exchange rates appeared to be the abolition altogether of exchange rates among the members of the European Union. This was the conclusion and recommendation of the Delors Report, prepared by a group of experts/practitioners, which comprised the leading central bankers of Europe.[54]

The following were the main features of the new system, which was probably the boldest common initiative in the field of monetary matters by a group of highly developed free and sovereign countries:

- The creation of a new common currency that would replace all the national currencies.
- The transfer of all sovereign power in the area of monetary policy to a new European Central Bank (ECB) that would be at the center of a common system of national central banks.

54

Table 1.5 Government debt, 1998–2010: Average annual growth rate

	Germany	France	Italy	Spain	Netherlands	Ireland	Portugal	Hungary	Poland	UK
	12	12	12	12	12	12	12	12	12	12
1998	754	790	1233	285	197	41	54	24	56	567
2010	1342	1310	1738	549	337	147	157	74	184	1269
	5.38%	4.71%	3.17%	6.14%	5.00%	12.31%	10.19%	10.78%	11.42%	7.60%

Source: Euronet.

- The conduct of monetary policy by independent officials who were not to take orders from any of the individual member states, from the members acting together or from any of the other institutions of the European Union.[55]

Fighting inflation became the central mandate of the new common monetary authority. Policies to stimulate growth or to fight unemployment were seen implicitly as potentially incompatible with monetary policies focusing on price stability. This, as much as independence, was obviously the central thesis of the Bundesbank doctrine.

Next to "concern for growth and employment," the other great absent among the tasks of the ECB and its management was the rate of exchange of the Euro against other currencies. Both in the Delors Report and in the final treaty creating the Monetary Union and the common currency, the new "Euro zone" or "Euro land" was projected as an island (a fortified island) far, far away from other "monetary areas," where other currencies were being managed by other central bankers with similarly narrow mandates. This was clearly a make-or-break issue for the Bundesbank and its allies in the German government and public. The fact that the French fought for a different approach—which would recognize the importance of the external value of the Euro—was proof for the Bundesbank that France remained "soft" on the inflation issue.[56]

Key elements of the Economic and Monetary Union are the so-called Maastricht criteria, concerning inflation, fiscal indicators (debt and deficit), interest rates and exchange rates (Table 1.5). The role of the Maastricht criteria is to determine, first of all, whether a country qualifies to enter the Monetary Union and, subsequently, whether members pursue sufficiently convergent policies required by a common currency and monetary policy. The so-called Growth and Stability Pact was adopted essentially in order to give added political weight to monitoring the policies of the member countries with respect to these criteria.[57]

1.4.3   The EMU and "limited government"

The creation of the Economic and Monetary Union in the 1990s also coincided with the heyday of the new orthodoxy: a combination of libertarianism, financial deregulation and globalization. This trend, similar to other theories that had turned into dominant doctrines, was marked by a number of paradoxes both in Europe and the United States.

While the common political values of the various components of these trends were freedom and the respect for diversity (the foundations of a free-market economy), the new orthodoxy became increasingly intolerant in defining what was and was not compatible with the market economy. Along with freedom, the respect for democracy, representative government and free political institutions were rightly regarded as cornerstones for the success and the political acceptance of the market economy. Yet, the new orthodoxy became increasingly intolerant when it came to the scope of the decisions of freely elected democratic governments. According to this doctrine: "governments could never do anything right" whereas "markets could never do anything wrong."

Limiting government power meant not only reducing and even eliminating the right of governments to "interfere" with cross-border economic and financial transaction (strict immigration control has been an exception to the liberalization of cross-border movements), but also the definition and imposition of binding limits on the policy choices and freedom of governments on a range of issues. The definition of what is and is not compatible with "market economics" has often been the result of the work of non-elected bodies—experts, industry associations, think tanks and international bureaucracies. The term "democracy deficit" is characteristic for a range of binding international economic and financial rules.

Competition is a key aspect of the proper functioning of the market economy. Thus, one would expect that the advocates of free markets and an open "globalized" economy would be particularly concerned that excessive concentrations of economic and market power should not undermine the advantages of a liberal, open market economy on a global scale. Many of the advocates of globalization (and also of European integration) exaggerate the advantages of "economies of scale" and the frequency of "natural monopolies." They do not pay enough attention to the negative consequences of the creation of mammoth companies that dominate large portions of global markets. Obstacles to mergers are thought to be undue interference, whereas predatory takeovers (and elimination) of business rivals are considered a normal practice.

The creation of the European Union coincided in time with growing arguments that "financial integration" could be a self-regulatory process and not require supervision by the authorities in charge of maintaining monetary stability. Thus, the "costs of integration" and the "recessionary effect" of the requirements of convergence toward stricter macroeconomic discipline were to be more than offset by full, seamless, financial integration not only within the European Union, but world-wide. Thus, any national efforts to slow down or control the takeover of national banks by foreign entities, or the attempt to maintain a modicum of national control or influence, were considered the epitome of forbidden state interventionism and anti-market behavior. The consequences of the absence of some limits or tools to oversee the excesses of the increasingly concentrated cross-border financial giants (including those that took over much of the Eastern and Central European banking market) have been well illustrated both during the expansionary phase and during the contractionary phase of the current crisis.

According to Otmar Issig (2004), at the time Chief Economist of the European Central Bank:

> The new insights stress the endogeneity of the structure of the economy and are part of the so-called new optimal currency area literature. ... A first insight of this literature is that a currency union can use financially integrated capital markets more easily to share risk.[58]

It is believed today both in academic circles and in the broader public (especially in the business community) that discretionary decisions by governments are inferior to decisions based on legislation, international agreements, judicial decisions and pre-determined rules in general. Politicians are depicted as self-serving, interested only in "popular favor and re-election" and thus less respectful of the true interests of the community. National and international rule-making and legislating on the basis of often untested and controversial economic theories have been a characteristic of the post-war decades. At times these initiatives and innovations have produced very positive results. However, many of the rules thus adopted have proved to be not only ineffective but often outright harmful.

1.4.4 The issue of fiscal balance

Fiscal policy—whereby governments collect part of the income of populations which they will then spend or distribute—is perceived and analyzed by economists, political leaders, officials, households and businesses from five perspectives:

1. The first has to do with ownership, the power to decide and the question of private and individual interests vs common interests (the interests of the community).
2. The second has to do with the division of tasks or division of labor between the government and the private sector.
3. The third perspective is the role of government spending and revenues in stimulating or slowing down economic activity (the issue of "effective demand" and the full use of resources—the "Keynesian" issue) and the contribution of fiscal policy to equilibrium or imbalances in the economy, including the issue of deficits and surpluses and the level of government debt.
4. The fourth issue has to do with the structure and efficiency of the fiscal system, on both the income and expenditure sides, the financing of spending (taxation or borrowing), etc.
5. Lastly, fiscal policy can have a more or less important function of income redistribution (social justice).

The relative weight of these factors tends to differ not only between countries but within the same country depending on which party is in power. In practice, fiscal policy is a complex and controversial area of economic science and practice. There is a tendency by all governments and public administrations to throw a veil of mystery and prudish discretion over what goes on in the enormous accounting machinery of receipts and expenditures of the multiple levels of the "public sector." Often too little information is the problem. But not surprisingly, in many cases too much data can also be a source of confusion and misinformation. The "information revolution" of the last 20 or 30 years, and the new technologies available for collecting, analyzing, storing and diffusing fiscally relevant data should have made fiscal policies more transparent and more reliable and the outcomes more accurate. This has not been universally the case, partly because of the volatility of the link between fiscal and non-fiscal variables.

The question of how to achieve fiscal balance, through "higher taxes" or "lower government spending," has provoked acrimonious and recurring political and social debates throughout the OECD countries during the last 40 years. Allegedly neutral "technical economists" have often lacked objectivity in this context, and their advice has led to greater, rather than less, confusion. Today there is no consistent theory of how to deal best with the fiscal issue, and consequently with the debt issue. Some points are fairly obvious, and there is a consensus around them. Credit and thus debt are an important part of the modern economy, and this includes government debt. Government debt plays (i.e., is supposed to play) an important role as the most reliable or ultimate instrument of "storage of value," both for banks and non-financial actors including households. Also, "government paper" is one of the traditional tools for central banks to implement monetary policy. It is also generally accepted that beyond a certain point both government debt and private debt become unsustainable (for debtors and creditors or for the system as a whole).

Should there be a rule-based economy or a market-based economy? The answer by both economists and the real actors in the economy is that there is a need for both—and the two approaches have to be compatible and not create excessive distortions, injustices and inefficiencies. The approach that politicians favor is one of trial and error and political negotiations. This approach involves innovation and frequent compromises on principles, in particular in order to obtain the necessary consensus for action. Economists tend to deride this tradition. Their approach has been that either you are right or you are wrong. A compromise between the two solutions is not a "second best" but a "third worst outcome." Yet "pure economists" are rarely able or willing to give an objective interpretation of the advantages and disadvantages of conflicting theories and policies, and which theory, at what point, will produce the better results.

1.4.5   Fiscal policy, sovereignty and European and world-wide integration

For any objective observer, one of the important characteristics of the process of European integration has been, from the start to the present day, how small the share first of the European Community and now of the European Union has been in the total of the public sector revenues and expenditure of the member states. The basic rule throughout the years has been: the public sector's income is earned, collected and spent in and by the states where it is originally generated. The common programs, including those that involve resource redistribution among the member countries, represent, despite the constantly recurring complaints of the "net payers," a fairly small proportion of both the GDP, public sector income and spending in the European Union.

If the *de facto* and *de jure* fiscal sovereignty of the member states had not been respected, the project of European integration and European unification would have come to a halt at an early stage—probably several decades ago, without any serious chance of a "relaunch." The introduction of the so-called Maastricht criteria and the Growth and Stability Pact represented the first important step toward greater relevance of the Union in the planning and implementation of fiscal policy at the national level. The principle of fiscal sovereignty, in particular the amount of spending and the way the government's resources were collected, was not weakened. The so-called excessive debt procedures represented the first systematic direct intervention by the EU bureaucracy in the fiscal decision making of the member states. These procedures have not been particularly successful[59]—especially when it became evident that the principle of equal treatment was not fully respected by the Commission. Thus, similarly to the tradition of the IMF, the smaller and more vulnerable the member states, the harsher the language and threats (and increasingly the measures) aimed at correcting the behavior of the culprits.

1.4.6   Monetary sovereignty vs fiscal sovereignty

The question of how much "national fiscal sovereignty" was compatible with international monetary integration (and with a rule-based international monetary order) has been part of the debate at least since the Werner Report. This issue was discussed during the creation and throughout the life of the European Monetary System. It was also a major issue in the negotiations on the European Monetary Union. There remained, however, a sharp contrast in terms of "limits on fiscal sovereignty" as defined in the Maastricht criteria and the Stability and Growth Pact, on the one hand, and the revolutionary limitations (or even elimination) of "national monetary sovereignty" brought about by the creation of the European Central Bank and the common currency, on the other. The ECB and the Euro represent an unprecedented transfer of sovereignty in an essential area affecting economic prosperity and involving major policy responsibilities not only to a common institution but also to one that is meant to have an iron-clad guaranty of its independence against any attempts to interfere by the member states.

The visceral resentment manifested towards the idea of the common currency and a European Central Bank—not only in Britain, but also in Germany—had to do as much with the political dimension of the issue of sovereignty as with the economic question: would the European Central Bank be able to do a good job, during both good times and during crises? One may argue, however, that it was not so much the transfer of sovereignty that threatened to make the ECB a "fair-weather" institution, but the serious limitations imposed on its mandate—not in the name of national sovereignty, but in the name and spirit of a particular economic theory, the one advocating floating exchange rates to prevent inflationary contamination from the rest of the world.[60] These limitations reflected the Emminger-Tietmeyer interpretation of the role of the central bank and of the origins of the success of the Deutschmark and the German economy as a whole.[61]

During the 1970s, 1980s and 1990s through the publications of the Bundesbank, and especially of the speeches and articles published in the widely distributed *Auszüge aus Presseartikeln*, this doctrine was hammered home to the business community and the general public systematically week by week, month by month, year after year. No week went by without a member of the Board, the President or other officials making a speech at annual meetings, openings of industrial fairs, etc., talking about the threats to the stability and the prosperity of the German economy. The bulk of these real or alleged threats came from the outside. The speeches, the analyses and reports conveyed a veritable siege mentality. The message of the Bundesbank, of the supreme *Währungshüter* of the country, was that Germany has to defend itself against contagion from rest of the world—first and foremost against the contagion of inflation.

The message that was systematically impressed on the business community and politicians, the press and the general public was that the German economy—the most dynamic exporter in the world, the world's third largest economy—was vulnerable. All that Germany could do was to isolate itself—isolate one of the most foreign-trade dependent economies in the world. Germany could not and should not take any international initiatives to create a more stable and better functioning monetary system—which maybe would not only reduce the threats to the deutschmark but also help the rest of Europe and the world deal with the real or alleged problems created by the imbalances engendered by German surpluses.

The contrast between German activity at the European and Atlantic level in terms of political and security cooperation and the doctrine of passivity with respect to international monetary reform preached by the Bundesbank has been a constant of European and world history since the 1950s virtually to the present day. What would have happened if the rest of Europe, and the rest of the world, had isolated itself from the German economy? On this point there was no doubt or hesitation in the convictions and message of the Bundesbank: this would be protectionism, and protectionism is evil and a threat to prosperity and peace. It was argued that what the Bundesbank was preaching was not protectionism but monetary nationalism, and that was allegedly legitimate and compatible with a liberal, internationalist outlook.[62]

From the start, the Bundesbank was opposed to the idea of a European Monetary Union.[63] The virus of inflation could not be eradicated in the vast majority of countries (if one listened in private: for virtually ethnic reasons). It was Chancellor Helmut Kohl and his Finance Minister, Theo Waigel, who pushed through the project against the rearguard action of the Bundesbank and its allies. However, if the European Central Bank was to become a reality, the price to be paid to the Bundesbank would be the incorporation into the rules of the new institution the Bundesbank's sense of vulnerability and its narrow and defensive vision of the world beyond the EMU's borders. There were no clear indications of what the exchange-rate policy should be. There was no right to be worried about economic activity.[64]

An irony of history and of institutions is that too much independence combined with a too narrow interpretation of the scope of their responsibility may lead to inaction, with at times disastrous consequences. Thus, ultimately, it may be argued that it was because of a tight curb of their mandate that the "Guardians of stability" at the ECB in Frankfurt fell asleep on their watch with respect to the impending two giant crises of the first decade of their activity: the corruption of financial assets by the deregulated banking sector and the corruption of financial assets by reckless governments. To say that these developments were surprising would be to accuse the highly experienced professional staff of the ECB of incompetence and negligence. To accept the argument that it was not the responsibility of the ECB to warn with all its power of persuasion across Europe (the way the Bundesbank used to spread its message in Germany) that this was not part of its mandate, would mean a very narrow and corrupt interpretation of the duty to "assure monetary stability."

1.4.7 The political dimension of the European Union: Theory and practice

European integration has been one of the most complex and successful examples of institutional innovation and attempts to reconcile the respect for diversity and national autonomy with the requirements of economic, monetary and financial integration. This process has also been marked by trends in the broader Western community and the "national models" and the debates and preferences of member states. The evolution of rules and policies at the European level and the so-called *acquis communautaire* at any given time also mirrors the interaction of economic and social theories and the shifting position of new intellectual fashions and once powerful dominant doctrines.

Is there insufficient or too much political integration in the European Union? Does the center—the Council, the Commission and the Parliament, not to mention the Court and the ECB—lack sufficient legislative and executive powers compared with the member states, or are the continued progress and even the survival of the Union, the European project, dependent on concentrating even more issues at the "common" level, and reducing the scope even further for diversity—and for democratic preferences—at the national level? Is subsidiarity only a "fair weather" concept?

Although during the last 20 years the European Union has increasingly assumed "State-like" characteristics, there are still many complaints that Europe has not gone far enough toward a "political union" compared with progress in the economic and monetary area.[65] Two points should be mentioned in order to put these complaints about the alleged lack of sufficient "political union" within the European Union into the right perspective. They are equally relevant for understanding both the complexity of the decision making within the European Union and the sources of the innovation and progress of European integration achieved so far and the reasons for at least qualified optimism about the continued strength and resilience of the European project in the future.

Comparing "progress at the economic level" with "lack of progress at the political level" is a common (and convenient) fallacy. Contrary to widespread opinion, at all stages of European (and Western) integration political objectives and decisions preceded purely economic objectives. Economic integration, while important by itself, was from the start and remains today primarily a tool to achieve the shared political objectives of peace, freedom, independence and security.

The other factor that tends to be overlooked frequently by those who voice their frustration about the "lack of political will" or the "lack of political unity" within the European Union (as well as within the broader Western community) is that democracy and diversity are not secondary or "collateral" issues in the European and Western community, but the very essence of the project. The European Union as well as the Western community of free nations were devised, developed and upheld through good times and crises, ever since the 1940s, in order to build and strengthen democracy and to respect and live with diversity without which democracy becomes an empty shell. This also implies that the debate on specific "European" or broader "Western" issues, the debate for "more Europe" or "less Europe," is first and foremost not a debate *between* national states, but *within* the political community of each member state, between the right, the left and the center, the Greens, Conservatives and Social Democrats, the Liberals and the Environmentalists (and the Democrats and Republicans in the United

States). This is true no matter how the different parties and coalitions define themselves, from Luxemburg to Germany, from Hungary to Britain, from France to Greece and Ireland. To ignore this debate, and especially to try to ignore the changing national electoral outcomes of this debate, would be depriving the entire European (and Western) project of legitimacy.[66]

A central issue in the debt crisis is to what extent governments (and their fiscal policies) are at the core of the problem and what their role is in the solution. What should be the division of tasks and of the share of the control of the GDP between government agencies, on the one hand, and the private sector, on the other, is the single most important issue in the debate about economic theory and economic and social issues. The debate is both about "efficiency" and about "equity"—in fact about the values and objectives of modern society.

Beyond ideological preferences, the "pragmatic" questions are: what is the minimum level of government share in national income below which the cohesion and the efficacy of modern society (the social compact) are threatened? Where is the maximum level of government control over the spending and distribution of income, beyond which not only the efficiency of the economy is gravely reduced but also the basic freedoms of citizens are seriously threatened? What should be the degree of international cooperation and common international rules and institutions in the monetary and fiscal area, not only in Europe but also among the leading liberal economies?

There is a close connection between politics and legislation, the legal framework and specific rules, and economic and social theory. Institutional and policy innovation directly or implicitly reflects the influence of theoretical explanations and expectations of the working of the economy and society at large. Actual systems, however, do not follow the strict definitions and conditions of the underlying theories. Legislators and policy makers are by definition forced to see the issues and problems to be solved in a broader perspective than academic scholars, and are forced to accept compromises.

1.5 Competing theories and economic, monetary and societal models: The future of the "social market economy"?

1.5.1 The need for clear signals: globalization and the role of "indicators"

At the center of the political and economic debate there is constant reference to a certain number of key indicators, such as, the deficit/GDP ratio, the debt/GDP ratio, the current account deficit or surplus expressed in terms also of the GDP, nominal and "real" exchange rate, or the "Maastricht criteria," the discount rate, the Libor, etc.

A paradox of the modern globalized economy is the growing importance of "aggregate indicators" in influencing decisions at all levels at a time when the economy has become more complex, and more detailed quantitative and qualitative information is available than ever before. Some of the indicators are of a regulatory type—"traffic signals"—others are aggregate statistical estimates (e.g., the GDP and its components), while others again are based on the judgment and assessment of private or public organizations, with "sovereign credit ratings" currently receiving particular attention.[67]

Much of the debate about the origins and consequences of the debt crisis turns around the question of the "acceptable size of government deficits and sovereign debt/GDP ratios." The theoretical and pragmatic answers to these questions influence policies, private financial markets, and the income and wealth of households and companies throughout the world. There is a common need throughout the economy for decision makers, from individual households to the largest companies and governments of the major economies, to compress the vast amount of information available in the world today into a relatively small number of key indicators. These indicators are interesting on their own. More importantly, they act like traffic lights or warning signals, and thus have much greater global importance than their actual information content and real impact on the rest of the economy. They are important primarily because there is a consensus that they are important.

Some of these indicators are fixed for the long term or adjusted periodically by the "authorities"; others are the result of "markets." The introduction or abandoning of indicators may be the result of systemic changes and/or may be the cause of such changes.

The principal economic, monetary and financial actors can be grouped into the following broad categories:

Producers, Savers, Spenders
- Households and companies
- Governments

Monetary and Financial Institutions
- Banks and other financial intermediaries
- Central banks

These actors both need information and are important sources of information. The actions and plans of the numerous actors in each of these categories are determined by information that is specific to their own individual situation or position, specific to the broad category to which they belong or important for all four major categories listed earlier.

Theory and information failure

Since the mid-1930s under the impact of the "Great Depression" a profound methodological revolution has taken place in economic analysis and policy making. Three stages can be distinguished in this intellectual, but also political and technical, process.

The first stage was the Keynesian revolution and the invention of macroeconomic aggregates for the purpose of analysis, prediction and policy. The second stage was the statistical revolution (part of it carried out by the disciples and students of Keynes, such as the late Sir Richard Stone, who was awarded the 1984 Nobel Prize in Economics for his "fundamental contributions to the development of systems of national accounts [that] greatly improved the basis for empirical economic analysis"). The third stage was the "information revolution" with its powerful hardware and software of which both economists and policy and business decision makers could not have dreamt even as recently as 15 or 20 years ago.

Has this last stage, which is far from over, made the accomplishments and debates of the first two stages obsolete? The answer to this question is an unqualified "no." The enormous progress of statistical/empirical tools has not solved some of the basic theoretical (and policy) arguments and disagreements about the virtues and shortcomings of the various policy instruments (fiscal, monetary, regulatory or institutional), or of the behavior of markets. Also, the degree of effectiveness of policy measures and the time lags with which they will achieve the desired effects (if not the opposite ones) remains largely a guessing game. Most importantly the powerful analyses of vast amounts of past data (daily, weekly, monthly, quarterly and yearly time series) have not provided convincing tools for forecasting major turning points, and thus the basis of anticipation for avoiding them or attenuating their effect.

One of the characteristics of current theories and policies is the important role played by a small number of key indicators in assessing developments, guiding policies and trying to predict future developments. Most of these indicators are symbolic rather than directly affecting the functioning of the national and world economies. They often contribute to the attempt to fine-tune policies on the basis of relatively minor fluctuations in the level of these values. Positive or negative judgments are based on differences of less than 1%, even in areas where the initial statistical errors maybe of 1% or 2% on either side of zero.

An illustration of the problems encountered with indicators in the recent past (and of the attempt to learn from these problems) is the new "Scoreboard" prepared by the European Commission for assessing the economic situation and the conformity of national policies with EU policy guidelines and objectives.[68] This "scoreboard" includes the following 10 sets of "alert indicators for macroeconomic imbalances":

- Current account balance
- Net international investment position
- Real effective exchange rate

- Export market shares
- Unit labor costs
- House price index
- Private sector debt
- Private sector credit flow
- General government sector debt
- Unemployment rate.

The first *Alert Mechanism Report* was completed in February 2012.[69]

In the debt area one can mention the "Fiscal Monitors" prepared by the IMF at regular intervals for all members of the Fund and for major country groupings. The indicators also include projections for two to three years ahead.

Indicators and financial markets

It is widely recognized that international capital movements have played an important and often destabilizing role in the financial and monetary crises of the last 40 years. Over time, the BIS and other institutions (including private banks and research and consulting organizations) have developed useful systems to statistically track these flows. Yet, this data remains far from complete and sufficiently reliable and homogenous. More importantly, there is no clear understanding of the links between these flows, on the one hand, and the monetary policies of central banks and the "real transactions" related to trade or long-term investments, on the other.

In today's complex, even cacophonic, financial and monetary system, official actors have increasingly adopted a "trial and error approach." The problem has been aggravated by the view, which prevailed for many years among both economists and policy makers, that it is up to "private markets" to bring order and rationality into the financial and monetary system. Systematically, "authorities" have been seen not as the solution but as the principal source of the problems. It has been argued that, given the often contradictory signals (interest rates, money supply, fiscal policies, etc.) coming from officials, it is little wonder that even "perfect markets" would sometimes fail.

Yet, financial markets, however important, are far from perfect. (One of the dangers of the current situation is to nurture a visceral anti-bank attitude.) Even consistent defenders of the market economy and the convertibility of currencies in an integrated world economy recognize that markets, and in particular financial markets, need clear signals from the "authorities." It is the lack of such clear signals (or outright "wrong signals"), or the ignoring of them by market actors, which are mainly responsible for creating the conditions for monetary and financial crises.

1.5.2   The role of theory and research

There is a lively debate at the national and international level about the possible long-term solutions to the debt crisis and about the hierarchy of objectives, policy tools and options for short-term policies. A positive aspect of the current situation is the energy and imagination with which economic research—in academic institutions, government agencies, international organizations, research centers and central banks—has responded to the challenge of the debt crisis and the need for understanding, for realistic and reliable forecasting and reasonable policy options. This research, however, also reflects the fluidity of the situation and the frequent revisions that are made both about the order of magnitude of the debt problem and the relative importance of the various issues. There are also frequent adjustments and differences of opinion on the policy priorities.

The various positions and preferences reflect different interests—within and between states—and political ideologies. However, directly or indirectly, the debate also reflects the influence of various economic theories and schools of thought. The monetary and financial crisis has given a new impetus to both applied research on the debt issue and the debate on theory—to the development of new concepts and approaches and to revisiting earlier crises and theoretical controversies, in particular the interwar period and the Great Depression of the 1930s.

1.5.3 Current views and recent research

A worrying aspect of the current systemic crisis is that it will have lowered not only the short-term growth rate of the OECD economies but also the rate of potential long-term growth. This could be the case, in particular, if the international monetary system was to continue exerting a deflationary and recessionary influence. Freely floating exchange rates tend to exert, through the high degree of uncertainty and actual and potential instability, a strong deflationary influence, in particular on "weaker economies." The message from most of the recent research is clear. There is a need for both strong growth and for political and structural adjustments.

The severity of the debt crisis and the dramatic long-term consequences of the continuation of current trends in the OECD countries are illustrated in a working paper prepared by the Bank for International Settlements in 2010.[70] In this widely read article, the authors present three sets of long-term scenarios for the size of public debt as a percentage of GDP for a number of OECD countries. According to one of the authors,[71] the paper

> should have been titled "The *impossible* future of public debt" because our idea is not that this *will* happen, it is that this *cannot* happen. ... Our message is also that even fairly big adjustments are not enough to stabilize debt for a surprisingly large number of important countries. For most countries in fact, recent crisis-related spending plus the coming onset of ageing pressures mean that brutal policy choices will have to be made if we are to get public debt under control.

Their scenarios show that by the year 2040, for a number of major European countries, including Germany, without drastic corrections, the share of public debt could reach or even exceed 300%. For the UK, this number could be close to 400%. This would be the case also for the United States, for which the best-case scenario still shows a public debt representing 150% of GDP. The worst case—a real outlier—is Japan where, according to the authors' calculations, public debt could represent between 350% and 500% of GDP. The scenarios take into account the structural changes occurring in the OECD area as a result of the demographic trends of ageing populations and the decline in the share of the active working force in the total population. (This makes the problem of high levels of youth unemployment—and of precarious, low-paying, low-skilled jobs that discourage people from having more or even any children—all the more dramatic.)

To quote at some length:

> (The) examination of the future of public debt leads us to the ... important conclusion ... (that) fiscal problems confronting industrial economies are bigger than suggested by official debt figures that show the implications of the financial crisis and recession for fiscal balances. As frightening as it is to consider public debt increasing to more than 100% of GDP, an even greater danger arises from a rapidly ageing population. The related unfunded liabilities are large and growing, and should be a central part of today's long-term fiscal planning. ... It is essential that governments not be lulled into complacency by the ease with which they have financed their deficits thus far. In the aftermath of the financial crisis, the path of future output is likely to be permanently below where we thought it would be just several years ago. As a result, government revenues will be lower and expenditures higher, making consolidation even more difficult. But, unless action is taken to place fiscal policy on a sustainable footing, these costs could easily rise sharply and suddenly.

The authors also "note the risk that persistently high levels of public debt will drive down capital accumulation, productivity growth and long-term potential growth," referring to "a recent study suggests that there may be non-linear effects of public debt on growth, with adverse output effects tending to rise as the debt/GDP ratio approaches the 100% limit (Reinhart and Rogoff)."[72]

In fact, the work of Reinhart and Rogoff, the authors mentioned in the aforesaid BIS Working Paper, is among the most widely quoted among the historical and quantitative analyses of debt crises.[73] Among the issues and conclusions of Reinhart and Rogoff, the following points should be mentioned: (1) the vicious circle, based on regression results, showing that above a debt/GDP ratio of around 80 to 100 the potential growth rate tends to decline significantly; (2) the widespread occurrence in the recent or more distant past of "sovereign debt default"; and (3) their use of the concept of "financial repression"—that is, any official measures of "interference" with international capital movements and markets.[74]

Another important theoretical and practical development is the so-called Golden Rule, that is, the enshrining of the obligation of a balanced budget into the constitution. The principal example is the German *Schuldenbremse* (break on debt) adopted in 2009:

> The debt brake enshrined in Article 109 III of the Basic Law explicitly requires that, as a general rule, central and state government must achieve balanced budgets without incurring new debt, and it therefore differs substantially from the previous investment related borrowing limit. The debt brake does not merely set a target; it imposes a ceiling that must not be overshot. Suitable safety margins are therefore needed to allow governments fiscal leeway under the new rules. Given the clarity of the rules, any planned contravention of the borrowing limit could at least be halted by the constitutional courts if someone were to file a suit.[75]

This was essentially the model followed by the European Union[76] in the "Treaty Establishing the European Stability Mechanism" and "Treaty on Stability, Coordination and Governance in the Economic and Monetary Union" in early 2012 ("Fiscal Pact").[77] It remains to be seen to what extent this concept will stand the test of time, both during recessions and during phases of expansion.

An often-heard argument is that it is the "small countries" that have brought on the crisis of the Euro zone. This argument is the pendant of the one about the weight of the undisciplined "periphery" on the virtuous "core" of the European Union and of the Euro zone. This reasoning leads to some outright fallacious conclusions. The principal one is that the "sooner the virtuous countries in the Euro zone" get rid of the perennial deficit-makers and problem countries the better it will be for everyone concerned.

> It may seem ironic that euro area countries with relatively modest fiscal gaps are the victims of a virulent debt crisis whereas other countries with much larger fiscal gaps enjoy very low bond yields at present. This partly reflects concerns about potential needs for intervention in euro area banking systems, but also that euro area debt essentially corresponds to foreign currency denominated debt for the individual country. In the absence of corrective action, higher interest rates could lead to substantial increases in debt, in particular in high debt countries (e.g., Japan and Greece) but also for countries running large structural deficits (e.g., the United Kingdom, Ireland, New Zealand and the United States).[78]

The balance of payments and "fiscal devaluation"

Another issue raised both in official statements and by researchers in central banks and international organizations as well as by academic economists is the need to improve the "competitive position" of the highly indebted countries in order to improve their balance of payments. This is the case where a large part of the government debt is held outside the country in question, such as the United States or Greece. As often as not, the recommendations include a devaluation of the currency. However, while there is no consensus on the effectiveness of devaluations in improving the current account position in the long run—and this is especially the case for countries with a relatively small manufacturing base—the issue of "balance-of-payments improvement" (and debt reduction) through devaluation becomes even more questionable for members of the Euro zone. This is in fact the most frequently invoked argument for inducing Greece and possibly other deficit countries to leave the Euro zone. The favorite solution for this dilemma for those who advocate both devaluation and staying in the Euro zone is the so-called fiscal devaluation approach.[79]

A balance-sheet recession

Another widely discussed author is Richard Koo, Chief Economist of Nomura Research. In his writings Koo has applied the concept of "balance sheet recession" to the analysis of both the origin and nature of the financial and economic crisis in Japan in the 1990s and to the current "great recession." He also argues that applying this concept to the depression of the 1930s helps better explain the nature of that economic, financial, social and political catastrophe than the monetarist explanation of Milton Friedman and Anna Schwarz.[80]

The Japanese example is particularly relevant in the current context for a number of reasons: it includes a very large debt problem, a major asset-destruction at the start of the crisis (it has been estimated that the crisis destroyed the equivalent of two or three years of GDP, some of which, however, had been pure hot air created by the preceding speculation), and the issue of the consequences of financial deregulation. The question of the "internal social and economic" model is also very much at the center of the Japanese story as it is in the current European and American debate. According to Koo:

> It is critical that President Obama and other world leaders understand the relevance of the Japanese experience and make use of it to avert global depression. ... (S)ome democracies may collapse if the global contraction is allowed to continue. Countries with the right economic policies but the wrong political agenda may also expand their influence, as happened in the 1930s.[81]

1.5.4 Economic theories, the lessons of the Great Depression and the failure of "modern economics"

The financial, monetary and debt crisis in the leading economies of the world has revived the debate about economic theory and the link between theory, forecasting and the various policy models and options. Modern economic theories are directly or indirectly the result of the Great Depression and the lessons learned from this traumatic experience with wide-ranging consequences. Historians and the general public agree to this day that without the Great Depression and the international monetary and economic crisis, the world could have been spared the National Socialist regime and the Second World War for which this regime was responsible. Many of the laws, policies, institutions and innovations that have marked the period since the end of the Second World War were adopted in response to the experience of the 1930s (and in fact of the entire inter-war period).

Since the outbreak of the world-wide financial crisis there has been a revival of interest in the subject of the Great Depression—its causes, manifestations and consequences—and in the debate about how it could have been avoided. The current crisis has also led to new interest in the origins and the nature of the depression of the 1930s and in the lessons that can be drawn for understanding the current problems and their implications for the future. The coining of the term the "Great Recession" on the model of the "Great Depression" suggests that there is a fear that the past might repeat itself.

Thus, there is concern that the bold belief, prevailing for most of the period since the late 1940s, that the power of modern economic analysis and the sophistication of the tools of contemporary policy making would render for ever impossible the recurrence of the calamities of the first half of the twentieth century, might not be justified after all. This fear has also been revived by the recent history of the Japanese economy, which during the last 20 years has defied all attempts to find the way back to a bright future and the dynamic growth prospects that used to be taken for granted.

There is no room or need to go into the details of this debate and the rapidly growing literature on this subject. It is clear that the differences are as important as the similarities between the current situation and that of the 1920s and 1930s.

1.5.5 The legacy of Keynes

At the level of economic theory, the most obvious legacy of the Great Depression (and in fact also of the decade leading up to the Great Crash) was the oeuvre of John Maynard Keynes—both his writings and his role in the creation of the basic concepts and institutions of the post-war international economic and monetary order—and the spreading of "Keynesianism" as the dominant doctrine for virtually three decades after the end of the Second World War.

Those who were not Keynesians—including his most virulent critics before and after the end of the war—were also influenced by his ideas. Keynes defined to a large extent the terms of the debate. There were also those, like the liberal economist Wilhelm Röpke, who were critical (especially of the qualification "general") of Keynes's theory advocating the need to stimulate demand through government spending, but who shared the view that under exceptional circumstances (the Great Depression) exceptional government measures were necessary and justified.[82]

Röpke wrote in 1931 about the report of the so-called *Braun-Komission* concerning the objections to government measures to combat crisis:

> *Der soeben betrachtete Einwand läuft auf einen konjunkturpolitischen Liberalismus hinaus, der in seinen Konsquenzen zu einer wahrhaftigen konjunkturpolitischen Nihilismus führt. Bei aller Sympathie für den Liberalismus als allgemeines wirtscheftpolitisches Program muss ich gestehen, dass ich je länger, desto weniger Verständnis für diesen Standpunkt aufbringen kann.*[83]

After the war, Röpke wrote about the "austerity policy" of the British Labour Government: "Austerity is schlechte Nationalökonomie und eine falsche Rechnung, weil sie dem heute so notwendigen Arbeits- und Sparwillen entgegenwirkt."[84]

Keynes and "Keynesian" ideas are at the center of the debate on how to deal with the debt situation.[85] The main questions are:

1. Is there room and a need for fiscal stimulus at the time of large deficits and unprecedented debt/GDP ratios in order to prevent a lasting recession (or even depression) that would further aggravate the deficit and debt problem?
2. Is it possible to effectively deal with the debt problem without debt and asset destruction through inflation (and if yes, how to make sure that inflation does not get out of hand)?
3. Is it economically and politically necessary and justified to provide Central Bank guaranty to governments that otherwise would face insolvency?

The positions and solutions proposed concerning the debt issue and the international monetary system are closely related to the perception of the existing problems and preferences of the economic and social models. This is true for the political parties, political leaders and decision makers, the academic debate, and most importantly for national and international officials.

1.5.6 Fiscal discipline vs growth? The risks of relative-price and asset-price deflation

What should come first: fiscal discipline or economic growth? This question dominates both the debate among economists and the policy differences at the national, the European and global levels. At the two extremes there are those who insist on an either/or answer: (1) one group that includes both the Keynesians ("increase government transfers and spending") and the die-hard supply-siders ("tax cuts will reduce the deficit"), and (2) another group that argues that cutting the deficits *now* is the only way to avoid a calamity.

Most people concluded that the optimum approach would be to try to promote growth and reduce the deficits and the debt. Thus, according to the President of the European Central Bank, Mario Draghi:

> First of all: there is absolutely no contradiction between a growth compact and a fiscal compact. In fact, growth is sustainable in the long run if it is based on a variety of pillars, one of which is fiscal stability. The second observation is that I certainly agree when you say that we have to put growth back at the centre of the agenda. What does this growth compact mean? It refers to a variety of ideas that have been expressed in a number of places, and I certainly don't claim any patent on this concept.[86]

It is not clear, however, whether the various suggestions, coming from official or unofficial sources will achieve the combined objective of deficit and debt reduction and sustaining and stimulating economic growth. The following illustrate the wide range of policy suggestions (some of which are already being implemented):

1. systematic and often severe cuts in wages and employment (both in the public and "productive" sectors)
2. pressure on prices (and wages) to improve productivity and competitive positions
3. actual or "fiscal" devaluation to reduce balance-of-payments deficits
4. labor market reforms to increase "mobility and flexibility"
5. reducing "resource transfers" from the "virtuous" (low-deficit) to the "undisciplined" (high-deficit) countries and taxpayers
6. *de facto* or *de jure* debt default (in particular sovereign debt default), and finally
7. breaking up the Euro zone.[87]

At the end of May 2012,

> the European Commission has adopted a package of recommendations for budgetary measures and economic reforms to enhance financial stability,

boost growth and create employment across the EU. ... Unemployment, and in particular youth unemployment, is a severe problem—and though there is no quick fix, immediate action should be taken to increase productivity and better match skills and training to labour market needs ... twelve Member States concerned face macroeconomic imbalances which need to be corrected and closely monitored. ... One key lesson from the crisis has been that more attention needs to be paid to macroeconomic imbalances and divergences in competitiveness between EU countries. In some cases, current account imbalances and divergences in price competitiveness have reached unprecedented and unsustainable levels, and this goes well beyond a natural catching-up process or demographic determinants of the past decade. ... They also conclude that the adjustment of economic imbalances is broadly proceeding, as reflected in reductions in current account deficits, convergence in unit labour costs, retrenchment in credit flows or corrections in housing prices. However, in some cases it is not clear to what extent the adjustment is complete and durable, or whether the speed of adjustment is adequate. In many cases, the accumulated internal and external imbalances continue to pose a formidable challenge, for example with regard to private and public sector indebtedness.[88]

There is no question that taken individually many of these measures make good economic and even political sense. In the light of the current situation and past experience, it is probable that some of the policy suggestions aimed at correcting the main sources of "structural imbalances" contain major deflationary risks. In the immediate aftermath of the "subprime crisis" (Stage I) the expansionary fiscal reaction of most countries was welcomed even by the most prudent monetary experts. Thus, for example, Alexandre Lamfalussy, former Head of the European Monetary Institute and of the Bank for International Settlements, argued in April 2009:

(Part of the) good news concerns fiscal policy. Quite rightly, given the deleterious impact of the financial crisis on economic activity, all governments have accepted the deterioration of their fiscal balances. In the case of the European countries this meant that they let the automatic stabilizers do their work, and on top of this added discretionary stimulative measures. The size and the nature of these measures vary considerably among the countries, but most of them go in the right direction. Of course, as time goes by, increasing attention will have to be paid to the exit scenario. As we all know these measures had to be timely (broadly speaking, they respected this criterion), they had to be well targeted (this was also more or less respected), but now we have to make sure that there will be no doubt about their temporary nature. And, about this, doubts are beginning to arise.[89]

As it became rapidly evident, these counter-cyclical fiscal policies aggravated the fiscal situation across the OECD countries and contributed to what has become the current debt crisis. The fact that these "discretionary stimulative measures" did not lead to a robust growth by now (although as many rightly argue they may have prevented the "Great Recession" from turning into a "Great Depression II") and thus have made a fiscal reversal and debt reduction (the "exit scenario") more onerous if not impossible. According to the European Commission (as quoted by the European Central Bank) the "aggregate euro area government deficit" was expected (in the autumn of 2011) to decline in 2011 to 6.2% of GDP in 2010 (and a similar level in 2009 compared with 2.1% in 2008 and 0.7 in 2007) and was forecast to fall to 3.1% in 2012 and to the "magic" 3.0% level by 2013. The "bulk of the fiscal adjustment in 2011 results from a fall in government spending."[90]

Irving Fisher and the debt-deflation theory of great depressions

Already in the 1930s Professor Irving Fisher had identified "excessive indebtedness" as one of the two principal causes of depression (the other was "deflation"):

> In the great booms and depressions, (all the other) factors (have) played a subordinate role as compared with two dominant factors, namely overindebtedness to start with, and deflation soon after; also that where any of the other factors do become conspicuous, they are often merely effects or symptoms of these two.[91]

It is not a far-fetched view that the level of indebtedness reached by now—and especially the level that could be reached in the medium and long term—should warrant a fear of a second Great Depression in the Western world in less than a century.[92] What seems to be "good news" in the context of Irving Fisher's theory is that there has been no "deflation" so far (i.e., a collapse and downward spiral of prices and wages) in the original sense of the word, and as it had happened in the 1930s. Since the 1930s, we know that "deflation" means not just an absolute decline in prices but also a downward pressure of "relative prices"—and (with Keynes) a "decline in aggregate demand." It is well known by now that "asset-price deflation" is a powerful recessionary force, not only through the corporate and bank "balance-sheet" effects, but through the impact on household savings, retirement security and income as well. As it is widely (and rightly) argued, the effects of "asset-price deflation" become particularly pernicious as a result of an "aging society" and in economies where (as in most of the OECD countries), over the last decades, there has been a marked and deliberate shift from wage income to income from financial assets (including through asset-price inflation).

1.5.7   International economic disintegration: The lessons from the Great Depression

In his outstanding history of the Great Depression, Charles Kindleberger insists on the complexity of the causes of the depression and warns against using a single theory or set of policies to explain what happened. Kindleberger also emphasizes the importance of the international interdependence of the major economies and the fatal consequences of the breakdown of the international monetary and trading system.[93] The main lesson from the Great Depression both for economists and for political leaders after 1945 had to do with its international dimension. This was also Wilhelm Röpke's thesis in 1942 in his pioneering book on *International Economic Disintegration*.[94] It was already accepted during the war that the depression had both complex international causes and devastating international consequences through its impact on the international monetary system, international trade and ultimately output and employment. The rise of protectionism and of an increasingly restrictive web of exchange controls was also a source and effect of political crises and of the ground gained by totalitarian regimes.

Thus, the restoring of a functioning international monetary system and the gradual reduction of barriers to international trade were not only major economic objectives but also of political importance for the Western democracies.[95] It is the memory of the lessons of the 1930s that ultimately has been the most powerful obstacle to the return of protectionism and a fragmented trading system during periods of recession and financial and monetary crises during the last 40 years. International cooperation and determined leadership for an open world economy have been the mainsprings of integration and prosperity since the 1950s. Should the leadership and cooperation weaken or turn into outright conflict, the consequences would be disastrous. At the end of his book Kindleberger evokes the threat of "disaster scenarios" for international economic instability and conflict:

> The three outcomes to be avoided because of their instability are: 1) the United States, Japan and the EEC vying for leadership of the world economy, 2) one unable to lead and the others unwilling as in 1929 to 1933, and 3) each retaining a veto power over programs of stability or strengthening of the system without seeking to secure positive programs of its own.

These warnings are as timely as in 1986 when the revised edition of the *World in Depression* was published.[96]

1.5.8   The "Anglo-Saxons" vs the "Continentals"

There is frequent reference—especially in France and some of the other continental European countries—to the "Anglo-Saxon" model and the differences between this model and the "European" model. In fact, there is considerable diversity both in the "Anglo-Saxon" and the "European" model at any given time, and there has been considerable evolution in all these models not only since the late 1940s and early 1950s—the initial period when the institutional and policy foundations of the economic and social order in the Western World were created—but also in the last quarter century which was marked by the end of the Cold War and the successful trend of globalization.

1.5.9 The theory and practice of the "social market economy"

One of the most successful models was and remains the so-called social market economy.[97]

Germany is the largest member state of the European Union. As all the other member states, and in fact as all the other countries in the Western community, it has had its share of crises and tensions and had to go through often painful periods of economic and social adjustment. On balance, ever since the late 1940s, it has benefitted greatly from the success of European integration and of the Western market economies as a whole—as it has been a major contributor to this unique global success story of the liberal and democratic economic and societal model.

Most people agree that the "German success story"—beginning with the original *Wirtschaftswunder* of the post-war decade—has been the combined result of a favorable external environment and a "home-grown" economic and social model: the "social market economy." The concept of the "social market economy" is based on the recognition of the need to reconcile the apparently conflicting requirements of a competitive, liberal market economy with social responsibility, and an impressive list of major State responsibilities for the common good with the upholding of private initiative and individual freedom. The core tenets of the "social market economy" include the fight against inflation, the concern about public finances, the importance of liberal trade policies and finally social solidarity.

Over the decades the interpretation of this concept, the question of what is compatible or incompatible with the "social market economy" has been at the center of the political and economic debate in Germany, both between the major political parties and within the parties themselves. However, at no point has the model of the "social market economy" been repudiated by either the governing coalitions on the center-right or the center-left of the political spectrum—coalitions that have alternated during the more than six decades long history of the Federal Republic.[98] Thus, Germany has not experienced the often quite radical economic and societal "model changes" that could be observed in some of its major partners in Europe and in the United States—between Keynesianism and monetarism, between state interventionism (including wholesale nationalizations) and market fundamentalism and privatizations *à outrance*, between the welfare state and Thatcherism and Reaganomics and price and wage controls and massive government subsidies.

This does not mean that Germany and the model of the "social market economy" were not affected by these trends. The policy debate was also vigorous in Germany, and there are many traces of the influence of Keynes, Friedman, Hayek and others both at the level of theory and policy in the Federal Republic. There were multiple and sometimes conflicting interpretations of the concept of the social market economy itself, in particular with more or less emphasis on the social dimension and with more or less criticism of the increasing weight of large companies in Germany and abroad. Yet, the radical conflicts and shifts between economic models at the level of theory and policy that could be observed both in the "Anglo-Saxon" world and some of the European countries (in particular in France) tended to create the sense of the "uniqueness" of the German model among both experts and political leaders. It was felt that "the social market economy is not an export model." This consensus prevailed not only in Germany, but also in most of the other OECD countries, and importantly among the experts of the major international economic organizations. In the past, in major debates about various "economic and societal" models with the leading Western countries, German leaders sought less to convince their partners of the benefits of the general acceptance of the German model, but to make sure that Germany could safeguard its model intact and would not be infected by the excesses of other governments. This was true not only in the wider framework of the Atlantic and Western community, but also in the close (and highly successful) cooperation between France and Germany in the process of building the European Union.

The special position of Germany in the efforts to deal with the consequences of the monetary and financial crisis and the debt problem, the rescue of the Euro and in the longer term creating a global international monetary system, is due not only to the weight of the German economy in the European Union and in the world at large. It is also because more than before "interpreting and implementing the concept of the social market economy" has become central not only to the German debate but to the European and transatlantic debate as well. There is no question that Germany has played a major—positive—role in the international efforts during both Stage I and Stage II of the "debt crisis"—and will have to continue, and is ready, to play a positive role in Stages III and IV, which are looming on the horizon of the European and world economy.

Today, accepting the German influence is widely seen as opting for recession and lower long-term growth prospects. Having "to submit" to the economic model inspired by the German experience is seen as severe punishment. The model of the "social market economy" is perceived not only as "recessionary" but also as profoundly anti-social. It is true that Germany drove a hard bargain, in particular during the rescue efforts between 2010 and 2012, and the outcome of these efforts to a significant extent bears the marks of both German fears and preferences. There is no doubt that for Chancellor Merkel and Germany the solutions to be adopted both at the European Union and the European Monetary Union and the country level (in particular the "Greek rescue") had to be acceptable not only to "German taxpayers," but also be compatible with their definition of "responsible economic governance"—in other words, in tune with the model of the "social market economy." This represents both a problem and a challenge for Germany and its partners, and a major, unexpected opportunity not only for Germany but also for the European and world economy.

Probably the most important problem is that most people outside Germany have only a rather vague and superficial understanding of the "social market economy." Many people, including economists and other experts, confuse the concept with the "welfare state," and some think it is a mild form of socialism. Most observers tend to confuse the original concept of "neo-liberalism"—a concept situated between the extreme nineteenth-century version of liberalism (which had contributed to the economic and social crisis of the 1930s) and the state interventionist doctrines that had been so popular in the post-war period in Britain, Scandinavia and also the United States—with the current "libertarian" version of "neo-liberalism"-based market fundamentalism. The lack of understanding of "foreigners" is partly due to their lack of familiarity with the language. Trying to understand all the nuances of what goes on today and has been going for 60 years in a dynamic society and economy of the size and complexity of Germany only in English translation is an arduous task. Most foreign (especially American and British, but also French) experts and commentators who write about Germany and the German economy interpret the English translation of the German context and the German debate through the mental image of the American and British way of thinking or through a "globalized" common view of the world.[99]

The lack of a thorough understanding in Europe and the world of what the "social market economy" was and still represents today is also the fault of the Germans themselves. There is a shortage of good texts on the subject—not only in English or French, but also in German. The second problem is that, like with all economic and social concepts and models, there is no single "authoritative" interpretation even of some of the core concepts and tenets and the extent to which they are present or absent in the actual legislative and institutional structure and policy making. Today there is no pure version of the social market economy (and probably never was) just like there was no pure "Keynesian" model.

Three issues on which there has been controversy in the past and also affect the debate on the German position in the European Union and in the Euro zone and in the international economic and monetary policy debate are: (1) the social dimension of the social market economy and the issue of "solidarity" at the national and international level, (2) the question of growth vs stability and (3) the gains and risks of German participation in the process of European integration, the fear of "contamination" and the need to protect the German model.[100]

Historical record shows that the "social dimension" has been an essential feature of the German success story and of the original model of the "social market economy": this was true in the 1950s and 1960s, and it was again proved during the process of German reunification. The original call for "prosperity for all," *Wohlstand für Alle* by Ludwig Erhard was not populist propaganda but a realistic and feasible objective. It remained feasible because it was based not on redistribution of income but on economic efficiency and growth. Finally, trying to "protect the German model" through isolation from "contamination" is contrary to the way dynamic open economies interact. Turning the social market economy into a successful "export model" is as much in the interests of Germany as of the rest of Europe and the world. In order to succeed, this has to be done not as a "punishment" but as a stimulus for growth and prosperity.[101]

1.5.10 The world needs the Euro

The frontal attacks on the Monetary Union are the culmination of two years of debt crises—of Stage II of the global international monetary and financial crisis. This is further proof, after Iceland and Ireland, of the close connection between the debt issue and the volatility of the international monetary system.

The attacks come from all directions and with growing intensity. They come from economists and political leaders, from government officials and rating agencies, from the "markets" and from those who claim to speak in the name of taxpayers. They come from inside the Euro zone—in the "North," especially Germany[102] and in the "South"—and from outside, from the Anglo-American skeptics and from young market-savvy fund managers. Many of those who argue that the end of the Euro is inevitable, or even that it would be desirable, seem to forget the historic precedents and their consequences: the abandoning or blowing up of an imperfect but functioning major system of international monetary cooperation and integration. The last times this happened were 1971–3, 1929–33 and 1914. Those who insist on dismantling the Euro zone—step by step or in one big meltdown—forget how serious and unpredictable are likely to be the financial and real economic consequences of such a revival of monetary nationalism in both the short and the long term. An integrated world economy needs an integrated and functioning international monetary system that fulfills all the required functions: to help avoid financial excesses (including asset price inflation and deflation) and to provide the framework for the sustained growth of trade and output.

Yet, while lacking historical memory, the common characteristic of these attacks is that they offer no consistent and workable long-term alternative for Europe or for the world economy. Some of them, even among those with the best scholarly pedigrees, exhaust their arguments in trying to prove that there should not be, there cannot be, a functioning monetary union among such a diverse group of countries as the members of the Euro zone and even more the entire European Union. (If this argument had the validity that their advocates claim it has, European integration would never have advanced beyond the stage of an extended EFTA—one that would have swallowed the EEC, rather than the inverse happening in reality.) Some want the return of national currencies—with the deutschmark at the top of the list. Others predict the return of the pure gold standard.

There are, however, also in Germany strong voices, such as the Council of Economic Experts, who warn against misplaced nostalgia for the past and about the consequences of pushing Greece or other countries out of the EMU:

> If German commentators repeatedly say it would have been better to stick with the deutschmark, they fail to see how difficult it is for a national economy focused on exports and stability to assert itself given global financial markets that are as integrated as they are volatile. ... Greece's exit is also no solution. From Greece's viewpoint it might seem beneficial at first glance to quit the euro and by devaluing the newly introduced currency improve the country's competitiveness at one fell swoop. Such a strategy would involve risks that are hard to assess. ... It seems as good as impossible that Greece would manage to prevent its entire financial system collapsing. ... What would (also) be completely unclear is how an exit from the EMU would impact on contracts with non-nationals. From the perspective of the euro area as a whole, an exit by Greece would above all be problematic as it could trigger a chain reaction in the other problem countries, and there is no foreseeing where that would lead.[103]

A systemic financial and monetary crisis is both a challenge and an opportunity, an opportunity if not seized, which could precipitate the next and possibly even more serious crisis. This is the sense of the comments made by the IMF's historian about international monetary reform in the wake of the "subprime crisis":

> The international financial architecture over the past century evolved in response to circumstances of the moment. ... Each of the major attempts to revise the international financial architecture came in response to a crisis. When they succeeded, they did so only partially. This observation leads to (the) lessons (that) ... if revising the rules of international finance dominates the agenda, the opportunity to find better ways to deal with other issues could be lost, possibly for many years.[104]

Defending and bolstering the EMU, however, is not only in the interest of the European economies but of the world economy as a whole, and in

Table 1.6 Gross and net debt position: Major country groups

Country	Concept	Unit	2006	2007	2008	2009	2010	2011	2012	2013	2014	2015	2016
Total Reporting Countries (Average)	Gross debt position (Gen. Govt.)	Percent of GDP	61.599	59.819	62.348	69.150	73.897	73.985	74.080				
Total Reporting Countries (Average)	Net debt (Gen. Govt.)	Percent of GDP	44.789	42.883	46.285	54.343	58.671	62.758	64.978				
Advanced economies	**Gross debt position**	Percent of GDP	74.3	73.4	79.7	91.9	98.1	102.9	106.1	108.0	108.7	109.0	109.4
Advanced economies	**Net debt**	Percent of GDP	46.0	45.0	50.2	60.0	65.7	70.2	74.1	76.6	78.0	79.2	80.3
Euro Area	**Gross debt position**	Percent of GDP	68.6	66.4	70.1	79.7	85.8	88.6	90.0	90.2	89.3	88.0	86.6
Euro Area	**Net debt**	Percent of GDP	54.3	52.0	53.9	62.1	65.9	68.6	70.1	70.5	70.0	69.3	68.6
Emerging Countries	**Gross debt position**	Percent of GDP	36.6	35.9	34.7	36.7	40.9	37.8	36.0	34.3	33.0	31.9	30.9
Emerging Countries	**Net debt**	Percent of GDP	29.7	26.2	23.3	27.9	28.7	28.5	27.5	26.9	26.2	25.7	25.3

Source: IMF Fiscal Monitor.

particular of Europe's partners in the OECD countries (Table 1.6). Also, it is unlikely that it will be possible to strengthen and reform the Euro zone in the long term in isolation from the rest of the world economy, however drastic the measures proposed to curtail the sovereignty of the member states not only in the monetary field but also in the fiscal area and the economic and social policy sphere in general.[105] Thus, the need to support and reform the EMU should be seized as an opportunity, both by Europeans and their principal partners—the United States and Japan—to start addressing the issue of the rebuilding a global international monetary order.

1.6   Conclusion: Is there a way out?

The answer to the question of whether there is a way out of the debt crisis and the crisis of the international monetary system has to be positive. This is based not on vague idealistic optimism but on the seriousness of the situation and the successful record of the Western democracies during the last 60 years in dealing time and again with major crises threatening their prosperity and freedom. The solution has to be primarily political, based on innovation and cooperation not only among the European countries but across the entire Western community.

In terms of the title and the topic of this chapter, that is, "international monetary system and the debt problem," the main conclusion is that a reform of the international monetary system is both possible and indispensable if the twin problems of the debt and its recessionary impact are to be solved. Solving the "Euro zone crisis" is also part of this reform challenge. The planning and the implementation of the reform of the international monetary system have to be common projects of the three pillars of the Western liberal political and economic order: Europe, Japan and the United States. The solution is neither Bretton Woods nor a return to the gold standard. The objective is to develop a rule-based system that will provide both stability and flexibility.[106]

The OECD countries are simultaneously facing a structural, a systemic and a cyclical crisis. This means that solutions have to address these three aspects of the situation at the same time. In this process, they will have to take into account three major sets of factors:

1. "Crisis management" and the "long-term reforms" can only succeed if there is a revival and solid performance of the "real economy."
2. Sustained and sustainable growth cannot be achieved without restoring confidence in financial assets, including government debt.
3. "Too much market" has led to the financial excesses of the past and the current crisis, and "too much government" could stifle innovation and ultimately prosperity and social progress as has happened in the past.

The current crisis is not a "regional crisis," it is not just the crisis of the Euro zone—the same way that the "subprime crisis" was not just the crisis of the US economy, but a global, systemic crisis of the international monetary and financial system. While some may have been hurt more than others (other countries, sectors or sections of the population), there have been no winners since 2007–8. Effective—*ex ante* and not only *ex post*—burden-sharing and solidarity will reassure not only the financial markets but even more importantly the actors in the "real economy" who are responsible for innovation, investments and job creation, and thus reduce the costs for all of dealing with the debt issue.

The exit or the suspension of the membership of one or several countries in the Euro zone would create great risks not only for the countries leaving, but also for the countries remaining within the Euro. The possibility of a "domino effect" cannot be discarded. Doubts about the future of the Euro would not cease, they would rather increase whatever the reassurances issued in Frankfurt, Brussels or in the national capitals. Both the so-called strong and weak countries would suffer from this uncertainty. In the medium and long term, a return to a *de facto* split along the lines of "virtuous" and "unreliable" economies would lead to a lasting slowdown of the European economy and a profound political and institutional crisis of the European Union.

The crisis is not "just an economic crisis." From the start it has been an economic, social and political crisis. Among economists there is no consensus about which theory yields the perfect solution, and many economists tend to ignore the social dimension. Most economists, however, tend to blame "the politicians" for both the origins of the crisis and the failure so far to have found a reliable way out. Yet, both the short-term crisis management and the search for long-term solutions are eminently political tasks. The record shows that the errors of the interwar period were first and foremost the sins of politicians. History also shows that the achievements since the 1940s have been the results of political innovation. Today, once more, there is no acceptable alternative to a solution built on political initiative and cooperation.

Trying to find a solution to the twin problems of the large debt burden and the risk of reduced actual and potential growth ultimately is an issue of the "societal model" and of the balance between the "individual interests" and the "common good." The last 100 years have amply demonstrated the shortcomings of the two extreme versions of economic, political and social order. On the one hand, there is the collectivist (in its extreme form totalitarian) system where individual interests are denied and all (bureaucratic) decisions are declared to serve the collective interest. On the other hand, the extreme version of nineteenth-century liberalism (and current libertarianism and market fundamentalism) denies the legitimacy of common interests and of social solidarity between the successful and less successful.

The unprecedented success of the "Western model" in terms of economic prosperity and social progress since the middle of the twentieth century was largely due to the division of tasks between markets and governments, to the search for balance between competition and solidarity at the national and international level. This was also the main strength of the concept of the "social market economy," arguably one of the most successful societal models, in terms of reconstruction and economic growth and social progress. The principal conclusion of the author is that the broad principles that had inspired the *original model of the "social market economy"* could be a promising common basis for the search of the societal model and for the political solution of the current crisis, which are so urgently needed in Europe and in the Western community.[107]

Notes

1. Some of these had already been raised by the author in earlier years and again more recently. See, for example, Otto Hieronymi (1998) "Agenda for a New Monetary Reform," *Futures*, Vol. 30, No. 8, pp. 769–81; Otto Hieronymi (ed.) (2009) *Globalization and the Reform of the International Banking and Monetary System*, Basingstoke: Palgrave Macmillan; Otto Hieronymi (2009) "Rebuilding the International Monetary Order: The Responsibility of Europe, Japan and the United States," *Revista de Economia Mundial* (Madrid), No. 29, pp. 197–226, October.
2. See Hieronymi, "Rebuilding the International Monetary Order."
3. "In 'Equilibrium and Disequilibrium: Misplaced Concreteness and Disguised Politics' (1958), Machlup argues that the most prevalent use of the equilibrium concept in economics is as a methodological device in abstract theory, a 'useful fiction' that is a part of a mental experiment designed to analyze causal connections between 'events' or 'changes of variables.'" Carol M. Connell (2011), "Why Economists Disagree: Fritz Machlup's Use of Framing at the Bellagio Group Conferences," *PSL Quarterly Review*, Vol. 64, No. 257, pp. 143–66. See also Fritz Machlup (1966, 2003) *International Monetary Economics*, London: Routledge.
4. Otto Hieronymi (ed.) (1980) *The New Economic Nationalism*, London: Macmillan, passim.
5. Friedrich A. Hayek (1976, 1978, 1990) *Denationalisation of Money: The Argument Refined. An Analysis of the Theory and Practice of Concurrent Currencies*, London: Institute of Economic Affairs; on the importance of exchange-rate stability, see Friedrich A. Hayek (1937, 1964) *Monetary Nationalism and International Stability*, New York: Augustus M. Kelley, Reprints of Economic Classics.
6. Robert Mundell in Hieronymi, *The New Economic Nationalism*, pp. 34–5.
7. International Monetary Fund (2011) *Annual Report on Exchange Arrangements and Exchange Restrictions 2010*, Washington, DC: IMF, pp. 13–14.
8. Ibid., p. 20.
9. Robert Skidelsky (1992, 1994) *John Maynard Keynes: The Economist as Saviour, 1920–1937*, London: Macmillan. Richard N. Gardner (1956) *Sterling–Dollar Diplomacy: Anglo-American Collaboration in the Reconstruction of Multilateral Trade*, London: Oxford University Press.

    Otto Hieronymi (1973) *Economic Discrimination Against the United States in Western Europe, 1945–1958: Dollar Shortage and the Rise of Regionalism*, Genève: Librairie Droz.

D. Michael Bordo and Barry Eichengreen (eds) (1993) *A Retrospective on the Bretton Woods System: Lessons for International Monetary Reform*, A National Bureau of Economic Research Project Report, Chicago: University of Chicago Press.

10. Hieronymi, *Economic Discrimination Against the United States*.
11. On the "end of Bretton Woods," see Hieronymi, *Globalization and the Reform of the International Banking and Monetary System*, Chapter 1 and the literature discussed there.
12. See Connell, "Why Economists Disagree." The numerous Princeton *Essays in International Finance* give a fair idea of the intensity and the wealth of the debate on reform of the international monetary system.
13. "While the Bretton Woods Agreement has been identified with Western unity and cooperation, from 1958 to 1968, when the Bretton Woods system was at its height, a whole series of agreements, regimes rules and institutions were needed to ensure the system worked (including the creation of the Organization for Economic Cooperation and Development, which was tasked with problems of money and exchange, 1961; swap agreements between central banks, 1961–2, the General Agreement to Borrow, 1962; the Gold Pool, 1964; and the Special Drawing Rights (SDRs) of the International Monetary Fund, 1965–7.) Nevertheless, the imbalance in international payments and flows of short-term capital that emerged in the late 1950s and the early 1960s became increasingly hard to resolve. Hence, so far as the International Monetary Fund, Organization for Economic Cooperation and Development and the Group of Ten were concerned, the use of flexible rates as a 'disequilibrating' change was off the table. Nevertheless, in policy and academic circles, everyone had a preferred solution in his back pocket—whether it required increasing the price of gold, moving from a single reserve currency to a basket of currencies, creating new reserves under the aegis of the International Monetary Fund, or freeing exchange rates to vary with the market." Connell, "Why Economists Disagree."
14. The Bush Administration's policies after 2001–3 closely followed this pattern of fiscal laxness—with the addition of massive tax cuts. See Alan Greenspan (2007) *The Age of Turbulence: Adventures in a New World*, New York: The Penguin Press, passim.
15. International Monetary Fund (2011) *Articles of Agreement*, Washington, DC: IMF, and International Monetary Fund (2006) *Article IV of the Fund's Articles of Agreement: An Overview of the Legal Framework*, Washington, DC: IMF, 28 June.
16. Quoted in Rudiger Dornbusch (1983) *Flexible Exchange Rates and Interdependence*, NBER Working Papers 1035, Cambridge, MA, National Bureau of Economic Research, Inc., p. 25.
17. Hayek, *Monetary Nationalism and International Stability*. See also Otto Hieronymi (1982) "In Search of a New Economics for the 1980s: The Need for a Return to Fixed Exchange Rates," Otto Hieronymi (ed.) *International Order: A View from Geneva*, Annals of International Studies, Institut Universitaire de Hautes Etudes Internationales, Geneva, Vol. 12, pp. 107–26; Hieronymi, *The New Economic Nationalism*.
18. Harry Johnson, 1969, quoted by Dornbusch, *Flexible Exchange Rates and Interdependence*, p. 3.
19. Connell, "Why Economists Disagree."
20. Dornbusch, *Flexible Exchange Rates and Interdependence*, p. 25.
21. Joseph Gold (1978) *The Second Amendment of the Fund's Articles of Agreement*, Pamphlet Series No. 25, Washington, DC: International Monetary Fund.

22. See British Cabinet Office documents for August 1971 and the 1976 UK sterling crisis and the IMF loan.
23. John Maynard Keynes (1920) *The Economic Consequences of the Peace*, New York: Harcourt, Brace and Howe, and also Keynes (1922) *A Revision of the Treaty, Being a Sequel to the Economic Consequences of the Peace*, London: Macmillan and Co. Ltd. On the transfer issue, see also The American Economic Association (1950, 1958) *Readings in the Theory of International Trade*, London: George Allen & Unwin, Ltd, and The American Economic Association (1952, 1956) *Readings in Monetary Theory*, London: George Allen & Unwin, Ltd.
24. "The grant-in-aid which Keynes had failed to win in Washington in 1945 eventually came in the form of $13bn worth of Marshall Aid, of which Britain's share was $2.7bn." Robert Skidelsky (2000) *John Maynard Keynes: Fighting for Britain, 1937–1946*, London: Macmillan.
25. See Gardner, *Sterling–Dollar Diplomacy*.
26. Hieronymi, *Economic Discrimination Against the United States in Western Europe*.
27. Otto Hieronymi (1996) "The International Financial Institutions and the Challenge of Transition and Reconstruction in the Former Communist Countries of Central and Eastern Europe," Miklos Szabo-Pelsöczy (ed.) *Fifty Years After Bretton Woods* (Sixth Conference of the Robert Triffin-Sziràk Foundation, Brussels 1994), Aldershot: Ashgate, pp. 129–40; Otto Hieronymi (1996) "International Capital Markets and the Financial Integration of the Transition Countries," Unpublished manuscript, Geneva.
28. Gerhard A. Ritter (2006) *Der Preis des deutschen Einheit, die Wiedervereinigung und die Krise des Sozialstaates*, Munich: Verlag C. H. Beck; Deutsche Bundesbank (2004) *Monthly Report*, Frankfurt am Main, March, p. 18.
29. For detailed arguments for flexible exchange rates from before August 1971, see Egon Sohmen (1969) *Flexible Exchange Rates*, rev. edn, Chicago: University of Chicago Press.
30. Ibid., p. 35.
31. Jagdish Bhagwati (2004) *In Defense of Globalization*, Oxford: Oxford University Press, p. 7.
32. A prominent example was the former Chairman of the Federal Reserve Board, Alan Greenspan. See Greenspan, *The Age of Turbulence*.
33. «La position qu'a prise Calvin à l'égard du prêt à intérêt a été considérée comme un acte tout à fait décisif dans l'histoire de l'Occident, un 'turning point' de son évolution», André Biéler (1959, 2008) *La Pensée Economique et Sociale de Calvin*, Genève: Georg Editeur, p. 453.
34. Margaret Garritsen de Vries (1986) *The IMF In A Changing World, 1945–1985*, Washington, DC: International Monetary Fund, p. 183.
35. Paul Volcker and Toyoo Gyothen (1992) *Changing Fortunes: The World's Money and the Threat to American Leadership*, New York: Times Books, pp.163–84.
36. Ottó Hieronymi (2011) "The Economic and Social Policies of the Orbán Government—A View from Outside," *Hungarian Review*, Budapest, Vol. II, No. 3.
37. Bank for International Settlements (2011) *81st Annual Report, 1 April 2010–11 March 2011*, Basel, 26 June, pp. 33ff.
38. To quote the late Professor Machlup: "no deficit can come into being without its being financed." Fritz Machlup "The Three Concepts of the Balance of Payments."
39. Alexandre Lamfalussy (2000) *Financial Markets in Emerging Markets: An Essay on Financial Globalisation and Fragility*, New Haven and London: Yale University Press, pp. 57–8.

40. Ibid., p. 60.
41. Ibid., pp. 172–3.
42. Venezuela is a typical illustration of this phenomenon and Hugo Chavez an illustration of the legacy of the "structural adjustment programs."
43. The OECD Economic Surveys on Japan provide an interesting overview of the sequence of these developments from the late 1980s through the early 1990s. See OECD (1988, 1989, 1990, 1991, 1992, 1993, 1994) *Economic Surveys: Japan*, Paris.
44. Richard C. Koo (2009) *The Holy Grail of Macroeconomics: Lessons from Japan's Great Recession*, rev. and updated edn, Singapore: John Wiley & Sons (Asia), p. 16.
45. Joseph A. Schumpeter (1950) *Capitalism, Socialism and Democracy*, 3rd edn, New York: Harper & Row, in particular Chapter VII; see also Schumpeter (1939) *Business Cycles: A Theoretical, Historical and Statistical Analysis of the Capitalist Process*, New York: McGraw-Hill Books [Reprinted by Porcupine Books, 1982].
46. Philippe H. Trezise (ed.) (1979) *The European Monetary System: Its Promise and Prospects*, Washington, DC: Brookings Institution, p. 57.
47. Larry Summers (1997) "Testimony before the Senate Budget Committee" reported in *The Financial Times*, October 22.
48. In October 2011 at the 10th Annual Meeting of the Geneva-based Observatoire de la Finance.
49. Barry Eichengreen (2011) *Exorbitant Privilege: The Rise and Fall of the Dollar and the Future of the International Monetary System*, New York and Oxford: Oxford University Press, p. 153.
50. See Koo, *The Holy Grail of Macroeconomics*.
51. Stephen Cecchetti (2011) "Fiscal Policy and Its Implications for Monetary and Financial Stability," 10th BIS Annual Conference, Lucerne, June; see also Stephen G. Cecchetti, Madhusudan S. Mohanty and Fabrizio Zampolli (2010) *The Future of Public Debt: Prospects and Implications*, BIS Working Papers, No. 300, Basel, March.
52. Alexandre Lamfalussy (2011) "Keynote Speech," 10th BIS Annual Conference, Lucerne, June.
53. Sachverständigenrat zur Begutachtung der gesamtwirtschaftlichen Entwicklung (2011) *Chancen für einen stabilen Aufschwung*, Jaresgutachten 2010/2011, Wiesbaden, p. 96.
54. European Community (1989) *Rapport sur l'Union économique et monétaire dans la Communauté européenne*, Brussels, 12 avril.
55. This degree of independence, *de jure* and *de facto*, goes even beyond the much-vaunted independence of the German Bundesbank, which was, of course, the model for the ECB. The decision by Chancellor Kohl and the German Government to fix the rate of exchange between the D-mark and the East German currency at the time of reunification at a much higher rate than favored by the Bundesbank was a dramatic demonstration of the limitations of central bank independence in pre-Euro Germany.
56. On the negotiations and on the position of the major actors, see Kenneth Dyson and Kevin Featherstone (1999) *The Road to Maastricht: Negotiating Economic and Monetary Union*, Oxford: Oxford University Press.
57. According to the European Central Bank's "Glossary": "The four criteria set out in Article 140(1) TFEU that must be fulfilled by each EU Member State before it can adopt the euro, namely a stable price level, sound public finances (a deficit and a level of debt that are both limited in terms of GDP), a stable exchange rate and low and stable long-term interest rates. In addition, each EU Member State must ensure the compatibility of its national legislation, including the statutes of

the national central bank, with both the TFEU and the Statute of the European System of Central Banks and of the European Central Bank."

58. Otmar Issing (2004) "The New EU Member States: Convergence and Stability," EU Enlargement and Monetary Integration, Speech by Otmar Issing, Member of the Executive Board of the ECB, Third ECB Central Banking Conference, Frankfurt am Main, October 22.

59. "The high debt-to-GDP-ratios that many Member States had already accumulated even before the crisis, showed that the EDP (Excessive Deficit Procedure) had not been effective in curbing debt developments. The reform therefore introduced new provisions to render operational the debt criterion of the EDP. ... On 23 November 2011, the European Commission tabled a proposal for two new regulations to further strengthen fiscal discipline and surveillance in the euro area. The proposal is often referred to as the 'two-pack.' This is still under discussion in Parliament and Council. For euro area Member States in the EDP, the planned rules introduce a new system of monitoring. If adopted by the Council, this would more regularly provide the Commission with the information needed to judge whether or not there was a risk of non-compliance with the deadline set by the Council to correct the excessive deficit." European Commission (2012) "Commission Sets Out the Next Steps for Stability, Growth and Jobs," Press release, Brussels, May 30.

60. See Chapter 1 in Hieronymi, *Globalization and the Reform of the International Banking and Monetary System.*

61. Dyson and Featherstone, *The Road to Maastricht*, pp. 292–4.

62. See Hieronymi, *The New Economic Nationalism.*

63. The following are recent representative examples of German anti-Euro writings. Former Budesbank Directors are prominently represented among the following authors:

Bruno Bandulet, Wilhelm Hankel, Bernd-Thomas Ramb, Karl Albrecht Schachtschneider, Udo Ulfkotte (2011) *Gebt uns unsere D-Mark zurück: Fünf Experten beantworten die wichtigsten Fragen zum kommenden Staatsbankrott,* Rottenburg: Gebundene Ausgabe, May.

Thilo Sarrazin (2012) *Europa braucht den Euro nicht: Wie uns politisches Wunschdenken in die Krise geführt hat,* Frankfurt: DVA.

Wilhelm Hankel (2011) *Das Euro-Abenteuer geht zu Ende: Wie die Währungsunion unsere Lebensgrundlagen zerstört.*

64. *Article 127* (ex Article 105 TEC):

1. The primary objective of the European System of Central Banks (hereinafter referred to as 'the ESCB') shall be to maintain price stability. Without prejudice to the objective of price stability, the ESCB shall support the general economic policies in the Union with a view to contributing to the achievement of the objectives of the Union as laid down in Article 3 of the Treaty on European Union. The ESCB shall act in accordance with the principle of an open market economy with free competition, favouring an efficient allocation of resources, and in compliance with the principles set out in Article 119.

2. The basic tasks to be carried out through the ESCB shall be:
   — to define and implement the monetary policy of the Union,
   — to conduct foreign-exchange operations consistent with the provisions of Article 219,
   — to hold and manage the official foreign reserves of the Member States,
   — to promote the smooth operation of payment systems.

Article 219 (ex Article 111(1) to (3) and (5) TEC):

1. By way of derogation from Article 218, the Council, either on a recommendation from the European Central Bank or on a recommendation from the Commission and after consulting the European Central Bank, in an endeavour to reach a consensus consistent with the objective of price stability, may conclude formal agreements on an exchange-rate system for the euro in relation to the currencies of third States. The Council shall act unanimously after consulting the European Parliament and in accordance with the procedure provided for in paragraph 3.

   The Council may, either on a recommendation from the European Central Bank or on a recommendation from the Commission, and after consulting the European Central Bank, in an endeavour to reach a consensus consistent with the objective of price stability, adopt, adjust or abandon the central rates of the euro within the exchange-rate system. The President of the Council shall inform the European Parliament of the adoption, adjustment or abandonment of the euro central rates.

In European Union (2010) "Consolidated Versions of the Treaty on European Union and the Treaty on the Functioning of the European Union, and the Charter of Fundamental Rights of the European Union," *Official Journal of the European Union*, C83, Vol. 53, Brussels, March 30.

65. (Schmid): ,,'Jeder in Europa muss sich darüber im Klaren sein, alles was wir wirtschaftlich erreicht haben, können wir auf Dauer nur bewahren, wenn wir es auch politisch absichern. Eine Wirtschaftsunion ist nur dann überlebensfähig, wenn sie sich auf eine politische Union stützen kann.' Das sagte Helmut Kohl in einer Regierungserklärung im Jahre 1992. ... (Waigel): Wir haben mit dem Vertrag von Maastricht den ökonomischen Teil gut bewältigt. Das gilt für den politischen Teil nicht. Da hätte es schneller und früher zu einer stärkeren Einigung kommen müssen. Die Anstrengungen dazu waren ungenügend. Auch hier waren es Frankreich und Großbritannien, die vor allem auf ihre nationale Identität geachtet haben. Die politische Union ist nicht an Deutschland gescheitert.',, Schmid, Thomas (2011) "Theo Waigel gibt dem Euro noch weitere 400 Jahre," Interview with Theo Waigel, *Welt am Sonntag*, Hamburg, December 25.

66. On this vital issue, the members of the European Union still have much to learn from a small non-member country, Switzerland. In Switzerland the government never resigns when it loses a vote either in Parliament or in a referendum. Also, the idea that one of the "Cantons" would have to leave the Confederation for reasons of "financial excesses," either by the markets or by the elected officials, would be considered absurd in Switzerland, a country with one of the best fiscal record in the OECD.

67. Some of the leading international banks had been involved in falsifying for years the "Libor" (London interbank offering rate). The Libor has been one of the iconic market indicators for decades, a symbol of the working of the free market as distinguished from central bank or government intervention in interest rate formation. Barclays was fined almost $500 million for its role in this scheme. Cf. Peter Ràsonyi (2012) "Schamlose Libor-Manipulationen bei Barclays," *Neue Zürcher Zeitung*, June 28.

68. European Commission (2012) *Alert Mechanism Report*, COM (2012), 68 Final, Brussels, February 14. European Commission (2012) *Scoreboard for the Surveillance*

of Macroeconomic Imbalances, European Economy, Occasional Papers 92, Brussels, February.

69. European Commission, *Alert Mechanism Report*.
70. Cecchetti, Mohanty and Zampolli, *The Future of Public Debt*, p. 16.
71. Cecchetti, "Fiscal Policy and Its Implications for Monetary and Financial Stability," pp. 3–4.
72. Cecchetti, Mohanty and Zampolli, *The Future of Public Debt*.
73. Carmen M. Reinhart and Kenneth S. Rogoff (2009) *This Time is Different: Eight Centuries of Financial Folly*, Princeton and Oxford: Princeton University Press, and Carmen M. Reinhart and Kenneth S. Rogoff (2011) *A Decade of Debt*, Washington, DC: Peterson Institute of International Economics. Carmen M. Reinhart and M. Belen Sbrancia, with discussion comments by Ignazio Visco and Alan Taylor (2011) *The Liquidation of Government Debt*, BIS Working Papers, No. 363, Basel, November.
74. "A more subtle form of debt restructuring takes the form of 'financial repression' (which had its heyday during the tightly regulated Bretton Woods System). Limiting investment choices of the private sector importantly facilitated sharper and more rapid debt reduction from the late 1940s to the 1970s than would have otherwise been the case." Reinhart and Rogoff, *A Decade of Debt*, p. 3.
75. Deutsche Bundesbank (2011) *Monthly Report*, Vol. 63, No. 10, Frankfurt am Main, October, pp. 16–17.
76. European Union (2012) "Treaty Establishing the European Stability Mechanism," Brussels.
    "Where, on the basis of its own assessment or that of the European Commission, a Contracting Party considers that another Contracting Party has not taken the necessary measures to comply with the judgment of the Court of Justice referred to in paragraph 1, it may bring the case before the Court of Justice." Article 8, European Union (2012) "Treaty on Stability, Coordination and Governance in the Economic and Monetary Union" ("Fiscal Pact"), Brussels.
77. "The signatory Member States commit themselves to implement in their legislation a fiscal rule which requires that the general government budget be balanced or in surplus. The fiscal rule is considered to be respected if the annual structural balance meets the country-specific medium-term objective and does not exceed a deficit (in structural terms) of 0.5% of GDP. If the government debt ratio is significantly below 60% of GDP and risks to long-term fiscal sustainability are low, the medium-term objective can be set as low as a structural deficit of at most 1% of GDP." Deutsche Bundesbank (2012) *Monatsbericht, März 2012 64, Jahrgang Nr. 3*, Frankfurt am Main, March, p. 101.
78. OECD (2012) *Fiscal Consolidation: How Much, How Fast and by What Means?* An Economic Outlook Report, OECD Economic Policy Papers No. 01, Paris, April, p. 12.
79. "We show that even when the exchange rate cannot be devalued, a small set of conventional fiscal instruments can robustly replicate the real allocations attained under a nominal exchange rate devaluation in a standard New Keynesian open economy environment." Emmanuel Farhi, Gita Gopinath and Oleg Itskhoki (2011) "Fiscal Devaluations," http://www.economics.harvard.edu/faculty/gopinath/files/fiscal_devaluations.pdf, December 6.
80. Koo, *The Holy Grail of Macroeconomics*, and Koo (2011) "The World in Balance Sheet Recession: Causes, Cure, and Politics," *Real-World Economics Review*, No. 58, December 12, pp. 19–37. According to Tyler Durden: "The key difference between an ordinary recession and one that can produce a lost decade is that in

the latter, a large portion of the private sector is actually minimizing debt instead of maximizing profits following the bursting of a nation-wide asset price bubble. When a debt-financed bubble bursts, asset prices collapse while liabilities remain, leaving millions of private sector balance sheets underwater. In order to regain their financial health and credit ratings, households and businesses are forced to repair their balance sheets by increasing savings or paying down debt. This act of deleveraging reduces aggregate demand and throws the economy into a very special type of recession. ... More importantly, when the private sector deleverages in spite of zero interest rates, the economy enters a deflationary spiral because, in the absence of people borrowing and spending money, the economy continuously loses demand equal to the sum of savings and net debt repayments. This process will continue until either private sector balance sheets are repaired or the private sector has become too poor to save (i.e., the economy enters a depression)." See Koo, "The World in Balance Sheet Recession."

81. Koo, *The Holy Grail of Macroeconomics*.
82. Wilhelm Röpke (1963) *Economics of the Free Society*, Chicago: Henry Regnery, see Chapter VII.
83. In Bombach, G., Netzband, K.-B., Ramser, H.-J. and Timmermann, M. (eds) *Der Keynesianismus III, Die geld- und beschäftigungs-theoretische Diskussion in Deutschland zur Zeit von Keynes*, Berlin, Heidelberg and New York: Springer-Verlag, p. 327.
84. Wilhelm Röpke (1951) "Austerity," reprinted in Wilhelm Röpke (1962) *Wirrnis und Wahrheit* Erlenbach-Zürich: Eugen Rentsch, p. 151, quoted in Hieronymi, *Economic Discrimination Against the United States in Western Europe,* p. 113.
85. Robert Skidelsky (2009, 2010) *Keynes: The Return of the Master*, London: Allen Lane (revised and updated edition published by Penguin Books).
86. Mario Draghi (2012) "Press Conference," Meeting of the Board of the European Central Bank, Barcelona, May 3.
87. See the so-called Bogenberg Declaration organized by the IFO Institute of Munich:

    "Germany was not the euro winner, as some politicians argue, but is benefiting from free trade. The euro itself was a leading cause of this crisis. ... The euro is not suffering from a mere confidence crisis that can be resolved by assuaging the markets; it is experiencing a profound balance-of-payment crisis that is being prolonged by the expansion of public financial aid. ... Countries that are not competitive enough to repay their foreign debts should, in their own interest, leave the Monetary Union." IFO Institute (2011) "Bogenberg Declaration: Sixteen Theses on the Situation of the European Monetary Union," Munich, October 15.

88. European Commission, "Commission Sets Out the Next Steps for Stability, Growth and Jobs."
89. Alexandre Lamfalussy (2009) "The Specificity of the Current Crisis," The Belgian Financial Forum and the Robert Triffin International Foundation, Brussels, April 30.
90. European Central Bank (2012) *Monthly Bulletin*, Frankfurt am Main, March.
91. Irving Fisher (1933, 2010) *The Debt-Deflation Theory of Great Depressions*, Pakthongchai, Thailand: ThaiSunset Publications, p. 21.
92. The calculations of such conservative organizations as the BIS, IMF or the OECD, mentioned earlier in this chapter, seem to suggest such orders of magnitude.
93. Charles P. Kindleberger (1986) *The World in Depression 1929–1939*, rev. edn, Berkeley: University of California Press.

94. Wilhelm Röpke (1942) *International Economic Disintegration*, London: William Hodge.
95. John Lewis Gaddis (2011) *George F. Kennan: An American Life*, New York: The Penguin Press; Gardner, *Sterling–Dollar Diplomacy*; Skidelsky, *John Maynard Keynes, Fighting for Britain, 1937–1946.*
96. Kindleberger, *The World in Depression 1929–1939*, p. 305.
97. On the "social market economy," see Otto Hieronymi (2005) "The 'Social Market Economy' and Globalisation: The Lessons from the European Model for Latin America," Emilio Fontela Montes and Joaquin Guzmàn Cueva (eds) *Brasil y la Economia Social de Mercado*, Cuadernos del Grupo de Alcantara, pp. 247–300. Otto Hieronymi (2002) "Wilhelm Röpke, the Social Market Economy and Today's Domestic and International Order," Otto Hieronymi, Chiara Jasson and Alexandra Roversi (eds) *Colloque Wilhelm Röpke (1899–1966). The Relevance of His Teaching Today: Globalization and the Social Market Economy*, Geneva: HEI-Webster University, Cahiers HEI, Vol. 6. Von Philip Plickert (2008) *Wandlungen des Neoliberalismus*, Stuttgart: Lucius & Lucius. Anthony J. Nicholls (1994) *Freedom with Responsibility: The Social Market Economy in Germany, 1918–1963*, Oxford: Clarendon Press. Rolf H. Hasse, Hermann Schneider and Klaus Weigelt (eds) (2005) *Lexikon Soziale Marktwirtschaft, Wirtschaftspolitik von A bis Z, 2., aktualisierte und erwiterte Auflage*, Paderborn, München, Wien and Zürich: Ferdinand Schöningh. Wolfgang Rudzio (1983, 2006) *Das politische System der Bundsrepublik Deutschland, 7, aktualisierte und erweiterte Auflage*, VS Verlag Für Sozialwissenschaften. Ritter, *Der Preis des deutschen Einheit, die Wiedervereinigung und die Krise des Sozialstaates.*
98. On the issue of the differences between Chancellor Kohl and the orthodox "Ordo-liberals" in the context of the EMU negotiations, see Chapter 6 of Dyson and Featherstone, *The Road to Maastricht.*
99. On the "transferability of the German model," see Dyson and Featherstone's remarkable history of the Maastricht negotiations:

"A key feature of the EMU negotiations was the assumption that Germany offered the most appropriate policy model on which to base the design and operation of EMU. French Trésor negotiators would have liked to introduce the US Federal Reserve mode as a basis for seeking more effective arrangements for democratic accountability, but they bowed to the political realities created by the need to 'bind in' Germany to the negotiations. Broadly speaking, most—if not all—EMU negotiators saw that the superior performance of the German economy offered an argument for imitating it as a model. Some—especially the central bankers—went further and identified with the German economy as a normative model. Whatever the basis of this policy—utilitarian, strategic or normative—there was a widespread view that the German model was the one around which to negotiate. ... But questions arise of whether the German model was transferred to the EC level and whether it could ever be transferred there. The EMU agreement in fact shifted the ideology of the German model to the EC level (notably in its stress on open and free markets and price stability) and an isolated institutional aspect of that model (central bank independence) to the EC level. However, the deeper institutional underpinnings were not and could not." Dyson and Featherstone, *The Road to Maastricht*, p. 794. The last sentence shows an excessively "cultural" interpretation of the "German economic and social model" that unfortunately continues to prevail both in Germany and abroad, and that has been one of the principal stumbling blocks in the search for solution in the present crisis.

100. One of the most vocal "isolationists" in Germany today is Thilo Sarrazin, a former member of the board of the Bundesbank who had to resign because of his xenophobic views. On the "German standards" and the Euro: "Die Europäische Währungsunion erfordert wenn sie funktionieren soll, dass sich die Volkswirtschaften und Gesellschaften aller teilnehmenden Staaten mehr oder weniger so verhalten so wie es deutschen Standards entspricht. Das ist ein ungeheuer ehrgeiziges Unterfangen, und dieses überhaupt zu verlangen, empfinden nicht ganz zu Unrecht viele in den btroffenen Ländern als deutsche Arroganz." Thilo Sarrazin (2012) *Europa braucht den Euro nicht: Wie uns politisches Wunschdenken in die Krise geführt hat*, Frankfurt: DVA, p. 416.

101. See Hieronymi, "The 'Social Market Economy' and Globalisation" and Hieronymi, "Wilhelm Röpke, the Social Market Economy and Today's Domestic and International Order."

102. Wilhelm Nölling, former President of the Landeszentalbank of Hamburg and former member of the board of the Bundesbank writes about the "ride to hell with the Euro"—"die Euro-Höllenfahrt." Nölling has been one of the initiators of a series of complaints against the German Federal Government at the German Constitutional Court against the Euro, against the measures to help Greece, etc. Wilhelm Hankel, Wilhelm Nölling, Karl Albrecht Schachtschneider, Dieter Spethmann, Joachim Starbatty (2011) *Das Euro-Abenteuer geht zu Ende: Wie die Währungsunion unsere Lebensgrundlagen zerstört*, Rottenburg: Kopp, pp. 56–103.

103. Sachverständigenrat zur Begutachtung der gesamtwirtschaftlichen Entwicklung, *Chancen für einen stabilen Aufschwung*, pp. 157–9.

104. Mark Boughton (2009) "A New Bretton Woods?" *Finance and Development*, Vol. 46, No. 1, Washington, DC: IMF.

105. Mario Draghi (2012) "Introductory Statement," Hearing on the ESRB before the Committee on Economic and Monetary Affairs of the European Parliament, May 31.

106. Hieronymi, "Rebuilding the International Monetary Order: The Responsibility of Europe, Japan and the United States." Hieronymi, *Globalization and the Reform of the International Banking and Monetary System*, Chapter 2. Otto Hieronymi (1995) "The Case for an 'Extended EMS': A New International Monetary Order to be Built by Europe, Japan and the United States," Miklos Szabo-Pelsöczy (ed.) *The Global Monetary System After the Fall of the Soviet Empire* (In Memoriam Robert Triffin, 1911–93, Sixth Conference of the Robert Triffin-Sziràk Foundation, Sziràk, 1993), Aldershot: Ashgate, pp. 57–67. Hieronymi, "Agenda for a New Monetary Reform."

107. Hieronymi, "The 'Social Market Economy' and Globalisation."

2

The Dual Debt Problem in the US and in Europe: Are Policy Makers Addressing the Right Issues?

Michael Sakbani*

Title of this chapter indicates that the US and the heavily indebted countries in the Euro zone have a dual debt problem: a balance of payment deficit, engendering the need to borrow from other countries, and a sovereign debt problem, engendering a need to borrow from anywhere. The chapter discusses the nature and the order of magnitude as well as the possible solutions of the dual debt problem of the United States and the case of Greece and Italy to illustrate the situation in Europe and the Euro zone. The thrust of the argument is that there is need for both fiscal correction and for sustained growth, and for improving the competitive position of the indebted deficit countries on both sides of the Atlantic.

2.1 The size of the debt problem

The size of the US public debt may be assessed by relating it to the US Gross Domestic Product. At the end of 2010, the public debt stood at $14.96 trillion whereas the GDP was $15.02 trillion, resulting in a debt ratio of 99.6%. It is certain that by early 2012 this ratio had well passed 100%. Excluding due payments to Social Security and Public Pensions, the privately held public debt was 68% of the GDP.[1] Among the developed industrial countries, only nine countries have a debt GDP ratio higher than 100%.[2] Naturally, 100% is a mere benchmark, which does not in itself mean a great deal.

This sizable debt has many consequences. The most immediate is the budgetary burden of the debt service. The net interest service of the debt amounts to 9.5% of the federal budget in the US. At the states level, 43 states have budget deficits.[3] According to the US' Bureau of Budget, unless the debt trend is inflexed, it will, on current trends, double between 2008 and 2015.[4]

The EU 27 members had in 2010 a collective indebtedness of $12.9 trillion. Their combined GDP stood at $16.3 trillion, resulting in a debt ratio of 80%. The Euro monetary zone total GDP in 2010 stood at $12,458 trillion, while their debt stood at little more than $9.1 trillion, thereby resulting in a debt–GDP ratio of 76%. Seven members are indebted at more than this average ratio. If one eliminates France (81%) and Austria (72.3%), Greece, Italy, Belgium, Ireland and Portugal in 2010 had debt–GDP ratios between 142% and 93%. For Greece and Italy, the ratio was certainly higher in.[5]

2.2   Why is the burden of the public debt so troublesome?

There is some demonstrable statistical confluence of a growth gap suffered by countries whose debt ratio exceeds 100%. According to Rogoff and Reinhart, these countries showed an average growth of 1.3% per annum less than those below this benchmark.[6] Naturally, this is not a causation finding, and several factors in addition to the deficit ratio might be responsible. Nonetheless, deficits do put pressure on interest rates, and that cannot be helpful to income growth.

One of the staple arguments of modern classical economists and monetarists is the "crowding out" effect of financing public deficits. This argument holds that private sector investors get crowded out of financial markets by public sector borrowings. This theoretical possibility would obtain if the financial markets were non-global or if all governments were financing deficits at the same time. During the Reagan era, the US expanded its annual military spending by $400 billion and financed the resultant deficits by borrowing from foreign savers. There was no evidence that crowding out took place as a result of these Treasury borrowings.

A prominent argument in the political–moral debate on debt is the burden shift to future generations. Neoclassical economists gave a slant to this argument by an economic hypothesis that holds that the debt would raise the level of anticipated taxation in the future, causing an equivalent cut in current spending. This is known as the Sergeant-Barrow equivalence hypothesis. In effect, the hypothesis negates the benefits of any current stimulatory fiscal action by counterpoising the deflationary consequences of cuts in current spending. This hypothesis, like much of recent rational economic theory, has no known empirical validity. It is no more or less than a hypothesis based on rational expectations of human behavior. In the aftermath of the 2008 financial crisis, such models of behavior have come under serious questioning (Sakbani 2010; Kaletsky 2009).[7]

A more valid argument invokes the structural budgetary problems caused by heavy indebtedness. In the case of the US, for example, the structural parts of the deficit, namely, the Pentagon budget, social entitlements, income support and debt service, leave a mere 20% (19.3% in 2010) of US expenditures as discretionary. That means, in effect, that necessary expenditures on education, development of new technology and R & D are starved of funds. Moreover, the limited margin of discretionary spending removes fiscal policy as an available policy instrument.

The heavy indebtedness of the US poses a grave problem to the international monetary system. Under the current international arrangement, the US dollar is the major asset of the system of international reserves. The dollar share in official international reserves is about 60%, three times the weight of the US GDP in the world economy. Most central banks intervene with US dollars. Indeed, the dollar share in foreign exchange turnover is a staggering 80%. Neither the Euro (26% of official reserves), nor the Yen nor the Yuan have evolved into valid alternatives. The size of US foreign official indebtedness has become out of proportion to the US exports and the politically permissible settlement by foreign holders of dollar balances. On more than one occasion, US authorities have banned foreigners from acquiring real US assets. A case in point is the Peninsular Steam Navigation Company, a Dubai-owned firm, which was barred from acquiring US real assets, namely New York and New Orleans port facilities.[8] This creates an international reserve system problem and undermines the US credit worthiness. Already China, a $2 trillion holder of dollar assets, has expressed its interest in replacing its dollar assets through international monetary reforms aimed at asset settlement in other than just US dollars (the Economist, September 2011).[9] And China, to be sure, is not the only country that is putting in question the borrowing credibility of the US.

On political terms, the US dependence on foreign borrowing and its sizable foreseeable need to finance its deficit by foreign borrowing creates political dependence. The recent financial crisis in Europe has thrown into sharp relief the limitations of political sovereignty of indebted countries; in a globalized setting, the financial markets can rob a heavily indebted country of its economic sovereignty.

Finally, the pattern of use of global international savings is both an economic and a development issue. That the richest country in the world borrows poorer-country savings because it does not or would not want to live within its means is a drag on the growth of developing countries and on international productivity.

2.3 The US situation

2.3.1 Why did the US get into a debt problem?

In one of the political ironies of recent US history, the Conservative Administrations of Ronald Reagan and George W. Bush, both elected on promises of fiscal conservatism, each borrowed more than their predecessors; each of the two Presidents added $4 trillion to the stock of the received US debt. Mr Reagan borrowed principally to finance his expansion of military expenditures near the end of the Cold War, and Mr Bush borrowed to finance his tax cuts and the wars in Iraq and Afghanistan and that on terror.

The imbalance between US saving and national investment is a main cause of the expansion of US indebtedness. This imbalance is partially the result of the US payments deficit caused by a combination of factors: the decline in US exports of manufactured goods and chemicals as well as strong demand for energy and foreign goods such as cars and consumer electronics. Now for several decades, the US trade account has been in chronic deficit. Only in a handful of years since 1960 has the current account shown surplus. While services, especially financial and cultural services, have paid for a part of the trade deficits, lagging US exports in many traditional industrial sectors are a main cause for US foreign indebtedness. And this has not been helped by the emigration of US jobs from the US to foreign countries in pursuance of global comparative cost reduction and new consumers by global companies.

Another reason for the US debt problem is the structural problems of the US federal budget. In the recent business cycle, it has been estimated that 58% of the deficit is due to structural factors and 42% is due to the economic conditions (see Table 2.1).[10] The structural problem is the result of political failure in Washington to deal with the underlying reasons. Since the Reagan Administration in the 1980s there has been a demagogic political rhetoric in the US about taxes. Even though US taxpayers pay only 18.3% of GDP in taxes at all three levels of government, a share by far lower than any industrial country, the American public has been goaded by the politicians to believe that taxes are much too high. And this stance of the public is rooted in the reality that the US Federal government does not provide many services to the public; it spends the tax dollars on the military, the social entitlements programs, the debt service and on running the Federal administration. At the same time, there is public resistance to cutting some of these very programs. The two main political parties have played demagogic games with this public confusion. The Republican Party has elevated refusal to impose taxes to a political *sine qua non*, while the Democrats have made preservation of social entitlements their basic populist plank. Both parties, however, do not dare to raise the question of the appropriate size of the military budget (US Budget, Wikipedia, November, 2011).[11]

In an attempt to reach some common grounds, the President and Congressional leaders formed the Bowels-Simpson Commission to propose measures to solve this problem. The commission worked hard for several

Table 2.1 Principal factors responsible for the deterioration of the US financial position since 2001

- Cyclical revenue decline (28%)
- Increased defense expenditure (15%)
- War on terror (2%)
- Bush tax cut (13%)
- Increase in net interest payments (11%)
- Other tax cuts (8%)*
- Obama's stimulus (6%)
- Increases in Medicare costs (2%)
- Other reasons (8%)

* These tax cuts were made in a compromise deal by President Obama and the Republican leadership in 2010.
Source: "US Budget," *Wikipedia*, 2011.

months and issued a sensible report, which recommended raising taxes by a variety of reform measures and new taxes, some 3% over a period of time and cutting expenditures (Bowels and Simpson 2012)[12] Neither the President nor the Congressional leaders followed up on this sensible report. Soon afterwards, a committee of six senators from the two parties produced proposals along the same lines. But again, no follow-up was in evidence. The resultant gridlock has effectively taken the real solutions out of the agenda. Instead, the budget compromise in 2011 committed the President to cut Federal expenditures by $13 trillion over ten years as aquid proquo for the Republican acceptance of raising the debt ceiling.

Examining the Federal Budget, the following picture emerges. The US Federal Budget in 2010 stood at $3.5 trillion, of which 25% was spent on the military and on wars, 9% on servicing the net interest of the public debt, 52% on various mandatory entitlements and 19% discretionary (the Daily Bail, 2012).[13] This picture did not change in 2011.

2.3.2 The deterioration of the US' financial position since 2001

President Clinton bequeathed to his successor George W. Bush a Federal Budget running a $232 billion surplus.[14] This surplus arose from the mid-1990s' reforms in the welfare system, a non-interrupted buoyancy of the economy and the peace dividend. Early in his term, President Bush decided to cut taxes, a move whose benefits accrued mostly to well-off taxpayers and which was to be responsible for 13% of the US budget deficit up to 2011. President Bush was faced soon after by the events of 9/11, which launched the war on terror. Those events led to the wars in Afghanistan and in Iraq, which in total increased security expenditure. This increase has been responsible for 17% of the average deficit. Table 2.1 summarizes the contribution of various factors to the deterioration of the financial position of the US since 2001.

The breakdown shows that the US recession is responsible for 42% of the deficit, while structural factors account for 58%. It should be noted in this context that 48% of Americans do not pay Federal income tax. All of this means that a revision of the revenue and expenditure pattern of the Federal Budget is indeed overdue. A step in the right direction was embodied in the 2012 budget, which promised to cut the deficit by $1.3 trillion over ten years.

The orthodoxy on dealing with the debt problem in both Europe and the US is through budget austerity, emphasizing expenditure cuts. For any country standing alone this view is rather sensible. The International Monetary Fund has advocated such a view for most of its history. However, in the present global situation, this view has a fallacy of composition. If all countries retrench at the same time, growth of international trade would be practically shut down. Growth, not just austerity, is the appropriate way to fix the debt problem; after all, is not the debt problem defined in terms of the GDP? How can open economies like those in Europe grow if all their trading partners retrench at the same time? The lagging current performances in Britain, France and Italy, to cite a few examples, are testimony to the failure of the stand-alone view of the orthodoxy.[15] The US administration under Mr Obama has dissented from this view and advocated the more coherent one that the debt problem must be attacked in the short run by growth policies, and in the long run, that is, when the economy picks up steam, with budget retrenchment. President Obama gave formal expression to this view in his address to the G20 in June, 2010[16] Unfortunately, this view has not received wide support by policy makers in Europe, nor a favorable response in the financial markets and the President has failed to muster enough Congressional support for it.

The US economy has not recovered from the 2008 recession. It was running at 8.4% unemployment the end of 2011. Official statistics of the US Bureau of Labor. By September 2012, unemployment was still 7.8 of the active labor force. Unemployment might be as high as 10–12 if one factors in part-timers and people who have dropped out of the active labor force. Investment in plant and equipment and housing has not recovered from the 2008 recession. Business is not investing because consumer spending, which used to run at 67% of aggregate demand (AD), is now only about 61% of AD. At the time of writing (June 2012), the corporate sector in the US has profits twice those of 2007, but it produces 10% less in value added to GDP. This vicious cycle will not be broken until consumers are relieved of their massive debts. An appropriate strategy has to have multiple elements: supporting investment by small and midsize businesses to create jobs, rebuilding US manufacturing industries, diversifying the export product base, encouraging investments in new technologies and green energy, repairing US infrastructure and offering relief to indebted households. These were all envisaged by the recovery act of 2009, but hardly implemented because of the shortage of appropriations. Looking beyond that, the US has to cut the US Federal deficit.

2.3.3   Conclusions on the US situation

1. US public indebtedness is for the foreseeable future out of control unless major changes in the tax and expenditure structures are made; the US cannot afford current levels of the entitlement programs and military spending.
2. The US has hardly any room to use discretionary spending to steer its economy or to undertake investments in infrastructure in new technologies and in any social or educational domains. This threatens future growth.
3. The US economy has not satisfactorily recovered from the recession for reasons that have yet to be dealt with effectively.
4. The debate on dealing with the large deficits has had no strategic design; there is a wide consensus on cutting the budget without factoring in the adverse impacts on economic growth in the short run. Indeed, growth is more effective in reducing the growth of debt than mere austerity.

5. Washington is in a gridlock about what expenditures to cut and what taxes to increase.
6. There is massive need for investments in new technology, human resources, R & D and infrastructure if the US wants to safeguard its leading economic position.
7. Large segments of the public harbor a deep sense of social injustice, as the top 1% of income earners in the US have doubled their share in the GDP to 20% in the last decade.
8. US global firms have moved away many jobs to garner global profits, and these jobs have not been replaced by more intensive skilled jobs.

2.4   Europe: The EU and the Euro zone

2.4.1   A statistical picture

The EU 27 members in 2010 had a collective indebtedness of $12.9 trillion. Their combined GDP stood at $16.3 trillion, resulting in a debt ratio of 80%. The Euro monetary zone total GDP in 2010 stood at $12,458 trillion, while its debt stood at little more than $9.1 trillion, thereby resulting in a debt–GDP ratio of 76%. Seven members of the Euro zone are indebted at more than this average ratio. If one eliminates France (81%) and Austria (72.3%), Greece, Italy, Belgium, Ireland and Portugal in 2010 had debt–GDP ratios between 142% and 93%. For Greece and Italy, the ratio was certainly higher in 2011 (Wikipedia 2012).[17]

Except for five countries—Germany, Sweden, Slovakia, Poland and Finland—other countries are either in recessionary conditions or running anemic growth. Euro zone combined growth over the three first quarters of 2011 was only 0.2%.[18] The European economies are, in general, burdened by social compacts involving a great measure of social solidarity. Most of them have not effected the necessary economic reforms needed to stimulate growth, again for political and social reasons. Without significant increases in productivity and human and other resources, Europe cannot afford its social compacts. European countries have severe demographic problems, which are not amenable to immigration solutions inasmuch as the European societies dislike multiculturalism and most European countries have no clear immigration policies. As a result, European pension systems are in stress and need significant adaptations and reforms. Similarly, European labor markets are rigid and in need of deep structural reforms. The reforms introduced by Chancellor Gerhard Schröder in Germany, and other similar reforms in Poland and Slovakia, show that deep structural labor reforms are a requisite for healthy growth. With a diversified export base and more flexible markets, Germany has been an exception to arthritic European growth.

As was mentioned earlier, macroeconomic policies in Europe have been restrictive all at the same time. With intra trade among EU members constituting the greater part of their trade,[19] the orthodoxy of European policy makers is certainly not helpful for solving Europe's debt problems. Just like the US, Europe needs trade-led growth and investment in productivity and new technologies to lead the way out of its debt problems. François Hollande's victory in the French elections, despite many serious questions about his macroeconomic proposals, might furnish some room for debating the question of growth in Europe. Economic data now show the UK, Spain, France and the Netherlands all experiencing a double dip into recession.

2.4.2   The Euro zone

The Euro was launched as a political project without sufficient consideration of its economic design. It is a monetary union in which the Central Bank (ECB) does not have a "bank of last resort" function, and is barred from lending to its member states. The fiscal policies of the member states have been independent and, in recent years, non-convergent. Until the new treaty signed in February 2012 there have been no enforcement and control provisions regarding fiscal policies. Although there are common convergence criteria, there were no mechanisms of enforcement in place. Until the new treaty, there was no European Union authority over sovereign fiscal decisions by member states. With no federated authority, the EU has no sovereign governmental authority to allocate resource transfers when needed.

The Euro zone incorporated, knowingly and purely on political grounds, states whose economies are inefficient and uncompetitive (Portugal, Greece, Spain, Italy and Ireland). The fulfillment of the convergence criteria was in many candidates the result of creative accounting.[20] The internal balance of payments deficit of the weak countries shows up in significant debt positions of their respective national central banks vis-à-vis the ECB (Wolf 2011).[21] In effect, the Euro zone is not an optimal currency area, inasmuch as labor, capital and public transfers are, for a variety of sociological and political reasons, not completely mobile. The European political reality is such that if resources of capital, labor and firms were perfectly mobile, public opinion in most member states would not accept the national consequences of such mobility.

The crisis of the Euro zone in the second half of 2011 revealed all these defects. European leaders faced the stark choice of either cutting loose weaker members or furthering the integration of the Euro zone and putting in place enforcement mechanisms in all domains, especially on the fiscal side. They opted for the latter. Chancellor Merkel and President Sarkozy both brought up this issue by end November 2011. In the summit of late January 2012, the European Council approved a draft treaty, which 25 members indicated that they would sign. The revisions included stronger fiscal integration and a modified common monetary mandate for the ECB, and also created enforcement mechanisms for the three Euro criteria (debt ratio, deficit ratio, balance of payments ratio). There is furthermore a veto power in the hands of the Commission on budgetary decisions by member states.

Twenty-seven members agreed on March 2, 2012 to the revisions of the Euro zone treaty proposed by Chancellor Merkel and President Sarkozy. On the margin of the treaty, the EU leaders also doubled the size of the European Financial Safety Facility (EFSF) to Euro 840 billion. Together with the new treaty, the European leaders agreed to deep structural reforms and austerity measures in the affected countries. In return, Greece and Italy received massive financial aid by the troika (see further), and offered written guarantees for the required measures by the political players in both countries.[22]

These treaty changes address the gaps in enforcement that have allowed the development of the present crisis, but they do not, as we will show below, remedy the prevailing crisis of confidence.

2.4.3 Greece, Italy and Spain

The problematic countries in the Euro zone include Italy, Greece, Spain, Portugal and Ireland. Ireland seems to have made the right adjustments and is now relatively clear of the danger zone. Portugal, a small economy, has an inefficient and uncompetitive economy, and its problems have not yet erupted. Spain has a major unemployment problem, large public deficits and an overstretched and thinly capitalized banking system. After recent elections, the new Spanish government has undertaken considerable austerity measures. But the solution to Spain's problems is to grow its economy and carry out the necessary labor market reforms to tackle its massive unemployment problem. Spanish banks are undercapitalized inasmuch as they carry significant non-performing assets. Their capitalization needs are estimated by the IMF at Euro 50 billion. However, we estimate these needs in excess of Euro 100 billion. Spain's is the fourth largest economy in the Euro zone. If it falters, the Euro zone will have a massive problem on hand.

Greece and Italy are countries in crisis. We will take them up in this order.

Greece

The Greek economy is little more than 2% of the economy of the Euro zone. It is an economy that has been mismanaged for at least three decades. Since 2008, its real GDP has declined by 12% through the end of 2011, and is expected to continue doing so in 2012. Greek public finances have been in disarray. The budget has been bloated for decades; until 2010 the public sector used to pay higher salaries and pensions than the private sector, and on a 14-month basis. Since 2007, the general government balance has been negative: Greece's budget deficit was 9.8% of GDP in 2008, 15.8% in 2009 (a final figure from Eurostat after revision of GDP), 10.6% in 2010 and 9.2% in 2011, with an estimated 8% in 2012 (EU statistics, 2012).[23] By comparison Spain's deficit was 8.6%.

In addition to this budgetary deficit, Greece's balance of payments are also in current account deficit; BOP was 4% of GDP in 2006, 7% in 2007, 6% in 2008, 4% in 2009 and 2.5% in 2010.[24] The CA deficit is a reflection of the poor competitiveness of Greece: the export labor unit for comparable goods cost 44% more to import from Greece than from the adjacent Turkey. From 2001 to 2009, unit labor costs increased by 20% relative to the EU. However, these costs have been declining since 2010.[25] The export sector is dominated by tourism. Thus, domestic prices dictate services sold to foreigners. Outside maritime transport, Greece does not have world-class large export firms.

Greek banks have weak capital positions and deteriorating assets. They are principally owned by Greeks and thus cannot in principle, depend on outside sources.

The crisis hit Greece with full force in 2010. Mr Papandreou's government had to undertake a one-third cut in the budget and finance, with deteriorating revenues, making a massive public debt amounting to 168% of GDP. Greece needed outside help to stave off default. The EU responded in August 2011 by loaning Greece some Euro 126 billion. The EU imposed a troika composed of the EU, IMF and the European Central Bank to supervise the required adjustment and fiscal management. The first loan, however, was not enough, and Greece needed another loan of Euro 130 billion before March 20, 2012. The troika demanded three things: further cuts in the budget and meaningful guarantees for the adjustment measures; negotiating a restructuring of Euro 200 billion debts held by private creditors; and written guarantees by all leaders of Greek political parties that they would abide by governmental promises to the EU (see also Chapter 4 in the present volume on the Greek bailout instruments).[26] On the political side, Mr Papandreou resigned and a government of technocrats led by former ECB Vice Governor Lucas Papademos was installed.

Greece did all these things and, in early March 2012, it was given the second loan.

Does that mean that the crisis was over? Almost all commentators have expressed doubts. The Euro rescue plan for Greece formulated in October 2011 had several pillars. It established a European Financial Safety Facility or EFSF (Euro 840 billion with unexplained gearing potential); approved a package of Euro 130 billion lending to Greece by the IMF, the ECB and member states under conditionality instituting performance and monitoring clauses; forced specific austerity measure on Greece's budget; and forced restructuring of Greek private debts down to 50% of their book value. After this haircut, Greek debt ratio was predicted to go down from 168% to 120% of GDP.

Why the skepticism?

The first reason is political. Can Greek governments maintain the austerity and severe cuts in the Greek standard of living and still maintain power? That is doubtful no matter what written promises signed. The results of the Greek elections, which gave prominence to right-wing extremists who reject the European fiscal restrictions, is a proof of this if one is needed. The repeat of the elections, even if the results were different, will make Greek politicians think twice before accepting the Euro dictates.

Secondly, can Greece eliminate its balance of payment deficit by increasing its productivity and competitiveness in a reasonably short time? The answer is perhaps no. Thirdly, the interest yield on 10-year Greek bonds has passed 7%, some 511 basis points higher than the German comparable yield. At 2.1% inflation, the real interest rate is 4.9%. To pay this interest on the stock of the debt without deterioration in living standards, Greece must grow at about 5.88% in real terms. Greece's average growth rate during the period 2001–7 was 3.5%, although this was based on irresponsible borrowing. The Greek economy is expected to shrink in 2012 by 6%. Under the Euro system, it cannot adjust its exchange rate; it has to make income and price adjustment. Fourthly, if Italy or Spain collapse, then the EFSF will not be sufficient to weather that fall. Therefore, on objective grounds Greece cannot be sure that it can continue in the Euro zone without further help. And this help has become prohibitive to the political elected leaders of the EU.

Italy

Like Greece, Italy has suffered macroeconomic mismanagement for at least two decades. But unlike Greece, Italy has a diversified and large economy, although its fiscal management has been at best poor and at worst calamitous. After three governments and grave personal scandals, the long-serving Sr Berlusconi had resigned by the end of 2011, and a government of technocrats led by ex-EU Commissioner Mario Monti was put in place.

The third largest member in the Euro zone, Italy has a debt–GDP ratio of 120%. Italy must grow at 5.96% per year to keep its debt burden steady, whereas its actual performance was growth of 1.3% in 2010 and an expected shrinkage of 2.2% in 2012. It had shrunk by 1.3% in 2008 and 5.2% in 2009. The Italian economy is not competitive and its exports cannot be helped, as in the past, by currency devaluations. It needs substantial income and price adjustment along with deep structural reforms.

The positive aspect is that the Italian state owns significant and viable assets, which can be sold. Italy also does not run a significant budget deficit; its 4% deficit is modest by current European standards. Moreover, the majority of its public debt is domestically owned.

Italy's main problem, besides economic mismanagement, has been the deterioration of its productivity. While Italy has some world-class export firms, small and medium-size firms dominate. This is not helpful to increasing productivity and is a source of the large Italian underground economy. Sr Monti has performed well and the financial markets are showing confidence, expressed by the reduced yield on Italian bonds and the successful sale of bond issues in March 2012. Unfortunately, this reprieve did not last. The problems of Greece and Spain spilled over into Italy. In June, the Spanish Government had difficulties financing a loan, and that lack of confidence was reflected on Italian bond rates.

2.5   Conclusion: An assessment of Euro zone prospects

Italy, Spain, Greece, Portugal, Ireland and Austria are all in need of structural economic reforms. These include labor market liberalization, privatization of some state assets, pension reforms, tax and expenditure adjustments, and a variety of other measures to improve competitiveness within and outside the Euro zone. Despite its relative strength, France is also in need of such reforms.

If not treated, Euro zone sovereign debt problems will feed into a global banking crisis. Within the Euro zone, banks from France, Germany, Italy and Spain have large Greek and Italian assets. This crisis will have two main dimensions, namely, deterioration of bank balance sheet assets and capital inadequacy. It will also result in erosion of the value of collaterals and mutual default insurance contracts, as the value of these instruments fluctuates with the cycle. Globalization of financial markets synchronizes this fluctuation globally and renders banks everywhere simultaneously vulnerable.

The European fiscal package dealt with the lack of enforcement problem. However, the European leaders were reluctant to make two critical political decisions: to enable the European Central Bank to finance bank capital inadequacies and to pass on the question of joint European bonds. These two critical decisions would reestablish confidence, and Europe has the assets and means to do so. But the politicians know that the European public opinion, especially in Germany, would not tolerate the implied transfer of resources. This is hardly surprising because the European project was imposed from the top and the Euro zone was expanded beyond what was acceptable in the old founding membership of six or even 12 countries.

From an economic point of view, there are five ways in which the Euro zone may deal with its dual debt-deficit problems.

First, allow the European Central Bank to purchase bonds of member states, thereby printing money and in effect distributing the burden of the severely indebted countries to the strong economies. There is little political prospect of that.

Secondly, keep lending to Greece and potentially to Italy, Portugal and Spain on an unlimited basis, a recipe of symptom suppression under the current Euro zone arrangement. Besides, the funds required are beyond any feasible size of the projected EFSF at any workable gearing ratio. This alternative renders the EU a transfer union, which surely would be voted down by the public.

Thirdly, force adjustment in the form of structural reforms and austerity measures upon the weak economies and stimulate the strong ones to act as locomotives. That creates a two-tier Euro zone running at two different speeds.

Fourthly, force adjustment and austerity only on the weak deficit countries. In view of the rather restrictive policies of the core countries, the price and income adjustments therein would take a very long time; it took France close to ten years to adjust to the 1981 payments problem through automatic price and real income adjustment without a locomotive push from Germany.

Fifthly, allow controlled default and possible exit from the Euro zone. This can be done cooperatively and is perhaps easier than carrying on with the Euro zone's inherently faulty design.

The taboo of countries dropping out of the Euro is no longer unthinkable. It is better in the long run to have fewer members but a more cohesive and stronger Euro zone than the present limping structure.

2.5.1 A possible process of devolution?

The crisis of the Euro zone is now more than one year old and gives no signs of abetting. The markets have no confidence in the promises of Greece and the others. Moreover, there are five countries in question: Greece, Spain, Ireland, Portugal and Cyprus. This threatens to make the Euro zone one of alternating crisis from one country to another. Providing exit to all these countries is the surest way of ending the problem. However, that is costly. *The Economist* estimated that the total cost would be Euro 1.2 trillion. No political leader in Europe can face his or her public with such a bill. Dealing with Greece alone is one-third that total cost. The balance of cost-benefit according to *The Economist* is clearly in favor of a cooperative exit of Greece. Such an event must be done with utter confidentiality, lest there will be a running on the banks. Greece can revert to a new Drahma for all contracts signed forthwith and for all government taxes and payments under Greek law, thereby regaining its full monetary independence. Old accounts denominated in Euros would continue on bankbooks. The exchange rate of the new Drahma to the Euro would find its market rate at perhaps very low levels. Europe can help in mitigating the impact on Greek debtors in Euro and the deterioration of banks' asset values. Greece would also be helped in coping with its payments balance. There would be undoubtedly significant inflation during the adjustment. The challenge is to contain inflation so as to assure gains in real competitiveness as a result of the fall in exchange rates. These developments are a tall order in any democracy. But exit will be easier than staying within the Euro trying to service the escalating cost of the debt and live with unending austerity.

A strong and healthy Euro is a common international good for the International Monetary System; a viable Euro is needed as an alternative to the US dollar in the IMS.

Notes

* The research for this chapter was partially supported by a research grant from Webster University, Geneva.

1. "US Debt," *Wikipedia* [consulted on December 11, 2011].
2. "EU Economic Statistics," *Wikipedia* [consulted on November, 11, 2011].
3. Ibid.
4. *US Bureau of Budget*, 2011.
5. "EU Economic Statistics," *Wikipedia* [consulted November, 2011].

6. Carmen Reinhart and Kenneth S. Rogoff, *Growth in Time of Debt*, NBER Working Paper No. 15639, January 2010.
7. See, for a discussion, Michael Sakbani (2010) "The Global Economic Recession: Analysis; Evaluation and Implications of Policy Response and System Reforms Proposals," *Journal of Studies in Economics and Finance*, June; Anatole Kaletsky (2009) "Economists are the Forgotten Guilty Men. Academics—and their Mad Theories—are to Blame for the Financial Crisis. They too Deserve to be Hauled into the Dock," *Financial Times*, London, June 2.
8. Peninsular Steam Navigation Company, a firm owned by a Dubai holding company, was barred from buying the port facilities of NY and New Orleans in the US in 2010.
9. *The Economist* (2011) "Climbing Greenback Mountain," September 24–30, 2011, pp. 13–18.
10. "US Budget," *Wikipedia* [consulted November, 2011].
11. For a full discussion of the Washington gridlock, see Michael Sakbani (2011) "The US Budget Impasse: Dogma v. Economic Sense," in michaelsakbani.blogspot.com, August 1.
12. Erskin Bowels and Allen Simpson (2012) *The National Commission on Fiscal Responsibility and Reform*, Washington, DC, January 31.
13. *The Daily Bail* (2012) "Wake Up America: The Real US Budget Problem: Defense and War Spending," in OZHOUSE.org.
14. Various sources, *New York Times*, *Washington Post*, December, 1999.
15. For detailed statistics on the performance of the EU economies on faltering growth in Europe, see http://epp.eurostat.ec.europa.eu/cache/ITY_PUBLIC/2-26042011-AP/EN/2-26042011-AP-EN.PDF.
16. The Administration views were expressed by President Obama's statement before the G20 in its meeting in Toronto on June 27, 2010.
17. "EU Economic Statistics," *Wikipedia* [consulted January 10, 2012].
18. Europe economic statistics can be found in the source given in note 12.
19. The majority of European exports go through intra EU trade. In some cases more than 70% is intra trade.
20. At the inception of the Euro zone, the convergence criteria were a maximum budget deficit of 3% of a country's GDP, no more than 70% debt to GDP, and exchange rate and interest convergence over the previous three years. See for details, Michael Sakbani (1998) "The Euro on Schedule: Analysis of its European and International Implications," Miklós Szabó-Pelsőczi (ed.) *European Monetary Integration*, Avebury and the Robert Triffin Foundation.
21. Martin Wolf (2011) "Thinking through the Unthinkable," *Financial Times*, London, November 9, p. 9.
22. *The Wall Street Journal* (2012) "Greece Sets Austerity Plan: Leaders Approve Unpopular Cuts; Europe Wants Vote to Secure Another Bailout," February 10.
23. EU, IMF and Bank of Greece statistics. Reported by *Financial Times*, London, February 15, 2012.
24. Ibid.
25. Ibid.
26. The first Greek bailout, amounting to Euros 110 billion, was implemented by means of pooled bilateral loans from Euro zone members of Euros 80 billion and IMF loan facility of Euros 30 billion. The second Greek bailout, amounting to Euros 130 billion, will be implemented by means of EFSF loans of Euros 110 billion on behalf of the Euro zone countries and Euros 20 billion by the IMF.

3
The Illusion of Monetary Sovereignty

Péter Ákos Bod

3.1 Introduction

In our modern age, most economies are open—if economic and financial openness is defined as exposure to cross-border flows of goods, services, labor and financial funds. Openness has become the normal state of contemporary market-based economies: they are organically engaged in foreign trade, and are parties to international conventions and organizations as a matter of fact. Some states are even members of trade and monetary blocs.

Economic and financial openness has become one of the defining aspects of globalization. As a result, the term "national economy" has progressively been reduced to a statistical concept: one can talk of the "Dutch economy" or the "Estonian economy" but, in reality, these and similar market economies have become genuinely international as far as their institutional order, ownership structure, technological norms, financial standards, accounting and business practices, consumption and saving patterns, and many other modalities of economic activities are concerned.

Openness has consequences on all states, and not only on small and medium-sized economies: even the US—a very large, advanced and diversified economy—is compelled to react instantly to external market conditions. American business players respond vigorously to events such as changes in world prices of crude oil or exchange rates fluctuations. American federal debt management is directly influenced by foreign investors' appetite for US government bonds.

Thus, openness shapes national policies, and leads to policy interconnectedness: government policy makers must consider key market events taking place elsewhere in the world. Globalization is, in fact, *institutionalized economic openness*: policy options of nation states are influenced and constrained by international rules. It is hard to deny that membership in international organizations such as the International Monetary Fund or World Trade Organization limits what governments do, even if national policy makers will attempt to secure for themselves as wide a room of maneuver as possible.

Institutional constraints are not the only factors to tie the hands of officials: the simple logics of economics will also limit what governments can attain. Let us look at Robert Mundell's oft-quoted "impossible trinity" (or "trilemma") claiming that a country cannot simultaneously maintain three policy goals: (1) free movement of capital, (2) an independent monetary policy and (3) a fixed exchange rate.[1] Once a country pegs its currency to another currency or it joins a currency zone, and at the same time its rules guarantee free flow of capital, a requisite characteristic of financial openness, the authorities will have to realize soon that they cannot set interest rates as they wished or as they could do earlier in a less advanced stage of openness or when the exchange rates were not fixed. Hence the trilemma: authorities could only have a combination of any two of the three components of the trinity.

By the late 1990s, definitive financial openness—full convertibility and lack of effective capital controls—had become the policy norm not only in advanced but also in emerging and transition countries. Policy options thus were reduced to choosing the exchange rate regime: fixed or floating or something in between. The eventual choice, in turn, will determine the degree of interest rate flexibility: with floating rate, monetary authorities could set interest rates rather freely, while in the case of a long-term currency peg or permanent fix of the exchange rate, they cannot exercise interest rate discretion.

Whether driven by economic logics or by the spread of "best practice" in monetary matters during the boom years of the 1980s and 1990s, most governments became followers of the internationally accepted rules and norms, and thus they decided to give up, in a piecemeal manner, part of their monetary sovereignty. But that was before the recent outbreak of financial turbulences that arrested the previous long-term tendency towards a general policy culture of non-interventioist, rule-based and self-restrained economic and monetary policy in market-based societies.

Crises, however, lead to changes in rules and norms. The "Great Recession" of 2007–9 was no exception. During and after the eruption of financial disturbances, many governments, mostly in advanced nations, decided to resort to activist policy measures, ranging from massive Keynesian fiscal stimuli to enacting market protection schemes.

Governments are notoriously reluctant to step back after having assumed a prominent role in society even if the exceptional circumstances that once justified their activist stance do not apply any more. This was a lesson from the Great Depression of the 1930s, and we could witness something similar in major market economies right after the recent financial crisis. European states beefed up their regulatory roles; many of them resorted to discretionary industrial policy measures, and most increased public expenditure. But will the frenzied state activity last? Or is it, in fact, a transitory phenomenon to be followed by a return to the previous status quo? These are the obvious questions raised in academia as much as in public discourse.

This chapter will not attempt to provide an authoritative answer. It is too early to conclude whether hectic crisis management activities in many countries herald a new era of state activism in economic affairs in general, and in matters of finance, in particular, or it is just a limited period of "unconventional policies" in economies experiencing market failures and private sector weaknesses. Still, there is a growing body of knowledge about the states' behavior during and after the recent crisis to offer certain conclusions and lessons. The particular country case of Hungary, an emerging economy and a new member state of the European Union, will be examined here in detail. Its government has taken a series of unorthodox measures attempting to enlarge its room of maneuver in financial affairs through a controversial "financial freedom fight" and "fight against debt." This case illuminates an important question: do crisis times increase or decrease margins of maneuver of governments?

3.2 Notes on sovereignty and periphery, and on sovereignty in the periphery

Originally a constitutional concept, the term "sovereignty," or the adjective "sovereign," has rarely appeared in economic policy discourses until recently. That should not surprise us: it is hard to define the proper meaning of the term outside legal contexts. Jean Boden's age-old definition of sovereignty was relevant at a time when the ruler exercised his or her unquestioned rights within the borders of the realm concerning the legal system, taxation, coinage, signing international contracts, deciding on war and peace.[2] Those prerequisites of the rule of a sovereign laid soon the foundation of the norms of national sovereignty under the Westphalian system: a modern state is independent—from other states or monarchs—in determining its legal system, border control, excise and taxation rules, national currency regime (in due time: in establishing a central/national bank), building key national institutions ranging from nationwide industrial standards to national railways or later national airlines. One may add a variety of non-economic institutions such as a national team at the Olympics or a nation's representative in international song contests, to name but a few customary elements of what seemed to make a contemporary state.

But this is past history in economic matters; we live in a post-Westphalian era. Not all nations, including quite advanced ones, have all the mentioned constituents. Gradually, starting after the Second World War but more pronouncedly since the 1980s, states have tended to give up areas of full (albeit formal, in many aspects) economic sovereignty for memberships in international accords, conventions and associations aiming at providing safety and mutual benefits. Let us point out the nearly universal membership in the International Monetary Fund (IMF or Fund), which *de jure* is an association of sovereign nations but its articles of association do in fact imply a certain limitation of financial sovereignty.[3]

The European Union is, by definition, supranational in certain respects. Euro zone nations, on top of being members of a "common market"—a term not much used today—have even given up a very important part of their economic sovereignty by introducing the common currency. You may argue that this is a case of pooled sovereignty in monetary affairs: a number of otherwise sovereign states exercise their sovereign rights via joint institutions such as the European Central Bank (ECB) and the European System of Central Banks. But the fact remains: a national currency (like national airlines, railways and so on) is no more a *sine qua non* of state sovereignty in Europe and some other places. What is particularly noteworthy in this respect is that the states that first entered into monetary arrangement were not weak, poor or instable states but they were those, at least in the European context, that belonged to the center of economic, technological and political development.

Patterns of government activities, as we have witnessed recently, much differ across nations during crisis years. Most emerging nations, exposed to the dramatic events of the financial theatres, typically reacted with more caution and policy restraint than a number of core countries.[4] This is interesting since less advanced nations had experienced a long history of government activism: many developing nations had previously tried to use the public sector extensively to cope with external challenges, or had attempted to speed up economic development by relying heavily on the state activity. In contrast, governments in most emerging economies during the recent crisis even resisted the lure of Keynesian spending, and some even followed the classical, pre-Keynesian policy line of restrained public spending,

This is less surprising, though, once you take into account the lessons of previous crises, notably the one concerning the nature of capital flows to emerging countries. As Kaminsky, Reinhart and Végh put it:

> capital flows to emerging markets are markedly procyclical. Procyclical capital inflows, in turn, reinforce the tendency in these countries for macroeconomic policies to be procyclical as well. The fact that capital inflows collapse in a recession is perhaps the principal reason that emerging markets, in contrast to rich countries, are often forced to tighten both fiscal policy and monetary policy in a recession, exacerbating the downturn.[5]

Advanced nations, on the other hand, tended to apply massive fiscal stimuli in Keynesian counter-cyclical policy textbook fashion, and some even applied protectionist measures to soften the blow to their economies during contraction in 2009. While a number of advanced countries as well as some emerging market economies resorted to conventional (Keynesian) policy measures, there were dissimilarities in monetary policy. As D. Mohanty, executive director of the Reserve Bank of India, has pointed out: credit easing and quantitative easing was more limited and fiscal policy remained cautious in the emerging world.[6]

The marked differences in policy behavior between advanced nations and emerging markets have contributed to the recent revival of professional and media interest in the concept of core versus periphery of capitalist development as elaborated by Immanuel Wallerstein.[7] The use of the term "periphery" has become customary in policy debates after the eruption of sovereign risk crises in Europe, even if the term is rather vague in this context. Is Ireland a country in the periphery of Europe, with its above-average GDP per capita data? If Greece is, what about Slovenia, a new member state of the EU with a similar level of development, but with incomparably less financial problems? What about then with other, less advanced new member states in the Baltics and in Central-Eastern Europe, or much poorer Balkan countries: Romania, Bulgaria? Is it justified at all to use the term "periphery" for a European country? Despite their towering financial problems, countries in Europe are more advanced than truly peripheral nations further away in terms of geographical distance and of material advancement.

Thus it seems useful to have a look here at the factors that make a country core, peripheral or semiperipheral. The fact that a number of open, mostly small, countries of the European Union have lately experienced an explosion of their sovereign risk adds a new angle to the debate on what constitutes a core (center) and what a periphery economy under contemporary circumstances.

Even a quick glance on the policy behavior and crisis management style of some European economies can convince us that the very existence of best practice in policy making has been questioned in countries, whether in the European core or further away in geographical and income terms. National policies significantly differ from each other in times of crisis. States have not faded away; just the opposite. This may come as a surprise only for the believers of the view that "the world is flat" and that globalization (mondialization) has made global markets so interdependent that nation-states do not really matter in economic affairs.

The role for governments in market economies, according to the best practice of yesteryear, was to maintain the social order without intervening directly in economic matters, particularly in financial affairs. The emergence of the European Union strengthened the concept of the gradual vanishing of the nation-state. But if this was the mainstream, it dried out with the present financial crisis. Simply put, the whole concept of "best practice in economic policy" seems to have lost its relevance.

3.3   Diversity of policies in crisis times

Let us look at recent evidence: once the fiscal turbulences hit Europe, some—but not all—EU member states ran a huge budget deficit in order to soften the blow, in a good Keynesian manner. In 2009 the largest government deficits as percentage of GDP were recorded by Ireland (–14.3%), Greece (–13.6%), the United Kingdom (–11.5%), Spain (–11.2%), Portugal (–9.4%), Latvia (–9.0%), Lithuania (–8.9%), Romania (–8.3%), France (–7.5%) and Poland (–7.1%), according to the European statistical service.[8]

When things turned bad, differences in starting macroeconomic positions were realized with a certain amazement by analysts as well as the general public. Economic conditions have, in fact, always much differed across Europe, and public finance situations vary tremendously at present. That such variance exists within a union that had established common economic policy guidelines, institutions and structures aiming at long-term nominal and real convergence tells a lot about the degree of efficiency of EU-wide convergence policies. Let us take a key indicator: public sector indebtedness, as measured by debt per GDP ratio, which had a span in the Euro zone from Greece with over 140% to Estonia with less than 7% in 2010.

Nation-states do no seem to fade into insignificance. Moreover, they are more numerous than ever: the number of sovereign states in Europe is much higher than 50 or 100 years ago. There are more currencies (monetary regimes) in Europe now than a century ago!

The recent crisis led thinkers and policy makers to rethink the hitherto abstract contradiction between national policy sovereignty and the supra-national nature of contemporary world economy. The former Finance Minister T. Padoa-Schioppa quipped that "Interdependence has developed to such a degree that all of the Union's member states—the strong and the weak, the virtuous and the sinners—have now lost their full economic, and even political sovereignty."[9] Well, being a strong member state, or put differently, being in the core, helps when it comes to compliance with the ground rules of interdependence. But what about non-core nations? Have they really lost most of their sovereignty? And if it is so, what have they got in return?

Whether one calls new member states (that is, the 12 countries that joined the EU in two groups in 2004 and 2007) emerging economies, as is custom-ary in market analysts' circles, or refer to them as periphery countries, as has become fashionable since the outburst of the European sovereign debt crisis, there are certain common features of group EU12. First, in spite of their individual specificities, most such economies had a very successful decade behind them in terms of economic growth, ranging from four to over ten per cent annual rate before the crisis—Hungary being an exception, as we will see later. On the back of their robust growth, European and national policy mak-ers did not take due cognizance of asset price movements and of the build-up of credit imbalances, notably the curiously high loan-to-deposit ratio in the banking system of the new member states. Thus, rather than being ham-strung by visible (official) and invisible (market) forces, new member states could attain unprecedented room of maneuver—until the crisis.

This policy neglect suddenly backfired when liquidity was drastically tightened in interbank markets of core economies in 2008. Banks in most new member states (note: mostly foreign-owned banks) experienced an end to easy access to foreign exchange funding—to which they had become accustomed in the pre-Lehman Brothers period. Spillover (contagion effect) hit suddenly a number of overheated emerging European economies. The events took them unprepared—in contrast to non-European emerging economies in the "genuine periphery."

The differences between the former and the latter in respect of the conditions of the real economy, asset prices, level of international reserves and general government balances are striking. New EU member states, having experienced massive inflows of official funds as well as of private funds for years before, during and right after their accession to the EU, seemed to have taken their benign funding positions for granted, assuming a certain macroeconomic and macrofinancial protection from the EU, in the unlikely (it seemed at that time) case of financial tensions. While non-European emerging economies and most prominently, but not only, China amassed high international reserves, similar buffers turned out to be inadequate in some new member states: official reserve levels were clearly below recommended benchmarks in the Baltic countries and in Hungary in the period preceding the intensification of the global financial crisis.[10]

Genuine emerging economies had been cautious with their fiscal policies, remembering how some star countries (South Korea, for example) had run into deep problems a decade before. In contrast, new EU member states seemed to care less about budget deficit and public debt with the exception of countries where the authorities truly aspired to enter the Euro zone and thus had to meet the Maastricht criteria for Euro zone entry.

Based on these differences in situation and policies, one can in fact classify the EU12 group plus the "problem" Euro zone economies (Greece, Ireland, Portugal and Spain) as "semi-periphery" to distinguish them for the countries of "real periphery."

3.4   Fragility of economic and financial systems in semi-peripheral European economies

What are the determining characteristics of a semi-periphery economy? The level of economic development measured by gross domestic product (GDP)? There must be something more than the customary measures of economic output. Let us take the Irish case: Irish GDP per capita was much higher than Germany's during the run-up to the European crisis; and still it was Ireland that had to turn to the EU/IMF for financial help. It is obvious that in the Irish case—and to a lesser degree in the case of all other semi-periphery economies—gross domestic product is not the best measure of the advancement level of the given country, GNI (gross national income) being much closer to reality. As C. Ryan warns, although Ireland shot to the top of the European league table of GDP per capita by 2008, second only to tiny Luxembourg, this rise was illusory.[11] The difference between GDP and GNI data, typically of the order of one to two per cent in big and rich economies, amounts to 20 per cent in the Irish case, mostly owing to a phenomenal inflow of foreign direct investment (FDI) for a long time: between 1998 and 2003 the country had the largest net FDI flow per capita of any country in the world. Similar, even if less spectacular, data characterized Hungary, Estonia, Slovakia and other new member states during the years before the crisis. Consequently, the genuine national income of these capital importer countries, in the absence of other sources of revenues, turned out to be much less than their GDP. On the semi-periphery, the difference between GDP and GNI or the indicator of disposable national income is generally much more than simply nuances of statistics.[12]

The choice of adequate statistical indicators of national income flows has an important impact on how a semi-periphery economy appears in international comparison, but even with a 20 per cent reduction of GDP, this given country should, in principle, belong to the class of core nations—and this is not the case with Ireland at present. A detailed country study points out various socioeconomic aspects that may have explanatory power for the travails of this semi-periphery country: the underlying economy with its structural characteristics; size and efficiency of the public sector; and quality of government institutions responsible for monitoring and regulating the economy, in particular financial activities.

But country cases also reveal that development is much more than improvement in flow variables; what seems to make a difference is better described by stock indicators measuring the accumulated amount of financial and physical assets, and of human capital. Fast-growing (very successfully emerging) nations can at some point in time reach a national income (i.e., a flow variable) level that is as high as that of an established, mature, rich core country—without reaching a similarly high level of credit rating or a comparable political, financial position in international affairs. In short: without getting core status.

Growth rates and income levels can also quickly change for the worse, and a phenomenal growth period may be followed by a similarly fast contraction, while a stock variable such as national wealth (real and financial) will change more slowly. Talking of national assets, we should add a particular (and hardly measurable) asset class, namely, institutions. The quality or reliability (credibility) of national institutions certainly appears among the factors that distinguish core and periphery nations: when investors, small and big, vote with their funds in turbulent moments, they invariably turn to markets underpinned by strong and reliable economic and social institutions, such as Switzerland, the USA and Germany. How to measure the institutional quality of a country is another issue—one may use proxies for analytical purposes, such as place in the corruption index, level of trust in society or administrative costs as percentage of GDP.

3.5   States can borrow money but not credibility

To translate the previous reasoning about core and periphery (semi-periphery) to policy issues, let us take a phenomenon that tends to characterize less advanced nations: indebtedness in other nations' currency. This is a curious phenomenon since borrowing in foreign currency carries obvious risks for the borrower. In an often-quoted paper, Eichengreen and Hausmann analyzed the financial situation that emerges as a consequence of what they dubbed the "original sin": market participants, including the state agencies, in need of funds borrow not in their domestic currency but take up instead funds in foreign (hard) currencies.[13] Under such circumstances, borrowers run an exchange rate risk emanating from a currency mismatch: projects that generate local currency will be financed with foreign currencies. This risk adds to another one resulting from a maturity mismatch: long-term projects are financed with short-term (foreign exchange-denominated) loans.

The monetary phenomenon called "dollarization" originates in the Latin American context, characterized by scarce domestic savings. A similar process, this time not involving the US dollar, has emerged in Central and Eastern Europe in recent times: banks, households (mostly through the intermediation of banks), firms and the governments have gradually engaged to borrow in Euros or Swiss Francs.

The factors behind this particular episode of dollarization of households in new EU member states are many: they include the availability of foreign funds, interest rate differentials and the rosy expectations of future income catching up.[14] Certainly, the mere prospect of full membership in the European Union accelerated financial flows into the region. The year 2004, the date of entry into the EU, opened a new chapter eliciting increases of both credit demand and credit supply. Household borrowing started from a modest level, picking up in 2003–4, and growing very fast until the Lehman moment.

The prevalence of foreign currency (FX) borrowing by neighboring states shows a distinct pattern in the region concerned: FX share became dominant in Estonia and Latvia, high in Hungary and Romania, while virtually non-existent in the Czech Republic and Slovakia. Interestingly enough, the phenomenon appeared in a less serious form also in Austria, a member state of the Euro zone where Swiss Franc lending reached a certain proportion in the years before the crisis.

The Baltic or Central European cases of "euroization" had strong drivers: most of the banking sector in the region is owned by foreign investors, with easy access to foreign exchange funding. Thus foreign-owned banks offered foreign currency-denominated loans to domestic customers as a matter of course. Their practice was soon copied by domestic banks. Households and corporate borrowers found the lower interest rates on foreign currency-denominated loans attractive, even though most borrowers earned no income in the same funding currency, and consequently they, as clients, had no natural hedging against foreign exchange risk. Banking supervision agencies make sure that the banks do not keep open positions or they hedge their exposures, thus the banks' FX-positions are broadly balanced. But this also means that private and corporate domestic borrowers are those who run the exchange rate risk. This sort of risk became a major item in the Hungarian case in the years before the crisis: over half of bank lending to the nonfinancial sector was denominated in foreign currency (mostly in Swiss Francs and the Euro).

3.6   The Hungarian government attempts to get loose from financial bonds

One of the particularities of Hungary is that this country started its transition process in 1990 with the highest per capita external debt of all Central and Eastern European nations, due to a complex history of greater openness to trade and financial flows even under Communist rule. Transformation into a market economy, perhaps the most successful among transition nations in the early 1990s, further increased financial openness. Accession to the EU obviously triggered additional financial inflows in the form of EU funds on top of private funding. By the end of 2007, Hungary's external debt amounted to about 100 percent of GDP—not high by core nations' standards but quite an exposure for an emerging economy even in good times. But 2008 turned out to be anything but good.

In October of 2008, amid the turmoil in international financial markets, the Hungarian government (a Socialist-Liberal coalition) decided to turn to international institutions for financial support. The request was accepted: the EU and the IMF offered a massive loan of Euro 20 billion, saving the country from a looming sovereign default.

The events leading to the IMF loan, the first ever to be granted to a member of the EU, started with sharp drop in the exchange rate of the forint (HUF), the national currency, in September and October 2008 (see Figure 3.1). International investors lost interest in Hungarian sovereign debt instruments; the debt agency of the Hungarian Treasury was unable to sell government bonds at reasonable prices for weeks, and later at all. Cross-border banking credit lines were suspended, evoking the specter of a sudden stop in capital inflows. The Hungarian government, already very unpopular for reasons of political scandals and zigzags in policies, and being surrounded by an air of corruption, balked at tough domestic measures, and asked for external help instead.[15]

Within weeks, a joint EU/IMF team finalized the loan package. The economic policy conditions of the loan were elaborated, approved and monitored jointly by the European Commission (EC) and the IMF. In this

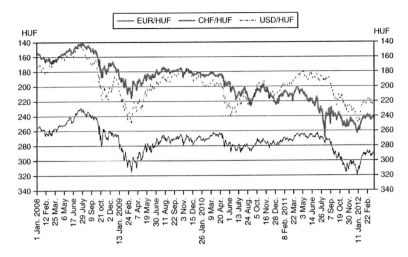

Figure 3.1 Exchange rates, 2008–12
Source: Hungarian National Bank, Chartpack. Downloaded on April 7, 2012.

case, as later with Greece, EU decision makers were motivated to team up with the Fund in the deal not only for funding reasons: they also acknowledged that the Fund was better prepared to set quantitative loan conditions and to oversee debtor government than the EU. The corporate governance of the Bretton Woods institutions differs from the EU's: decision making is much faster in Washington, DC than in Brussels.

The sensitive issue of sovereignty also comes into the picture. Granting of a standby loan is conditional on the borrower's willingness to take particular economic policy measures as determined by the provider(s) of the funds. The borrower is a member state of the EU, thus the parties to the deals face an awkward situation: it is hard for the EU to force politically unpopular loan conditions on a member state, particularly when core nations are also experiencing fiscal difficulties. Note that this event took place at a time when coercive mechanisms for European economic policy harmonization agreements were still soft or vague. This is not so with the IMF; throughout its long existence, sovereign borrowers have learnt to accept IMF tutelage in return for loans at short notice from the Fund.

In order to avoid formal limitation on sovereignty, it is the borrower that "offers" economic policy conditions to the lender, detailed in a request letter sent to the IMF. In this particular case, the letter of intent set out the Hungarian government's planned budgetary, tax and regulatory measures as agreed upon during prior visits of joint IMF/EU representatives:

> The 2009 budget will be amended to reflect the deterioration in the economic outlook and to further reduce the government's borrowing

requirement. The revised budget envisages a general government deficit of 2½ percent of GDP, which implies a structural fiscal adjustment of about 2½ percent of GDP. Revenues, which are difficult to project precisely in the present environment, are expected to decline somewhat as a percentage of GDP, reflecting the slower growth of the tax base and the effect of the spending measures outlined below. The tax cuts previously envisaged for 2009 will be cancelled and we will not make any changes in the tax code that could lead to lower net revenues.[16]

The wording of such a request letter should not deceive us: the government applying for an IMF loan can only include its "own" planned items in the letter once the measures have been reviewed and accepted by the Fund's mission. This is why the approval of such a request at the IMF Board meeting is close to formality; the planned measures being tabled by the government are the very ones that the IMF expects from the applicant.

The particular loan conditions of the IMF/EU loan fell into the Fund's practice of determining quantitative performance criteria and targets, as well as structural measures. Performance criteria included target figures on the central government primary balance, inflation, international reserves, external debt and stock of central government debt. Structural issues included the enactment by the Hungarian parliament of a law on financial supervision, a scheme to recapitalize Hungarian banks, and the introduction of new forms of taxes, such as one on property.

Soon after, it turned out that not every policy promise could be delivered even if the government had really tried hard. The economic reality proved to be rather different, with implications for the state budget as well. 2009 will go down in Hungarian economic history books as a year of deep contraction of output, when budget revenues were strongly impaired by the economic downturn. Eventual deficit and debt data varied from those written into the loan documents back in 2008. Still, the drawdown of the loan went ahead, as the Fund/EU team acknowledged the efforts of the government (a reshuffled Socialist government since April 2009, a sort of caretaker administration in office until the general election in April 2010).

The consequences of the EU/IMF loan were heavy on society: cuts in pensions, a salary freeze and suspension of public investments. The economy suffered a deep contraction (close to 7% in 2009), unemployment increased, real wages declined. Households, in addition, suffered from the depreciation of the domestic currency. As mentioned above, banks had mostly lent to households and businesses in *foreign* currencies until end of 2008. When the HUF deeply depreciated against funding currencies, the debt servicing costs of the debtors shot up.

Bad news like company: major rating agencies downgraded Hungary's sovereign risk to BBB– in summer of 2008. Clearly, markets became edgy about Hungary. The perception of the country risk was reflected in CDS spread: the 5-year CDS spread of Hungary reached its peak level at around 600 bps in October 2008. By comparison, the Polish CDS spread was less than 300 bps in October 2008, and the Czech spread was less than 250 bps. The risk of default of Hungary was therefore perceived to be substantially higher than a default for Poland or the Czech Republic (see Figure 3.2).

Once the initial shocks were over, domestic bond issues were restarted after a couple of months of suspension, and the Hungarian government tapped international capital markets by issuing a EUR bond in 2009. It was significantly oversubscribed, making the authorities declare the issue a big success. However, the funding cost was high: the price of the bond exceeded the German government bonds of corresponding maturity by 432 basis points, resulting in an effective Euro interest rate of around 6.8%.

The year 2010 started more promisingly for emerging economies. Hungary issued its first US dollar-denominated bond after a five-year interval in January 2010. The ten-year bond's yield was set 265 basis points over US Treasuries; this was much higher than the spread of Turkey's corresponding USD bonds.[17]

The above pricing data show that an otherwise far from cheap IMF/EU loan was still less expensive than bonds issued to a skeptical capital market. Still, the incoming center-right Hungarian government under the premiership of Viktor Orbán decided in July 2010 to terminate borrowing cooperation with the IMF.

The roots of disagreements seemed to be the following. The new center-right government wanted to negotiate a higher deficit for 2011 than the

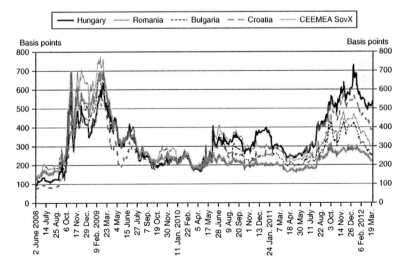

Figure 3.2 Five-year sovereign CDS spreads in emerging markets
Source: Hungarian National Bank, Chartpack. Downloaded on April 7, 2012.

original loan condition (less than 3% of GDP), in order to fulfill its election promise to "restart the engines of the Hungarian economy" by applying a fiscal stimulus. However, the European Commission and the IMF insisted on the original debt schedule. Prime Minister Orbán still wanted to go on with the promised decrease of personal income tax (PIT) as a growth-enhancing measure—even if a flat tax at a reduced rate would, in the short run at least, also reduce government revenues. The government, noting the collapse of "best practice in economic policy" in Europe, decided to resort to unconventional measures of its own, starting with a heavy levy on financial institutions, designed to raise nearly 1% of GDP in 2010. But that led to another clash with official lenders: they did not like the financial sector levy ("bank tax"), claiming that such a one-off measure would help cut budget deficit only temporarily but at the cost of damaging economic growth through reduced financial intermediation. The IMF/EU team also noted that government declarations on reforms in transport and health care, and on reorganizing state-owned enterprises, were not clear enough—while the new government felt it was too early to present detailed plans. The lenders' team was reported to worry about the independence of the central bank: the government moved unilaterally to enforce a public sector pay ceiling at the Bank, which much reduced the central bank governor's pay, a move also objected to by the European Central Bank.[18]

The HUF exchange rate immediately weakened on news about the departure of the IMF; investors sensed clouds over the future of Hungarian finance. What they must have found also confusing, if they cared to listen to what politicians said to their domestic audience, was a series of public speeches about "an economic freedom fight" against "distant global powers."[19]

A number of foreign commentators joined the debate over "life without the IMF"—or used the Hungarian case to illuminate their views and beliefs.[20] Rating agencies became nervous about the Hungarian economy; this was probably as much about its macroeconomic policy twists and turns as about the fundamentals.[21]

The IMF was not the only, let alone the main, obstacle to the new Hungarian government's desired unorthodox policy course: it was the EU. The Hungarian general elections in April 2010 remained a local issue in Europe at a time when the Greek sovereign debt crisis had become the critical story. As a consequence of the crisis, European governments were soon forced to take measures to calm financial markets.[22] The mood thus changed in the summer of 2010 in the European Union, partly because of a parallel change in winds in the financial markets. There remained no room for maneuver for the new Hungarian government, however justified it would have been to apply a dose of anti-cyclical public spending to kick-start the stagnating economy. Neither fellow European politicians nor financial market players felt sympathy for the incoming Hungarian administration in its endeavors. Still, the cabinet went ahead with its policy goals.

What followed turned out to be a busy period in Hungarian economic policy making. The "bank tax," introduced mid-year with retrospective effect in summer 2010, was soon followed by another set of sector taxes ("crisis tax") levied mostly on foreign-owned corporations. Ownership was not mentioned in the original official argument for the sector taxes—it is illegal to discriminate among taxpayers by their nationality within the EU—but most companies involved happened to be foreign-owned; and the prime minister himself referred repeatedly to these levies as "tax on multi-nationals." The series of unorthodox measures included soon a moratorium on foreclosures in 2010.

But what really hurt the vital interest of banks was legislation in the autumn of 2011 to allow homeowners to repay foreign exchange-denominated mortgages in a lump sum at government-determined exchange rates. This preferential repayment exchange rate certainly helped debtor households: those with enough free cash or access to bridge loans could repay Swiss Franc mortgages at 20% discount *vis-à-vis* going market rates—causing similar losses to the banks. The latter, mostly under foreign ownership, complained publicly and turned to European institutions for a remedy. The mortgage loan scheme led to tensions with the governments of parent banks (Austrian banks were particularly exposed to Hungary). A modification of the Act on central banking was also brought into law in December 2011, enabling the cabinet to enlarge the policy interest rate-setting board by two more external members, and creating a position for an additional deputy governor at the National Bank—a not much camouflaged attempt to take control of the decision-making process at the central bank.

Each one of the mentioned measures could be justified in the particular Hungarian context, knowing the numerous mistakes that had led to the stagnation-turned-recession of 2006 through 2009, but the frequency and the mere number of the changes turned out to be too much for important interested parties. What the Hungarian government probably did not foresee was the response of rating agencies, and the instant reaction in the EU. The series of the mentioned and similar non-conventional policies had already been negatively commented upon by major risk-rating firms. Soon, they reduced the sovereign rating of the Hungarian Republic from BBB to BBB– in 2010—downgrades that were vehemently criticized by Hungarian officials. But the real blow followed the Act on FX-loan repayment: all three major agencies (Moody's, S&P and Fitch) downgraded Hungary to non-investment grade (BB–) in the period from November 2011 to January 2012.

The Hungarian government, in fact, at first tried to avoid a downgrade by a surprise statement about restarting talks with the IMF in November 2011, but that maneuver came late and did not impress Moody's. Other rating agencies followed suit. After the downgrades, government bond yields kept growing and exceeded temporarily ten per cent both on short and long maturities. The forint depreciated again, steeply. The Hungarian government had no other option than to turn to the IMF in earnest for financial help.

Here the EU came into the picture. Just as in 2008, any new policy loan to a member state was to be provided jointly by the Fund and the EU; therefore loan conditions were determined by both institutions. By early 2012, the Commission had already compiled a list of unresolved issues with the Hungarian government, including the legal position of the central bank. Such frictions made the new loan preparation process harder and more political than in 2008. For long months, there was no progress in loan negotiations between the Hungarian government and the twin team of lenders. Meanwhile, financial market conditions deteriorated for the Hungarian state as a borrower. At the time of this writing, the attempt to get rid of the tutelage of the international financial institutions and to finance the sovereign debt instead through the markets, presumed to be "non-political," seems to have failed.

3.7   Conclusions

A period of "no best practice" in the developed world certainly enlarged the margin for country-specific policy experiences; the particular circumstances evoked an invitation to experiment with policy innovations and apply trial-and-error measures, and even to return to long-forgotten pre-globalization measures, such as taxing cash-rich (foreign) investors. Policy innovations turned to be less frequent in emerging markets; the peculiar contrast between conservative emerging markets and core countries experimenting with "unorthodox" measures tells a lot about the importance of institutional credibility when it comes to disputed practices. The European semi-periphery, an antithesis to prudence in periphery, was caught in a particularly fragile situation by 2009: high exposure to spillovers without proper protection from the side effects of massive capital flows.

With the benefit of hindsight, it is obvious that fast-growing semi-periphery countries fell victim to a false sense of security in the Euro zone concerning current account deficits—of shockingly huge proportion in some country cases. But where were the international bodies and the supranational authorities when it all happened? The soul-searching at the IMF led later to the admission that the Fund had made mistakes in the run-up to the crisis, partly as a result of the particular mindset at the Fund, namely that financial crisis in large advanced economies was unlikely, and financial markets were fundamentally sound and rational.[23] The same report of the Evaluation Office of the IMF admits that advanced economies were not included in its vulnerability exercise, and thus not much scrutinized before the crisis—even if some so-called advanced nations were none other than crisis-prone semi-periphery markets.

A thorough Breugel report on IMF and Euro zone surveillance identified the following factors behind the regulatory failure: IMF surveillance had failed to identify spillovers between Euro-area countries; the Fund fell victim to a "Europe is different" mindset; warnings about the dismal state of Greek fiscal reporting were raised with Greek authorities but EU institutions were not warned; and the urgency of problems in Greece was not properly captured in Article IV consultation in 2009.[24]

Certain capital market processes also proved to be faulty: risk appetite remained too strong for some time even when tension signs had already appeared on the European horizon, and then, suddenly, market players panicked when the genuine risks of sovereign defaults were noticed and translated into (late, and with questionable) justification by rating agencies.

National decision makers in the European semi-periphery did not fail to notice the growing room for policy maneuver in the crisis period and right after it. But as the financial crisis evolved into a sovereign debt crisis, the window of opportunity narrowed immediately. It is, anyway, a mistake to confuse a larger margin of maneuver with economic sovereignty.

Western Europe soon put into motion its bureaucratic machinery to initiate an exit from the exceptional period of expansive fiscal and monetary policies of 2009—and that happened to undermine the attempts of some governments (as in the Hungarian case) that tried to copy these policies at a later stage. It may be too early to declare the advent of a "new normal," but in major capitals of Europe a new crisis management (or a new best practice) may emerge gradually, thus closing the "low risk" experimentation window. What looked to politicians like the end of the self-confident, even arrogant, "neo-liberal" mainstream of "markets are always right," turned out to be a lull. Interdependence, and not independence, is the name of the game, with its heavy consequences for all those involved, politicians and their voters alike.

Notes

1. See Michael Burda and Charles Wyplocz (1993) *Macroeconomics: A European Text*, Oxford: Oxford University Press.
2. Jean Boden (1576) *Les Six livres de la République*, translated by M. J. Tooley (1955), Oxford: Basil Blackwell, http://www.constitution.org/bodin/bodin_.htm.
3. François Gianviti (2004) *Current Legal Aspects of Monetary Sovereignty*, Seminar Paper, Washington, DC: IMF.
4. IMF (2010) *Central Banking Lessons from the Crisis*, Policy Paper, May 27, Washington, DC: IMF.
5. Graciela L. Kaminsky, Carmen M. Reinhart and Carlos A. Végh (2004) "When it Rains, It Pours: Procyclical Capital Flows and Policies," *NBER Macroeconomic Annual 2004*, ed. Mark Gertler and Kenneth S. Rogoff, Cambridge, MA: MIT Press, pp. 11–53.
6. Deepak Mohanty (2011) "Lessons for Monetary Policy from the Global Financial Crisis: An Emerging Market Perspective," Bank for International Settlements' central bankers' speeches, April.
7. Immanuel Wallerstein (1979) *The Capitalist World-Economy*, New York: Cambridge University Press.

8. Eurostat (2010): *Newsrelease—Euroindicator* 55/2010. 22 April 2010.
9. Tommaso Padoa-Schioppa (2010) *The Debt Crisis in the Euro Area: Interest and Passions*, Notre Europe Policy Brief No. 16.
10. Zdenek Cech and Anton Jevcak (2011) "International Reserves in the CEE8—Lessons from the Financial Crisis," *ECFIN Country Focus*, Vol. 8, No. 3.
11. Cillian Ryan (2011) "The Euro Crisis and Crisis Management: Big Lessons from a Small Island," *International Economics and Economic Policy*, Vol. 8, No. 1.
12. Irish government debt in year 2008, amounting to a mere 64% of GDP, would be—if measured against Irish GNI—78%, placing the country close to the danger zone already prior to the climax of the crisis. See Ryan, "The Euro Crisis and Crisis Management."
13. Berry Eichengreen and Ricardo Hausmann (1999) *Exchange Rates and Financial Fragility*, National Bureau for Economic Research Working Paper 7418, Cambridge, MA: NBER.
14. Attila Csajbók, András Hudecz and Bálint Tamási (2010) *Foreign Currency Borrowing of Households in New EU Member States*, Occasional Paper No. 87, Magyar Nemzeti Bank (Hungarian National Bank), Budapest.
15. Péter Ákos Bod (2010) *Hungary Turns to the International Monetary Fund in 2008—Anatomy of a Crisis*, Gazdasági Élet és Társadalom, WSUF, No. I–II.
16. MNB (Hungarian National Bank) (2008) *Letter of Intent*, http://english.mnb.hu/engine.aspx?page=mnben_stand-by_arrangement.
17. Turkey was ranked non-investment grade by major rating agencies, while Hungary stood at BBB–, the lowest investment-grade category, at Standard & Poor's; at Baa1, two notches higher, at Moody's, and was ranked BBB by Fitch, two ranks above non-investment (or 'junk') grade.
18. Péter Ákos Bod (2011) "On Business–Government Relations: The Hungarian Case," *Hungarian Review*, Vol. II, No. 5.
19. The Economics Minister put it this way in a television programme: "the cabinet remains intent on maintaining the country's financial independence and regaining economic self-determination." Portfolio.hu: "EcoMin says Hungary will not 'break its back' to cut deficit in 2011," August 6, 2010.
20. See supporters of the Hungarian new government's position: for example, Paul Krugman (2010) "Give Me Your Tired, Your Poor, Your Hungary," *The New York Times*, August 4; Mark Weisbrot (2010) "To Viktor Go the Spoils: How Hungary Blazes a Trail in Europe," *The Guardian*, August 9; while as for critical opinions, see *The Economist* (2010) "Orban out on a Limb: Hungary's New Prime Minister Takes on the World," August 5; Krisztina Than (2010) "Hungary Risks Markets' Goodwill with IMF/EU Failure," Reuters Analysis, July 23.
21. Standard & Poor's (2010) *Credit Trends: Global Potential Fallen Angels*, September 10.
22. Not only Greece but also Spain, Portugal and Ireland declared drastic budgetary actions. Even the nation with the best ranking joined in: in June the German government announced a package of measures that would save around €80 billion by 2014. Chancellor Angela Merkel said Germany was to set an example of budgetary discipline to other Euro zone countries. The French government also declared it would act to trim its deficit by abolishing tax exemptions.
23. IMF Independent Evaluation Office (2011) *IMF Performance in the Run-up to the Financial and Economic Crisis: IMF Surveillance in 2004–07*, Evaluation Report, Washington, DC: IMF.
24. Jean Pisany-Ferry, André Sapir and Guntram B. Wolff (2011) *An Evaluation of IMF Surveillance of the Euro Area*, Bruegel Blueprint Series XIV, Brussels: Bruegel.

4
Building Firewalls: European Responses to the Sovereign Debt Crisis

Constantine A. Stephanou

4.1 Introductory remarks

The financial crisis, originally affecting banks and subsequently sovereign borrowers, may be considered as an episode in the continuous confrontation between states and markets. Previous confrontations have led to major adjustments or even breakdowns of international regimes. Market forces were successful at breaking down the Bretton Woods system in 1973, thereby allowing exchange rates to fluctuate freely. Financial innovations, including the securitization of debt, its dispersion resulting from the development of secondary markets and the multiplication of financial derivatives, such as credit default swaps (CDSs), have put added strains on governments and the management of public debt.

The current sovereign debt crisis constitutes a "novelty," because it involves members of a monetary union, thereby undermining trust in the union's currency. It is often argued that a monetary union goes hand in hand with an economic and fiscal union. Such a union involves a lender of last resort, along the lines of the US Federal Reserve, committed to redeeming the debt of the Union and its members in case of default.[1] The European Union treaties and, specifically, the Treaty on the Functioning of the European Union (TFEU) embody no-bailout provisions,[2] which can be read as absolute impediments to the creation of a fiscal union. These provisions and other constraints on government spending were actually founded on the moral hazard argument; they aimed at deterring both sovereign borrowers and private creditors from irresponsible behavior. Profligate borrowers were expected to live within their means and strengthen their competitiveness, since they were no more in a position to devalue their currency. Investors were expected to reward the best and punish the worst performers; the latter were expected to adjust so that, in the end, the market mechanism would lead to a convergence of interest rates. From a political viewpoint the constraints aimed at soothing taxpayers in fiscally responsible countries who were worried that they might have to pay the debt of other members of the currency union.

When the provisions on Economic and Monetary Union (EMU) were introduced by the Maastricht Treaty (1992) into the European Community Treaty (TEC), it was unclear which countries would participate in the Euro Area. Moreover, it was understood that countries aspiring for membership would fulfill all the economic convergence criteria, including the levels of government deficit and debt. After joining the Euro, it was expected that the no-bailout and economic governance provisions embodied in the Treaty would guarantee fiscal discipline. These expectations proved to be wrong.

Firstly, some countries were allowed to join the Euro, even though their government debt exceeded not the reference value of 60% but 100% of their GDP.[3] Secondly, after accession to the Euro Area the key provision for ensuring fiscal discipline was the prohibition of excessive deficits, that is, deficits exceeding 3% of the GDP. In contrast, however, to the bulk of EU law, in this specific case infringement proceedings could not be brought against a non-abiding Member State.[4] The Council could exert pressure against such a state by imposing sanctions on it, including huge fines, at the end of a long and painstaking procedure. Very soon after the launching of the single currency, the threat of sanctions proved ineffective. The Commission recommended to the Council the enforcement of these rules against France and Germany but the Council refrained from doing so.[5] Compliance with the 3% threshold was an overwhelmingly political issue, and most countries seemed to have valid excuses for exceeding it.[6]

The current sovereign debt crisis has demonstrated the limits of the system. The fall of interest rates expected to occur in high interest-rate countries, rather than benefiting these countries, led to irresponsible borrowing. On the other hand, the fact that Euro Area government bonds were zero-weighted for bank capital purposes encouraged investors to ignore the fundamentals of less competitive countries.

The reaction of the Euro Area has been slow, due to the inadequacy of economic governance, as well as political opposition to bailouts in the Northern members and to reforms in the Southern ones. The current process, described as one of muddling-through, is time-consuming and subject to challenges by impatient market players. Nevertheless, in response to market pressures, the Member States and, in particular, the members of the Euro Area, committed to the survival of the single currency, established mechanisms for bailing-out members facing liquidity problems although, in at least one case, the liquidity problem masked a solvency problem.

As long as sovereign borrowers kept their high ratings, the inadequacies of the EU treaties went unnoticed. The situation changed when the rating agencies started detecting the fiscal imbalances of Euro Area members. Up to 2009 all sovereign borrowers of the Euro Area were rated by the three American agencies with variations of A. Two years later, the sovereign debt of three members had been reduced to junk status and the Euro Area was racing to save these and other members from default. The rating agencies had failed to notice the deterioration of the public finances of the Euro Area peripheral members prior to the 2010 crisis. The rapid fall of interest rates, which occurred in these countries following their incorporation into the Euro Area, had led to irresponsible borrowing. In the case of Greece, government borrowing soared, being politically more acceptable than cutting government expenditure on the welfare state or extending income tax coverage to small business and the self-employed. On the other hand, rating agencies have also contributed to the sovereign debt crisis, by their hurried downgrading of the debt of the aforementioned countries; their predictions amounted to self-fulfilling prophecies.

4.2   The birth of the bailout mechanisms

4.2.1   The first Greek bailout

The first major test for the Euro Area came in the early weeks of 2010. Following the change of government that took place in Greece in October 2009 and the discovery of a hidden fiscal deficit,[7] the spreads on the interest rates of Greek government bonds skyrocketed. On December 2, 2009 the Council established in accordance with Article 126 (6), TFEU that Greece had taken no effective action to curb its deficit in response to a Commission report of April 27, 2009. On February 16, 2010 the Council adopted decision 2010/182/EU, giving notice to Greece in accordance with Article 126 (7), TFEU to take measures to correct the excessive deficit by 2012. Greece announced deficit-cutting measures of over 2% of GDP, which were judged satisfactory by the European Council meeting held on March 25; in the relevant declaration it was also mentioned that Euro Area members were ready to provide coordinated bilateral loans at non-concessional interest rates and subject to strong policy conditionality. Nevertheless, markets were not convinced. By April, when it became a certainty that Greece would soon be unable to refinance its debt from the international bond market, the Greek government submitted a formal request for financial assistance. In early May, the Member States of the Euro Area and the IMF agreed to extend loan facilities of unprecedented amounts to Greece, described further.

Under a five-year Loan Facility Agreement with a three-year grace period, signed on May 8, 2010 by the European Commission on behalf of the Euro Area members, the latter agreed to extend to Greece pooled bilateral loans amounting to Euros 80 billion; the agreement was subsequently ratified by them, with the exception of Slovakia. The loan facility carried floating interest rates, that is, three-month Euribor, plus a spread of 300 basis points rising to 400 points for amounts outstanding beyond three years; evidently, these interest rates, as opposed to those of the IMF, were non-concessional and very attractive for the lending nations, even more so for Germany, whose bond offerings with similar maturities carried interest rates inferior to 2%. On May 10, the Council gave a revised notice to Greece under decision 2010/320/EU, based on Article 126 (9), TFEU, as well as article 136, TFEU on coordinated action by members of the Euro Area, extending by two years, that is, to 2014, the deadline set earlier to Greece for putting an end to its deficit and embodying the necessary implementing measures.

Whatever views one might have about the expediency of financial assistance to Greece, it constituted a major innovation in the governance of the Euro Area. It is true that the Treaty embodies a provision (article 143, TFEU) on mutual assistance to a Member State facing difficulties as a result of "an overall disequilibrium in its balance of payments, or as a result of the type of currency at its disposal." Such mutual assistance is granted by the Council or by other Member States subject to their agreement. This provision, which has been applied to Member States with balance of payments difficulties, is inapplicable to members of the Euro Area. Moreover, the Treaty does not provide for mutual assistance in the case of a sovereign debt crisis. It actually prohibits bailouts, as explained previously.

IMF participation in the Greek bailout also constituted a novelty because, for the first time, a recipient of IMF assistance was a member of a currency union, which should normally be self-reliant; moreover the recipient was unable to implement a key element of IMF medicine for its recovery, that is, the devaluation of its currency. The sum of Euros 30 billion was extended to Greece under a stand-by agreement approved on May 9 by the IMF Executive Board under the Fund's fast-track Emergency Financing Mechanism procedures. The expediency of IMF participation was questioned inside and outside the Euro Area. The Greek government was criticized for having contacted the IMF prior to the discussion in the Euro Area. Although elites committed to the European cause objected to IMF involvement in an intra-European problem, the German government supported IMF participation on the ground of the IMF's expertise in the management of policy conditionality. From the point of view of the IMF itself, the amount of Euros 30 billion represented the largest access granted to a member country and was out of proportion with previous loans granted by the IMF, which were usually limited to 10–15 times the borrower's quota—Euros 900 million euros in the case of Greece.[8] The IMF rescue was questioned in the US Senate, bearing in mind its potential implications—the United States being the largest shareholder of the IMF.

Strict policy conditionality meant that prior to the conclusion of the loan agreements, the Greek Parliament had to endorse a Memorandum of Understanding (MoU) containing three documents: a Memorandum of Economic and Financial Policies, a Memorandum on "Specific economic policy conditionality," setting forth the conditions for the quarterly loan disbursements, and a Technical Memorandum of Understanding.[9] Greece committed itself to implement dramatic deficit-cutting measures for 2010, amounting to 6% of its GDP. Greece also accepted inspection at regular intervals by the so-called Troika, composed of representatives of the Commission, the ECB and the IMF. The three institutions were required to deliver an opinion before the disbursement of each installment. Entrusting the IMF, a non-EU institution, with the duty to monitor the economy of a Euro Area member was well received in financial circles but was perceived as a failure in the governance of the Euro Area by the aforementioned elites. In Greece, the undertakings under the MoU were branded unconstitutional by opposition parties, though they were obviously related to the state of emergency of the Greek economy.

After a first period of successful implementation, involving very substantial cuts in civil servants' pay and state pensions, as well as public health expenditure, resulting in the reduction of the government deficit by one-third—it declined from 15.8% to 10.6% of GDP in 2010—the government embarked in a process of reorganization of the public sector, including the tax collection system, with an uncertain outcome. While the deficit of 2011 was further reduced in absolute terms, its ratio to GDP declined only slightly, from 10.6% to 9.2%, because of the unexpected recession of the economy, reaching 7% of the GDP. It is now recognized that the austerity package has dramatically affected domestic demand and, by implication, tax revenue and social security contributions. On the positive side, the austerity package led to a dramatic decline of the balance of payments deficit from a world record of 15% of the GDP to less than 10%, with a declining trend.

The expediency of the financial package has been a controversial issue from the beginning of the crisis. Daniel Gross, the Director of CEPS, observed that the package was designed to cover the financing needs of Greece for a couple of quarters and to contain the interest burden following the sudden rise of spreads; Gross pointed out that interest savings would make very little difference because as long as the public deficit remained high the financing needs of Greece would continue to rise; the real problem for Greece was not one of liquidity but one of solvency; the key was therefore whether Greece was willing to undertake the huge domestic effort required to achieve a sustainable fiscal position.[10] Greece's problem was eminently political—the country was living beyond its means; its insurance-based social security system was kept alive with annual subsidies amounting to Euros 15 billion or, approximately, 6% of the GDP of 2009. On the other hand, the shock therapy applied by the IMF to developing countries for reducing government deficits proved inappropriate in the Greek case, due to unforeseen political opposition. The Greek bailout postponed default but, a year later, a second bailout had to be arranged and political consensus for its implementation was uncertain.

4.2.2   The provisional stability mechanisms: The EFSM and the EFSF

The birth of the bailout mechanisms coincided with the Greek bailout. The reasoning behind their creation was the "severe deterioration of the borrowing conditions of several member States beyond what can be explained by economic fundamentals."[11] The Portuguese bailout, which occurred a year after the establishment of the bailout mechanisms, was the typical example of a country whose borrowing conditions deteriorated following successive downgrades by the credit rating agencies; its levels of public debt and deficit were far better than those of Greece.

The need to involve the EU as such and the Euro Area Member States in bailout operations led to the creation of two separate instruments. Thus, on May 9, 2010, the Council decided the creation of an EU instrument to be known as the European Financial Stabilisation Mechanism (EFSM) and a "Special Purpose Vehicle" among the members of the Euro Area, to be known as the European Financial Stability Facility (EFSF). The EFSM and EFSF were intended only as temporary bailout mechanisms (to expire in 2013), in part due to the lack of a legal basis in the EU treaties at that time.

On May 11 the Council adopted Regulation 407/2010, establishing the European Financial Stability Mechanism (EFSM)[12] with a capital of Euros 60 billion. The EFSM is based on a solidarity clause in the Treaty that enables the Council to grant financial assistance to a Member State facing difficulties caused by "natural disasters or exceptional occurrences beyond its control" (Article 122 par. 2, TFEU). The possibility of grounding on this provision a derogation from the no-bailout provision of Article 125, TFEU has been a matter of controversy. The issue was raised in the context of an appeal before the German Constitutional Court, which was dismissed following a stimulating exchange of arguments, the most important being that financial assistance from the EFSM carried non-concessionary interest rates and did not constitute a bailout.[13]

Moreover, under an agreement signed on June 7, the Euro Area members established the European Financial Stability Facility (EFSF), in the form of a limited liability company incorporated in Luxembourg, with an authorized capital of Euros 440 billion. A Decision of the Representatives of the Governments of the Euro Area Member States meeting within the Council of the European Union committed their respective governments to provide guarantees of up to this amount in proportion to their share in the capital of the ECB.

The EFSM and the EFSF raised funds on the capital markets. Bond offerings by the EFSM were backed by collateral from the EU budget, whereas bond offerings by the EFSF were backed by guarantees given by the Euro Area members. The triple A rating and the effective lending capacity of the EFSF estimated at Euros 250 billion very much depended on the triple A rating of its main guarantors, Germany and France.

The EFSM and the EFSF participated, together with the IMF, in the Irish and Portuguese bailouts. In the Irish case, the sovereign debt crisis was the outcome of the banking crisis that occurred in this country and was of direct concern to Britain's banking system. Prior to the bailout, the Irish government had injected considerable liquidity into the ailing banks, actually nationalizing one of the biggest (Anglo-Irish Bank). Moreover, Irish banks could refinance themselves from the ECB, by offering as collateral Irish government bonds. However, the ECB notified Irish banks that this method of financing had reached a peak (approximately Euros 115 billion) and said the Irish government would have to seek alternative sources of financing. Ireland sought direct financial support for the bailout of its banks, rather than indirect financing through sovereign borrowing. The banking crisis deepened, however, as a result of massive deposit withdrawals. Following a request on November 21, a joint rescue operation was organized by the EFSM on behalf of the EU, the EFSF on behalf of the Euro Area, non-Euro area members (Britain, Sweden and Denmark) and the IMF. Under loan facilities providing for a four-year grace period and a seven-year repayment period, the EFSM agreed to extend Euros 22.5 billion and the EFSF Euros 17.5 billion, out of a total amount of Euros 85 billion. A few months later, in April 2011 and in the context of the Portuguese bailout, the EFSM provided Euros 26 billion and the EFSF Euros 26 billion, out of a total amount of Euros 78 billion. The Euros 60 billion lending capacity of the EFSM was practically exhausted with its contribution to the Irish and Portuguese bailouts.

The EFSM and the EFSF were intended to provide loans to Euro Area members in distress, which sign up to financial support programs. The deterioration of the fiscal situation of Italy in the beginning of July 2011 led to important amendments to the EFSF during the second half of 2011, with a view to enhancing the capacity of this instrument. The Euro summit of July 21 decided to allow the EFSF to act on a precautionary basis by purchasing bonds of Euro Area members that were not finding buyers, thereby reducing interest rate spreads—subject, however, to a positive opinion by the ECB. Moreover, the EFSF could also provide loans to Euro Area members, including states outside bailout programs, who could use the funds to redeem high-interest bonds or to recapitalize their banks. The ratification of the aforementioned amendments by the Euro Area Parliaments was completed on October 13, 2011.

The EFSF's limited "firepower" remained, however, a matter of concern. German opposition to a further increase of the capital guarantees led to alternative arrangements. At the Euro summit of October 26/27, 2011 it was agreed to leverage the resources of the EFSF by offering credit enhancements to purchasers of Euro Area members' debt in the primary market, on part of the value of the respective bonds. It was also agreed to create "Special Purpose Vehicles," which would combine EFSF resources with resources from private and public institutions for achieving the aims of the EFSF. The IMF and sovereign wealth funds of China and other economic powers were considered as potential participants. At the Euro summit of December 8/9 Member States decided to provide up to Euros 200 billion to the IMF in the form of bilateral loans, to ensure that the IMF had adequate resources to deal with the crisis. Thus the IMF would be in a position to supplement EFSF assistance.

4.2.3   The European Stability Mechanism (ESM)

The provisional character of the aforementioned bailout mechanisms led to a decision by the European Council in December 2010 to establish a permanent stability mechanism. The new mechanism, to be known as European Stability Mechanism, was scheduled to assume the roles of the EFSM and the EFSF when these mechanisms expired. In order, however, to conclude the agreement among Euro Area members, an enabling clause had to be inserted in the Treaty. The European Council agreed to insert into Article 136, TFEU a paragraph 3, which reads as follows:

> The member states whose currency is the euro may establish a stability mechanism to be activated if indispensable to safeguard the stability of the euro area as a whole. The granting of any required financial assistance under the mechanism will be made subject to strict conditionality.

In March 2011, the European Parliament approved the Treaty amendment after receiving assurances that the European Commission would play "a central role" in the preparation of the ESM macro-economic adjustment programmes and the monitoring of their implementation. Thereafter, the Treaty amendment was approved by a formal decision of the European Council,[14] and submitted to the Euro Area members for approval by their Parliaments, in accordance with Article 48 par. 6 of the Treaty on European Union (TEU).

Moreover, the Treaty establishing the ESM was signed on July 11, 2011 among the Euro Area members, following difficult negotiations during the first semester of 2011. According to this treaty, the ESM is an intergovernmental organization under public international law, located in Luxembourg. Its authorized capital amounting to Euros 700 billion consists of paid-in shares amounting to Euros 80 billion and callable guarantees amounting to Euros 620 billion. Its effective lending capacity was estimated at approximately Euros 500 billion. The large amount of paid-in capital in the form of cash deposits was a source of concern in a number of Member States. The distinguishing feature of the ESM is that its method of action combines financial assistance with debt restructuring through private sector involvement (PSI), described below (4.3). Moreover, in addition to "stability support" the purchase of bonds of the beneficiary on the primary market is envisaged under the "primary market support facility."

At the Euro summit of December 8/9 it was decided to accelerate the entry into force of the ESM Treaty, as well as to adjust some of its provisions.

A revised version of the Treaty signed on February 2, 2012 was scheduled to enter into force as soon as Member States representing 90% of the capital commitments had ratified it; moreover, the trigger for bailouts was made more flexible with the replacement of unanimity by an 85% majority in case the Commission and the ECB conclude that an urgent decision related to financial assistance is needed. A clarification on private sector involvement (PSI) was also to be included in the preamble of the Treaty.

4.2.4   The second Greek bailout

Very soon after the granting of pooled bilateral loans to Greece it was realized that the country required further debt relief. The Euro summit decided on March 25, 2011 to reduce the floating interest rates applicable to the loans by 100 basis points and to extend their maturity to 7.5 years, in line with the IMF. On July 12, the Council gave a revised notice to Greece under decision 2011/734/EU (amended in November 2011 and in March 2012) with revised conditionality criteria. At the July 21 Euro summit it was decided that future EFSF loans to Greece would involve maturities of 15 to 30 years (with a grace period of 10 years) and would carry interest rates "close to, without going below, the EFSF funding cost": the same terms were made applicable to the loans of Ireland and Portugal. More importantly perhaps, the summit decided for the first time a 21% voluntary "haircut" on the face amount of privately owned Greek debt estimated at Euros 200 billion, with the granting of credit enhancements by the EFSF in order to ensure the voluntary character of the restructuring. Negotiations on private sector involvement (PSI) were launched in September 2011, but an IMF report endorsed by the Troika determined that the July package including the haircut would not ensure the long-term sustainability of the Greek debt.[15]

On the basis of the aforementioned report, the July bailout was revised at the October 26/27 Euro summit; the haircut was set at 50% of the face value of bonds in the hands of private investors and was to be achieved by means of a voluntary bond rollover. Finally, the Euro Area members undertook a political commitment regarding the participation of the official sector, which, according to the declaration, "stands ready to provide additional programme financing of up to 100 bn euros until 2014, including required recapitalization of Greek banks."[16] The IMF contribution was expected to be equivalent to the previous one, although a large part of it had not yet been disbursed.[17] An important part of the new program would help cover Greek government deficits, essentially debt servicing, until 2014, when it was estimated that Greece would run a primary surplus.[18] The Eurogroup specified the conditions of the second bailout at its meeting on February 21; on March 14 it decided that Greece had fulfilled the requirements described as "prior actions" for the disbursement of the first tranche of the loan facility.

4.2.5　Principles governing bailouts

Trigger mechanism

The wording on the trigger mechanism has varied. Thus, the European Council stated in its declaration of March 25, 2010, prior to the first Greek bailout, that the mechanism of coordinated bilateral loans "has to be considered *ultima ratio*, meaning in particular that market financing is insufficient." Later the ESFM Regulation stated that "financial assistance may be granted to a Member State which is experiencing, or is seriously threatened with, a severe economic or financial disturbance caused by exceptional occurrences beyond its control."[19] Although the revised EFSF has made easier the access to its resources under the precautionary approach described earlier, the stigma attached to such access has deterred potential candidates from seeking EFSF assistance. The ESM Treaty allows on its part the provision of financial assistance to an ESM Member "when its regular access to the market financing is impaired."[20] In practice, bailouts have been decided when Member States in distress were unable to borrow on markets at acceptable rates. Rates above 6% on ten-year bond issues are generally deemed unacceptable because they make debt servicing unsustainable.

Policy conditionality

A crucial element in financial assistance under the bailout mechanisms is "strict policy conditionality" under an economic adjustment program, which entails economic policy obligations for the sovereign borrower, in addition to the usual loan obligations. The conditionality principle, originally embodied in the "structural adjustment programs" accompanying IMF loan facilities, is now a key element of the bailouts in the Euro Area. Conditionality would be impossible to implement if bailouts were assigned to the ECB. As things stand today, the bailout mechanisms are activated after a country program has been negotiated with the European Commission and the IMF, and such program has been unanimously approved by the Eurogroup (Euro Area Finance Ministers) and, finally, a Memorandum of Understanding (MoU) embodying the policy conditionality has been signed. Policy implementation is monitored by the so-called Troika, consisting of representatives of the European Commission, the IMF and the ECB.

4.2.6　The ECB: A "hidden" lender of last resort

The ECB has played a crucial role in defending the Euro from speculative attacks, by providing adequate liquidity to banks since the 2008 crisis and, later, by accepting as collateral, low-rated government bonds.[21] In doing so it saved the Greek banking system, and subsequently those of Ireland and Portugal from collapse. Moreover, on May 10, 2010 the ECB decided to buy bonds from the secondary market under its "Securities Market Program"[22] in order to stabilize the bond market. The decision was still in force when the ECB decided to intervene massively by means of the Long Term Refinancing Operations (LTROs) to contain speculative attacks against Italian and Spanish government bonds. LTRO 1 (December 2011) and LTRO 2 (February 2012) involved amounts of approximately Euros 500 billion in the form of three-year loans carrying a 1% interest rate. According to a BIS study, banks in Italy and Spain used the new funds to significantly boost their holdings of government bonds.[23] Thus the ECB's action achieved two goals: it prompted the banks to purchase bonds from the countries that were unable to refinance their debt at sustainable interest rates, while also averting a banking crisis that would have resulted from the large exposure of European banks to these countries. George Magnus, the Senior Economic Adviser at UBS, pointed out, however, that even though banks may have increased their lending to governments, much of their increased access to ECB liquid funds has ended up back at the ECB, and there was no evidence that the European economy would benefit from an increase in credit.[24]

4.3   Debt restructuring

4.3.1   The issue of private sector involvement (PSI)

The moral hazard argument leads to the conclusion that the way to deal with irresponsible behavior by private bondholders is to make them incur losses on their investments. In the EU context, this view was vigorously promoted by Germany; it served as a *quid pro quo* for the setting-up of the permanent bailout mechanism under the ESM Treaty. Under Article 12 of the Treaty the beneficiary of ESM assistance is required to put in place an "adequate and proportionate form of private sector involvement (PSI) ... in line with IMF practice." Depending on the outcome of the negotiations and the sustainability of the beneficiary's debt, the restructuring will be voluntary or compulsory. It is explicitly provided that ESM loans will enjoy preferred creditor status, junior only to IMF loans. The idea is to make default possible with only a minor risk to the budget of creditor nations.[25] On the other hand, the preferred status of official lenders (IMF, ESM) reduces the funds available for private creditors in case of default or restructuring, thereby increasing the risk premium and the cost of servicing the debt. It is worth noting that according to recital no. 10 of the preamble, preferred creditor status will **not** apply to an ESM financial assistance program, which follows a European financial assistance program existing at the time of the entry into force of the Treaty, that is, previous EFSM- and EFSF-sponsored programs. Claims under such programs will rank *pari passu*, that is, on the same terms with private creditors' claims.

Moreover, the ESM Treaty stipulates that, after its entry into force, all new Euro Area government bond offerings should include standardized and identical collective action clauses (CACs).[26] CACs allow compulsory "haircuts" to be decided by qualified majorities of bondholders. Under English law, applicable to many bond issues, haircuts decided by qualified majorities of bondholders[27] at assemblies by bond series are binding on the minorities and do not constitute default events. Recourse to CACs allows for an orderly restructuring of government debt and has been recommended in the past by the G-10,[28] the IMF[29] and the EU.[30] It does not necessarily increase the cost of borrowing; thus, the yield curve of new bonds issued in the context of Mexico's 2003 rollover was not affected by the inclusion of CACs in these bonds.[31]

The model CACs elaborated by the Economic and Financial Committee and approved in the form of a *Common Understanding* by the Ministers of Finance and the Governors of the central banks of the EU members at their meeting in Stresa on September 13, 2003 enable majorities of at least three-quarters (75%) by face amount of a quorum of these bonds to approve exchange offers and amendments of redemption provisions.[32]

4.3.2   The Greek PSI

The context

Soon after the decisions of the Euro summit of October 26/27, 2011 on the PSI issue Greece entered into negotiations for the implementation of the PSI provisions with the International Institute of Finance (IIF), representing the major bondholders. The agreement reached by mid-February 2012 was the outcome of difficult negotiations regarding the interest rates and maturities of the new bonds.[33] These negotiations were carried out in a completely new context, outside the caucuses of the Paris and London Clubs involved in previous debt restructuring operations, and with the active support of the sovereign borrower by the IMF and the Euro Area whose primary concern was to ensure the long-term sustainability of the Greek debt.

Under the informal agreement reached in mid-February, a 53% haircut on the face amount of privately owned debt[34] or 75% in net present value terms was agreed. The haircut involved a write-down of over Euros 100 billion and was the largest in history; the official lenders were not affected by the restructuring but the Greek State Pension Funds were included in the haircut. The success of the PSI relied on credit enhancements by the EFSF, amounting to Euros 35,5 billion and, as regards Greek banks, which were the most exposed to the haircut, an amount of up to Euros 50 billion was earmarked for their recapitalization.

The PSI process was triggered upon the finding by the Eurogroup on February 21, 2012 that Greece had fulfilled the so-called prior actions referred to in the new MoU on economic conditionality. The Greek government statement on the bond swap, embodying an exchange offer and a consent solicitation, was published on February 24, 2012 and set a deadline until March 8, 2012 for the acceptance of the offer.

The exchange offer

The exchange offer permitted private sector holders to exchange bonds for:

1. new bonds issued by Greece on the PSI settlement date having a face amount equal to 31.5% of the face amount of the exchanged bonds, to be governed by English law;
2. EFSF notes described in the PSI Liability Management Facility Agreement concluded with Greece as EFSF debt securities, with a maturity date of two years or less from the PSI settlement date and having a face amount equal to 15% of the face amount of the exchanged bonds;
3. detachable GDP linked securities issued by Greece, having a notional amount equal to the face amount of each holder's new bonds.

Greece also committed itself to deliver short-term EFSF notes on the PSI settlement date (March 12, 2012), in discharge of unpaid interest accrued up to February 24, 2012 on exchanged bonds, amounting to Euros 5.7 billion.

The consent solicitation

The consent solicitation was applicable to Greek-law governed bonds issued prior to December 31, 2011 and having an aggregate outstanding amount of Euros 177 billion, that is, 93% of the total amount of Euros 185 billion in private hands. The Greek government sought the consent of the affected bondholders to the amendment of these bonds, relying on the recently enacted Law 4050/2012 (the Greek Bondholders Act). The amendments provided for the redemption of the affected bonds in exchange for the PSI consideration mentioned previously. Under the collective action clauses introduced by the Greek Bondholders Act with retroactive effect,[35] the proposed amendments would become binding on the aforementioned bondholders if at least two thirds (66.6%) by face amount of a quorum of these bonds, voting in aggregate, without distinction by series, approved these amendments. One half (50%) by face amount of the aforementioned bonds would constitute a quorum for these purposes. It was also provided that the government would solicit consents in favor of equivalent amendments from the holders of its foreign-law governed bonds, in accordance with the terms of these bonds.

The outcome

The exchange offer was accepted by bondholders representing 85.8% of the amount governed by Greek law, that is, Euros 152 billion out of a total of Euros 177 billion. This acceptance rate above the 66.6% threshold enabled the Greek government to activate the CACs inserted in these bonds and to include the rest of these bonds in the swap. The exchange offer was also accepted by bondholders representing 69% of the amount governed by foreign law, that is, Euros 20 billion out of a total of Euros 29 billion, although the period of acceptance of the offer was extended in order to comply with foreign law requirements. As for the remaining Euros 9 billion, which included a Euros 450 million note expiring on May 15, there was some concern that under foreign applicable laws it might be possible for bondholders voting by series rather than in aggregate, as had been the case with Greek-law bonds, to block the exchange offers and pursue legal action in their respective jurisdictions. The Greek government finally decided to honor its commitments.

Evaluation

Participation in the Greek PSI finally reached 97% of total bond issues and the write-down Euros 106 billion, a historical record. With the help of CACs, its voluntary character had been safeguarded and the "free rider" problem adequately addressed.[36] The ISDA determined, however, that an event of default had occurred, triggering thereby the payment of credit default swaps.[37] A closer examination of the debt rollover leads to the conclusion that the net gains in terms of Greece's debt burden were significant but not as impressive as originally thought; practically, an important part of the debt owed to private creditors was converted into debt owed to official lenders.[38] On the other hand, the lower interest rates and the extended maturities of the new bonds were expected to relieve substantially, by up to Euros 5 billion, the annual debt service burden, representing 2.5% of Greek GDP at the end of 2012.

Arguably, however, the most important outcome of the debt restructuring operation was the avoidance of a full-blown crisis involving Greek exit from the Euro and the contagion effects that such a move would unleash. The official view was that the debt restructuring operation had given Greece valuable breathing space in order to restructure its economy and reduce its debt burden to 116% of GDP by 2020 under the Troika's scenario.[39] Pessimists argued, however, that this scenario was unrealistic under the conditions of extreme austerity imposed on the country, entailing dismal effects on growth. At the time of writing, an economic recovery program for Greece, referred to as a Marshall Plan, was being considered by the Commission and official lenders, involving fast-track procedures for EU budget transfers under the structural funds and substantial guarantees from the EU budget for loans by the European Investment Bank (EIB).

4.4   Overall assessment of the European bailout mechanisms

4.4.1   The contested logic of bailout mechanisms

Moral hazard

The moral hazard argument is central in dealing with the issue of bailouts; bearing in mind moral hazard the Rey Commission report argued that "neither debtor countries nor their creditors should expect to be insulated from adverse financial consequences by the provision of large-scale official financing in the event of crisis."[40] The no-bailout provisions in the TFEU aim at deterring Euro Area members and their creditors from irresponsible behavior. Private sector involvement (PSI) in bailouts aims at deterring and punishing the same creditors, although the idea of punishment, central in the moral hazard argument may not always be applicable.[41]

The decisions regarding the second Greek bailout were declared "unique and exceptional" at the Euro summit or December 8/9, 2011. Nevertheless, the implementation of the massive Greek bond swap and the acceptance of the idea of losses by private bondholders under the ESM Treaty provisions on PSI have undermined the assertion that government bonds are risk-free. The spreads in interest rates between the German bund and the bonds of the other Euro Area members have increased. German insistence on preventing moral hazard and making creditors pay for their irresponsible behavior has actually benefited Germany. In absolute terms, the interest rates of German bunds decreased, while those of the other Euro Area members increased.[42] Risk aversion towards the bonds of the European periphery made the fiscal position of the respective countries unsustainable.

A side effect of the crisis—and of the acceptance of PSI—may be the reconsideration of the basic assumption regarding government bonds in the new EU capital adequacy directive, freeing until now the banks from the obligation of holding capital against sovereign bonds. Such a development would entail the restructuring of the international bond business, while also attaching quasi-permanent stigma to sovereign borrowers benefiting from debt relief of any kind. It is unlikely that EU sovereign borrowers will endorse a directive with such far-reaching consequences; on the other hand, the British government may try to avoid full harmonization of the relevant national regulations, in order to establish compulsory risk assessment criteria for government bonds.[43]

Risks of contagion

Arguably, any bailout mechanism creates moral hazard. Nevertheless, the counter-argument regarding risks of contagion has weighed heavily in the shaping of public policy. A prime example is that of the recapitalization of banks that have invested in government bonds; if these banks are systemically important they will not be punished for their irresponsible behavior, in order to avoid contagion. A related argument is about the contagion effect that would result if a Euro Area member was allowed to fail. Should it be allowed or even encouraged to leave the Euro Area? The voluntary restructuring of the Greek sovereign debt reflected a delicate assessment of risks of contagion. The Euro Area has apparently been spared contagion by a disorderly Greek default, but its peripheral members remained at risk.

4.4.2   The effectiveness of European bailout mechanisms

The Euro Area institutions have been running behind the markets—and Parliaments have been held hostage. The precautionary approach embodied in the EFSF following the July 21, 2011 Euro summit and the decision to leverage its resources taken at the October 26/27 summit were rightly perceived by the press as representing too little and coming too late to deal with the sovereign debt problem. By the end of 2011, renewed anxiety over the Italian debt prompted the ECB interventions described above (4.2.6). Arguably, the speculative attacks could have been contained at a lower cost, had the ECB not just acted as a lender of last resort to banks unable to access the markets, but had also stated its intention to provide unlimited support to Member States in financial trouble. Fears on the reversibility of the euro prompted the ECB on September 6, 2012 to launch a new program entitled 'Outright Monetary Transactions' (OMT's) in secondary bond markets, thereby ending the Securities Market Program (SMP). The OMTs would be considered for future cases of EFSF-ESM macro-economic adjustment programs or precautionary programs, without *ex-ante* limits. It seems therefore that, notwithstanding the ECB's role in containing speculative attacks against sovereign borrowers, effective European bailout mechanisms, able to impose policy conditionalities on sovereign borrowers, will be needed as long as the no-bailout provisions of the Treaty remain in force.

On the other hand, the problems faced by larger Euro Area economies could drain the resources of the bailout mechanisms and affect their lending capacity. If countries such as Italy or Spain became "stepping-out guarantors" and, more importantly, if France lost its triple A rating,[44] the EFSF would also lose its triple A rating and its lending capacity would be reduced accordingly. The Commission has called for the co-existence of the EFSF and the ESM during a transitional period; the latter was originally perceived as a replacement of the former, taking up the previous EFSF commitments and effectively reducing its lending capacity.[45] On March 30, 2012 the Eurogroup decided to raise the ESM capacity from Euros 500 billion to Euros 700 billion.[46] This is still far from the goal of one trillion euros—or the doubling of the ESM capacity— recommended in the course of 2011, before the ECB's massive interventions.

Last but not least, in the early months of 2012 difficult negotiations took place regarding IMF participation in Euro Area bailouts. Although the IMF decided to participate in the second Greek bailout after the successful haircut of the Greek debt,[47] its response to the Euro Area request for a substantial increase of its lending capacity to cope with future challenges was cautious; the decision was linked to the outcome of the negotiations regarding the increase of the capacity of the ESM. Clearly, the risks of contagion were understood by the non-European members of the IMF but the Europeans were expected to assume the primary responsibility for bailouts in their realm. On April 20, 2012 it was decided at a special meeting in Washington to raise the resources "for crisis prevention and resolution" by $430 billion, in addition to the quota increase under the 2010 reform that had not yet entered into force;[48] half of the amount was pledged by EU members of the IMF.

4.5   The reform of the Stability and Growth Pact

4.5.1   Addressing fiscal indiscipline

The asymmetry between weak economic governance and strong monetary governance has been a matter of concern ever since the adoption of the Maastricht Treaty provisions on Economic and Monetary Union (EMU). As pointed out earlier, infringement proceedings cannot be brought against a Member State exceeding the 3% deficit limit. The Stability and Growth Pact (SGP) implementing the treaty provisions on economic policy[49] is embodied in two regulations and a resolution of the Council adopted in 1997.[50] The regulations, as amended in 2005,[51] did not address the weaknesses of the system. Jean-Victor Louis observed that these weaknesses "are not due to the Pact or its reform. They concern the loose concept of coordination and the weight given to peer pressure in the treaty itself, for the sake of preserving national sovereignty";[52] moreover, according to the same author, "the soft procedures of surveillance and the hard procedures of correction are both relying on peer judgment, i.e. ministers are in a situation of conflict of interest."[53]

The facts seem to confirm the view that the revised SGP and, indeed, its "hardest" part, implementing the provisions of Article 126, TFEU and the Protocol (no. 12) to the Treaties on the "excessive deficit procedure" (EDP) have not deterred fiscal indiscipline. The implementation of the EDP reached a climax in the case of the Greek, Irish and Portuguese deficits entailing the application to these countries of the provisions of Article 126 (9), which involve binding measures for the correction of excessive deficits and apply only to Euro Area members.[54] Interestingly, the application of the EDP, rather than being an exception became the rule. In the middle of the international financial crisis several Member States were forced to take fiscal measures that induced them to deviate boldly from their budgetary plans.[55] According to the latest assessment by the Commission services, the 2011 Autumn Forecast, published on November 10, 2011, all the Member States with the exception of Estonia, Finland, Luxembourg and Sweden were subject to the EDP. Five among them—Greece, Ireland, Portugal, Romania and Latvia—were benefiting from a financial assistance program; the balance of payments program for Latvia was successfully implemented and expired in January 2012. The assessment showed that the majority of countries had implemented the Council recommendations under Article 126 (7), TFEU for the correction of their excessive deficits, but for Belgium, Cyprus, Hungary, Malta and Poland the assessment indicated that a timely and sustainable correction of their excessive deficit was clearly at risk, as the deadline for correction was imminent or close. On November 11, 2011, the Economic Affairs Commissioner Olli Rehn addressed letters to the Member States concerned to treat as a matter of urgency the adoption of a 2012 budget that would include additional measures, so as to ensure a timely and sustainable correction of their excessive deficit. In order to avoid the imposition of sanctions, the aforementioned Member States adopted or announced additional measures, which in most cases—for Belgium, Cyprus, Malta and Poland—were considered sufficient.

Nevertheless, two cases retained the attention of the EU institutions. At the Council meeting in Copenhagen on March 12–13, 2012 the Council dealt differently with the cases of Hungary and Spain. In the case of Hungary, the Ecofin Council determined, upon the recommendation of the Commission and in accordance with Article 126 (7), TFEU, that no effective action has been taken in order to bring an end to the situation of an excessive government deficit and decided in accordance with Council Regulation 1084/2006 to suspend as of January 1, 2013 Cohesion Fund handouts to Hungary amounting to Euros 495 million, if the country failed to present by June 22, 2012 convincing measures for the correction of its deficit. In the case of Spain, whose government deficit had reached 8.51% in 2011, the Council conceded that it would be impossible for Spain to fulfill the goal of 4.4% set in this country's stability plan; it set the target for 2012 at 5.3%, while insisting that Spain should reduce its deficit under the 3% threshold in 2013. The Council declined to give a retroactive effect to the recently revised EDP provisions applicable to Euro Area members, which require the imposition of a fine (see next section).

4.5.2   The "six-pack" legislation on the European Economic Union

General outline

The two regulations implementing the Stability and Growth Pact (SGP) adopted in 1997 and substantially amended in 2005 came up for a further revision at the outset of the sovereign debt crisis. The so-called six-pack on the European Economic Union, also involved the adoption of three new regulations and a directive. All these legislative acts, which entered into force on December 13, 2011,[56] entail a substantial strengthening of the instruments of economic governance of the EU and the Euro Area; three regulations and a directive aim at promoting *fiscal discipline* while two regulations aim at effectively preventing and correcting emerging *macroeconomic imbalances* within the EU and the Euro Area. The former introduce major improvements in the budgetary surveillance of Member States, but the latter are the most innovative, in the sense that they impose for the first time on the Euro Area members binding commitments on non-fiscal aspects of their economic policy. In a common recital in the preamble of the five regulations, reflecting a holistic approach to economic and financial governance, it is stated:

"The improved economic governance framework should rely on several interlinked and coherent policies for sustainable growth and jobs, in particular a Union strategy for growth and jobs, with particular focus on developing and strengthening the internal market, fostering international trade and competitiveness, a European Semester for strengthened coordination of economic and budgetary policies, an effective framework for preventing and correcting excessive government deficits, a robust framework for preventing and correcting macroeconomic imbalances, minimum requirements for national budgetary frameworks, and enhanced financial market regulation and supervision, including macroprudential supervision by the European Systemic Risk Board".

Fiscal discipline

a. Regulation 1175/2011 "on the strengthening of the surveillance of budgetary positions and the surveillance and coordination of economic policies" amends Regulation 1466/97, which constitutes the legislative underpinning of the preventive part of the SGP, based on Article 121 TFEU. It embodies the new rules on the so-called European Semester for Economic Policy Coordination, which aim at aligning national budgetary frameworks with the objectives of multilateral surveillance in the Union. The amended regulation enables the Council to provide "timely and integrated policy advice on macrofiscal and macrostructural policy intentions"[57] to Euro Area members implementing stability programs, as well as non-Euro Area members implementing convergence programs. Member States have to adopt prudent fiscal policies in "good times" (i.e., during economic growth) in order to build up the necessary buffer for "bad times" (i.e., during a recession). Country-specific "medium-term objectives" have to be included in the national medium-term budgetary frameworks, in accordance with Directive 2011/85 (see below). These objectives are implemented by means of "adjustment paths" monitored by the Commission. Faster adjustment paths are required for Member States faced with a debt level exceeding 60% of GDP or with pronounced risks in terms of overall debt sustainability. Temporary departures from adjustment paths are allowed on very strict terms.

b. Regulation 1177/2011 "on speeding up and clarifying the implementation of the excessive deficit procedure" amends Regulation 1467/97, which constitutes the legislative underpinning of the corrective part of the SGP, based on Article 126, TFEU. According to recital 4 of the preamble, the amendments build on "the experience gained and mistakes made during the first ten years of the economic and monetary union."

In accordance with the amended regulation, the evolution of government debt to GDP ratio should be followed more closely and put on an equal footing with deficit developments as regards decisions related to EDP. Henceforth, Member States will be benchmarked as to whether they can sufficiently reduce their debt. Those whose debt exceeds 60% of their GDP have to take steps to reduce it at a satisfactory pace, defined in the amended Article 1 of the Regulation as a reduction of 1/20th of the difference with the 60% threshold over the last three (3) years. Moreover, under amended Articles 3 and 5 of the Regulation, Council recommendations and decisions pursuant to Article 126 (7) and (9), TFEU respectively, shall provide for a minimum annual improvement of at least 0.5% of GDP as a benchmark in the cyclically adjusted balance, net of one-off and temporary measures. Finally, the amended Article 11 of the Regulation facilitates the application of Article 126 (11), TFEU regarding the imposition of sanctions to Euro Area members whose deficit exceeds the 3% threshold; in this case "a fine shall as a rule be required" comprising of a fixed component equal to 0.2% of the GDP and a variable component.

c. The aforementioned amendments of the SGP are backed up, through the provisions of the Regulation 1173/2011 "on the effective enforcement of budgetary surveillance in the euro area" by a new set of financial sanctions and fines aimed at ensuring compliance with the recommendations and decisions addressed to Euro Area members, before resorting to Article 126 (11), described by Jean-Victor Louis as the "atomic bomb" of sanctions.[58] The gradual imposition of sanctions to ensure early compliance is envisaged in the context of both the preventive and the corrective parts of the SGP. In the case of the preventive part, they take the form of an interest-bearing deposit, which is released once the Council has been satisfied that the sanction-related situation has come to an end; in the case of the corrective part, a non-interest bearing deposit, amounting to 0.2% of GDP would follow a decision to place a Member State in excessive deficit. This non-interest-bearing deposit would be converted into a fine in the event of non-compliance with the recommendation to correct the excessive deficit. Fines are finally envisaged for the punishment of the manipulation of statistics by Member States.

In substance, the revision of the EDP by the aforementioned regulations reflects a transition from soft law to hard law. The EDP has become more rule-based and sanctions will be the normal consequence for the Euro Area members' failure to implement the measures decided by the Council.[59]

Equally important, however, is the strengthening of the Commission's role in the implementation of EDP; thus, under the provisions of the so-called economic dialogue between the institutions, "the Council is as a rule expected to follow the recommendations and proposals of the Commission or explain its position publicly";[60] moreover, under the decision-making process of "reversed qualified majority voting" the Commission's proposal for a sanction will be considered adopted, unless the Council overturns it by qualified majority.[61]

d. Finally, in accordance with Directive 2011/85 "on requirements for the budgetary frameworks of the Member-States," each Member State shall by the end of the period of transposition of this directive (December 31, 2013) have in place numerical fiscal rules which effectively promote compliance with its obligations deriving from the TFEU in the area of budgetary policy over a multi-annual horizon for the general government as a whole. Recital 18 of the preamble to the directive underlines that such rules will help avoid pro-cyclical fiscal policies and promote fiscal consolidation in good times. The aligning of national fiscal rules with the provisions of the TFEU reflects the idea that compliance can be promoted by the "national ownership" of the relevant rules.

Macroeconomic imbalances

The two innovative regulations on macroeconomic imbalances are based on the enabling clause of Article 121 (4), TFEU added by the Lisbon Treaty, which empowers the Commission and the Council to intervene when it is established that the economic policies of a Member State are not consistent with the broad economic policy guidelines or that they risk jeopardizing the proper functioning of the economic and monetary union.

a. Regulation 1176/2011 "on the prevention and correction of macroeconomic imbalances" introduces a new element in the EU's "economic surveillance framework": the "excessive imbalance procedure" (EIP). This procedure comprises a regular assessment of the risks of imbalances in a Member State based on a "scoreboard" composed of economic indicators. According to the provisions of this regulation:
   - Once an alert has been triggered for a Member State, the Commission will launch a country-specific, in-depth review in order to identify the underlying problems and submit recommendations to the Council on how to deal with the imbalances;
   - For Member States with severe imbalances or imbalances that put at risk the functioning of the EMU, the Council may open the EIP and place the Member State in an "excessive imbalances position";
   - A Member State under EIP would have to present a "corrective action plan" to the Council, which will set deadlines for corrective action;

- Repeated failure to take corrective action will expose the Euro Area member concerned to sanctions.

b. Under Regulation 1174/2011 "on enforcement measures to correct excessive macroeconomic imbalances in the Euro Area," if a Euro Area member repeatedly fails to act on Council EIP recommendations to address excessive imbalances, it will have to pay a yearly fine equal to 0.1% of its GDP. The fine can only be stopped by a reversed qualified majority vote.

4.5.3   Further reforms designed to apply to the Euro Area

On November 23, 2011, the day of publication of the aforementioned six-pack in the *Official Journal*, the Commission submitted two proposals for further reforms:

1. A proposal for a regulation "on common provisions for monitoring and assessing draft budgetary plans and ensuring the correction of excessive deficits of Member States in the euro area."[62] The provisions on the draft budgetary plans complement the European Semester provisions by requiring the submission of the medium term fiscal plans by Euro Area members, together with their stability programs by April 15 and their budgetary plans and independent macroeconomic forecasts for the forthcoming year by October 15, enabling the Commission to deliver its opinion by November 30. The draft regulation also provides for the submission of reports on in-year budgetary execution and related information on a six-month basis for Member States at the Article 126 (7) stage of EDP and on a quarterly basis for those at the Article 126 (9) stage of EDP.

2. A proposal for a regulation "on the strengthening of economic and budgetary surveillance of Member States experiencing or threatened with serious difficulties with respect to their financial stability in the euro area."[63] In the preamble it is explicitly stated that "the economic and financial integration of the Member States whose currency is the euro calls for a reinforced surveillance to prevent contagion from a Member State experiencing difficulties with respect to its financial stability to the rest of the euro area." The proposed regulation provides for enhanced surveillance, commensurate to the severity of financial difficulties. Such surveillance will take due account of the nature of the financial assistance received, which may range from a mere precautionary support to a full macroeconomic adjustment program involving strict policy conditionality. In the former case, the proposed regulation provides for wider access to the information needed for a close monitoring of the economic, fiscal and financial situation, whereas, in the latter case, the draft regulation provides for the suspension of other processes of economic and fiscal surveillance, including the submission of stability programs and the monitoring and assessment provisions of the European Semester under amended Regulation 1466/97.

4.6   The Treaty on Stability, Coordination and Governance in the Economic and Monetary Union

4.6.1   Treaty objective

The Treaty on Stability, Coordination and Governance in the Economic and Monetary Union, hereafter referred to as the "Fiscal Compact Treaty,"[64] was signed on March 2, 2012 by the EU members except the UK and the Czech Republic, after difficult intergovernmental negotiations carried out under the chairmanship of the President of the European Council, Herman van Rompuy. The Treaty is not part of EU law but accepts the primacy of the latter. It aims at further enhancing fiscal discipline and facilitating the governance of the Euro Area. As mentioned in the introductory remarks, in contrast to the bulk of EU law, in the case of economic policy, infringement proceedings cannot be brought against a non-abiding Member State. The compliance issue emerged as a central topic in the debate on economic governance following the suspension of the EDP procedure against France and Germany in 2004. The reform of the SGP in 2005 did not solve the compliance problem, which ultimately required a redefinition of the fiscal autonomy of Member States in the context of a monetary union. The sovereign debt crisis presented a unique opportunity for such an exercise: the setting-up of the bailout mechanisms served as a token of solidarity that could be used as leverage by the main guarantors of these mechanisms, Germany and France, to push on with the necessary reforms on economic governance and fiscal discipline. On the other hand, the revision of the EDP in the context of the aforementioned six-pack and, more specifically, France's reluctant acceptance of decision making by reversed qualified majority, had shown the limits of further transfers of powers to European institutions.

Enhancing fiscal discipline without further transfers of powers seemed totally unrealistic before Germany came out with the idea of embedding a fiscal break, also known as "balanced budget rule" and an automatic correction mechanism in the constitutions of Member States. The innovations amounted to an application of the "national ownership" principle, in the sense that the responsibility for the enforcement of the fiscal break would be entrusted to the political system of each Member State, without prejudice, however, to the implementation of the EDP by EU institutions.

The final wording of the undertakings by the Contracting Parties takes into consideration the particular situation of Member States that do not have written constitutions or whose constitutional revision procedures are time-consuming. Thus, the provisions on the fiscal break described in Article 3 of the Treaty under the heading fiscal compact "shall take effect in the national law of the Contracting Parties at the latest one year after the entry into force of this Treaty through provisions of binding force and permanent character, preferably constitutional, or otherwise guaranteed to be fully respected and adhered to throughout the national budgetary processes."

Germany's insistence on the introduction of a fiscal break or "balanced budget rule" in the constitutions or equivalent legislation of Euro Area members could have been implemented by means of an EU directive addressed to these countries, in accordance with Article 136, TFEU. The idea, however, that a constitutional amendment may be sought by a directive rather than an international treaty was bound to raise delicate legal and political issues in many, if not all, the Euro Area members. Alternatively, an amendment of the TFEU would have required unanimity; Britain would have availed itself of the opportunity to include in the package the repatriation of powers to national parliaments or the return to the unanimity rule in various areas where its interests were at issue. Thus, the idea of an intergovernmental agreement compatible with the EU Treaties and making use, as far as possible, of the Commission and the ECJ for its enforcement came to be seen as the only realistic alternative. To facilitate its entry into force the unanimity principle was put aside. After some hesitations it was decided that the Treaty would enter into force on January 1, 2013, provided that 12 Euro Area members have ratified it, or after 12 have ratified it, whichever is the earlier; moreover, to enhance participation, access to ESM funds was made dependent on the ratification of both the ESM and the Fiscal Compact Treaty.

4.6.2 Treaty implementation

Article 3 of the Treaty commits the Contracting Parties to put in place at national level the balanced budget rule and the automatic correction mechanism. The balanced budget "shall be deemed to be respected if the annual structural balance of the general government at its country-specific medium-term objective, as defined in the revised Stability and Growth Pact, with a lower limit of a structural deficit of 0.5% of the GDP at market prices." As regards the correction mechanism the Treaty provides that the Contracting Parties shall put it in place "on the basis of common principles to be proposed by the European Commission, concerning in particular the nature, size and time-frame of the corrective action to be undertaken, also in the case of exceptional circumstances, and the role and independence of the institutions responsible at national level for monitoring compliance. ... Such corrective mechanism shall fully respect the prerogatives of national Parliaments." The Commission is actually requested to draft a fiscal compact embodying the common principles to be inserted in the constitutions or equivalent legislation, prior to any action by the Contracting Parties.

Many treaty provisions correspond to the recently revised legislation on the Stability and Growth Pact. Thus, for example, the required speed for reducing government debt (by a 20th a year of the portion of the debt exceeding 60% of GDP) is exactly the same as the speed required under the revised SGP. Worth mentioning, however, for their novel character are Articles 5, 6 and 11 of the Treaty, which provide respectively for the adoption of budgetary and economic partnership programs detailing structural reforms for Member States under an excessive deficit procedure, *ex-ante* reporting of public debt issuance programs and *ex-ante* discussion—and, where appropriate, coordination, of all major economic policy reforms planned by the Contracting Parties.

4.6.3 Treaty enforcement

The Treaty does not avoid transfers of sovereignty; it provides for the judicial review of its application by the European Court of Justice (ECJ), under a special arrangement in the framework of Article 273, TFEU. The Commission is assigned the task of monitoring compliance of the Contracting Parties with the provisions of Article 3 (2), but only the Contracting Parties will be able to institute infringement proceedings before the ECJ for failure to comply with the aforementioned provisions. Subsequently, upon a request of a Contracting Party the Court may impose on the Contracting Party in breach of its obligations, a lump-sum or penalty payment "that shall not exceed 0.1% of the GDP."

4.7 Concluding remarks

4.7.1 Solidarity

The containment of the sovereign debt crisis is a typical example of reactive policy making in the EU context. Martin Wolf has rightly pointed out that "the scale of the crisis has made it necessary to remedy what can be remedied, under huge pressure. At every stage, the eurozone has done more than one might have expected, yet it has not done enough."[65] The crisis has been contained by means of bailout mechanisms, which reflect the Euro Area's acceptance of the solidarity principle. Nevertheless, solidarity was not open-ended: it was linked to fiscal discipline and structural reforms. Thus, at the time of writing, three economies of the European periphery (Greece, Ireland and Portugal) were implementing strict policy conditionalities, in exchange of financial support programs; Spain and Italy were under enhanced budgetary surveillance. Arguably, however, self-preservation and risks of contagion were the determining factors in the setting-up of the bailout mechanisms. Moreover, private sector involvement in debt restructuring, implemented in the second Greek bailout and embodied in the permanent stability mechanism, the ESM, reflected a new approach to state insolvency, involving a delicate balancing of moral hazard and risks of contagion.

The bailout programs, as well as ECB's role as a "hidden" lender of last resort, departed from the spirit but not from the letter of the Maastricht Treaty. The same cannot be said of various formulas and ideas that were recently submitted for the purpose of alleviating the sovereign debt problem, such as the gradual and/or partial "mutualization" of the debt of Euro Area members and the issuance of European "stability bonds"[66] or Jacques Attali's proposal on the establishment of a European Debt Agency, able to access markets on behalf of Euro Area members.[67] Nevertheless, moving towards a debt union, prior to other policy adjustments, may be premature. More feasible, because it would not require a treaty amendment, would be the issuance of European "project bonds"—they are actually foreseen in Europe's 2020 Strategy for the purpose of complementing the funding of Trans European projects by the EU and Member State budgets.

4.7.2 Sovereignty

Participation in the Euro Area is usually perceived as entailing the surrender of monetary sovereignty to the ECB and far-reaching restrictions in the exercise of fiscal sovereignty. From a formal/legal point of view, sovereignty is safeguarded, to the extent that Euro Area members may recall the transfers and constraints affecting their sovereignty and may even exit the EU, in accordance with an explicit provision (Article 50, TFEU) inserted by the Lisbon Treaty. Nevertheless, from a substantive/political point of view, fiscal sovereignty, in the sense of decision-making autonomy, has been curtailed to a point where national budgets now have to be reviewed by the Commission prior to being approved by national parliaments, putting thereby at risk the political consensus on participation in the Euro Area. Cynics would argue that the whole concept of fiscal sovereignty is irrelevant in the era of financial globalization, to the extent that borrowing conditions are determined by rating agencies and speculators. It should rather be admitted that in our post-modern world the concept of sovereignty is changing and adapting to the current conditions of global interdependence, where state and non-state actors promote more or less successfully their goals and interests. State interests may be served by participation in international regimes, as well as by staying out of them. Weak economies benefit the most from international regimes, although strong economies may benefit too. In the European context, Germany chose to participate in the Euro Area, while Britain remained outside. George Magnus rightly observed, however, that "Germany has displayed a continuing ambivalence, torn between its own sovereign interests and its interests in preserving the integrity of the Euro Area, from which its export industries and people derive enormous benefits."[68]

4.7.3 Policy adjustment

As mentioned, fiscal discipline came to be regarded as a precondition for fiscal solidarity. Under German guidance, fiscal discipline was drastically enhanced by means of the revised SGP and the Fiscal Compact Treaty. Distinguished economists have challenged this policy orientation by pointing out that debt sustainability, especially in the peripheral members of the Euro Area, very much depends on these countries' growth prospects. Paul Krugman recently argued that "because investors look at the state of a nation's economy when assessing its ability to repay debt, austerity programs haven't even worked as a way to reduce borrowing costs"; he then went on to criticize the European leaders who signed a fiscal treaty "that in effect locks in fiscal austerity as the response to any and all problems."[69]

Domestic politics and constitutional impediments played a critical role in the Euro Area crisis. Thus, before and after the French presidential election on May 6, 2012, François Hollande made clear that the ratification of the Fiscal Compact Treaty by his country would depend on the adoption of a clear commitment to growth in the EU context. In the case of Germany, there were constitutional impediments to the "mutualization" of debt, including partial "mutualization" by means of the redemption fund proposed by the German economic advisers known as the "wise men." To the extent, however, that the German Lander enjoyed fiscal autonomy and, by implication, the Bund was not responsible for their debt, it was unthinkable for Chancellor Merkel to make Germany responsible for the debt of other Member States of the Euro Area.

The breakthrough achieved at the Euro Area summit of June 29, 2012 was hastened by market pressure. The need to recapitalize the Spanish bank Bankia and other ailing banks drastically increased the yields of Spanish bonds. The Spanish government had to request EFSF support, insisting however that such support should be granted directly to ailing banks and should not affect Spain's debt position or involve policy conditionalities and related restrictions of sovereignty. The Eurogroup agreed to an EFSF loan facility of up to Euros 100 billion, which would be transferred to its successor, the ESM, whose entry into force depended on German ratification. At the Euro Area summit of June 29 it was confirmed that the EFSF facility would be transferred to the ESM "without gaining seniority status."

More importantly for the European integration process—and following German insistence, the direct recapitalization of banks—requiring changes in the relevant instrument in accordance with the enabling clause of Article 19 of the ESM Treaty—was made dependent on the establishment by the end of 2012 of a Europe-wide banking supervisory mechanism, involving the ECB for banks in the Euro Area, in accordance with the enabling clause of Article 127 (6), TFEU. The debt position of Spain—and Ireland for that matter—would be alleviated once the aforementioned components of the banking union were in place and the recapitalizations were reflected under the new rules. Another important element of the aforementioned summit was the decision to address Italy's refinancing problem "by using the existing EFSF/ESM instruments in a flexible and efficient manner in order to stabilise markets for Member States respecting their Country Specific Recommendations and other commitments."

The French demand for a pro-growth agenda was reflected in a policy document entitled "Compact for Growth and Jobs" annexed to the Danish Presidency conclusions of the 27-member European Council. The document referred to action on the national level and to the contribution of European policies to growth and employment. The most significant part was the increase of the paid-in capital of the EIB by Euros 10 billion, "with the aim of strengthening its capital basis as well as increasing its overall lending capacity by EUR 60 billion and thus unlock up to EUR 180 billion of additional investment, spread across the whole European Union, including in the most vulnerable countries." There had been no convergence, however, on more ambitious plans, allowing for example the EU budget to be funded by Europe-wide taxes.[70]

In conclusion, the sovereign debt crisis provides clear evidence that in the era of financial globalization, European integration is a market-driven and reactive, rather than proactive, process. The crisis has led to the creation of solidarity mechanisms and demands for sovereign debt "mutualisation". These raised sensitive redistribution issues, which make a new "grand bargain" necessary for the survival of the Euro Area. Bearing in mind, however, the opposition of taxpayers in North European countries to debt "mutualisation", the answer may lie in another reform of the ESM, allowing it to borrow from the ECB. Such a reform addresses two fundamental constraints discussed in the present paper: the limited "firepower" of the ESM and the inability of the ECB to act as a lender of last resort to Euro Area members.

The sovereign debt crisis has also led to major encroachments to the fiscal sovereignty of Euro Area members. Not only did those under the adjustment programmes surrender their sovereignty but all the other members have accepted substantial restrictions to theirs, by means of the revised Stability and Growth Pact and the Fiscal Compact Treaty. The latter ensures the "ownership" of fiscal discipline by the ratifying states but, under the revised SGP, the "power of the purse" of national parliaments may be severely curtailed, thereby creating a democratic legitimacy problem. Thus, moving ahead towards fiscal union sets the stage for political union, thereby confirming the validity of the Monnet / Schuman / Delors method of "indirect" integration. The emerging package has been skillfully designed in the report entitled "Towards a Genuine Economic and Monetary Union" presented by the President of the European Council, in cooperation with the Presidents of the European Commission, the Eurogroup and the ECB. The report sets out "four essential building blocks" for the future EMU: an integrated financial framework, an integrated budgetary framework, an integrated economic policy framework and strengthened democratic legitimacy and accountability to compensate for the transfers of sovereignty.

Notes

1. The view that the Union is the ultimate guarantor of the debt of states and local authorities is contested. New York City was saved from bankruptcy with federal funds, although on October 29, 1975 President Ford had declared his opposition to a bailout.
2. Article 123, TFEU precludes bailouts by the ECB, and Article 125, TFEU precludes the "mutualization" of debt among EU Member States.

3. Italy and Belgium participated from the outset (January 1, 1999) and Greece from January 1, 2002, after the Commission had established, in accordance with Article 104 (2b), TCE that their government debt to GDP ratio "was sufficiently diminishing and approaching the reference value at a satisfactory pace." Actually, it was politically unthinkable to prevent Italy and Belgium from joining the Euro Area, bearing in mind that they were founding members of the original six-member EEC. The same flexible interpretation was subsequently applied to Greece, whose corresponding ratio was better compared to the ratio of the aforementioned countries at that time. Later it was also found that the government deficit to GDP ratio of Italy and Greece had exceeded by 0.3–0.7% the 3% threshold for admission to the Euro Area.

4. Article 126 (10), TFEU.

5. Upon request of the Commission, the conclusions of the Council suspending the excessive deficit procedure against France and Germany were annulled, without, however, any practical outcome because the Commission cannot force the Council to adopt its recommendations. See ECJ, 13.7.2004, case C-27/04 (Commission/Council), *ECJ Rep.*, 2004 I-6649. For a comment of this case and its aftermath, see Jean-Victor Louis (2004) "Economic and Monetary Union: Law and Institutions," *CML Review*, Vol. 41, pp. 575–608, at 577–9.

6. Thus, for example, since 1990 Germany has carried the financial burden of its reunification. Greece was facing a continuous threat from Turkey's military establishment since the invasion and occupation of Northern Cyprus in 1974 and had the highest per capita defense expenditure—and the sixth in absolute terms—among EU Member States.

7. The projected deficit under the country's revised stability and growth plan adopted on February 5, 2009 had been 3.7% and the final deficit sealed by Eurostat was 15.8%.

8. IMF (2006), *Guidelines on Conditionality*, Decision No. 12864-(02/102), as amended by Decision No. 13812-(06/98), November 15, 2006, Section A.5: "The Fund will ensure consistency in the application of policies relating to the use of its resources with a view to maintaining the uniform treatment of members."

9. European Commission, DG Economic and Financial Affairs (2010) *Economic Adjustment Programme for Greece.*

10. Daniel Gross (2010) "Only Athens has the Power to Rescue Greece," *Financial Times*, April 15.

11. See recital 4 of Regulation 407/2010, establishing the EFSM.

12. Published in the *OJ*, 2010, L 118.

13. On September 7, 2011 the German Constitutional Court dismissed the appeals against the German Law of May 22, 2010 enabling the participation of Germany in the EFSM and against the law enabling its participation in the Greek bailout. For the EU law aspects related to these cases, see Jean-Victor Louis (2010) "Guest Editorial: The No-Bailout and Rescue Packages," *CML Review*, Vol. 47, pp. 971–86.

14. EU Official Journal (2011): European Council Decision, L 91.

15. This determination entailed policy implications. According to its rules, the IMF can only be active when there is a refinancing guarantee for 12 months.

16. According to the official statement, the maturities, grace periods and interest rates applied by the EFSF would be determined in accordance with the guidelines adopted at the July 21 Euro summit.

17. Before the second bailout, Euros 73 billion had been disbursed to Greece (including Euros 20 billion from the IMF facility); Euros 37 billion were still available (including Euros 10 billion from the IMF facility).

18. European Commission (2012), *The Greek Loan Facility*, DG Economic and Financial Affairs, Brussels, March.
19. See Article 1 of Regulation 407/2010.
20. See recital 10 of the preamble.
21. On lending to Euro zone credit institutions, see the contribution of Christos Gortsos in the present volume, at section 6.2.2. and Figure 6.1.
22. ECB, Decision of May 14, 2010 (ECB/2010/5). The ECB practice has been strongly challenged in Germany. Nevertheless, the Federal Government and the Bundestag took the view that only direct loans or purchase of bonds in the primary market were prohibited by the Treaty; see the joint cases before the German Constitutional Court, note 13.
23. Bank for International Settlements (2012) "European Bank Funding and Deleveraging," *BIS Quarterly Review*, March 12, especially Graph 4.
24. George Magnus (2012) "Allons enfants: The Euro Crisis and the French Elections," UBS Investment Research, *Economic Insights*, February 6.
25. Wolfgang Münchau (2011) "Muddling Through Will Not Work This Time," *Financial Times*, March 14.
26. The Euro summit of December 8/9, 2011, referring to PSI, declared that "we will strictly adhere to the well established IMF principles and practices. This will be unambiguously reflected in the preamble of the treaty. We clearly reaffirm that the decisions taken on 21 July and 26/27 October concerning Greek debt are unique and exceptional; standardised and identical Collective Action Clauses will be included, in such a way as to preserve market liquidity, in the terms and conditions of all new euro government bonds."
27. Two-thirds majorities of those present and voting are required, subject to a quorum of 50%.
28. Group of Ten (1996) *The Resolution of Sovereign Liquidity Crises: Report to the Ministers and Governors Prepared under the Auspices of the Deputies*, May, report available on the BIS website: http://www.bis.org/publ/gten03.pdf; the report is usually referred to as the Rey Commission Report. See also Group of Ten (2002) *Report of the Group of Ten Working Group on Contractual Clauses*, September 26, report available on the IMF website: http://www.imf.org/external/np/g10/2002/cc.pdf.
29. IMF (2002) *Collective Action Clauses in Sovereign Bond Contracts: Encouraging Greater Use*, IMF publication, prepared by the Policy Development and Review, International Capital Markets and Legal Departments, Washington, DC, June 6, 29pp.; also, IMF (2003) *Collective Action Clauses: Recent Developments and Issues*, IMF publication, prepared by the International Capital Markets, Legal and Policy Development and Review Departments, Washington, DC, March 25, 28pp.
30. European Union (2004) *Implementation of the EU Commitment on Collective Action Clauses in Documentation of International Debt Issuance*, Economic and Financial Committee, Brussels, ECFIN/CEFCPE(2004)REP/50483 final, November 12.
31. See Anna Gelpern (2003) "How Collective Action is Changing Sovereign Debt," *International Financial Law Review*, Vol. XXII, pp. 19–23, and Nancy P. Jacklin (2010) "Addressing Collective-Action Problems in Securitized Debt," *Law and Contemporary Problems*, Vol. 73, pp. 173–91, at 185.
32. European Union (2004): see note 30.
33. The new bonds had maturities from 11 to 30 years and carried an average interest rate of 4% depending on these maturities.
34. In net present value terms, investors would incur losses amounting to 75% on their investment.

35. The International Securities and Derivatives Association (ISDA) determined that the retroactive introduction of CACs did not constitute an event of default. Subsequently, however, ISDA determined that the activation of the CACs constituted such an event.

36. For a thorough discussion of the free rider problem in sovereign debt restructuring, see the contribution of Daniel Kaeser in the present volume.

37. The amount of Euros 3.2 billion were paid during 2011 for risk premiums. The value of the bonds covered by CDSs had been estimated at four to five times the amount of these premiums. Following, however, the auction that took place in London on March 19, 2012, the institutions that had issued the CDSs were called upon to pay 78.5 cents for each Euro of the insured value.

38. The new debt owed by Greece to the EFSF as a result of the debt rollover included up to Euros 50 billion to be provided by the EFSF for the recapitalization of Greek banks.

39. An essential element of the sustainability scenario was the implementation of a privatization program, initially set at Euros 50 billion, for the purpose of debt reduction.

40. See the Executive Summary of the report cited previously.

41. Thus, from the beginning of the crisis, Greek banks with excellent ratings were pressurized to purchase Greek government bonds.

42. Another factor that played in favor of the German bund was the growth performance and prospects of Germany.

43. The British government's attitude toward harmonization in the area of financial regulation reflects its commitment to promote the interests of the City of London. In some cases, it is opposed on principle to harmonization, deemed to curtail the operation of financial markets while, in others, such as the one under consideration, it wishes to impose more stringent rules. These cases correspond to the well-known regulatory competition models of "race to the bottom" and "race to the top."

44. At the time of writing, one of the rating agencies had downgraded France by one notch.

45. These commitments included EFSF contributions of Euros 17.5 billion for Ireland and Euros 26 billion for Portugal. To these should be added EFSF commitments under the second Greek bailout amounting to Euros 109.1 billion in loans and Euros 35.5 billion in credit insurance in the context of the PSI.

46. The commitments undertaken by the EFSF amounting to approximately Euros 200 billion were included in the enlarged ESM capacity. On the other hand, it was decided that the Euros 240 billion of unused funds of the EFSF could still be accessed during a transitional period during which the two funds will coexist (until January 1, 2013).

47. The IMF agreed to provide Euros 19.8 billion, which included an undisbursed amount of Euros 10 billion from the previous facility. IMF exposure to Greece would not exceed the amount of Euros 30 billion agreed under the first facility, because disbursements would coincide with repayments.

48. See Joint Statement by the International Monetary and Financial Committee and the Group of 20 Finance Ministers and Central Bank Governors on IMF resources, IMF Press Release No. 12/144, April 20, 2012.

49. Articles 120–6, TFEU.

50. Council Regulations (EC) 1466/97 and (EC) 1467/97 were published in the *OJ*, 1997, L 209 and the Resolution of the European Council on the Stability and Growth Pact was published in the *OJ*, 1997, C 236.

51. Council Regulation (EC) 1055/2005, amending Regulation (EC) 1466/97 on the strengthening of the surveillance of budgetary positions and the surveillance and coordination of economic policies, and Council Regulation (EC) 1056/2005 amending Regulation (EC) 1467/97 on speeding up and clarifying the implementation of the excessive deficit procedure. They were published in the *OJ*, 2005, L 174.
52. Jean-Victor Louis (2006) "The Review of the Stability and Growth Pact," *CML Review*, Vol. 43, pp. 85–106, at 104–5.
53. Ibid. at p. 105.
54. Article 139, par. 1, indent b, TFEU.
55. Christos Gortsos (2011) Written evidence in House of Lords, *The Future of Economic Governance in the EU*, European Union Committee, 12th Report of Session 2010–11, Vol. II: *Evidence*, EGE 6, March 24.
56. They were published in the *OJ*, 2011, L 306.
57. The European Semester procedure is described in Section 1-A, article 2-a, inserted in Regulation 1466/97 by Regulation 1175/2011.
58. Louis, *supra* note 52, p. 103.
59. Gortsos, Christop (May 2011) "Comments on Evidence to the House of Lords", ECEFI Reporter, www.ecefi.eu.
60. Article 2a, inserted in Regulation 1467/97 by Regulation 1177/2011.
61. Reversed QMV applies to sanctions in the preventive and corrective parts of the SGP (Articles 4, 5 & 6 of Regulation 1173/2011). The threshold of qualified majority is amended upon every accession to the EU. Nevertheless, as of November 1, 2014 the qualified majority will be 55% of Member States representing 65% of populations of the Euro Area members (Article 238, par. 3, indent a), TFEU).
62. European Commission, COM (2011) 821 final, November 23, 2011.
63. European Commission, COM (2011) 819 final, November 23, 2011.
64. Although the original title of the Treaty was "International agreement on reinforced economic union," the Euro summit of December 8/9, 2011 used the term "fiscal compact" to describe the focus of the new treaty.
65. Martin Wolf (2012) "Banks are on a Eurozone Knife-Edge," *Financial Times*, April 25.
66. European Commission (2011) *Green Paper on the Feasibility of Introducing Stability Bonds*, COM (2011) 818, November 23.
67. *Agence européenne du Trésor* is the term used by Jacques Attali (2010) *Tous ruinés dans dix ans? Dette publique: la dernière chance*, Paris: Fayard, pp. 201–5.
68. Magnus, "Allons enfants."
69. Paul Krugman (2012) "Europe's Economic Suicide," *International Herald Tribune*, April 17.
70. A Europe-wide income tax has been proposed by Guy Verhofstadt, former Prime Minister of Belgium and co-chairman of the ALDE group at the European Parliament.

5
The Case for a Sovereigns' Bankruptcy Procedure

Daniel Kaeser

Introduction

The issue of a bankruptcy procedure for sovereign states has been addressed by many famous and less famous authors since the mid-1970s, that is, since the international financial markets experienced a strong and sometimes problematic development. The objective of organized bankruptcy procedures is to assure the protection of the legitimate interests of both debtors and creditors and to prevent a negative spillover ("domino effect") on the financial system and the rest of the economy. In the wake of the international debt crises of the 1980s and 1990s serious consideration was given within the International Monetary Fund to the development of an organized bankruptcy procedure for sovereign debtors. While at the technical level the concept of the "Statutory Sovereign Debt Restructuring Mechanism" proposed by the IMF staff appeared to be workable, the Executive Board decided not follow up on this initiative. The present chapter recalls this important moment in recent international financial history and contains suggestions, in the light of the current debt crisis, for reviving this approach and defines the conditions under which it could be implemented.

5.1 "Bankruptcy Procedures for Sovereigns": A concept developed within the IMF

In August 2002 Kenneth Rogoff and Jeromin Zettelmeyer of the IMF finalized a document entitled "Bankruptcy Procedures for Sovereigns: A Brief History of Ideas, 1976–2001" (IMF Working Paper 02/133).[1] This history shows inter alia that our topic has to be narrowed: a private enterprise can go bankrupt and die, leaving behind its debts and its assets; a sovereign state that is over-indebted will survive: it can default and live with the consequences, or it can seek an agreement with its creditors in order to restructure its debt. By analogy, Chapter 11 of the US Bankruptcy Code deals with the liquidation of insolvent private debtors, Chapter 9 with the debt restructuring of public entities. Therefore we should by now focus our attention on the ways and means to restructure the debt of sovereign states.

In my view, the best paper ever written on this subject is a "Note on an Adjustment Facility for Sovereign Debtors" by the Legal Department of the IMF, dated May 1995 (IMF EBS/95/90).[2] This note identified and discussed the issues that would have to be resolved for achieving an orderly and comprehensive adjustment of a country's external debt, as well as different options for its establishment.

At the beginning of the first decade of the present century, Anne Krueger, then First Deputy Managing Director of the IMF, promoted this issue and produced with the Fund staff a full-fledged proposal of a "Statutory Sovereign Debt Restructuring Mechanism" (Revised Report of the Managing Director to the International Monetary and Financial Committee, April 2, 2003, SM / 03/ 101/Revision 1). After numerous discussions in the Executive Board of the IMF, this proposal was buried alive in April 2003 at the Spring Meeting of the International Monetary and Financial Committee of the Fund. Why? The proposed mechanism would have had to be set up by way of an Amendment of the Articles of Agreement of the Fund, that is, of its Statutes, which requires the approval by three-fifths of the members, having 85 percent of the total voting power. As the United States—with their blocking minority—and some emerging countries did for different reasons oppose the proposal, it was impossible to go ahead. Since then this issue has been a sleeping beauty. Yet it is clear that the support of the United States is crucial to wake her up. Some influential American NGOs have been working on this issue for some time now, because in the present circumstances a sovereign debt restructuring mechanism is more needed than ever.[3]

5.2   The need to revive the IMF proposal

Today, when a country meets difficulties in servicing its external debt, the IMF will make its help conditional on a large and speedy downward economic adjustment, which in turn implies large cuts in government spending, including social programs. The idea is that an impressive austerity policy would make consumers and businesses more confident, so that their additional spending would offset the depressing effects of the government cutbacks. Furthermore, a country performing an impressive austerity policy would also restore the confidence of the financial markets in its resilience. Last but not least the credit extended by the Fund to that country would be used in part or in full to bail out the banks.

This is perhaps not fully in line with the Articles of Agreement, or Statutes, of the IMF according to which the Fund credit (art.1, point v) should give to a member country the opportunity to correct maladjustments in its balance of payments without "resorting to measures destructive of national or international prosperity." It is fair to say though that the austerity policies imposed by the Fund usually work, yet at a high price for the indebted country and its trading partners. The economy of Latvia, for instance, which successfully implemented such an austerity policy is by now roughly 18% smaller than before the country got into trouble.

However it may happen that heavily indebted countries fail to implement austerity policies, either because social unrest paralyzes the government, or because the economic environment deteriorates dramatically, for instance when the interest rates levied on the external debt raise abruptly, what should this country do then? The worst-case scenario for the country is to default on its external financial obligations, because it would make it extremely difficult to regain access to sources of external financing. It would in any case be better for the over-indebted country to seek an arrangement with its creditors.

If the country in trouble is mainly indebted to sovereign creditors, which is usually the case of low-income countries without access to the international financial markets, an orderly debt restructuring can usually be performed through negotiations with the Club de Paris, whose members are sovereign creditors. The Club will draft an agreement on the restructuring of claims owned by sovereign creditors or guaranteed by them, which are mainly export credits. Since the number of sovereign creditors is relatively small and since they have to stick together, the implementation of the negotiated agreement will usually not raise serious problems.

Yet if the over-indebted country has a relatively advanced economy with access to the international financial market, the restructuring of its debt has presently to take place in a legal "no man's land." Therefore, it can hardly proceed in an orderly way. Such a country is usually indebted to different categories of creditors (e.g., banks, private investors, private firms, sovereign states) that cannot be dealt with collectively. Furthermore, the debtor country cannot know all its creditors, especially if the debt has been securitized and is traded on different foreign markets. Last but not least, as the restructuring of a country's debt tends to raise the value of the claims not included in the restructuring agreement, rogue creditors, or "free riders," will prefer to keep away from such an agreement and go to court to press their claims or sell them on the market.

5.3 The main features of a "Sovereigns' Bankruptcy Procedure" and the conditions of implementation

What should be done? Without going into details, let us spell out what is needed to set up a mechanism that would allow the performance of an orderly and comprehensive sovereign debt restructuring.

First and foremost, the sovereign debt restructuring mechanism should be based either on an amendment of the Articles of Agreement of the IMF or the World Bank, or on a new international agreement. An amendment of the Articles would bind all members of the Fund or of the World Bank, but it requires the support of the United States since it must be approved by at least 85% of the Fund's quotas. Resorting to a new international agreement would be a second-best solution, because it would take years to become operational and because individual countries would be free to participate or not. Whichever, the mandatory approach would be the key of the mechanism. By creating international obligations that would become part of the domestic law of the signatory states, it would bind all creditors. This would prevent the emergence of the "free rider" problem, which is bound to poison any voluntary, consensual approach.

The mechanism should be managed by an independent organ of the Fund, or of the World Bank. Alternatively it would be managed by a new international agency if its creation is based on a treaty. This implementing authority would have to cooperate with existing bodies, like the Club de Paris for the sovereign creditors, the London Club for the commercial banks, and creditors' committees for the other creditors.

The second important element is the trigger mechanism: who should ask for a debt restructuring? It should be up to the sovereign debtor to take the initiative. The advice of the IMF will be required anyway, because the country in trouble would most probably be under the IMF's intensive care.

The sovereign debtor would have to list the eligible debts, that is, the debts that should be restructured. It should also list the non-eligible debts.

The third important element is the provision of an automatic stay. Once the restructuring process is initiated, creditors of eligible debts could no more take the debtor to court around the world. On the other hand, the debtor would have to refrain from making payments to creditors of eligible debts.

Fourth, provisions should be made for protecting lenders who provide interim financing to the debtor country during the debt restructuring period.

Fifth, the implementing authority would have to prepare a debt restructuring plan that is fair and equitable for the different categories of creditors, in collaboration with the Club de Paris, the London Club and the committees representing the remaining creditors. Once approved by a qualified majority of the creditors, the plan would bind all of them.

Sixth, the costs of the restructuring procedure should be fairly split between debtor and creditors.

Conclusion

One has to be realistic. It will not be easy to make a breakthrough on this issue. Nevertheless one should keep advocating the establishment of a mechanism for the orderly restructuring of sovereign debt, because it represents an important missing part of the financial architecture of our globalized world. The development of an international financial market calls for an international regulation. The deregulating mood that prevailed before the financial crisis and led to it has fortunately lost momentum. After all, it is in the best interest of the financial community to curb the "free rider" mentality.

Notes

1. Kenneth Rogoff and Jeromin Zettelmeyer (2002) "Bankruptcy Procedures for Sovereigns: A History of Ideas, 1976–2001," *IMF Staff Papers*, Vol. 49, No. 3, Washington, DC: International Monetary Fund; idem (2002) "Early Ideas on Sovereign Bankruptcy Reorganization: A Survey," *IMF Working Paper*, Washington, DC: Research Department, International Monetary Fund, March.
2. Anne Krueger (2001) "International Financial Architecture for 2001: A New Approach to Sovereign Debt Restructuring," Address by the First Deputy Managing Director of the IMF, Washington, DC: American Enterprise Institute, November 21; idem (2002) *A New Approach to Sovereign Debt Restructuring*, Washington, DC: International Monetary Fund, April. Jack Boorman (2002) "Sovereign Debt Restructuring: Where Stands the Debate?" Speech by the Special Adviser to the Managing Director of the IMF, Conference cosponsored by the CATO Institute and *The Economist*, October 17. International Monetary Fund (2003) "Communiqué of the International Monetary and Financial Committee of the Board of Governors of the International Monetary Fund," Washington, DC: IMF, April 12; idem (2003) "IMF Board Discusses Possible Features of a Sovereign Debt Restructuring Mechanism," *Public Information Notice* No. 03/06, Washington, DC: IMF, January 7; idem (2002) *The Design of Debt Restructuring Mechanism—Further Considerations*, Washington, DC: Legal and Policy Development and Review Departments, IMF, November 27; idem (2003) "Report of the Managing Director to the International Monetary and Financial Committee on a Statutory Debt Restructuring Mechanism," Washington, DC: IMF, April 8.
3. Carmen Amalia Corrales (2010) "Toward a Cosmopolitan Ethic in Debt Restructuring," *Law and Contemporary Problems*, Vol. 73, No. 93, Duke University. A. Mechele Dickerson (2004) "A Politically Viable Approach to Sovereign Debt Restructuring," Scholarship Repository, *Emory Law Journal*, Vol. 53, pp. 997–1041.

6

The Impact of the Current Euro Zone Fiscal Crisis on the Greek Banking Sector and the Measures Adopted to Preserve its Stability

Christos Gortsos

Introductory remarks

The present chapter examines the impact of the current Euro zone fiscal crisis on the Greek banking sector and the measures adopted to preserve its stability. It is divided into six sections:

1. Section 6.1 deals with the causes of the current Euro zone fiscal crisis.
2. Section 6.2 deals with the impact of the current crisis on the Greek banking sector.
3. Finally, Sections 6.3 through 6.6 deal with the measures adopted to preserve the stability of the Greek banking sector in 2008 (amidst the recent international financial crisis), and the institutional measures, micro-prudential supervisory and regulatory measures, as well as the reorganization measures and resolution tools adopted after the Euro zone fiscal crisis.

6.1 The causes of the current Euro zone fiscal crisis

6.1.1 The recent (2007–9) international financial crisis

Despite the existence of an extensive international regulatory financial framework, which was established gradually in the course of the last three decades,[1] a major international financial crisis erupted recently (2007–9). This crisis:

- was triggered by events in the financial system of the United States;
- spilled over to the world economy, seriously affecting the stability of the financial system in several other states around the globe; and
- had a serious negative impact on the real economy worldwide.[2]

The author uses the term "recent" (and not "current") to denote that this crisis lasted from 2007 to 2009 and came to an ending. This is without prejudice either to the fact that the financial systems of certain states remain vulnerable as a result of this crisis, or that in certain cases (especially in the Euro zone periphery) the current malfunctioning of the banking system is a corollary of the current "Euro zone fiscal crisis" which occurred, at least to some extent, as a result of the recent international financial crisis.

The analysis of the causes of this crisis is beyond the scope of the present study. Very briefly, it can be pointed out that the crisis mainly relates to the following aspects:[3]

1. The implementation of inadequate monetary and fiscal policies in several states.[4]
2. Failures by financial services providers, in particular[5] with regard to:
   - excesses in the asset securitization processes according to the "generate and distribute" banking model,[6] and excessive complexity of transactions;
   - poor lending practices (especially in the United States with regard to the household sector);
   - excessive leverage;
   - inefficient management of liquidity risk by banks; and
   - imprudent (*ex post* at least) remuneration policies adopted by several institutions.
3. Inefficiencies and failures in the regulatory framework of the financial system, such as:
   - lack of macro-prudential policies (both in terms of regulation and oversight);
   - lack of a regulatory framework for the operation of the "shadow banking system" (especially in the United States),[7] credit rating agencies and alternative investment vehicles (such as hedge funds);
   - other failures in the micro-prudential regulation of financial firms;
   - lack of transparency in trading of certain categories of financial instruments (namely bonds and financial derivatives);
   - inadequacy of certain valuation methods for financial instruments in accordance with international accounting standards; and
   - inadequacy of corporate governance rules for listed companies.
4. The subsequent extensive scope for regulatory arbitrage among financial products, markets and states.
5. Last but not least, major failures in the conduct of micro-prudential supervision of financial service providers in several states.

6.1.2 The impact

The consequence of this crisis was that several banks and other financial institutions around the world (small or big, even "systemically important" institutions[8]) were not able to absorb the losses from their risk exposure. This resulted, inter alia, in negative effects on the real economy, obliging several governments (especially in the United States and the European

Union) to adopt rescue packages and recovery plans[9] in order to support or even bail out individual banks (and, in some cases, the entire banking system[10]). Such government interventions weighed on state budgets and, in some cases, created serious fiscal imbalances, some of which evolved to fiscal crises,[11] which, in turn, spread to become financial crises.[12]

The study of the Committee on the Global Financial System (CGFS) identifies four main channels of transmission:

i. the impact of negative sovereign ratings on (individual) bank ratings;
ii. losses incurred by banks from their sovereign debt holdings;
iii. the "collateral/liquidity channel;" and
iv. losses from state guarantees granted to banks (explicit and implicit).

Adding to these channels is the negative impact on the performance of bank loans (in the event of recession).

The Euro zone fiscal crisis was triggered by the exceptionally severe fiscal imbalances in Greece,[13] which were then transmitted to other EU Member States of the "Euro zone periphery."[14] This crisis is the main cause of the current severe instability in the European banking sector, which cannot be fully assessed yet, neither as to the severity of its implications nor as to its potential spillover effects on a global scale.[15]

Amidst this crisis, apart from the initiatives undertaken at the European level in order to enhance the existing institutional and regulatory framework governing the operation of the "economic pillar" of the European Economic and Monetary Union (the "EMU"),[16] governments and central banks in several Euro zone Member States resorted to institutional, supervisory and regulatory measures in order to preserve the stability of their domestic banking sectors (and, more generally, financial systems). The case of Greece will be discussed in more detail in sections 6.3 through 6.6 of the present study.

6.2   The impact of the current crisis on the Greek banking sector

6.2.1   The Greek banking sector

In April 2012, the Greek banking sector consisted of 53 credit institutions[17] with 4,005 branches and 63,400 employees.[18] There are four main categories of credit institutions operating in Greece:

- 17 commercial banks incorporated in Greece and operating under a license by the Bank of Greece, and 13 cooperative banks incorporated in Greece and operating under a license by the Bank of Greece (both of which are hereinafter referred to as "Greek credit institutions"); as well as

.

Christos Gortsos   167

- branches of 19 credit institutions incorporated in other EU Member States, and branches of four credit institutions incorporated in third countries (outside the EU).

Credit institutions in Greece:

- manage an equivalent of 128% of the Greek GDP (loans to households and enterprises);[19]
- hold an equivalent of 96% of the Greek GDP in deposits and repos;[20] and
- lend Euros 113.4 billion for mortgage and consumer credit, an equivalent of €10,200 per inhabitant.[21]

With aggregate on-balance sheet assets at 217% of GDP, the Greek banking sector is not oversized compared to other economically developed countries.[22] In January 2012, the average loan-to-deposit and repos ratio was 146.5% (January 2011: 132.3%; January 2010: 119.9%), a development that is mainly due to the shrinking deposit base.[23]

6.2.2   The impact of the crisis

Greek credit institutions were not exposed to the risks that triggered the recent (2007–9) international financial crisis. As a result, the spillover effects on the Greek banking sector were limited. Accordingly, there was no need for a bank rescue package. However, liquidity conditions were strained during this crisis, since Greek credit institutions had restricted access to wholesale market liquidity for their lending operations, while maturing interbank liabilities put additional pressure on their liquidity position, thus rendering necessary the adoption of a recovery program.[24]

Despite these problems, Greek credit institutions have shown remarkable resilience and were able to overcome adversities thanks to a number of factors, such as, inter alia:

- a strong capital base and steadily increased provisions (more than 40% on a year-to-year basis);
- liquidity-support measures by the European Central Bank and the Greek government; and
- effective micro-prudential supervision by the Bank of Greece, which ensured the stability of the Greek banking sector.

As a result, the Greek banking sector remained healthy, adequately capitalized and highly profitable amidst the international financial crisis.

On the other hand, the Greek banking sector was negatively affected by the current Euro zone fiscal crisis. All the aforementioned channels[25] for the transmission of problems from the government to the banking sector were set in motion. In particular:

1. The successive downgrades of Greece's sovereign debt since late 2009 resulted in cuts also in the ratings of Greek credit institutions and severely tightened their liquidity position:
   a. Bank deposits and repos have declined by 19% since the end of 2010 (29% since the end of 2009).[26]
   b. Greek credit institutions' ability to raise liquidity on the international interbank market, as well as international bond markets has been almost totally constrained.
   c. Accordingly, there is a need to rely heavily on the Eurosystem credit facilities (see Table 6.1). ECB financing represents 18% of credit institutions' total liabilities.[27] Currently, Greek banks are also heavily reliant on the "Emergency Liquidity Assistance" (ELA) mechanism of the Bank of Greece, which acts as a lender of last resort to Greek credit institutions.[28]

      It is also worth noting that, as of February 2012, interest rates on household deposits with an agreed maturity of up to one year were the highest (4,86%) in the Euro zone (2.90%).[29] Interest rates on new deposits of non-financial corporations with an agreed maturity of up to one year were also the highest (4.08%) in the Euro zone (1.22%).[30]
2. Greek credit institutions suffered extremely severe losses from their participation in the Private Sector Involvement ("PSI") as far as their

Table 6.1 Financing of Euro zone credit institutions related to monetary policy operations denominated in Euro (1,000 Euros)

	December 2008	December 2009	December 2010	June 2011	December 2011
Main refinancing operations	22.765.300	2.355.000	18.023.000	28.439.000	15.177.500
Longer-term refinancing operations	15.584.000	47.300.100	78.382.800	74.600.600	60.942.000
Fine-tuning reverse operations	5.600	0	1.263.000	0	0
Total	**38.354.900**	**49.655.100**	**97.668.800**	**103.039.600**	**76.119.500**

Source: Bank of Greece, Financial Statements.

holdings of Greek government bonds are concerned. In this context, the following should be pointed out:

a. The July 2011 support program for Greece, aimed at strengthening economic policy coordination for competitiveness and convergence on condition of commitments by Greece, provided for total official financing of an estimated Euros 109 billion.[31]

b. On March 14, 2012, Euro zone Finance Ministers approved additional financing under the second economic adjustment program amounting to Euros 130 billion until 2014, including an IMF contribution of Euros 28 billion. They also authorized the EFSF to release the first installment of a total amount of Euros 39.4 billion, to be disbursed in several tranches. The release of the tranches will be based on observance of quantitative performance criteria and a positive evaluation of progress made with respect to the policy criteria contained in Council Decision 2011/734/EU of July 12, 2011 (as amended in November 2011 and March 2012) and the Memorandum of Understanding on economic policy conditionality, which was signed on March 14, 2012.[32]

c. The private sector involvement (PSI) in Greece's debt exchange offer was high. Out of a total of Euros 205.5 billion in bonds eligible for the exchange offer, approximately Euros 199 billion (96.9%) have been exchanged with a nominal discount of 53.5%. On April 20, 2012, the four largest Greek credit institutions (representing more than 60% of the Greek banking sector's assets) announced losses of Euros 27.9 billion.[33]

3. The "collateral/liquidity" channel has also been activated, since the European Central Bank has gradually been cutting the market value of Greek government bonds and the other assets provided as collateral by Greek credit institutions and currently referring them mainly to the ELA mechanism of the Bank of Greece.

4. Greek credit institutions also suffer losses on account of (explicit or implicit) Greek government guarantees granted to them, which cannot be honored in full given the current fiscal strains.

5. Finally, from the point of view of non-performing loans, the situation seems to deteriorate consistently: they increased to 14.7 % in September 2011 (from 10.5% at end-2010 and 7.7% at end-2009),[34] and the trend seems to be worsening owing to the ongoing economic recession in Greece, as 76% or Euros 24.9 billion in 2012 (December 2010: 74% or Euros 18.7 billion) of non-performing loans are secured loans—mainly loans to non-financial corporations and mortgage loans).[35]

It is also worth mentioning that there is minimal demand for new loans (with the exception of business loans for working capital).

6.3   Measures adopted to preserve the stability of the Greek banking sector in 2008 (in the middle of the recent international financial crisis)

As already mentioned,[36] the recent (2007–9) international financial crisis did not have a severe impact on the Greek banking sector, since Greek credit institutions were not exposed to the risk of holding "toxic assets" or other crisis-related risks.[37] Thus, the negative effects of the international crisis on the Greek banking sector were limited and, accordingly, there was no need for a bank rescue package, in contrast to several other countries, including EU Member States.

Nevertheless, in late 2008, in order to enhance the solvency and especially the liquidity of the Greek banking sector amidst the crisis,[38] following the bankruptcy of the investment bank Lehman Brothers Holdings Inc. (the "LBHI") on September 15, 2008,[39] the Greek government was urged to take initiatives, which led to the adoption of two legal acts by the Hellenic Parliament:

1. By virtue of Law 3714/2008, adopted immediately after LBHI's bank-ruptcy, the level of deposit guarantees provided by the then existing Hellenic Deposit Guarantee Fund[40] was raised to Euros 100,000 (from Euros 20,000 previously) per depositor (for each credit institution), in order to enhance depositors' confidence in the banking sector (success-fully averting a potential bank run).[41]
2. In addition, in December 2008 the Greek government adopted a "recov-ery program" (widely known as "the Euros 28 billion package") under Law 3723/2008 "For the enhancement of liquidity of the economy in response to the impact of the international financial crisis."[42] This pro-gram was mainly aimed at the enhancement of liquidity conditions in the banking system.

According to this Law's provisions, the government took the following liquidity-support measures in aid of Greek credit institutions:

1. A capital support of Euros 5 billion, through capital increases with the issue of preference shares rendering a fixed annual return of 10% (the "first pillar").[43]
2. Issuance of bank bond guarantees (with commission[44]) worth Euros 15 billion in order to facilitate fund-raising on international markets and bolster their liquidity (the "second pillar").
3. Issuance of "special" Greek government bonds (also with commission[45]) worth Euros 8 billion, in order to further bolster their liquidity and to ensure competitive terms for the financing of small and medium enter-prises, and also housing loans for households (the "third pillar").[46]

All these support measures fall into the category of state subsidies under European competition law and were authorized without objections by the Commission as compatible aid under Article 107, paragraph 3(b) of the Treaty on the Functioning of the European Union.[47]

It is also worth mentioning that in February 2009 the Hellenic Deposit Guarantee Fund was transformed into the Hellenic Deposit and Investment Guarantee Fund (hereinafter the "HDIGF") pursuant to Law 3746/2009.[48] The major development was the establishment of an "investor compensation scheme," alongside the "deposit guarantee scheme," in order to ensure that the customers of Greek credit institutions providing investment services would be adequately covered in accordance with the provisions of Directive 97/9/EC of the European Parliament and of the Council "on investor compensation schemes."[49] The HDIGF contains currently (i.e., in April 2012) three pillars (or "schemes"). For more details on the third pillar or "resolution scheme," see under 6.6.4.[50]

After the onset of the Euro zone fiscal crisis in 2010, however, the need to reinforce the stability of the Greek banking sector became imperative. This triggered important initiatives, which made use of:

- earmarked institutional measures (see under section 6.4);
- micro-prudential supervisory and regulatory measures (under 6.5);
- reorganization measures and resolution tools (under 6.6).[51]

In addition, the "second pillar" of Law 3723/2008 (mentioned under 6.3) has been further reinforced on three occasions, in 2010 with Euros 15 billion[52] and in 2011 with an additional Euros 25 billion,[53] and another Euros 30 billion.[54]

6.4 Institutional measures adopted after the Euro zone fiscal crisis

6.4.1 The Hellenic Financial Stability Fund

The Hellenic Financial Stability Fund (hereinafter the "HFSF") was established in 2010 by Law 3864/2010 as a legal person of private law.[55] This Law has repeatedly been amended by Laws 4021/2011,[56] 4051/2012[57] and 4056/2012,[58] as well as the Act of Legislative Content of 19.4.2012.[59]

The HFSF has full legal capacity and the right to bring an action in court (*locus standi*) and it does not come under the public sector. It enjoys administrative and financial independence, and operates exclusively in accordance with the rules of private economy.[60]

Its capital has been set at Euros 50 billion from the financial support mechanism for the Greek economy by Euro Area Member States, the European Central Bank and the International Monetary Fund.[61] An amount of Euros 25 billion has already been disbursed in April 2012.[62]

The objective of the HFSF is to maintain the stability of the Greek banking sector by strengthening the capital adequacy of Greek credit institutions (including the subsidiaries of Greek credit institutions whose parent company is established abroad), in case such a credit institution faces capital adequacy problems as laid down in Law 3864/2010.[63] In pursuing this objective, the HFSF has to manage its capital and assets and exercise the rights ensuing from its capacity as shareholder of credit institutions in a way that:

- preserves the value of its assets;
- minimizes risks for Greek taxpayers; and
- does not hamper or distort competition in the banking sector.[64]

On the other hand, it is not up to the HFSF to provide liquidity to Greek credit institutions, which is exclusively granted by the European Central Bank and the Bank of Greece (through the "Emergency Liquidity Assistance") in their capacity as lenders of last resort.[65]

Despite the fact that five Ministerial Decisions determining the exact role of the HFSF in the recapitalization of Greek credit institutions underway (especially after the PSI exercise) were still pending issuance on April 22, 2012, the Fund is already fully operative,[66] since the seven members of its initial Board of Directors were elected in September 2010.

According to the amendments introduced by Law 4051/2012, the governance of the HFSF has been delegated to two bodies: the General Board and the Executive Committee. The General Board consists of five members and the Executive Committee of three members (including its General Manager).[67]

6.4.2   The Hellenic Council of Systemic Stability

The Hellenic Council of Systemic Stability was established by virtue of Article 20 of Law 3867/2010.[68] Its objective is to analyze the dynamics between the various sectors of the financial system and continuously monitor them in order to proactively address stress situations and crises.

The Council consists of seven members, including the Minister of Finance, the Deputy Minister of Finance, the Bank of Greece's Governor and Vice-Governor responsible for financial stability issues, the President of the Hellenic Capital Markets Commission, and two persons with specific knowledge of the financial sector designated by the Minister of Finance.[69]

The Council has already convened on several occasions that were deemed necessary over the last three years in order to take decisions on the stability of the currently fragile Greek financial system.

The Hellenic Council of Systemic Stability is definitely distinct, with regard to its scope, from the Bank of Greece as a macro-prudential oversight body in Greece, according to the provisions of the European Systemic Risk Board's Recommendation of December 22, 2011 "on the macro-prudential mandate of national authorities."[70] The European Systemic Risk Board (the "ESRB"), which was established by virtue of Regulation (EC) 1092/2010 of the European Parliament and of the Council,[71] and is part of the European System of Financial Supervision (the "ESFS"),[72] has been entrusted with the macro-prudential oversight of the European financial system. The Governor of the Bank of Greece is a member of the General Council of the ESRB.[73]

6.5   Micro-prudential supervisory and regulatory measures adopted after the Euro zone fiscal crisis

6.5.1   Micro-prudential supervisory measures

Stress tests

1. According to the results of the EU-wide stress-testing exercise—which was conducted in 2010 by the Committee of European Banking Supervisors (hereinafter the "CEBS")[74] and national supervisory authorities in close cooperation with the European Central Bank in order to assess the overall resilience of the EU's banking sector to major economic and financial shocks—the results for the six largest Greek banking groups that participated in the exercise (representing more than 90% of the Greek banking sector's assets as a whole) indicated a net surplus of Tier 1 capital of Euros 3.3 billion above the 6% ratio of Tier 1 capital that was agreed as a benchmark solely for the purpose of the stress test (the "baseline scenario"). Under the adverse scenario, including sovereign shock, five of the six credit institutions passed the test. Four out of six credit institutions was above the benchmark, one achieved the benchmark of 6%, while the Tier 1 capital ratio of the remaining one was 4.4% at the end of 2011, indicating a shortfall of Euros 242 million.[75]

2. The 2011 EU-wide stress-testing exercise[76] conducted under the coordination of the European Banking Authority (hereinafter the "EBA") which succeeded the CEBS in January 2011,[77] in cooperation with the national banking supervisory authorities of the EU Member States, the European Central Bank, the European Commission and the European Systemic Risk Board, concluded that the above six largest Greek banking groups had a capital surplus of Euros 2.44 billion above the amount that corresponds to the Core Tier 1 capital ratio threshold of 5%. Under the adverse scenario, before taking into consideration additional mitigating measures, four out of six Greek banking groups were above the 5% threshold, one was marginally below the 5% threshold and one was significantly below the 5% threshold.[78]

Two key features distinguished the 2011 exercise from the stress tests performed in 2010:

- firstly, the threshold was set at 5% in 2011, compared to 6% in 2010; and
- secondly, the definition of capital used for the 2011 exercise was a Core Tier 1 capital ratio, compared to a broader Tier 1 capital ratio used in 2010.

However, following the completion of BlackRock's audit of Greek banks (see 6.5.1.2) and the PSI exercise (see 6.2.2(b)), these conditions have been totally reversed and the majority of Greek credit institutions need to resort to capital increases (and, as a last resort, to the HFSF for recapitalization) in the course of 2012.

Other supervisory measures

1. In 2011 the Bank of Greece resorted to BlackRock, a specialized external expert company, for a diagnostic study on the loan portfolios of Greek credit institutions in order to identify their exposure to credit risk from non-performing business, mortgage and consumer loans.[79] The study was completed at the end of 2011.
2. In addition, the principal banking Law (3601/2007), as amended by the aforementioned Laws 4021/2011 and 4051/2012, contains, inter alia, provisions on strengthening the Bank of Greece's micro-prudential supervisory powers and measures taken by the Bank of Greece. More specifically, if a Greek credit institution does not meet, according to the Bank of Greece, or if there are strong indications that it will not meet the requirements of the principal banking Law (3601/2007) and the relevant Bank of Greece Governor's Acts, it may be required to:
   a. hold own funds in excess of the minimum level laid down in its generally applicable decisions on capital adequacy;
   b. seek prior approval by the Bank of Greece of transactions which may be detrimental to its solvency;
   c. perform a recovery plan; and
   d. increase its capital according to the provisions of Article 62A of that Law.[80]

6.5.2   Micro-prudential regulatory measures

1. The framework on the micro-prudential regulation of Greek credit institutions has been shaped in accordance with the provisions of European banking law and is included in the principal banking Law (3601/2007) and in the relevant Bank of Greece Governor's Acts. In 2011, this framework was amended when two Directives of the European Parliament and

of the Council (2009/111/EC[81] and 2010/76/EU[82]), amending Directives 2006/48/EC and 2006/49/EC, were transposed into Greek law, respectively, by Law 4002/2011[83] and the aforementioned Law 4021/2011, as well by several Bank of Greece Governor's Acts.

2. In addition, based on the timetable for the implementation of the "Memorandum of Economic and Financial Policy,"[84] the Bank of Greece is currently requiring Greek credit institutions to:
   - develop and implement medium-term funding plans; and
   - maintain a minimum Core Tier 1 capital ratio of 9% (as of October 1, 2012) and 10% (as of July 1, 2013).[85]

6.6   Reorganization measures and resolution tools adopted following the Euro zone fiscal crisis

6.6.1   Introductory remarks

The aforementioned Law 4021/2011 also reinforced the provisions of the principal banking Law (3601/2007) on the reorganization of Greek credit institutions, while it also introduced for the first time legal provisions on resolution tools for credit institutions in Greece.

The provisions of this law on bank resolution (Articles 1–4) were adopted on the basis of the "Fourth Review Under the Stand-By Arrangement and Request for Modification and Waiver of Applicability of Performance Criteria" of IMF Country Report No. 11/175 (July 2011). In page 18 of this report the following is stated:

> However, the Greek legal framework lacks specific bank resolution tools— used in other countries with more comprehensive frameworks—which can provide a more orderly framework for dealing with bank problems, towards lowering the cost of resolving banks. In particular, there are no techniques to allow the continuity of banking operations, including sustained depositor access (e.g., the ability to undertake a purchase and assumption and to conduct resolution through a bridge bank). Reforms are also needed to ensure that the deposit insurance fund can be used to fund such techniques, and to establish depositor preference over unsecured creditors to better ensure recovery of guarantee funds.

In particular, Law 4021/2011 (as further amended by Law 4051/2012) introduced provisions with regard to:

- the conditions under which a Commissioner to a distressed credit institution (as the main reorganization measure under Greek administrative banking law) has to or may be appointed by the Bank of Greece, along with a definition of his/her powers (see under 6.6.2);

- resolution tools that may be implemented by the Minister of Finance and/or the Bank of Greece (see under 6.6.3);[86] and
- the creation of a "resolution fund" (see under 6.6.4).[87]

In this respect it is worth mentioning that the European Commission has taken initiatives for the creation of a European "bank resolution framework." Its most recent initiative is based on the Communication on "An EU Framework for Crisis Management in the Financial Sector,"[88] and it is strongly expected that in the course of the coming months it will submit a proposal for a Directive of the European Parliament and the Council on this issue area.[89]

In this Communication it is stated that the resolution tools should include, inter alia, "a sale of business tool which will enable authorities to effect a sale of the credit institution or parts of its business to one or more purchasers without the consent of shareholders."[90] Footnote 21 of the Communication notes also: "The Commission recognises that there will be circumstances in which a sale must be completed in a very short period to preserve financial stability."[91]

6.6.2   The enhanced role of the Commissioner

The new legislation distinguishes between conditions under which a Commissioner to a distressed credit institution *has to be* appointed or *may be* appointed by the Bank of Greece.[92] The Commissioner's powers are significantly strengthened, also with the ability to exercise (or collaborate to) the management of the credit institution.[93]

The Commissioner, who is subject to control and supervision by the Bank of Greece, is appointed for a period not exceeding 12 months. However, the appointment may be extended up to six months.[94]

6.6.3   Resolution tools

The relevant provisions of Law 4021/2011 introduce three resolution tools, which may be initiated by the Bank of Greece for the sake of protecting financial stability and boosting public confidence in the banking sector.[95] The Law contains detailed provisions on the conditions under which these tools can be activated, such as the impossibility of taking alternative measures of equivalent effect:

1. A capital increase of the credit institution by decision of the Commissioner following a request by the Bank of Greece.[96] Existing shareholders will not be allowed to exercise their right of preference in this case.
2. The sale of specific assets and liabilities of an insolvent credit institution to another credit institution or another legal entity and, in principle, the withdrawal of the former's authorization (which is under liquidation).[97]

This provision was enacted, for the first time, in December 2011 in the case of the T-Bank and the transfer of certain of its assets and liabilities to the Hellenic Postbank. The license of the T-Bank was withdrawn and the credit institution was set under liquidation.[98]

In this case, the European Commission stated that: "(...) where such funds intervene to assist in the rescue and/or restructuring of failing financial institutions, their intervention may constitute state aid. Whilst the funds in question may derive from the private sector, they may constitute aid to the extent they come within the control of the state and the decision as to the funds' application is imputable to the state."[99] This remark of the European Commission seems to contradict, in essence, its statement in its aforementioned Communication on "An EU Framework for Crisis Management in the Financial Sector" (see under 6.6.1), according to which: "In many jurisdictions resolution authorities are appropriately separately from supervisors and (...) such separation is important to minimise the risk of forbearance."

It is also worth mentioning that the Commission has to make a case on which there will be no precedent. There is no doubt that in the case of T-Bank there was:

- neither a state subsidy, since the financing was not provided by the state;
- nor a "control of the state," since it cannot be reasonably established that the Bank of Greece, being an independent supervisory authority according to its Statute (Article 5A), acted "within the control of the state."

In March 2012 this provision was also enacted with regard to three cooperative credit institutions (the deposits of which were transferred to the National Bank of Greece).[100]

3. The establishment of a "bridge bank," by decision of the Minister of Finance, upon a proposal of the Bank of Greece on grounds of public interest.[101] The bridge bank, which receives specific assets and liabilities of an insolvent credit institution (while the latter's authorization is withdrawn and it is set under liquidation) will receive own funds by the HFSF and may not operate for a period of more than two years.[102]

Its main objective is to ensure the continuity of provision of crucial banking services in order to maintain financial stability and protect depositors and investors. The sale of the bridge bank's shares has to take place through auction, to be determined by its Board of Directors following an assessment by an independent agency also designated by that Board.[103] This provision was activated immediately after Law 4021/2011 entered into force with regard to Proton Bank, whose license was withdrawn, and the bridge bank New Proton Bank was simultaneously set up. Proton Bank is currently under liquidation.[104]

Table 6.2 Chronological list of major institutional, supervisory and regulatory measures taken since 2008 in order to preserve the stability of the Greek banking sector (apart from measures relating to the implementation of European banking law Directives)

Date	Legal act	Content
A. The period before the current Euro zone fiscal crisis (2008–9)		
November 2008	Law 3714/2008	Increase of the deposit guarantee level to Euros 100,000 per depositor (per credit institution)
December 2008	Law 3723/2008	Enhancement of liquidity of the economy in response to the impact of the international financial crisis (three "pillars")
B. The period after the current Euro zone fiscal crisis (2010–12)		
July 2010	Law 3864/2010	Establishment of the Hellenic Financial Stability Fund ("HFSF")
July 2010	CEBS stress-testing exercise	
August 2010	Law 3867/2010	Establishment of the Hellenic Council of Systemic Stability
July 2011	EBA stress-testing exercise	
September 2011	Law 4021/2011	• enhanced micro-prudential supervisory powers and measures of the Bank of Greece (amendments to the principal banking Law 3601/2007); • enhanced powers for the Commissioner of troubled credit institutions (amendments to principal banking Law 3601/2007); • introduction of three resolution tools (amendments to the principal banking Law 3601/2007); • amendments to Law 3746/2009 on the HDIGF (including the introduction of a "resolution scheme"); • amendments to Law 3864/2010 on the HFSF
September 2011	Decisions of the Minister of Finance and of the Bank of Greece	• withdrawal of Proton Bank's license (currently under liquidation); • granting of license to the first bridge bank (New Proton Bank)
December 2011	Decisions of the Bank of Greece	• withdrawal of T-Bank's license (currently under liquidation); • transfer of specific assets and liabilities of the T-Bank to the Hellenic Postbank

(continued)

Table 6.2   Continued

Date	Legal act	Content
December 2011	Bank of Greece Governor's Act 2643/6.9.2011	Diagnostic study on Greek credit institutions' loan portfolios conducted by BlackRock on behalf of the Bank of Greece
February 2012	Bank of Greece Governor's Act 2653/29.2.2012	Establishment of a Resolution Measures Committee within the Bank of Greece
February 2012	Bank of Greece Governor's Act 2654/29.2.2012	Imposition of higher "Core Tier 1" capital requirements on Greek credit institutions
February 2012	Law 4051/2012	Amendments to Laws: • 3601/2007 (principal banking Law); • 3746/2009 on the HDIGF; and • 3864/2010 on the HFSF
March 2012	Law 4056/2012	Amendments to Laws: • 3746/2009 on the HDIGF; and • 3864/2010 on the HFSF
March 2012	Annex to Act of Legislative Content	Master Financial Assistance Facility Agreement between the European Financial Stability Facility, the Hellenic Republic as Beneficiary Member State, the Hellenic Financial Stability Fund as Guarantor and the Bank of Greece
March 2012	Decisions of the Bank of Greece	• withdrawal of the license of three cooperative banks (currently under liquidation); • transfer of the deposits (only) of these credit institutions to the National Bank of Greece
April 2012	Act of Legislative Content	Amendments to Laws: • 3601/2007 (principal banking Law); and • 3864/2010 on the HFSF

6.6.4 The "resolution scheme" of the HDIGF (Hellenic Deposit and Investment Guarantee Fund)

In accordance with the provisions of Article 7 of Law 4021/2011, a "resolution scheme" was established in 2011, as the third pillar of the HDIGF. This scheme is the only pillar of the HDIGF that is not (yet) premised on provisions of European law.

The resolution scheme, which is independent from the other two pillars (the deposit guarantee scheme and investor compensation scheme), provides funding, either in the case of the transfer of a credit institution's assets to another credit institution or another entity, or if a bridge bank is established under the provisions of Articles 63D and 63E of Law 3601/2007 (as mentioned under 6.6.3). The participation of all the Greek credit institutions (as well as Greek branches of credit institutions from third countries, non-EU Member States) in the resolution scheme is mandatory, as well as the payment of contributions to it.[105]

In this context, it is also worth mentioning that according to paragraph 12 of Article 9 of Law 4051/2012 (amending Law 3864/2010 on the HFSF), for a transitional period of 12 months from the date of enactment of that Law, it is the HFSF that will cover the difference referred to in paragraph 13 of Article 63D and in paragraph 7 of Article 63E of Law 3601/2007 rather than the HDIGF.[106]

In the author's view, this provision is adequate, taking into account that imposing additional contributions on credit institutions for funding the "resolution scheme" of the HDIGF (given the current liquidity strains) would not be appropriate (especially if the Ministry of Finance, Bank of Greece and HFSF decided, in the course of the recent restructuring of the Greek banking sector, to apply existing resolution tools laid down in Articles 63D and 63E of Law 3601/2007 to several credit institutions). Nevertheless, if the new Directive of the European Parliament and of the Council on deposit guarantee schemes (recast) (once finalized) requires "deposit guarantee schemes" to act also as "resolution funds," a new arrangement should be made.[107] (See Table 6.2 for a summary of the measures taken since 2008 to preserve the Greek banking sector.)

Conclusions

1. In the current conjuncture, the main challenges for the Greek banking sector are as follows:
   a. The first is the preservation of its solvency, with adequate recapitalization from the private sector and, as a last resort, the Hellenic Financial Stability Fund. Decisions on this will be taken in the coming months. In this respect, Greek credit institutions will also have to take deleveraging initiatives with regard to:
      - disposing of assets;
      - selling non-core foreign assets;
      - cutting claims on foreign financial institutions; and
      - reducing debt security holdings.[108]

      In any event, the primary objective is for *"private ownership [to] be maintained to the extent possible."*[109]
   b. The second is maintaining its liquidity, while creating conditions for gradual independence from European Central Bank and Bank of Greece financing.
   c. The third is granting credit to viable enterprises in order to support, as much as possible, the Greek economy's growth.

2. In the medium term, however, the Greek banking sector will also have to adapt to the European regulatory "tsunami" now underway. More specifically, Directive 2006/48/EC of the European Parliament and of the Council relating to the taking up and pursuit of the business of credit institutions (known as "CRD"), already amended by Directive 2009/111/ EC (known as "CRD II") and Directive 2010/76/EC (known as "CRD III"), will be repealed in the coming months by a Regulation and a Directive transposing into European law the Basel III regulatory framework[110] (known as "CRR IV and "CRD IV," respectively).[111] In light of this, it can be rightly argued that the current business model of EU credit institutions is in the process of a radical review.

Notes

Last updated: April 22, 2012. The author wishes to thank Professors Otto Hieronymi and Constantine Stephanou for their valuable comments, Lecturer Christina Livada and Vassilis Panagiotidis for their very useful support on the documentation and valuable comments, as well as Dr Sofia Ziakou and Ph.D. candidate Katerina Lagaria for their thorough editorial support.

1. On this see, by means of indication, Rosa M. Lastra (2006) *Legal Foundations of International Monetary Stability*, Oxford and New York: Oxford University Press, pp. 447–501, and Mario Giovanoli (2010) "The International Financial Architecture and its Reform after the Global Crisis," Mario Giovanoli and Diego Devos (eds) *International Monetary and Financial Law: The Global Crisis* (Oxford: Oxford University Press), pp. 3–39. On the evolution of the European financial law during that period see, inter alia, Lastra, *Legal Foundations of International Monetary Stability*, pp. 297–342, and Christos Vl. Gortsos (2011) *European Banking Law*, Notes for the post-graduate program of the Europa Institut, Universität des Saarlandes, http://www.ecefil.eu/Up1Files/monographs.
2. On this, see various relevant reports of the International Monetary Fund, available at http://www.imf.org.
3. There is a vast existing bibliography on this issue. See, by means of indication, John Kiff and Paul Mills (2007) *Money for Nothing and Checks for Free: Recent Developments in U.S. Subprime Mortgage Markets*, IMF Working Paper, WP/07/188, Washington, DC: International Monetary Fund; Claudio Borio (2008) *The Financial Turmoil of 2007–?: A Preliminary Assessment and Some Policy Considerations*, Bank for International Settlements (BIS) Working Paper No. 251, Basle, March, pp. 1–13; Charles W. Calomiris (2008) "The Subprime Turmoil: What's Old, What's New, and What's Next," paper for Jackson Hole Symposium *Maintaining Stability in a Changing Financial System*, Federal Reserve Bank of Kansas City, August; Barry Eichengreen (2008) "Thirteen Questions about the Subprime Crisis," paper for Conference of the Tobin Project *Toward a New Theory of Financial Regulation*, While Oak Conference and Residency Center, February; Charles A. E. Goodhart (2009) *The Regulatory Response to the Financial Crisis*, Cheltenham, UK and Northampton, MA: Edward Elgar, pp. 2–29; Johan Norberg (2009) *Financial Fiasco: How America's Infatuation with Home-Ownership and Easy Money Created the Economic Crisis*, Washington, DC: Cato Institute; Raghuram G. Rajan (2010) *Fault Lines: How Hidden Fractures still Threaten the World Economy*, Princeton: Princeton University

Press; Richard A. Posner (2010) *The Crisis of Capitalist Democracy*, Cambridge, MA and London: Harvard University Press, pp. 13–245; Rosa M. Lastra and Geoffrey Wood (2010) "The Crisis of 2007–2009: Nature, Causes and Reactions," *Journal of International Economic Law*, Vol. 13, No. 3 (September), pp. 537–45; Jean Tirole (2010) "Lessons from the Crisis," Mathias Dewatripont, Jean-Charles Rochet and Jean Tirole (eds) *Balancing the Banks: Global Lessons from the Financial Crisis*, Princeton and Oxford: Princeton University Press, Chapter 2, pp. 11–47; The Financial Crisis Inquiry Commission (2011) *The Financial Crisis Inquiry Report: Final Report of the National Commission on the Causes of the Financial and Economic Crisis in the United States*, Washington, DC: US Government Printing Office, January; and the reports of the Committee on the Global Financial System (on the latter see also in section 4 of this study, under A7.2).

For a comparison of the recent crisis with the international financial crisis of 1931 (both in terms of causes and in terms of regulatory reaction), see William Allen and Richchild Moessner (2010) *Central Bank Co-operation and International Liquidity in the Financial Crisis of 2008–2009*, BIS Working Papers No. 310, Monetary and Economic Department, Bank for International Settlements, June.

4. The primacy of this aspect is illustrated in Norberg, *Financial Fiasco* and Rajan, *Fault Lines*.
5. Lastra and Wood, in "The Crisis of 2007–2009," correctly point out the "usual suspects," that is, greed and euphoria in periods of rapid growth and extensive credit provision.
6. On this model, see analytically European Central Bank (2008) *The Incentive Structure of the "Originate and Distribute" Model*, European Central Bank, December.
7. According to the Financial Stability Board's report in 2011, *Shadow Banking: Strengthening Oversight and Regulation, Recommendations of the Financial Stability Board*, October (available at http://www.financialstabilityboard.org/publications/r_111027a.pdf): "The 'shadow banking system' can broadly be described as credit intermediation involving entities and activities outside the regular banking system."
8. There is an extensive literature on systemically important financial institutions. For more details see, by means of indication, Stijn Claessens, Richard J. Herring and Dirk Schoenmaker (2010) *A Safer World Financial System: Improving the Resolution of Systemic Institutions*, Geneva Reports on the World Economy 12, Geneva: International Center for Monetary and Banking Studies (ICMB), and the various contributions to Rosa M. Lastra (ed.) (2011) *Cross-Border Bank Insolvency*, Oxford and New York: Oxford University Press.
9. For an assessment of these measures, see Fabio Panetta et al. (2009) *An Assessment of Financial Sector Rescue Programmes*, BIS Papers No. 48, Monetary and Economic Department, Bank for International Settlements, July; Christos Vl. Gortsos (2009) "Assessment of the Banking 'Rescue' Packages and 'Recovery' Plans of the Member States in the European Union," *Banking Rescue Measures in the EU Member States— Compilation of Briefing Papers*, Report, European Parliament, Policy Department, Economic and Scientific Policy, IP/A/ECON/RT/2008–29, pp. 9–46; Ana Petrovic and Ralf Tutsh (2009) *National Rescue Measures in Response to the Current Financial Crisis*, ECB Legal Working Paper Series No. 8, July; and Bart De Meester (2010) "The Global Financial Crisis and Government Support for Banks: What Role for GATS?" *Journal of International Economic Law*, Vol. 13, No. 1 (March 25), pp. 27–63, concerning their compatibility with the provisions of the General Agreement on Trade in Services, known as "GATS."

10. The most striking example in this case is Iceland (see Claessens, Herring and Schoenmaker, *A Safer World Financial System*, pp. 51–3).
11. The most striking example is that of Ireland. With a sole exception, all Irish credit institutions were technically bankrupt after the financial crisis and needed to be recapitalized. For a more detailed discussion, see the references in note 10.
12. For more details, see Committee on the Global Financial System (2011) *The Impact of Sovereign Credit Risk on Bank Funding Conditions*, No. 43 (July), http://www.bis.org/publ/cgfs43.pdf.
13. On the causes of the Greek "fiscal indiscipline," see, by means of indication, George Alogoskoufis (2012) *Greece's Sovereign Debt Crisis: Retrospect and Prospect*, Hellenic Observatory Papers on Greece and Southeast Europe, GreeSE Paper No. 54, London School of Economics and Political Science, January. See also the contribution of Nikolas Haritakis in the present volume.
14. See, inter alia, Barry Eichengreen, Robert Feldmann, Jeffrey Liebman, Jürgen von Hagen and Charles Wyplosz (2011) *Public Debts: Nuts, Bolts and Worries*, Geneva Report on the World Economy, No. 13, Geneva: International Center for Monetary and Banking Studies, Centre for Economic Policy Research, pp. 47–64.
15. The only conclusion drawn at present is that the gravest impact was suffered by banks with sovereign debt holdings from countries severely affected by this crisis (namely Greece, Ireland and Portugal, and also—to a lesser extent—Italy and Spain).
16. For a thorough discussion of this aspect, see the contribution of Constantine Stephanou in the present volume.
17. Bank of Greece (2012) *List of Credit Institutions Authorized in Greece*, April. The term "credit institution," rather than "bank," is used hereinafter given its use in Greek (and European) banking law (unlike US law, which uses the equivalent term "depository institution"). According to the provisions of Article 2(1) of the principal Greek banking Law (3601/2007, Government Gazette A 178, 1.8.2007), a credit institution is defined as an undertaking whose business is to receive deposits or other repayable funds from the public and to grant loans or other credits for its own account.
18. European Central Bank (2001) *Structural Indicators for the EU Banking Sector*, December.
19. Bank of Greece (2012) *Governor's Annual Report*, April, Chart X.8, p. 157. Credit institutions in the Euro zone manage an equivalent of 170% of its GDP (loans to households and enterprises).
20. Ibid.
21. Bank of Greece (2012) *Bulletin of Conjunctural Indicators*, No. 142, January–February Table IV.15, p. 106.
22. Bank of Greece (2012) *Aggregated Balance Sheet of Credit Institutions*, February, and Hellenic Statistical Authority (2012) *Gross Domestic Product at Market Prices (Years 2000–2011)*.
23. Bank of Greece, *Aggregated Balance Sheet of Credit Institutions*. For the average ratio, total loans, as well as total deposits and repos to (domestic) residents and non-residents, are taken into account.
24. On this see under 6.3.
25. On this see under 6.1.2.
26. Bank of Greece, *Bulletin of Conjunctural Indicators*, Table IV.9, p. 96.
27. Bank of Greece, *Aggregated Balance Sheet of Credit Institutions*, as well as the Bank of Greece's monthly balance sheet. On the role of the ECB as a "hidden lender of

last resort" to credit institutions, see the contribution of Constantine Stephanou in the present volume, under 4.2.6.

28. In principle, there is no legislation on this issue area (according to the long-established principle of "constructive ambiguity"). The national central banks—as members of the Eurosystem—act as lenders of last resort at their discretion and in close cooperation with the European Central Bank, with adequate collateral. This should be distinguished from "unconventional monetary operations" conducted by the ECB. On this, see European Central Bank (2007) "The EU Arrangements for Financial Crisis Management," *ECB Monthly Bulletin*, February, pp. 80–1.

29. European Central Bank (2012) *Euro Area and National MFI Interest Rates*, Frankfurt am Main, February.

30. Ibid.

31. Council of the European Union (2011) *Statement by the Heads of State or Government of the Euro Area and EU Institutions*, Brussels, July 21.

32. Council Decision 2011/734/EU of July 12, 2011, addressed to Greece with a view to reinforcing and deepening fiscal surveillance and giving notice to Greece to take measures for the deficit reduction judged necessary to remedy the situation of excessive deficit, *OJ*, L 296, November 15, 2011, pp. 38–52 (recast); Council Decision 2011/791/EU of November 8, 2011, amending Decision 2011/734/EU ..., *OJ*, L 320, December 3, 2011, pp. 28–31; and Council Decision of March 12, 2012 amending Decision 2011/734/EU ... (unpublished in *OJ* at the time of writing). See also European Commission, *The Greek Loan Facility*.

33. Ibid. On the key terms of the PSI following the October 26, 2011 Euro Summit, see Hellenic Republic, Ministry of Finance (2012) "PSI Launch," Press release, February, http://www.minfin.gr/portal/en/resource/contentObject/id/7ad6442f-1777-4d02-80fb-91191c606664. For the final settlement of the PSI, see Hellenic Republic, Ministry of Finance (2012) Press release, April 25. See also the contribution of Constantine Stephanou in the present volume, under 4.3.

34. Bank of Greece (2011) *Monetary Policy Report 2011–2012* (March), p. 141.

35. In the second half of 2012 the relevant regulatory framework is expected to be amended in view of the restructuring of credit institutions' non-performing loans. The main principles governing this new regulatory framework will be to conduct targeted interventions (in line with fiscal and financial sector capacity), preserve the payment culture, avoid strategic loan defaults, maximize asset recovery and facilitate the distinction between rehabilitation of viable borrowers and efficient exit from the economy of non-viable borrowers. On this, see IMF Country Report No. 12/57 (2012) *Greece: Request for Extended Arrangement Under the Extended Fund Facility—Staff Report; Staff Supplement*; Press Release on the Executive Board Discussion; and Statement by the Executive Director for Greece, Washington, DC: IMF, March 16, p. 27.

36. See under 6.2.2.

37. As a matter of fact, 2008 was the year in which most Greek credit institutions (including major ones) managed to achieve a historically high level of profitability. See the published annual reports of these credit institutions for the period 2000–10 (available on their Internet addresses).

38. At that time, the main problem was that the international interbank market remained "closed" for several months (since there was no trust among banks as to their crisis-related risk exposures), a condition which impacted negatively on liquidity conditions for Greek credit institutions as well. The situation was gradually normalized at the beginning of 2009.

39. On this see, by means of indication, Claessens, Herring and Schoenmaker, *A Safer World Financial System*, pp. 42–5.
40. The Hellenic Deposit Guarantee Fund was established in 1995 pursuant to Law 2324/1995 (Government Gazette A 146, 17.7.1995), which incorporated into Greek law the provisions of Directive 94/19/EC of the European Parliament and of the Council "on deposit guarantee schemes" (*OJ*, L 135, May 31, 1994, pp. 5–14). Law 2324/1995 was repealed in 2000 by Law 2832/2000 (Government Gazette A 141, 13.6.2000) and then amended in 2009 with the currently applicable Law 3746/2009 (see further).
41. Law 3714/2008 (Government Gazette A 231, 7.11.2008), Article 6, amending Article 5, para. 2, of Law 2832/2000.
42. Law 3723/2008 (Government Gazette A 250, 9.12.2008).
43. Ibid., article 1. This support was deemed necessary on the ground of microprudential considerations, since no Greek credit institution was exposed (or was threatened to be exposed) at the time to insolvency.
44. The commission was set up, depending on the rating of each credit institution that made use of this pillar, by Decision of the Minister of Finance.
45. This commission was set up by Decision of the Minister of Finance.
46. Law 3723/2008, Articles 3 and 5. Beneficiaries of the measures provided for under (ii) and (iii) previously could be only credit institutions fulfilling the minimum capital adequacy requirements as determined by the Bank of Greece (see also Article 1, para. 1, with regard to measures under (i)).
47. Decision of the European Commission N 560/08, OJ C/125/6/5.6.2009, as continuously prolonged, available at http://ec.europa.eu/competition/state_aid/register/ii/doc/N-560-2008-WLWL-en-19.11.2008.pdf. For references, see Yassine Boudghene, Matthaeus Buder, Zetta Dellidou, Christophe Galand, Violeta Iftinchi, Max Lienemeyer, Christos Malamataris and Danila Malvolti (2011) *State Aid Control in a Stability Programme Country: The Case of Greece*, Competition Policy Newsletter, No. 1, pp. 45–9.
48. Law 3746/2009, Government Gazette A 27, 16.2.2009.
49. Directive 97/9/EC of the European Parliament and of the Council, *OJ*, L 84, March 26, 1997, pp. 22–31. On the contrary, the clients of Greek investment firms and Greek credit institutions that are members of the Athens Stock Exchange are covered by a separate investor compensation scheme (the "Athens Stock Exchange Members' Guarantee Fund," according to the provisions of Law 2533/1977, Government Gazette A 228, 11.11.1997).
50. On the functioning of the HDIGF, see http://www.hdigf.gr.
51. For a detailed analysis of the provisions of Greek administrative banking law (as of February 2012), see Nikos K. Rokas and Christos Vl. Gortsos (2012) *Elements of Banking Law*, Athens: Nomiki Bibliothiki Group (in Greek), pp. 11–177.
52. Law 3845/2010, Government Gazette A 65, 06.05.2010, Article 4, para. 8.
53. Law 3872/2010, Government Gazette A 148, 03.09.2010, Article 7.
54. Law 3965/2011, Government Gazette A 113, 18.05.2011, Article 19, para. 1.
55. Law 3864/2010 "Establishment of a Hellenic Financial Stability Fund," Government Gazette A 119, 21.7.2010.
56. Law 4021/2011 "Enhanced Measures of Supervision and Resolution of Credit Institutions—Regulation of Financial Issues—Ratification of the Framework Convention of the European Financial Stability Fund and its Amendments and Other Provisions," Government Gazette A 218, 03.10.2011.

57. Law 4051/2012 "Regulation of Pensions and Other Urgent Implementing Measures of the Memorandum of Agreement of Law 4046/2012," Government Gazette A 40, 29.2.2012.
58. Law 4056/2012, Government Gazette A 52, 12.3.2012.
59. Government Gazette A 94, 19.4.2012.
60. Law 3864/2010, Article 1. According to the same provision it is expressly stated that the purely private-law nature of the HFSF is not prejudiced by the fact that its capital shall be paid up in full by the Greek State or by the issuance of the decisions of the Minister of Finance contemplated in Law 3864/2010. See also Commission Decision of September 3, 2010 on State Aid Case No. 328/2010 "Recapitalisation of Credit Institutions in Greece under the Financial Stability Fund (FSF)" (*OJ*, C 316, November 20, 2010, p. 7) (as prolonged).
61. Act of Legislative Content, 19.4.2012, Article 1, para. 1(a).
62. For the requests, conditions to disbursements, financing and any other detail, see the Annex to the Act of Legislative Content, Government Gazette A 55, 14.3.2012 ("Master Financial Assistance Facility Agreement between the European Financial Stability Facility, the Hellenic Republic as Beneficiary Member State, the Hellenic Financial Stability Fund as Guarantor and the Bank of Greece").
63. Law 3864/2010, Article 2, para. 1. See also article 6 of this law with regard to the procedures for the activation of the HFSF.
64. Ibid., Article 2, para. 1.
65. On this, see under 6.2.2 (a–c).
66. As a matter of fact, the HFSF has already been set in motion through the necessary funding for the operation of the bridge bank "New Proton Bank."
67. Law 3864/2010, Article 4, as amended by Article 9, para. 3, of Law 4051/2012. According to para. 10 of Article 9 of this Law, the HFSF is governed by its existing Board of Directors until a General Board and Executive Committee are designated.
68. Law 3867/2010 "Supervision of Private Insurance, Establishment of a Guarantee Fund for Private Life Insurance, Credit Rating Agencies and Other Provisions of the Competence of the Ministry of Finance," Government Gazette A 128, 3.8.2010.
69. Currently these members are the Presidents of the HFSF and the Hellenic Bank Association.
70. *OJ*, L 41, February 14, 2012, pp. 1–4.
71. *OJ*, L 131, December 15, 2010, pp. 1–11.
72. See on this Christos Vl. Gortsos (2011) *The European Banking Authority within the European System of Financial Supervision*, ECEFIL Working Paper Series No. 2011/1, Section A (under 1 and 2), http://www.ecefil.eu/defaultEn.asp.
73. Regulation (EC) 1092/2010 of the European Parliament and of the Council, *OJ*, L 331, December 15, 2010, pp. 1–11, Article 6.
74. See CEBS, Press Release on the results of the 2010 EU-wide stress testing exercise, July 23, 2010, available at: http://stress-test.c-ebs.org/documents/CEBSPressReleasev2.pdf.
75. See "EU-wide Stress Testing 2010, Results for Greece," http://www.bankofgreece.gr/Pages/en/Supervision/stresstest.aspx.
76. See EBA, Press Release on the results of the 2011 EU-wide stress test, July 15, 2011, http://stress-test.eba.europa.eu/pdf/2011+EU-wide+stress+test+results+-+press+release++FINAL.pdf.
77. On the work of the EBA see, by means of indication, Gortsos, *The European Banking Authority within the European System of Financial Supervision*, Section A (under 1 and 2), pp. 24–44.

78. See "EU-wide Stress Testing Exercise 2011, Results for Greece," http://www.bankofgreece.gr/Pages/en/Bank/News/PressReleases/DispItem.aspx?Item_ID=3682&List_ID=1af869f3-57fb-4de6-b9ae-bdfd83c66c95&Filter_by=DT.
79. Bank of Greece Governor's Bank of Greece Governor's Act 2643/6.9.2011. Bank of Greece Governor's Acts are available at http://www.bankofgreece.gr/Pages/el/Bank/legal/Acts.sspx.
80. Law 3601/2007, Article 62, paras 1 and 2.
81. Directive 2009/111/EC of the European Parliament and of the Council, *OJ*, L 302, November 17, 2009, pp. 97–119.
82. Directive 2010/76/EU of the European Parliament and of the Council, *OJ*, L 329, December 14, 2010, pp. 3–35.
83. Government Gazette A 180, 22.8.2011.
84. Greece—Memorandum of Economic and Financial Policies, May 3, 2010, p. 66.
85. Bank of Greece Governor's Act 2654/29.2.2012.
86. Any bank resolution tool must be based on legislation, since the taking of the courses of action on "bank resolution" without a solid legal basis would negatively affect the rights of the existing shareholders, in breach of the provisions of European company law. This is undoubtedly an international practice (see, by means of indication, the provisions of UK law in Chan Ho Look (2011) "Bank Insolvency Law in the United Kingdom," Rosa M. Lastra (ed.) (2011) *Cross-Border Bank Insolvency*, Oxford and New York: Oxford University Press, pp. 276–381.
87. In addition, pursuant to the Bank of Greece Governor's Act 2653/29.2.2012 (which has been amended by Act 2657/20.3.2012), a "Resolution Measures Committee" has been established within the Bank of Greece.
88. COM (2010) 579 final, October 20, 2010. See also the very recent (April 2012) European Commission's discussion paper on the debt write-down/bail-in tool (available at http://ec.europa.eu/internal_market/bank/docs/crisis-management/discussion_paper_bailin_en.pdf).
89. Ibid., p. 3 (under 1, *in finem*).
90. Ibid., pp. 9–10.
91. Ibid., p. 10.
92. Law 3601/2007, Article 63, paras 2 and 1, respectively.
93. Ibid., Article 63, paras 6 and 10.
94. Ibid., Article 63, para. 13.
95. Ibid., Article 63B.
96. Ibid., Article 63C.
97. Ibid., Article 63D. According to the provisions of this Article: "If the value of the liability items transferred is higher than the value of the asset items, the Bank of Greece is determining the amount of the difference, which is covered ... by the resolution scheme of the Hellenic Deposit and Investment Guarantee Fund is providing the additional amount."
98. Decisions 25/1/17.12.2011, 26/1/17.12.2011 and 26/2/17.12.2011 of the Bank of Greece's Credit and Insurance Committee.
99. European Commission, Case SA.34115 (201/CP), Resolution of T-Bank (31.1.2012), p. 2.
100. Decision 34/18.3.2012 (items 1–3) of the Committee of Credit and Insurance Issues of the Bank of Greece, as well as Decision 1/23.3.2012 (items 1–9) of the Resolution Measures Committee of the Bank of Greece.

101. Law 3601/2007, Article 63E.
102. A derogation is permitted for another two (2) more years, by decision of the Minister of Finance, upon a recommendation by the Bank of Greece for reasons of financial stability (ibid., Article 63E, para. 9).
103. Ibid., Article 63 F.
104. Decision of the Minister of Finance 9250/9.10.2011 and Decision 20/9.10.2011 (items 1–3) of the Bank of Greece's Credit and Insurance Committee.
105. With the sole exception of the New Proton Bank, which is a bridge bank.
106. Law 3864/2010, Article 16B, para. 12.
107. COM (2010) 368 final.
108. IMF Country Report No. 12/57 (2012), p. 7.
109. Ibid., pp. 1 and 118.
110. On this, see Christos Vl. Gortsos (2011) "Basel III: The Reform of the Existing Regulatory Framework of the Basel Committee on Banking Supervision for Strengthening the Stability of the International Banking System," Werner Meng, George Ress and Torsten Stein (eds) *Europäische Integration und Gloablisierung, Festshrift zum 60-jährigen Bestehen des Europa-Instituts*, Schriften des Europa-Insituts der Universität des Saarlandes—Rechtswissenshaft, Band 84, Baden-Baden: Nomos Verlagsgesellschaft, pp. 167–84.
111. COM (2011) 452 final and COM (2011) 453 final, respectively.

7
Options, Decisions and Implementation under Extreme Market Conditions: Economic Policy in Greece the Day After

Nikolas G. Haritakis

7.1 Introduction

On the night of April 14, 1912, the RMS *Titanic* collided with an iceberg on her maiden voyage. Two hours and 40 minutes later it sank. The disaster came as a great shock because the vessel was equipped with the most advanced technology of the time, had an experienced crew and was thought to be practically "unsinkable."

For social scientists, evidence about how people behaved aboard the *Titanic* offers a quasi-natural field experiment, to explore behavior under extreme conditions of life and death. Studies proved that people in their prime age, people with high financial means (travelling first class) and crew members (who were better informed) managed to survive, as opposed to the poor, the old, the women and the children.

Analysis from a different viewpoint indicates how in such extreme cases, social cohesion disappears and selfish reactions predominate in human behavior. Counterfactually, while prudent and collaborative actions between individuals or members of a community are always the safest exit from an incident of social upheaval, in practice, individual self-preservation defeats expectations.

It is the purpose of this chapter to investigate how economic policy alternatives and decisions are not straightforward when they need to be implemented within a severe economic crisis, a classic example being the case of Greece since 2008. Tense financial conditions, the speed of global deleveraging following the economic crisis, fears of contagion from and towards other Euro zone partners, persistent local deficiencies such as tax collection ineffectiveness, or delays and capacity problems in delivering complex structural reforms proved to be highly inelastic factors of economic policy implementation. Using the current Greek experience, we will try to review the efficiency of the typical policy implementation techniques used in economic crisis relative to periods of non-crisis in order to derive policy recommendations.

There is one common aspect to the vast range of similar crises: the excessive debt accumulation in a booming period, irrespective of whether it is produced by government (the Greek case), by banks and corporations (the case of Ireland) or by consumers (the US case). The lesson to learn from the past is that most such booms end badly.

Therefore balancing risks and opportunities of debt is always a challenge—a challenge for policy makers, investors and ordinary people. In the case of Greece an additional problem has been the deadly combination of the so-called twin deficit, that is, fiscal as well as current accounts deficit. Policy measures should measure how we could tackle both and simultaneously under extreme macroeconomic conditions.

The Greek State is widely believed to be insolvent. Some economists have accepted unconditionally what former ECB chief economist Otmar Issing said: "Greece is not just illiquid, it's insolvent." Issing stands by a "perceived inability" of the Greek State to pay its debts, owing to a permanent deficiency in its economic performance and not to unanticipated monetary shocks. In general monetary shocks reduce the pledgeability of future income streams directly affecting either revenue by taxation or by privatizing future income streams from the wealth of its civilians combined with most EU monetary union beneficiaries.

On the other hand, ECB ex-president Jean-Claude Trichet stated: "default is not an issue for Greece." Logically therefore and in order to evaluate policy options we should first discuss if sovereign insolvency should always be considered as an incidence of default. And, assuming the answer is yes, then we should explain why the rules applicable to corporate debt, given the technical definition of insolvency (i.e., financial mismatching), in any legal and institutional setting are inappropriate for sovereign debt. At the end, we should focus upon a specific case of whether there is a distinction between sovereign debt with and without strong currency, and how we resolve the issue of policy recommendation in the Euro zone, given the presumed independence of the rating agencies.

In most of the literature the distinction between illiquidity and insolvency is typically described as the difference between short term versus permanent inability or unwillingness to pay. In this context we should explain how illiquidity and decisions for deleveraging restrict, firstly policy options, secondly decisions and finally the effectiveness of relevant implementation actions on otherwise optimal policy variables. The endgame scenario is the case where policy makers are asked to implement, at short notice, specific policy options in order to deleverage sovereign debt for a solvent but illiquid country within a strong currency area. We will show that under those restrictions, policy implementation is feasible only with external financial as well as administrative support. Rebalancing insiders' and outsiders' power in favor of outsiders is a vital decision if policy makers are after a success story, and local politicians are after the median voters.

In the opening paragraph of the economic adjustment program for Greece, the Directorate General for Economic and Financial Affairs claims the following:

> the objectives of the program are to preserve financial stability and adequate liquidity in the banking sector, a front-loaded reduction in fiscal deficit to restore public debt sustainability, and a change to a growth model based on exports and investment, in order to insure growth jobs and sustainability of external accounts

In simple economic terms the objectives are firstly to protect the banking sector and secondly to eliminate the so-called twin deficit, that is, a huge fiscal and current account negative balance.

In this chapter we make the case that quasi-rational models explaining default and illiquidity for a country in a loosely defined common currency area should be redefined when the economic crisis is "ante portas". In section 2 we will provide a reasonable explanation supporting the argument.

In section 3 we will present our theoretical reasoning in order to justify our claim, that Greece should meet its current liquidity shortfalls by counting first on both funding and market liquidity and then by announcing a fiscal consolidation plan, minimizing the fiscal policy duration effect. Funding liquidity refers to the right side of the balance sheet of the budget; it is meant to increase taxes and revenues, improve corporate governance and increase the pledgeability of public assets (reduce social noise and ineffective administrative operations by deregulation). The Greek state may also increase its funding liquidity by renegotiating existing claims and dilute existing claimholders, provided that it can get their consent (write-off). Market liquidity affects the left side of the balance sheet. It is the case where the government generates cash, over and beyond the current yields accrued from their assets on its balance sheet (i.e., privatization). All this can be done by prescribing a targeted fiscal stimulus package in order to resolve the exit problem from a balance sheet recession. The specific policy recommendation is justified in the case of large enough disruptions of credit supply. Illiquidity and credit rationing in financial markets impose financial frictions to the system and act as a tax on capital. Increasing the pledgeability of sovereign wealth by funding and market liquidity we increase the use of capital, GDP and finally employment.

In section 4 we will use all relevant information to clarify ambiguities about Greece's past macroeconomic performance focusing primarily upon the well-established twin-deficit problem.

Finally, in section 5 we will present a practical underpinning of the existing dilemma related with the argument "to stimulate or not to stimulate."

We will then discuss how overcoming liquidity problems is basically driven not only by market micro-structure but also by macroeconomic considerations. To our view it is not a policy choice but rather an issue of policy implementation. We strongly believe that the models we currently use in order to measure systemic risks cannot be adequate enough to support multi-country linkages and single currency unions with strong political independence. At this stage, based upon theoretical knowledge gained from recent experiences, we should start envisioning another fiscal and monetary regulatory mechanism. The missing element is the link between real-economy international trade no longer prevailing in a single optimal currency zone (US. dollar) but presumably within two to four major ones such us the US, Euro zone, China and Russia. A related argument was developed by Geanakoplos (2009) as well as Caballero and Krishnamurthy (2008). The policy recommendations introduced by both authors are an issue to be discussed at the final section.

7.2   Illiquidity, "no-default" equilibria and debt restructuring

Typically a domestic savings glut feeds in excessive sovereign debt. High real growth initiatives equally lead the aggregate economy initially into cashflow problems, and then into rationing dynamics in external financing. Economists can easily find arguments to explain why countries are able to borrow abroad despite the limited rights of creditors. But the arguments are surprisingly complex, suggesting that sustainable debt levels may be fragile as well. In an unexpected liquidity crisis, credit rationing events and fear for a generalized insolvency produce either local illiquidity or incidence of sovereign default. Both drastically affect in turn policy options, political decision making and, eventually, policy implementations on an otherwise non-defaulting nation.

An independent state is in liquidity shortage when an internal or external illiquidity crisis occurs and the country, even though it is willing and able to service its debt in the long run, is temporarily unable to roll it over. If under such conditions, in the presence of a strong macroeconomic shock (US), the economy is adequately capable of producing liquidity internally in order to partially absorb and partially export the unanticipated shock, the danger of an insolvency incident is partially or even permanently relaxed.

In contrast, insolvency is called the case where the country is "perceived" to be unwilling or unable to repay its debt over a long-term period or indefinitely. In such a case the country either defaults and/or reschedules (partially defaults), provided that most of its debt is held by a large and "willing to reschedule group" of lenders. According to the position taken by the lenders, a country may end up in a situation of multiple equilibria, that is, "default and no-default" conditions, where either a strong minority of lenders refuses to roll over, or a sufficient majority is willing to provide liquidity to the country in order to meet its long-run payments. For example, assume that the economy is incapable of providing excess liquidity at relatively undifferentiated tight spreads (Euro zone and periphery). Considering an extreme case, all economic agents in the country, private and public, face simultaneously a cost overrun. In such an event, outside liquidity should be provided by issuing publicly traded securities (bonds or other securities). Sovereign debt, being treated as risk-free, is expected to trade at relatively undifferentiated tight spreads. As turmoil spreads, one after the other, peripheral sovereign debts contaminate the pillars of the entire regulatory structure. At this stage two questions should be discussed. Under these conditions can we remove the risk-free sovereign tag either in relation to reserves or for counterparty risks? And beyond that, what does actually risk-free mean in a common monetary union regulatory framework?

When future historians look back at the early twenty-first century, they may reasonably wonder how the two most sophisticated financial industries of the world managed to gain an AAA rating, either by repackaging subprime US securities or by assigning "risk-free" status on sovereign debt produced by Southern European Euro zone countries. Trading at relatively undifferentiated and thus closely tight spreads was considered by—issuers, investors, private financial institutions, central bankers and regulators—a realistic choice.

By early 2008 the financial crisis forced all the players into a real paradigm shift. By 2010 woes mounted for most Euro zone countries and sovereign debt among them was no longer considered anymore as "risk-free" asset (Figure 7.1).

Deleveraging sovereign debt, implementing austerity plans for most Southern European Monetary Union members, partially relying on the IMF's conditional support and finally attempts to foster permanent fiscal discipline among Euro zone members were all strong indications of a shift from political denial to recognition.

Under these circumstances any country like Greece was therefore in an area of default on its debt. The problems were: first, if it was possible to receive another loan or keep the market open, at least at a palatable financial cost; second, to evaluate in advance the consequences of that decision on all other peripheral Euro zone countries; third to measure the level of reducing the balance sheet valuations of these countries' assets, which threatened the solvency of other European financial institutions; and finally, fourth, to determine how that policy could undermine the foundations of the monetary union on its own.

In a June 2011 paper, Anne Sibert, on behalf of the European Parliament's Committee on Economic and Monetary Affairs, proposed three options for bailing out Greece: first, exchanging the debt for new debt with a lower notional value; second, unilaterally changing it with the same face value but with a longer maturity and lower interest; and third, exactly the same

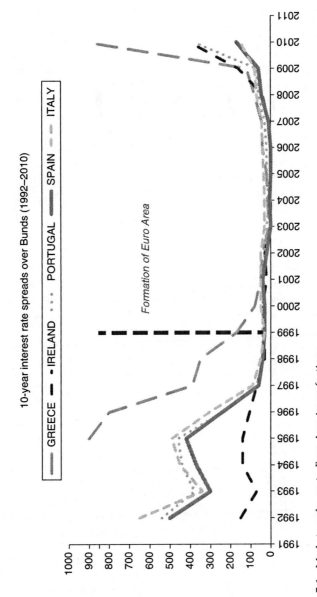

Figure 7.1 Markets wake up to Euro Area imperfections

as the second, but rather than imposing it unilaterally it could negotiate the terms with the creditors.

In reality a fourth option has been chosen. The deal negotiated directly with the creditors under the supervision of the major and fiscally sound Euro zone countries (Germany and France). The deal was structured in such a way that it was not to be interpreted as a "credit event," and thus reduced substantially (a 53.5% "haircut") the privately held Greek sovereign debt (75% in NPV), rescheduled maturity dates and finally imposed a lower than market-expected effective interest rate (2% on short-, 3% on medium- and 4.3% on long-maturity instruments) by transferring the holding of new debt from private financial institutions in total to Euro zone governments, the IMF and private financial creditors. Therefore by March 2012 Greece, in collaboration with the Euro zone, the IMF etc. managed to implement the first restructuring project for a Euro zone country and thus the sovereign CDS market throughout Europe undetermined substantially. Figure 7.2 compares economic and financial indicators for Greece and selected other EU countries.

The debt restructuring program presented above has a long history, starting one year after the global financial crisis in 2008. On the basis of the indicators in Figure 7.2, Greece seemed to be shooting itself in the foot after initial implementation of a strong austerity program (2010). Among other peripheral countries a choice to reform through the "carrot and stick approach" of the European Union and IMF should not be considered as the most probable. As we see, Greece's relative indexes were not among the worst compared with other members in the Eurozone. However, by mid-2010 Greece accepted its role in order to preserve domestic financial stability, restore debt sustainability and improve factors' productivity, real labor costs and competitiveness by deregulating state intervention—even though many other Euro zone periphery countries were at that time (2010) in the same or even a worse position.

	Germany	Portugal	Italy	Greece	Spain	UK	Ireland
GDP(tn)	2.4	0.2	1.2	0.2	0.7	1.7	0.2
Foreign Debt(tn)	4.2	0.4	2	0.4	1.9	7.3	1.7
GD/GDP (%)	83	106	121	166	67	81	109
FD/GDP (%)	176	251	163	252	284	436	1093

Figure 7.2 Economic and financial indicators for select EU countries
Source: Bank for International Settlements, IMF, World Bank, UN Population Division.

Why, then, among all others, was Greece the first choice? One simple but reasonable explanation is that in extreme macroeconomic conditions, problems explained in corporate finance in hierarchical organizations such as corporations are also relevant on horizontal decision-making systems such as liberal democracies. A perception well documented in corporate governance is that managers are most often unsupervised after ownership and control are separated. It happens then that in extreme cases (e.g., corporate crisis) the best managers are not in place and, even worse, they are not to be accountable. The same holds for politicians and public administrators. Inadequacy is obvious in extreme market conditions, and thus implementation of policy measures is not as effective as is prescribed by the traditional theory. Risk-taking behavior by civil servants is subject to the degree of severity of the economic environment.

Another line of reasoning could be the transition from an information-insensitive (i.e., before crisis) to an information-sensitive international banking environment (i.e., after crisis). The transition helps us understand why before the crisis trading partners were ill informed and why after the crisis they were scared and wanted to know so much more. A large literature (well analyzed by Richard Koo, 2011) describes how small shocks to one institution or to the economy may spread in the financial system with cross-exposure. Under those conditions one must ask what bilateral exposures are among various components of the system (Figures 7.3 and 7.4).

A common new expression in the literature related to regulatory evasion as well as with the opacity of the system is "too interconnected to fail"—a term explaining the severity of bilateral exposure in a common currency banking

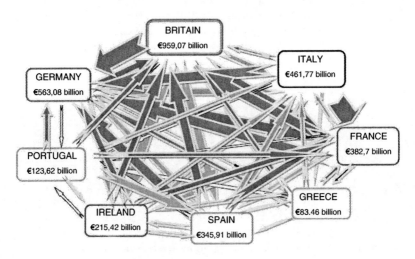

Figure 7.3 Too interconnected to fail

system. Unregulated institutions and countries are currently on rescue and monitoring programs, of course at the expense of taxpayers. Unfortunately, it is not for the first time in history (recall the rescue of LTCM). The EU very recently realized that the magnitude of a partial or global bailout for unregulated countries of the South was alarming. The European Union understood that during the pre-crisis these countries were unregulated and at the same time could avail themselves of access to a Euro zone safety net. They were allowed by "sophisticated" private lenders to borrow from other parties without being carefully monitored by them later. More importantly, both markets and regulators have little information about the consequences of "pulling the plug."

By now it is clear that bilateral exposure is motivated by the existence and use of decentralized information not held by a central banker or a global Euro zone regulator. The system should be protected from incidences of regulatory evasion by professionals, whether regulators or the banking industry. We should have known that an option to avoid the consequences of a financial shock was either to provide multi-government guarantees or to accept government bailouts. A well-protected multilateral exposure among common currency countries should really be about saying to each other: "I have information that makes me trust you and so I'm willing to accept the corresponding counterparty risk at least on the level of member countries."

The current crisis showed the existence of two problems: first was bilateral exposure and second was limited regulatory evasion, both being prerequisites in order to go forward and carefully issue a restructuring plan for long-term public debt. Then a new maturity structure for public debt may be carefully chosen ex-ante, and therefore ex-post variation in the market value of outstanding long-term debt may offset the unanticipated variations in the level of fiscal expenditures or the tax base. But such an optimal and forward-looking regulatory framework was far from existence in the EU before 2008.

The EU member countries and supranational institutions were therefore bound to navigate through excessive crisis events into non-optimal fiscal policy cases and non-optimal maturity structures for public debt. The analysis of public provision of liquidity, even in the presence of efficient international financial markets, is explained extensively in a recent book by B. Holmström and J. Tirole (2011).

The authors explain, from an economist's standpoint, how severe reductions on overall liquidity limit a government's ability to generate pledgeable income that is tradable in international financial markets. The paradigm is at its extreme edge when large and unexpected changes in economic activity call for drastic changes on pledgeable income. The market asks for specific actions, that is, cost reductions for public services, tax revenue increases, and a "fire sale" in public assets and rights in order to reduce imbalances and deplete the balance sheet of the public institution by triggering and facilitating strong deleveraging so as to avoid a cascade of defaults in the private sector. The actions demanded by the theory are fully in line with the policy suggested by IMF/EU Memorandum, initiative (memorandum 1, 2) for Greece.

Going beyond providing incentives for a more responsible administration, improving particular aspects of policy coordination without eliminating regulatory evasion produces bilateral exposure. Lee C. Bucheit and G. Mitu Gulati (2010) discuss "how the Eurozone officials could restructure Greece sovereign debt," during a time of global financial turmoil when fears for "systemic contagion" and need for a "mutual understanding" among institutions are preconditions for reforming and restabilizing the system.

Figure 7.4 reveals how sensitive the Euro zone financial system was during the crisis. In this context, policy makers tackled a legacy problem in the Euro zone banking sector, that is, massive recapitalizations of financial institutions in order to strengthen severity afflicted and opaque regulatory system. Officially the authorities proposed mutually agreed policy measures and induced forms of bailouts for all Euro zone periphery countries, resulting in serious bilateral support in the Euro zone, and avoiding, in many respects, spillover contaminations, as presented in Figure 7.5, and thus protecting efficiently the Euro zone's reputation.

In summary, this section has examined why Greece, contrary to a short-sighted view, was the best choice for support among other similar member countries. The choice reveals a common belief that the immediate monetary cost for the Euro zone system of a potential Greek default was not considered to be as large as with other members from the periphery. Significant uncertainties, however, in terms of Eurosystems, spillover contamination, policy decisions and emerging reputation evaluations about fiscal austerity programs moved the balance against Greek default, and in favor of collaborative and massive financial support.

7.3   Financial panics, cashflow inefficiencies and adverse selection in collateral markets: The case of Greece

The recent economic crisis was characterized by massive illiquidity. Unfortunately, liquidity constraints cannot easily be apprehended through a single statistic. In such an event, various markets—money, sovereign and corporate debt, securitization, collateralized debt obligations (CDOs) etc.—show danger signals. Investors run out of a variety of institutions. Authorities guaranteed a substantial fraction of the financial system. Markets closed for most illiquid entities at that time (from financial institutions to industrial companies to sovereign issuers) and finally illiquidity and all its corollaries appeared: markets freezes, fire sales and contagion. Insolvencies and bailouts became everyday phenomena. Massive injections

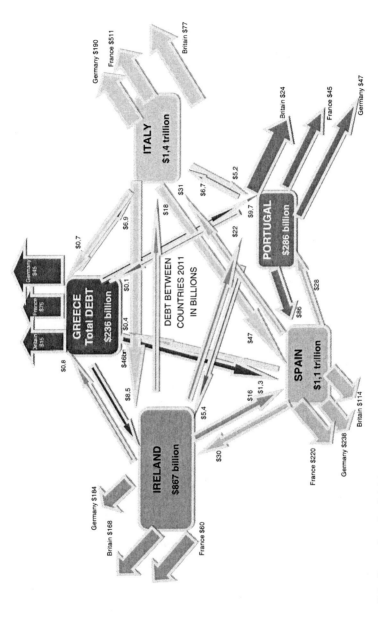

Figure 7.4 Europe's web of debt

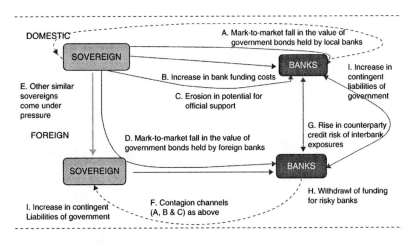

Figure 7.5   Spillovers and systemic contamination
Source: IMF.

of liquidity by both the Fed in the US and the Bank of England in the UK not only failed to prevent contractions in credit availability to the periphery, but also produced only minuscule increases in money supply.

The recent crisis unveiled the dire consequences of a maturity mismatch. The public bailout of the financial sector has taken many forms: in the US by the Federal Reserve (Quantitative Easing, rounds 1–3) and in Euro zone originally by the European Central Bank, next by the European Financial Stability Facility and in the near future most probably by ECB through an alternative of Q1 Fed policy. If asked to analyze this phenomenon, one may roughly deconstruct it into a monetary bailout combined with deleveraging and a fiscal prudency along with restructuring. The former consists in keeping extremely low short-run rates, as to allow institutions that depend on the wholesale market not to go under. The latter takes the form of recapitalization, liquidity support and asset repurchase.

It is the purpose of this section to explain why the twin-deficit reality grouped with an illiquid environment put Greece into an unlikely position. One may feel confident to support the argument that Greece is a typical event of a standard mechanism of a balance sheet-driven crisis—funding and margin spirals caused by and causing the fire sale of assets, a fight to quality and strategic hoarding of liquidity—all contributed to a large collapse on real activity. Politicians and authorities largely overlooked this systemic risk, or at least disregarded it (see also Koo, 2011).

Starting from a complete market model one knows that it views a panic as an exogenous tail event. It says nothing about how the panic may unfold since all contracts are made at the beginning of the crisis. Institutions ex-post are actually interdependent through cross exposure in interbank or derivatives markets. Liquidity is scarce when an ex-ante aggregate shock hits the market and there is no insurance (CDS) to cover it. Also in stages where liquidity is valuable (ex-post) but hard to define, insurance of any type (for example, CDS) is extremely expensive. Credit and liquidity rationing is a reality for both cases. The hypothesis that some agents foresaw the possibility of a collapse in Greek public debt financing is in doubt if we recall the fact that so few of them took action to face this possibility (out of the Euros 207 billion bailout facility only Euros 1.85 billion were paid in CDS). Either therefore they believed that the consequences would be relatively benign, or they deliberately gambled on the tail event.

In a simple form the setting of the model from an agent (such as a country) under a illiquidity shortage works as follows: formally the agent demands liquidity in anticipation of future financial needs either because it is cheaper to get financing now or because there is a risk that financing will not be available if it waits until the need for funding arises. A financial shock is the case when the agent (Figure 7.6) cannot get external funding unless it has arranged for such in advance. A credit rationing for such an event arises as in Figure 7.6. A common arrangement to guarantee that the agent will have enough resources at that time is the buying of insurance. CDSs allow agents to buy protection. Alternatively, the agent would either hoard liquidity or ask for internationally provided necessary funding.

There is a key difference between credit rationing at the initial financial stage and at the refinancing stage. In the latter case credit rationing can be

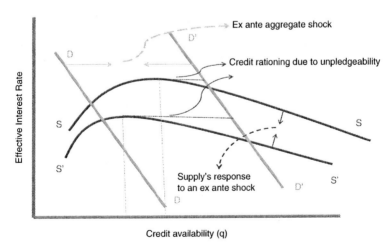

Figure 7.6 Financial panics, cashflow inefficiencies and adverse selection in the collateral markets

anticipated and therefore insured. The optimal design exhibits a trade-off between liquid and illiquid investments. The higher the insurance purchased by the agent in the form of illiquid backup the lower the investment is in illiquid assets. Put differently, the magnitude of a liquidity shock limits contracting possibilities for investment in real assets.

The role for the supra-national agent (e.g., IMF, EU) under these circumstances is to immediately redistribute wealth from taxpayers to the corporate sector, including the bailout of banks. For electoral reasons, governments in general prefer to avoid distortionary tax events resulting from unanticipated tax increases. The government could easily achieve a constant or in general non-anticipated tax change if it trades promises with the private sector or with the international financial markets that are conditional on the realization of future uncertainty. In reality, however, governments avoid that because the involved contingencies, that is, massive financial shocks, are hard to describe and verify. For that purpose in case government debt is only short-run, that is, completely independent of the realizations of shocks and uncertainties, the only feasible alternative is to raise both the tax rate and the level of public debt. Random variations in the budget should be offset by the government with appropriate adjustments in the tax rate. Increased taxation affects economic activity and a deflationary spiral results for the economy.

7.4   A few stylized facts about Greece: The twin deficit problem

Now having selected which questions to explore regarding the economic decision variables, as well as the options that theoretically were available at the time before the implementation period, it is time to turn to the data in order to incorporate specific country restrictions. Those restrictions describe the conditionality imposed by the facts on the economic system under consideration.

The main purpose of this section is to explain how important the twin deficit problem was during the implementation phase and why delays in the implementation of the economic measures requested by the international institutional partners of Greece proved to be critical for an unsuccessful result.

In an influential paper, two prominent economists, Carmen M. Reinhart and Kenneth S. Rogoff (2009), claimed that: "from 1800 until well after World War II Greece found itself virtually in a continuous default. Austria's record is in some ways even more stunning." From the same source and during the same period Greece is one of the few European countries that managed to succeed. For example, Greece increased its share in the world real GDP (1990 Geary–Khamis dollars) by 16% in a period of 77 years (1913–1990). In comparison during the same years the UK and Germany lost almost half of their share. Finally, and still in comparison with many other European countries far richer than Greece, Greece defaulted or rescheduled its sovereign debt from 1900 to 2010 only once (in 1932) when others did so between three and five times. Argentina, the reference point for Greece, did it five times (in 1951, 1956, 1982, 1989 and 2001). In most cases where Greece is described as defaulting (six in total), five occurred from 1821 to 1900.

It was claimed in the introduction of this chapter that Greece during the period of the global crisis was facing a twin deficit problem. Greece as a nation from 1990 onward was on an unsustainable fiscal path and because the economy enjoyed a growth rate at about 4% a year—double that in the Euro zone—Greece managed in the first place to increase its standard of living remarkably, but at the cost of a permanent deficit on international trade.

Starting from 1981, spending was rising and revenues were falling short, requiring the government to borrow huge sums each year to make up the difference. Greece is faced with staggering deficits. In 2011 public spending was expected to be nearly 30% of GDP, the value of all goods and services produced in the economy. Tax revenue stood at 23.5% of GDP and the budget deficit is just over 10%.

All peripheral countries benefited tremendously from the low interest rates and the financial stability brought about by the Euro. However, in the case of Greece the increase in the standard of living was twice as high as in the case of Spain and five times higher than in Portugal (see EU Commission, *Statistical Annex, European Economy*, Autumn 2010).

Tracing data from the longest period possible for the economy one can conclude that from 1880 to 2009 (see Reinhart and Rogoff, 2009) when the debt/GDP ratio was below 30%, the real growth rate of the economy was on average 4%. Respectively, between 30 and 60% it was 0.3%, between 60 and 90% it was 4.8% and finally from 90% it was 2.5%. Reasonably, therefore, we may claim that a strong relationship between the government debt/GDP ratio and economic growth is not supported by the data (Figure 7.7).

Assuming, therefore, that the next decade real interest rate will stay between 2 and 4%, Greece may drastically reduce its aggregate public debt as close as possible to 100% of GDP (that is, from Euros 350 billion to Euros 240 billion), with an average growth rate of 4%. Given that only 75% of a reduction in public debt is attributed to external lenders, we can readily associate the lower threshold of 90% to account for a portion of the actual reduction.

Historically, as we observe from Figure 7.7, at the beginning of 1970 the government was essentially breaking even. The deficit increased dramatically during the 1880s: in each year during that decade government expenditure exceeded revenue by an average 8.1% of GDP. Just before the international crisis Greek public borrowing was constantly below the Euro zone average, and while total spending was almost at the average level total revenues were lacking behind mainly due to widespread tax evasion.

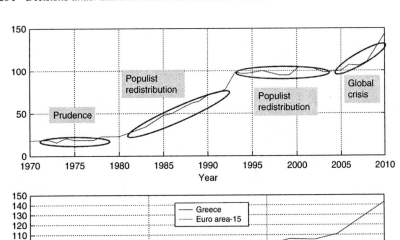

Figure 7.7   Total gross public debt as share of GDP (%)

On the basis of the data presented in Figure 7.8 one can make the following comments:

- During the period observed, total government spending as a share of GDP escalated from about 24% in the early 1970s to about 50%—catching up to the Euro area average—in the most recent years.
- Total tax revenues respectively increased from about 20 to 33%, remaining 10 percentage points below the Euro average.
- As a consequence of the above, the total government deficit was an ever-present feature of Greek public finance (the first out of two deficits). During the period considered its share skyrocketed from 20% in the early 1970s to 150% presently. During the 15 years to 2010 it was 35 to 67% higher than the Euro average. A remarkable feature of the deficit is that a substantial portion of it came from sources not included in the deficit (guarantees). Unlike other countries, 60% of it is held by foreigners.

On the revenue side the data are similar:

- Direct revenues as a share of GDP and effective tax rates on all types of income are substantially below the Euro average.
- Lower effective tax rates in Greece reflect the well-known tax evasion/ compliance and tax-collection problems. Whether the effective tax rates

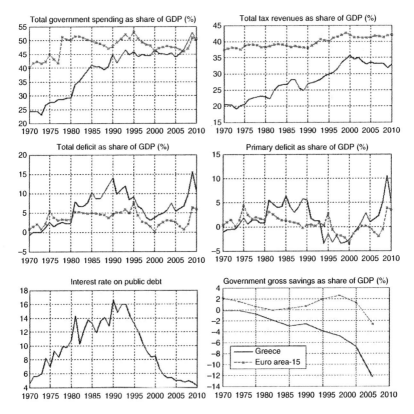

Figure 7.8 Twin deficit I: Public finances

will rise or fall depends on the progressivity of the tax rate system and the idiosyncratic characteristics of the system (see Figure 7.9).

Greece's external debt, defined as debt owed to foreigners, was 82.5% of GDP in 2009. In theory a country accumulates external debt when the government or the private sector borrows from foreign markets. Spanish banks were borrowing from foreign banks to give loans to Spanish citizens. In case of Greece the private sector did not. Savings of Greek citizens were enough to cover loans to the private sector. External borrowing was done by the government. Greece external debt essentially coincided with its external public debt.

These observations, however, present only a partial picture of the past financial landscape for Greece, particularly for private debt and for the years immediately following the crisis. Fortunately, private debt, in contrast to public, tends to shrink sharply for an extended period after any financial

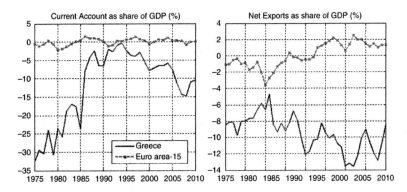

Figure 7.9   Twin deficit II: External trade

crisis. Just as rapid expansion in private credit fuels the boom phase of the cycle, so does serious deleveraging exacerbate the post-crisis downturn.

Finally, in order to explain the next deficit problem, that is, the current account of the balance of payments, a deficit that results from the low competitiveness of production and a systemic bureaucratic environment, it is necessary also to remember that during the same period:

- Inflation continued to be higher in Greece than in the Euro area even after entry to the EMU.
- Real effective exchange rates increased faster in Greece than in the Euro.
- Likewise unit labor cost, primarily in state-controlled and heavily unionized industries (energy, transportation, utilities), is higher in Greece. In regression the unit labor cost has a very strong negative effect on total factor productivity, a major obstacle to current and future competitiveness (Figure 7.10).

To summarize the current conditions in Greek public debt, drawing information from existing historical data, we should conclude that a sharp run-up in public sector debt proved one of the most enduring legacies of the 2007–10 financial crisis in Greece, but was not the cause of the crisis. As was expected from findings across both advanced and emerging markets, high debt/GDP ratio (+90%) is associated with notably lower growth rates. Any attempt therefore to stimulate the economy with traditional methods (of a Keynesian type) is unrealistic. Debt intolerance, at these levels, pushes risk premia up sharply and credit rationing will restrict growth potential.

The overall effect from the increased financial friction was to shift the economy into a lower capital mode. In order to finance the "twin deficits" Greece was obliged to compete in an after-crisis financial market with rising credit spreads and buyers "flying to quality". The Greek private and

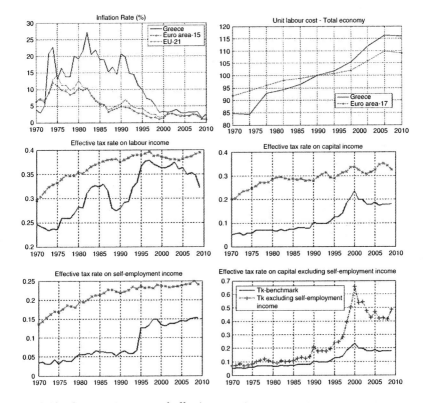

Figure 7.10 Competitiveness and effective tax rates

public borrowing options were closed. Investors suddenly started to express interest for high-quality debt versus lower-quality claims, and asset pricing through adverse selection or the "lemons model" became the reality for the economy.

7.5 To stimulate or not to stimulate?

Under these circumstances and in order to reduce the risk of a protracted economic "balance-sheet recession" it would be right to stimulate aggregate demand. How does a government face those challenges?

The reasonable approach for the authorities is to find ways of doing this without risking a loss of confidence in government debt. Bondholders should realize that the government policies are not designed to accumulate further public liabilities. Essentially bondholders look for actions that reassure them on this account. According to the economic theory of signaling an action by a "good type" it is revealing if a "bad type" would not prepare to imitate it. Government cannot base its reputation only on announcements of objectives, on what it says. Therefore in order to avoid that markets interpret a stimulus as a lack of resolve, a resolute government must be different from a weak one. This can be done only by designing a stimulus package, which despite increased spending may be unpopular.

A stimulus package designed to increase bondholders' confidence must involve cutting off popular but financially toxic expenditures.

How can Greece avoid fears of insolvency under a "good" stimulus package? Insolvency is not determined by the size of gross liabilities but by the balance sheet: liabilities relative to assets and not by inadequacies on cash flow. A deleveraged decrease in liabilities by a smaller increase in assets as well as the sale of non-performing or unpledgeable public assets (private rent-seeking returns, the underground economy, rights etc.) reduces the risk of insolvency and makes the bondholders happy.

The reforms that Greece has agreed on with its lenders (EU/IMF) aim at enabling it to repay its debt. A proportion of the existing reforms are expected to contribute to the goal by improving the government's finances. Others aim to raise competitiveness and growth. All of them are in parallel with the idea discussed previously, resulting in a debt maturity restructuring in order to shield debt servicing from unanticipated financial shocks.

Many of the Greek reforms are necessary and long overdue. A reason for this is that much of the debate, however, has focused on the short-run management of the crisis. Will Greece be able to repay its debt, or will it have to restructure, and if so under what terms? Will Greece exit from Euro? Will the European Union and the ECB decide to offer further assistance to Greece? Discussions of these issues are pointless. If reforms are not undertaken, Greece is bound to default. Moreover reforms are necessary not only for repaying the debt but also for long-run growth and prosperity. Even if Greece's debt were to magically disappear overnight, the same reforms would be needed.

All of the reforms suggested by the EU/IMF have been discussed before either by professionals or by international institutions (e.g., the OECD). But successive Greek governments have chosen to ignore the debate until they were forced into it by the crisis. That was either the result of lack of vision and courage, because of vested interest in the status quo or finally through lack of understanding of the economic realities. The populism and lack of leadership of the past must be replaced by political courage guided by the principles of modern economics.

Let us put aside any discussion about defaulting on the public debt and focus instead on the assumption that Greece will aim to fully repay its debt. Repaying the debt requires both that the government will stop running a primary deficit by not creating a new burden, and will reduce outstanding public debt.

How much of a primary surplus is needed? If the primary surplus is equal to the interest payments on debt the deficit will be zero and the debt will remain constant. While a primary surplus is effective to reduce debt, even a zero or slightly positive deficit can suffice. This is because the relevant quantity is not the level of debt but the debt/GDP ratio. If Greece's GDP doubled overnight, without any change in public debt, Greece would have a much smaller debt problem. Therefore, quick growth rates over the next decade drastically change the confidence burden for the economy.

The path for reform in order to improve productivity and competitiveness is the only solution to the problem. Nothing here is new. Running primary surpluses for the state budget, unbundling the restrictions and inefficiencies in the governance of the system by providing new institutional frameworks, increasing public sector productivity and effectiveness through cost reductions and rent-seeking activities, and finally implementing a "big" asset fire sale program in the form of privatization and rights transfer easily can reposition Greece in the financial market. Markets were not conspiring against Greece. They were merely reflecting economic realities well by protecting the interests of those who had lent their savings to Greece. The memorandum approach for all those issues is the right solution. At the same time, it is important to go even beyond these short-run reforms and think more on how to raise the growth rate in Greece in the long run.

Most of the economists in Greece currently believe that the reforms that Greece has agreed on with its lenders do not focus on the long run. Concerns on tax evasion, fighting corruption in the public sector, real reforms on social security and in the educational system are probably a few of the most important and critical.

In order to increase productivity in the public sector, Greece should engage in the extensive use of broad incentives on performance. Good performers are rewarded with higher salaries and better promotion opportunities.

The reason why productivity is low in the public sector is related to corruption. Some of the money allocated to public service provisions is diverted, and corruption also taxes citizens and firms more directly since they must bribe corrupt public servants to be served efficiently by them. According to recent research directed by the Bank of Greece (Angelopoulos et al., 2010), the annual cost of rent-seeking activities by public servants is estimated at 9% of GDP. Corruption is deeply engrained in the Greek economy and cannot be eradicated. But, as with tax evasion, one of the main reasons why corruption is deeply engrained is that not enough incentives are in place to discourage it.

7.6 Concluding notes

Liquidity mismatches and the overreliance on wholesale funding were at the core of failures and rescues in the recent crisis. Microeconomists interested in financial regulation can no longer ignore macroeconomic factors leading to market freezes. Greece stands as a typical example as well as a very interesting test to explore extreme case phenomena.

We have learned from this experience that moral hazard is a phenomenon flourishing in affluent economies and lax liquidity environments. Under those circumstances, ex-ante prudential regulation cannot protect the system from a strong ex-post deleveraging environment. From the current crisis we have realized that an important regulatory issue is whether one should append a liquidity measure to the solvency one. Put differently, a valid question is whether we can trust the institutions to properly manage their liquidity once excess leverage has been controlled by the solvency requirement.

Monitoring financial markets and global liquidity is not as easy as it was originally thought. We are far from understanding the analysis of multi-country collaboration and confrontation. However, a realistic approach demands that all sides collaborate at the final stage in order to avoid cross-country spillovers and financial contamination.

International bailouts as an issue *per se* in and for any financial system raise serious questions. But before addressing them, one should consider the different objections raised in the past for various international regulatory and monitoring framework initiatives (starting from Basel I, II and ending in the most recent Frank–Dodd). Realistically, world financial markets are still dominated by home-based regulations, which, up to now, are mutually incompatible.

Dealing therefore with problems of illiquidity and sovereign insolvency in order to capture a tractable insight one must use models with infinite horizons. Such models are not available as of now. As an alternative, in the short run, it is time to utilize cooperative understanding in order to safely navigate through shallow waters. In the long run one must properly undertake micro-monitoring for strong currencies on highly diversified economic structures before a permanent solution on maturity mismatching of sovereign debt can be found.

Finally, we still need a theory capable of providing a good understanding of the interconnections between corporate and public finance. Presently regulators and rating agencies focus on monitoring the quantity of liquidity, ignoring to a large extent the qualitative aspect of liquidity. But dealing with public insolvency is mostly qualitative and only partially a quantitative issue. Corporate finance is not of great help in this context. The bottom line is that monetary and fiscal bailouts are different in their workings. And efforts towards a common objective of restoring institutions' liquidity and solvency position should be conceived separately.

8
Quo Vadis Global Financial Governance?

André Baladi

8.1 Introduction

The title of this chapter alludes to the uncertainties of making reliable predictions for the governance of the global financial system. It stems from the thesis that global corporate governance endeavors could by osmosis influence global financial governance.

While the corporate governance concept exclusively concerns corporations, the relatively new "financial governance" terminology concerns the management of national economies in general. Could national economic administrations occasionally mirror the constraints of corporate management?

The European Commissioner for Internal Market and Services, Michel Barnier, now recommends developing EU proposals that could enhance national corporate laws with corporate governance principles. Corporate governance concerns have prevailed for a quarter of a century among major global institutional investors. They focused mostly on ensuring adequate long-term corporate returns for investors, via banks, insurance groups and particularly pension funds.

Certain corporations risk collapse sooner or later, if they do not balance their books, carry out adequate market research for their new products, or, even worse, cheat by hiding their losses. Moreover, corporations are encouraged to benchmark their corporate development objectives according to their "peer groups" (whether in the food or pharmaceutical industries, mining, etc.). They are also called upon to balance their accounts according to the International Financial Reporting Standards (IFRS) of the International Accounting Standards Board (IASB), or to the US Generally Accepted Accounting Principles (GAAP) of the Financial Accounting Standards Board (FASB); adopt the democratic "one share, one vote" principle; dissociate the chair and chief executive functions; refrain from hiding their losses or artificially inflating their incomes, so as to avoid the risk of being sued by their shareholders through securities class actions; ensure managerial accountability; avoid increasing the remuneration of their senior executives when their company underperforms; adopt corporate citizenship codes, and so on.

Economists who are concerned by the recent reiterated major financial crises could be inspired by the governance endeavors that have been carried out for two decades in the corporate world, so as to achieve adequate national financial reporting and budgetary equilibrium. Both the global financial crisis of 2007–8, often labeled "the subprime crisis," and the "sovereign debt crisis" of 2009–12, are considered to have significantly enhanced the importance of corporate governance throughout the financial arena.

This chapter reviews a quarter-century of global corporate governance developments, impacted by the questionable behavior of certain high-frequency traders and/or executives at several banks, corporations and credit rating agencies throughout 2009–12.

8.2   National economic governance dilemmas

Renowned economists around the world continuously express their views on how to resolve the current global economic crisis. For example, the 80-year-old debate between the disciples of John Maynard Keynes and those of Friederich von Hayek still continues today. British journalist and writer Nicholas Wapshott (in his interesting *Keynes–Hayek: The Clash that Defined Modern Economics*, W. W. Norton, October 2011) highlights the fact that, while the interventionist theories of Keynes appeared to be correct at a specific time (at least so as to delay the Second World War in Europe), the liberal theories of Hayek (inspired by the Austrian School led by Ludwig von Mises) appear to be gaining favor now.

A few economists recommend the reduction of national budget expenditures (which currently reach exceptionally high levels—for example, 40% in Germany and even 47% of GDP in France), after decades of budgetary profligacy. Could we then consider national economies as mirroring somewhat the characteristics of large multinational corporations? Actually, the latter are also progressively adopting corporate citizenship codes that emphasize social and environmental oversight criteria, thus replicating national economic criteria.

8.3   What is the global impact of corporate governance?

The gradual adoption of adequate corporate governance practices by major institutional investors and corporations could not prevent the S&P 500 drop of 49% in 2000–2, its 39% drop in 2008, and its wild gyrations since 2009.

Are stock market boom-and-bust situations (such as the 1609 losses of the Dutch East India Company in Amsterdam; the "Mississippi Bubble," which led to the 1720 collapse of the Banque Royale founded by John Law in France; the

1825 UK and 1836 US panics; the 1873 Vienna stock market crash; the 1907 US stock market crash; the 1929 Black Friday stock market crash on Wall Street; the 1987 Black Monday US stock market crash; the 2001–4 downfalls of Enron, Parmalat and World Com; or the bankruptcy in 2008 of Lehman Brothers) likely to occur at ever shorter intervals ?

Could long-term oriented investors (pension funds, insurance companies and high-net-worth investors such as Warren Buffet) be ultimately affected by split-second speculative swings by certain bankers or by mathematical wizards managing hedge funds? Shall we witness the return of high-frequency trading, collateralized debt obligations (CDOs) or credit default swaps (CDS), labeled by Warren Buffet as "weapons of mass destruction"?

8.4 Pension funds

Major pension funds have played a significant role for the development of global corporate governance.

The first pension funds were probably those set up in the Middle Ages by mining operations in Central Europe. Their concept was then expanded and diversified by the first German Chancellor, Prince Otto von Bismarck. The oldest pension fund still operational today, with up-to-date features, is the Caisse des Dépôts et Consignations (CDC), a sovereign wealth fund (SWF) founded 200 years ago in Paris.

Major modern global pension funds were only developed a quarter of a century ago, mostly in Anglo-Saxon and European countries (e.g., CalPERS, CalSTERS, New York City Pensions, and TIAA-CREF in the US; APG and PGGM in Holland; Hermes Pensions in the UK; Norwegian State Pensions; Pensionskasse Stadt Zürich in Switzerland), as well as worldwide, for instance Japan's Government Pension Investment Fund (considered to be the largest in the world).

Pension funds are reported to hold about 40% of major stock indexes (CAC 40, FTSE 100, S&P 500, etc.). As long-term oriented investors, via indexed funds invested in corporations all around the world, they try to avoid short-term speculations. Moreover, endowments of US universities (Harvard, Stanford, Yale, and also much smaller academies) often manage sizable assets. This pattern is developing in many other countries.

The corporate governance activism of these investors is clearly aimed at enhancing long-term shareholder values.

8.5 Foundation of the corporate governance movement

The foundation in 1985 of International Shareholder Services (ISS) by Robert (Bob) A. G. Monks, in Washington, DC, contributed to the birth of the global corporate governance movement. It coincided with the foundation of both the Council of Institutional Investors (CII) and the Investor Responsibility

Research Center (IRRC) in Washington, and preceded the interventions of Sir Adrian Cadbury on behalf of UK shareholders and the corporate governance board counseling of Ira Millstein at Bethlehem Steel, the Ford Foundation, General Motors, Walt Disney, etc.

Since its foundation, ISS has focused on enhancing the interests of shareholders, by encouraging leading US pension funds, as well as corporate board directors and executives, to adopt a wide range of adequate corporate governance principles. It intervened at American Express, Avon, Borden, Eastman Kodak, Exxon, Sears, Shearson Lehman Hutton, Texaco, Waste Management, Westinghouse, etc.

8.6   The main global corporate governance organizations

Over a hundred corporate governance-concerned organizations have been founded worldwide during the past two decades. The most important ones (with which the author has been closely involved for several years) can be classified as follows.

8.6.1   Governmental organizations

OECD

The Organization for Economic Cooperation and Development invited Sir Adrian Cadbury (author of the 1992 Cadbury Report of best practice, which served as a basis for reform of corporate governance in the UK and worldwide), the renowned US attorney Ira Millstein (who later founded the Millstein Center for Corporate Governance at Yale University), as well as several representatives from the International Corporate Governance Network (ICGN), including the author, to meetings at the OECD headquarters in Paris. This group set up a task force to develop and adopt the first OECD Corporate Governance Code in 1999. This Code was updated in 2004, and highlighted the following topics:

– **Basis for an Effective Corporate Governance Framework**
   The corporate governance framework should promote transparent and efficient markets, be consistent with the rule of law and clearly articulate the division of responsibilities between different supervisory, regulatory and enforcement authorities
– Rights of Shareholders and Key Ownership Functions
   The corporate governance framework should protect and facilitate the exercise of shareholders' rights, for instance:
   • secure methods of ownership registration;
   • participate and vote at general shareholder meetings;
   • elect and remove Board members, and share in the profits of the corporation;

- participate in, and be sufficiently informed on, decisions concerning fundamental corporate changes such as extraordinary transactions, including the transfer of all or substantially all assets, which in effect result in the sale of the company.
- **Equitable Treatment of Shareholders**
  The corporate governance framework should ensure the equitable treatment of all shareholders, including minority and foreign shareholders. All shareholders should have the opportunity to secure effective redress for violation of their rights.
- **Role of Stakeholders in Corporate Governance**
  The corporate governance framework should recognize the rights of stakeholders established by law or through mutual agreements, and encourage active cooperation between corporations and stakeholders in creating wealth, jobs and the sustainability of financially sound companies.
- **Disclosure and Transparency**
  The corporate governance framework should ensure that timely and accurate disclosure is made on all material matters regarding the corporation, including its financial situation, its corporate objectives, its performance, its ownership and the governance of the company.
- **Responsibility of the Board**
  The corporate governance framework should ensure the strategic guidance of the company, the effective monitoring of management by the Board, and the Board's accountability to the company and its shareholders.

  Board members should act on a fully informed basis, in good faith, with due diligence and care, and in the best interest of the company and its shareholders.

  Where Board decisions may affect different shareholder groups differently, the Board should treat all shareholders fairly.

  Boards should consider assigning a sufficient number of non-executive Board members capable of exercising independent judgment to tasks where there is a potential for conflict of interest.

  Board members should be able to commit themselves effectively to their responsibilities. Multiple Board memberships by the same person should be compatible with effective Board performance.

UNCTAD–ISAR

UNCTAD's Intergovernmental Working Group of Experts on International Standards of Accounting and Reporting (ISAR), in which the author participated for a decade in Geneva, is another major governmental organization involved in corporate governance.

UNCTAD–ISAR Reports aim to assist corporations in the preparation of corporate governance disclosures that address the major concerns of investors and other stakeholders worldwide.

The "Guidance on Good Practices in Corporate Governance Disclosure" was published in June 2006 (UNCTAD/ITE/TEB/2006/3), and the "Guidance on Corporate Responsibility Indicators in Annual Reports" in February 2008 (UNCTAD/ITE/TEB/2007/6).

UNCTAD also organizes corporate governance disclosure conferences in Geneva and around the world—for *example,* in *Brazil,* Dubai, Egypt, Morocco, Qatar, etc.

The World Bank–IFC

Last but not least, the International Finance Corporation (IFC), of the World Bank in Washington DC, organizes conferences throughout the world through its Global Corporate Governance Forum (in which the author participates), and publishes extensive reports such as the 500-page "Resolving Corporate Governance Disputes—Toolkit 4" of 2011.

8.6.2 Corporations

Major global corporations delegate representatives to several international financial and corporate governance conferences around the world. However, the main organizations representing corporations—such as the International Chamber of Commerce (ICC) and the World Economic Forum (WEF)—do not yet appear to have contributed significantly to the development of corporate governance principles.

8.6.3 Institutional investors

The US Council of Institutional Investors (CII) and the International Corporate Governance Network (ICGN) are the two major organizations representing institutional investors considered to be the leading global corporate governance monitoring organizations. Together, they bring together investors reported to hold worldwide stock securities assets amounting to some US$18 trillion.

The CII was founded in 1954 in Washington, DC, by investors reported to hold stock securities of over $3 trillion. It has "General Members" (more than 500 representatives, mainly from major North American pension funds), "Educational Sustainers", and a few "Honorary International Participants" (the author was nominated the first such representative two decades ago).

The CII edits several publications and reports. Moreover, it played a significant role in 1995 in the foundation in Washington, DC of the ICGN (see bellow).

8.7 International Corporate Governance Network (ICGN)

8.7.1 Historical profile

The ICGN is reported to be the premier global financial network, with members and participants reported to hold equity assets of some US$15 trillion. It aims at facilitating fruitful contacts, interventions and publications so as to promote adequate governance practices around the world.

The ICGN is a non-governmental and not-for-profit organization, which coordinates bankers and other asset managers, pension fund trustees, insurers, shareholder associations, investment clubs, governance experts, shareholder advocates, attorneys, auditors, proxy firms, corporate executives, stock exchange and regulatory officials.

The ICGN was founded in 1995 by leading institutional investors and corporate governance professionals. It has held annual conferences in: 1995 in Washington, DC, sponsored by the Council of Institutional Investors; 1996 in London, sponsored by the Corporation of the City of London; 1997 in Paris, sponsored by Paris Bourse; 1998 in San Francisco, sponsored by the California Public Retirement System (CalPERS); 1999 in Frankfurt, sponsored by the Deutsche Börse; 2000 in New York City, sponsored by TIAA-CREF, the New York Stock Exchange (NYSE) and NASDAQ; 2001 in Tokyo, sponsored by the Tokyo Stock Exchange; 2002 in Milan, sponsored by Borsa Italiana; 2003 in Amsterdam, sponsored by the Euronext Exchange; 2004 in Rio de Janeiro, sponsored by Bovespa; 2005 in London, sponsored by the London Stock Exchange; 2006 in Washington, DC, hosted by the US Council of Institutional Investors; 2007 in Cape Town, hosted by the Johannesburg Stock Exchange; 2008 in Seoul, hosted by the KRX Exchange; 2009 in Sydney, hosted by the Australian Superannuation Investors and Trustees; 2010 in Toronto, hosted by the Canadian Coalition for Good Governance with the Ontario Teachers' Pension Plan; and 2011 in Paris, hosted by Paris Europlace. The 2012 annual conference (at the time of writing) will be held on June 25–27 in Rio de Janeiro.

Spring and Fall meetings have also been held in France, India, Malaysia, the Netherlands, Sweden, the UK and the US.

The year-round activities of the ICGN are carried out by its various committees, including Accounting and Auditing, Awards, Board Nominations, Business Ethics, Corporate Governance Principles, Cross Border Voting Practices, Executive Remuneration, Non-Financial Disclosure, Securities Lending, etc.

The candidacy of Richard Bennett (CEO of Governance Metrics International, GMI) to replace Senator Olympia Snowe at the US Congress is considered a major breakthrough by the US corporate governance community, as he would become the first professional corporate governance congressman. He previously served as President of the Maine Senate, and was associated for many years with ISS founder Robert (Bob) Monks.

8.7.2   Main ICGN corporate governance principles

Corporate objectives
  - Optimize long-term growth benchmarked vs equity peer group, while also considering financial and shareholder return ratios.

Voting rights
- Uphold the "One Share, One Vote" principle throughout the world.

Disclosure and transparency
- Corporations should disclose all relevant material information on a timely basis.
- Corporations should disclose their systems of governance and whether they comply with a governance code.

Corporate boards
- Split chair and CEO functions.
- Majority of independent directors.
- No reciprocal cross-appointment of directors.

Executive remuneration
- Avoid guaranteed high remunerations.
- Align the financial interests of managers with those of shareholders.

Implementation of strategic corporate focus
- Major strategic core business shifts should be made with prior shareholder approval.
- Shareholders should be allowed sufficient time for their evaluations, before exercising their voting rights.

Peer group benchmarking
- Corporations should strive to excel in specific sector peer group benchmarking comparisons, regarding their respective financial and shareholder return ratios.

Accounting and auditing
- External auditors should be proposed by the Audit Committee of the Board, for approval by shareholders.
- Non-audit fees should be approved by the Audit Committee and disclosed in the Annual Report.
- A single global accounting standard should be developed.

Corporate citizenship
- Impact of Al Gore's global warming campaigns.
- Corporate citizenship codes—for example, OECD Anti-Bribery Code, Social Accountability SA 8000, Environmental Certification ISO 14000, and UN Responsible Investments Global Compact.

Corporate governance implementation
- Corporate governance disputes should preferably be addressed through dialogue, negotiation or arbitration, before resorting to class actions.
- Shareholders should have the right to sponsor resolutions or convene extraordinary meetings.

Additional information is available on: www.icgn.org

8.8   Rating agencies

8.8.1   Credit rating agencies

Fitch, Moody's and Standard & Poor's in the US have been criticized for not having adequately monitored the uncontrolled development of high-frequency trading with CDOs, CDs, etc. They are also criticized for being remunerated by the very institutions that they rate.

These credit rating agencies now also have to face new competitors (such as Dagong Global Credit Rating in China), which are not affected by such conflict of interest. Moreover, several US institutions (such as the House Financial Services Committee, the National Association of Insurance Commissioners, and the Securities Exchange Commission) now require credit rating agencies to implement additional professional investigations.

8.8.2   Governance rating agencies

These agencies strive to protect the long-term interests of pension funds and other major institutional investors. The most important worldwide are: Corporate Library with Governance Metrics International, ECGS (DSW, Ethos, PIRC, Proxinvest, etc.), Egan Jones, Glass Lewis, ISS (MSCI), Proxy Governance with Manifest, RiskMetrics Group, and Vigeo Group.

8.9   Financial dispute settlements

Over the past 400 years, international shareholder dispute settlements have been usually resolved via court litigation, and sometimes through arbitration or mediation. Securities class actions were developed recently, first in the US and now globally.

8.9.1   Arbitration of international financial disputes

The origins of arbitration probably date back to traditional dispute settlements prevailing before customs, rules and laws were established by ancient civilizations preceding Roman Law. In England, the earliest law dedicated to national arbitration was recorded in 1697. The French Revolution's first Constitution proclaimed in 1791, under Chapter V, Article 5, the right of all citizens to resort to arbitration in solving any dispute.

In 1919, the world's business community established the International Chamber of Commerce (ICC), which became a driving force for the promotion of both arbitration as a mechanism to resolve international commercial or financial disputes, and the need for international regulations to uphold and support the arbitration process.

International arbitration was first codified in the 1923 Geneva Protocol of the League of Nations, which was updated in the 1927 Geneva Convention on Foreign Arbitral Awards. In 1958, the New York Convention on the Recognition and Enforcement of Foreign Arbitral Awards (which replaced both the Geneva Protocol and the Geneva Convention) was established and became the cornerstone of international commercial and financial arbitration rules.

Today, the major arbitration organizations are the:

– London Court of International Arbitration
– Stockholm Chamber of Commerce
– International Chamber of Commerce in Paris
– American Arbitration Association
– China International Trade Arbitration Commission
– Hong Kong International Arbitration Center
– Singapore International Arbitration Center
– International Arbitration Organization (ARICI) in Geneva [co-founded by the author, which is likely to merge with the Geneva Chamber of Commerce Department of arbitration and mediation services]
– United Nations Commission on International Trade Law (UNCITRAL), which developed in 1970 Rules to cover all aspects of the international arbitration process

8.9.2   Shareholder securities class actions

The first recorded major shareholder dispute settlement was the Dutch East India Company litigation submitted to the Court in Amsterdam in 1609. This positioned Amsterdam early on as a leading global forum in this field.

Securities class actions were initially developed over 15 years ago in the US. They currently involve about three dozen law firms, for settlements estimated to amount to some $20 billion per annum in the US.

Securities class action settlements are now expanding from the US to Europe—for example, the Royal Ahold NV/US $1.1 billion settlement of 2004–6, or the current SCOR–Zurich Financial Services (ZFS), successive US–European Converium Insurance settlements totaling $143 million, of which the author chairs the pan-European settlement at The Hague (with Tal Schibler, at Schibler Hovagemyan in Geneva, as Secretary and Bart Groen, Deputy Judge at The Hague Court of Appeals and Dutch Arbitration Institute Arbitrator, as Treasurer). The US class action was approved in 2008 by the Southern District of New York, and the European class action on January 17, 2012 by the Amsterdam Court of Appeals.

This Converium class action involves several US and European administration and auditing settlement organizations (such as Bureau de Jong & Osborne at The Hague, Garden City Group at Melville, New York, and Mazars, formerly Paardekooper Hoffman, in Rotterdam), with half-a-dozen major US and European law firms (Spector Roseman Kodroff & Willis in Philadelphia, Bernstein Litowitz Berger & Grossmann in New York, Cohen Milstein in Washington, DC, Pels Rijcken & Droogleever Fortuijn in The Hague, Lemstra Van der Korst in Amsterdam, and Schibler Hovagemyan in Geneva).

These successive US–European Converium settlements were based on the June 2010 ruling of the US Supreme Court, which stated that the right to sue hinges on the location of the fraud, thus allowing the settlement resolution to be awarded first in the US and then in Europe. This ruling was largely based on the Morrison v. National Australia Bank case, which changed the landscape for investors worldwide, as it focuses on the locations where securities were purchased and sold.

This seminal Morrison v. National Australia Bank case has been referred to in professional reviews and reports (such as the March 2011 Quinn Emmanuel Business Litigation Report, or the March/April 2010 Pomerantz Monitor), and also in major news media (such as the April 21, 2010 European edition of *The Wall Street Journal* or *Time Magazine* of May 2010).

8.10   Sovereign Wealth Funds (SWFs)

These funds are currently considered to manage $5 trillion and are likely to exceed $10 (or even 15) trillion by 2015. Over half of them are based in major oil and gas producing countries—for example, Abu Dhabi Investment Authority (ADIA), Chinese Funds, Norwegian Pensions, Qatari Funds, Russian Funds, etc.

The Norwegian Pension Fund has been the most active SWF for a decade in promoting adequate governance principles.

8.11   Business ethics

In 2007, the ICGN set up a Working Group on Anti-Corruption Practices, which evolved in 2010 into a Business Ethics Committee. It was founded, and is still chaired, by George Dallas, Corporate Governance Director of F&C Management Ltd in London.

This ICGN Ethics Committee encourages companies to communicate openly on their anti-corruption policies and practices. According to Transparency International, the leading civil society organization in this field, "corruption is operationally defined as the misuse of entrusted power to private gain." This includes "private-to-public" corruption (where a private commercial party may bribe a public official so as to secure government business), as well as "private-to-private" corruption (where the commercial party offers an inducement to another, who has the decision-making authority to award a business deal opportunity).

In 2011, the US Securities Exchange Commission, the EU Competitiveness Council, and Transparency International joined forces to limit the reliance on corruption to secure important contracts. Certain major companies, like

Shell, are attempting to dilute such anti-corruption rules, which could affect their business in some countries.

8.12   Tax evasion

The main offshore financial centers, which were said to facilitate tax evasion, held assets approaching $6 trillion, according to a comprehensive article on "Tax Havens" in the December 1, 2008 issue of the *Financial Times*. This article mentions that these offshore financial centers include (in alphabetical order):

- The Cayman Islands, home to several global hedge funds
- Bermuda, a renowned leading global insurance center
- The British Virgin Islands, an important hub for offshore companies
- Guernsey, Europe's captive insurance domicile
- Jersey, mostly focused on fund management
- Lichtenstein, with concessions to secrecy after the LGT bank scandal
- Monaco, dubbed by the OECD as an uncooperative tax haven
- Panama, reported to operate strict bank secrecy procedures
- Singapore, a leading world financial center, considered as uncooperative and slow in answering requests by foreign law enforcement authorities
- Switzerland, where foreign assets make up to 35% of bank balance sheets
- Turks and Caicos Islands, mostly handling trust business

Delaware and the UK could also be considered as financial centers for facilitating tax evasion. However, Switzerland is currently considered by some to be the most important "tax haven."

This topic has been covered profusely in financial media, books and reports, such as in the Vanderbilt University Law School Ph.D. thesis of Niels Jensen, entitled "How to Kill the Scapegoat: Addressing Offshore Tax Evasion With a Special View to Switzerland."

The first major attempt to resolve Swiss banking secrecy issues with the US was probably the $780 million settlement negotiated in 2009 by US Secretary of State Hillary Clinton and then Swiss Foreign Minister (also twice President of the Swiss Confederation) Micheline Calmy-Rey. However, since the January 10, 2012 indictment of the oldest Swiss bank, Wegelin & Co., the banking relationships of the US authorities with Switzerland appear to be drifting toward uncharted territories. A similar pattern is also affecting the relationship of Switzerland with several EU countries.

Several Swiss banks (such as the Zurich Cantonal Bank or Raffeisen Bank) are now reported to have decided to refrain from dealing with US-based clients and even US citizens in general wherever they reside.

A so-called RUBIK approach, actively promoted since 2011 by the President of the Swiss Bankers Association, would allow payment of taxes by Swiss bank clients, through a fixed amount corresponding, for instance, to about 25% of their total assets, without revealing their names. However, this RUBIK formula might fail to ensure the participation of fiscal authorities in both the EU and the US before its announced 2013 implementation date.

8.13 Conclusion: Quo Vadis Global Financial Governance?

8.13.1 Reforming the banking sector

Reforms are required in the banking sector, to avoid repetitive financial breakdowns.

High-frequency trading, practised by "quant" professionals, is criticized by conservative investors. And the SEC fined Goldman Sachs a record $500 million for incomplete information in marketing the Abacus Fund.

Will the US Congress approve the Volcker Rule prohibiting banks from gambling with taxpayers' money?

Should the Glass-Steagall Act of 1933 (which established a firewall between commercial and investment banking until its repeal in 1999) be reconsidered? A great many corporate governance experts think so. However, such daring backtracking might be difficult to implement.

8.13.2 Promoting democratic governance principles

Efforts are required regarding the democratic "one share, one vote" tenet, which is less observed throughout the EU than in the US. The same goes for the equal treatment of all shareholders in cases of corporate mergers and acquisitions.

8.13.3 A single global corporate governance code?

Shouldn't there be a single global corporate governance code, instead of the approximately 200 national codes promulgated around the world? Are there justifications for having so many different strategic corporate objectives and peer group benchmarks, voting right tenets, corporate board structures, accounting disclosure standards, executive remuneration criteria or corporate citizenship norms? The CII, the ICGN, the OECD and the ICC could contribute to the formulation of such a code (published in the six official UN languages), thus mirroring somewhat the achievement of the 1948 Universal Declaration of Human Rights.

8.13.4 A single global accounting system?

Since the foundation of modern accounting by Fra' Luca Pacioli in his *Summa de arithmetica, geometria, proportioni e proportionalità* in 1494, the world has had to cope with several accounting systems, which have now been condensed to two: the International Financial Reporting Standards (IFRS) of the London-based International Accounting Standards Board (IASB), and the US Generally Accepted Accounting Principles (GAAP) of the Financial Accounting Standards Board (FASB). Although the author participated over the last decade in two dozen IFRS-focused sessions of the IASB in both London and at UNCTAD in Geneva, as well as to a dozen FASB sessions organized by the CII in Washington over the last decade, it is difficult to guess how close we might be to adopting a single global accounting system.

8.13.5   Upgrading credit risk rating agencies?

The role of Fitch, Moody's and Standard & Poor's during the 2007–8 financial debacle is challenged, as widely reported in the media. The main issue is whether these agencies should be appointed by investors rather than by corporate issuers, as is currently the case.

8.13.6   Court litigations, arbitration or class actions?

We should always endeavor to compare the merits of these different approaches to specific conflict resolutions, on a case-by-case basis.

8.13.7   Impact of the consolidation of stock exchanges

After the recently failed merger attempt between Deutsche Börse and NYSE Euronext, it is difficult to predict what other important mergers could follow the mergers of NASDAQ with OMX, or of the LSE with both Borsa Italiana and Borse Dubai. We could now be oriented either toward retrenchments, or toward a status quo consolidation, rather than to significant mergers and acquisitions, at least in the near future. It is, for instance, rumored that NYSE Euronext is re-examining its 20% stake in the Qatar Doha Securities Market.

8.14   Post Scriptum

The renowned economist Nouriel Roubini has highlighted in his speeches and publications the similarities of the current crisis with the Great Depression of 80 years ago, including huge bubbles in both stocks and real estate, minimal financial regulation and a flurry of highly speculative financial innovations. He has often stated that major Western economies have a 50% risk of recession, in the absence of more draconian budgetary economic constraints in the future.

The G20, the International Chamber of Commerce (ICC), the ICGN, the IMF, the OECD, UNCTAD, and the World Bank—among others—should strive to resolve the growing global financial governance imbroglio. They could, for instance, encourage the investment community to focus on long-term stock equities of major corporations that adhere to adequate governance principles, and to avoid high-frequency trading as well as other highly speculative short-term investments.

Should the endeavors of the G20 and other regulatory organizations fail to resolve the current crisis, certain financial pundits wonder whether the high equities investment ratio (even though recently reduced from 70% to less than 50%) of major pension funds—and of other institutional, as well as private, investors—should not be reduced in favor of Treasury Bonds, gold and other precious or rare metals, commodities, real estate or even farmland in the future.

In any event, the majority of governance-driven investments are long-term endeavors, which are not compatible with the relatively recent flood of speculative short-term stock investment schemes.

SEC Chair Mary Schapiro has expressed her concern about the increasing role of high-frequency traders in the stock market. She has stated that the SEC is likely to take aggressive action to curb such frenetic stock market activity (*The Wall Street Journal Europe*, February 23, 2012). Incidentally, Mary Schapiro is in close touch with the global corporate governance movement via the CII in Washington, where the author has often had the privilege of engaging in debate with her.

9
International Debt and Globalization

Alexandre J. Vautravers

Globalization can take many forms and has been defined in various ways. While some maintain that the phenomenon is unique and recent, others see an evolution reaching as far back as the sixteenth century.[1] Many still argue over its negative and positive aspects, in a form of "agony versus ecstasy" dialectic.[2] Our purpose, rather than judging the effects of the phenomenon, will be to investigate the ties between globalization—or interdependence—and its most severely criticized companion: debt.

The topic is highly relevant. The major industrialized countries' economies have not fully recovered from the 2008 subprime crisis and, since the 2010 debt crisis in several European countries, have started to feel its social and political consequences spreading through the Euro zone. Despite unprecedented international collaboration and intervention, despite a spectacular witch-hunt for fiscal paradises,[3] no satisfactory regulation has really been enforced at the global or national levels. No agreement has been reached on a common course of action in the G20. In particular, no sign is being given that industrialized countries will lower their public spending, reduce their debt or allow for a devaluation of their currency in order to increase their competitivity and improve exports.

On the contrary, beyond the rhetoric, the 2008–10 crisis has encouraged Organization for Economic Cooperation and Development (OECD) countries to spend and bailout generously, demonstrating solidarity with drifting economies—the UK for Ireland, France and Germany for Greece—which has only so far served to increase the debt and reinforce the interdependency and spillover risks among the Euro zone economies.

The OECD countries' public debt, and in particular that of the United States, continue to grow. The proposed solutions to reduce the debt are mostly short-term and involve the creation of more debt, the covering up of debt through the creation and exchange of private–public assets, or through a growing dependency on emerging countries–Brazil, Russia, India, China, South Africa (BRICS). Such policies are not sustainable, as the service of the debt carves out more and more of the national budgets. And as the ratio of debt to budget or debt to GDP rise, creditors and investors lose confidence in these economies and their governance.

Most authors will agree that the present policy of *laissez-faire* will run aground in the next decade. Few decision makers and economists are prepared today to take a chance in altering the course, following the principle of "you know what you lose, you don't know what you'll get." Experts and public opinion in democratic countries alike have become risk-averse and stuck on the 1990s twin paradigms of globalization and the dividends of peace.

In this chapter, we will aim to discuss whether economic growth, industrialization or globalization have been, historically, inherently responsible for the creation of excessive public debt, debt crises and, ultimately, defaults and their geopolitical consequences. We will argue that growth has been achieved, at different times, without recourse to debt, but through other social and geopolitical means. We will base some of our historical background on the research of Jacques Attali.[4] While recognizing the significance of his political essay, we will distance ourselves, however, from his future scenarios and recommendations.

We will also argue that the present surge of financial market globalization, triggered in the mid-1990s, has its roots in the loss of competitiveness of the United States' economy, and its situation of twin deficits. Despite the rift and growing tensions of the 1960s and 1970s, Western nations managed to strike deals. The situation, however, spun out of control with US President Reagan's deficit investment and market deregulation of the 1980s, exacerbated by President Clinton's "Great leap forward" stimulus package and financial deregulation in the 1990s.[5]

9.1 Public debt—An original sin?

The origins of public or sovereign debt can be found in the need for cities to raise their military defenses in times of war, to avoid defeat, destruction and dependence or occupation. Sparta is considered to be the first city to have raised a loan without interest, in 431 B.C. during the Peloponnesian wars against Athens. For this reason, the treasures of the Olympus and Delphi sanctuaries were mobilized.[6] With the war dragging on, Athens was also compelled to borrow money from the temples, between 426 and 422 B.C., in order to avoid bankruptcy.

Later, the militarization of Rome and the professionalization of its army required increased and permanent funding. Farmers were able to pay in order to avoid conscription. Personal borrowing by the emperors was instrumental in elections, in the military campaigns as well as in the large construction projects.

Loans occurred mostly without interest. But honors and privileges could be given, monuments erected. Debts were terminated with the death of one of the contractors; the principle of continuity only developing in the thirteenth century. At the same time, in Europe and in China, secondary markets, coins and fiduciary currencies were developed. They brought with them inflation and devaluation.

Reimbursement required gains after a military success[7] In Europe, lending became associated with religion. While lending with interest was not acceptable to the Church, the Pope exceptionally granted permission to certain monasteries and religious orders. Paradoxically, this led to both religious orders, the Templars and religious minorities—the Jews and the Protestants—to develop the foundations of the modern banking system.

In Italian cities, short-term high interest loans were progressively replaced by longer-term, shorter rates—typically 5% for *il Monte*, the institution later to become Venice's public treasury. Investment was strictly regulated, and reimbursement with interest or "indemnities" took place only from the redistribution of spoils of war. Payment was generally suspended during times of conflict.[8]

The French King Francis I repeatedly resorted to public loans, necessary to fund his military campaigns in Italy. Adding to the sovereign debt, his son Henry II institutionalized a system of *fermiers généraux*[9]—later *offices* in the sixteenth century—in effect, selling royal titles and rights to levy taxes.

The sovereign royal debt was a dangerous business. Despite the influx of precious metals from the Americas, Spain defaulted 13 times between 1500 and 1900.[10] Mercantilist theories discouraged the use of gold as a method of payment. Taxes were difficult to collect; military campaigns and gains were uncertain. Political intrigues were commonplace, and the sovereign could turn against his creditors, at times confiscating their fortune.

The sixteenth to eighteenth centuries witnessed a centralization and an industrialization of sovereign debt. Theorists argue on the positive and negative consequences of public debt: for John Law and his followers, "the debts of a State are debts of the right hand to the left hand."[11] On the contrary, David Hume called it a "major peril for society."[12]

The stabilization of European monarchies allowed bankers and financers to become significant powers in the entourage of the kings. Criticism against the *rentiers* and the *financiers* grew, in particular in the wake of Louis XVI's tormented reign. Resentment and alienation, in conjunction with the development of a working class, crystallize in the "class struggles" of the nineteenth and twentieth centuries. Despite the succession of financial experts at the head of the French Treasury—Turgot, Necker, Calonne and Necker again—the recipes to bring the finances out of the gutter are generally similar: short-term loans, then trying to achieve budgetary balance and hopefully austerity. The continued overspending of the crown ultimately condemned these efforts to failure.

In the young United States of America, the debate between budgetary rigor and investment opposed Thomas Jefferson and James Madison. On

June 20, 1790, Alexander Hamilton agreed to the creation of a perpetual sovereign debt, in exchange for the establishment of a federal district and a capital city, Washington, DC.[13] The debt grew rapidly, cumulating the costs of the war of independence, the printing of a federal currency and the purchase of Louisiana. Ironically, most of this debt was contracted through the Barings bank, in the United Kingdom—the former enemy, whose loans served to pay France—the latter's present foe.

9.2   Debt and industrialization

The economic collapse after the French Revolution, the nationalization and confiscation of the Church's assets, the attempt at creating paper money and its imposition by force, the wars and the surge of public debt, rapidly led to disaster. In February 1797, the new currency or "mandate" was worth less than 1% of its original value. Dominique Ramel had no other choice than to cancel the public debt.[14] Two years later, the Minister restructured France's Treasury, imposed a balanced budget and transparency in public spending.

The Directory introduced a period of rigor, upheld under Napoleon, who created the National Bank in 1802. Military operations during the Napoleonic wars were funded by the spoils of victory and occupation taxes. As the conservative monarchies went into deep debt—the British debt reached 275% of GDP—they made the Rothschild family rich. France's debt under Napoleon never exceeded 20%.[15] It rose, however, with the return to the monarchy, and tripled in just five years.

The nineteenth-century's industrialization took place essentially without recourse to public debt. Durable peace, provided by the 1815 Treaty of Vienna's architecture, colonization and private investment, with simultaneously liberal and reactionary governments, allowed several countries to reduce their debt levels. The UK saw its debt shrink from 250% of GDP in 1820 to a mere 25% in 1910.[16] The French debt was halved, and the American debt was even entirely eliminated in 1836 under President Andrew Jackson, leading the Congress to redistribute the federal profits to nine States who had declared bankruptcy after refusing to raise their taxes.[17]

The situation worsened, however, with the Union expanding West, requiring a war with Mexico, the building of a navy,[18] as well as overseas campaigns in Eastern Asia. In the second half of the century, France's economy fell victim to repeated speculation and depression.[19] Many new countries emerged from colonization and decolonization, especially in Latin America. Unfortunately, half of these were bankrupt before the end of the nineteenth century.[20]

The last years of the century saw several substantial wars, creating major debt for the USA (30%) and France (87% of GDP). Militarization, *revanche* ideology, rearmament and the arms race of the Cold War led defense spending during peacetime to attain and maintain levels previously only reached during times of war.[21] The cost of the American Civil War and of the two World Wars bled many countries' economies and converted the US Treasury into the world's creditor.

Wars do not explain everything. While most of the nineteenth century's industrialization was privately and locally funded, the second wave of industrialization, initiated in the 1880s and reaching into the 1960s, was mostly financed by governments, publicly funded research institutions, local and semi-public savings and credit institutions, supporting local industry's rapid "catch-up."[22] As the prime movers of industrialization saw their markets saturated, so then could the profits be invested abroad, where higher yields could be expected in the new industrializing countries. The early twentieth century was therefore the age of public investment, credit and speculation. With the establishment of the Gold Standard, inflation also became a characteristic of the period. In this context, even the seemingly dissonant appeal by John Maynard Keynes in the 1930s for governments to support employment, insurance and welfare,[23] shows consensus on the necessity to accept inflation and public debt as necessary evils.

Debt also became a geopolitical issue. As Jacques Attali notes, the pattern is for creditors to influence their debtors and overtake them when they default. Such was the case of Egypt, the Netherlands or Greece in the last decades of the nineteenth century. Debt is no longer simply an economic instrument; it has become a political tool of influence. Debt is no longer meant to be reimbursed. To demonstrate this change of paradigm, one sees that "the US Government, which owed 5 billion dollars to European bankers in 1914, invested at the same time 2.5 billion overseas, in Canada, Mexico and Cuba."[24]

The World Wars brought European countries to their knees: in 1919, the British and French debt amounted to 150% of their GDP. The US debt was only 28%.[25] Despite the Versailles plan to impose a 3%-GDP-a-year reparation, the British and French economies were again hit by the 1929 Wall Street *Krach*, and saw their debt level reach 191% and 150% of GDP in 1932 respectively. US President Roosevelt's "New Deal" increased public spending sixfold over President Hoover's last year in office.[26] The debt levels were so high that institutions had to be created to manage the crisis. In 1930, the Bank for International Settlements (BIS) was created in Basel.[27] The Lausanne conference met in 1932; two years later, the USA agreed to the partial default of the UK, France and Germany.

Despite dialogue between the central banks with substantial government involvement and an economic upturn in 1935, the debt levels remained high in 1939: 44.2% GDP in the USA, 125% in the UK and 110% in France. These levels were even higher after the Second World War, in 1945: 108% in the USA, 250% in the UK and 110% in France.[28]

In 1945, the establishment of the Bretton Woods system of monetary management and the International Monetary Fund (IMF) broke away from the protectionist inflationary policies of the interwar years. Fixed exchange rates and consultation, regulation and international arbitrage allowed for a return to balanced budgets, economic growth and debt reduction. By 1955, the US public debt was halved to 57.4% and the French debt dropped to 30% of its GDP.[29]

The creation of a new German currency imposed a default of the Reichmark. European economic cooperation was fueled by the "Marshall Plan" or European Recovery Program (ERP), and access to a larger and more common market. The post-war years were, however, marked by two concerns. First was the growing tensions between the USA and its Western European and Japanese economic partners. As the latter recovered from the war in the mid-1960s and accumulated "Eurodollars," the US Government feared a new run on the dollar, or the conversion of these reserves into gold. The 1971 interruption of the dollar–gold exchange standard created a crisis of floating currency exchange rates and stimulated European integration. The 1973 and 1979 oil shocks exacerbated the stagflation crisis and the tensions between the OECD countries. The resolution of these tensions, in particular the undervaluation of the Deutschemark and the Yen, was the object of a secret meeting of the G5—Canada and Italy were left out—at the Plaza Hotel in New York, on September 22, 1985.[30] One of the outcomes was the entrance of Germany and Japan into the multilateral system and, once again, substantial military sales to redress the US balance of payments.[31]

The second set of concerns involved an increasingly interdependent and rapidly changing world economy.

9.3 Debt and globalization

Decolonization from the 1950s to the 1970s led many Third World countries to a situation of economic disorganization and dependency. The reliance on raw materials and extraction was doomed from the onset by the law of declining returns and the competition between developing countries. The lowering of tariffs and rapidly growing economies in the Northern countries,[32] as well as the establishment of common markets, represented immense challenges for new entrants in the globalizing economy, faced with an "unlevel playing-field."[33]

The "Paris Club"—grouping the principal creditor countries—was created in 1956 to address sovereign debt defaults. In 50 years, it signed over 400 agreements with 81 debtor countries, for a comprehensive sum of US\$ 523 billion.[34] The "London Club"—grouping the main commercial banks lending to sovereigns—was created from the British Corporation of Foreign Bondholders (BCFB), originally established in 1868. Both institutions played a significant role in debt negotiations and reevaluations, especially after the 1974 creation of the G7 at the Rambouillet meeting. This concerned, in particular: Argentina, Peru, Zaïre, Turkey, Sudan, Poland, Ecuador in the 1970s,

Mexico, Brazil, Chili and Ecuador again in the 1980s. The increasing need for the refinancing of the debt of Third World countries encouraged closer collaboration with the International Monetary Fund.

The US-led IMF was encouraged by the US Government to introduce "Special Drawing Rights" (SDR) in 1969 and "Brady bonds" in 1989, for the specific handling of sovereign debts.[35] The creation of these instruments stimulated increased lending to developing countries. The guidelines of the "Washington Consensus" and "Structural adjustment programs" of the IMF were meant to offer the necessary guarantees for public and, increasingly, private lenders and investors.

In the summer of 1996, Thai bonds crashed. The poor handling of the crisis led to the spread of the crisis of confidence to Indonesia, Malaysia and the Philippines. Before the end of the year, South Korea, Taiwan, Singapore and Hong Kong were also hit. Elsewhere, Russia, Ecuador and Argentina had to face increasing international financial supervision.

The overvaluation of the US Dollar relative to the German DM and the Japanese Yen in the 1960s, the oil shocks and "stagflation" crisis of the 1970s, markedly deteriorated the situation of the US economy, characterized by high debt (35% of GDP in 1975), rising inflation, and a "twin deficit" of the budget and the balance of payments.[36] The South East Asian conflicts and the arms race affected US defense and public spending to such an extent that the brief *détente* period rapidly gave way to President Reagan's "supply-side economics," characterized by a substantial increase in the defense budget and the launch of a new arms race, epitomized by the "Star Wars" or Strategic Defense Initiative (SDI).

From the early 1980s onwards, investment in the United States became increasingly funded by devaluation and debt. This represented only 46% of the US GDP in 1990. In France and the UK the situation was similar, with 35% for both French and British debt.[37] But as these economies grew considerably thereafter, thanks to the lowering of tariffs and globalization, so too have the sums and risks involved. In 1991, Japan's real-estate bubble burst, leading to a two-decade-long recession. Sweden fell into a crisis in 1993, Canada in 1995.

If the main lesson of the 1929 crash has been to bail out the banks, the lesson from the 1970s crisis has been to avoid massive structural unemployment. For this, maintaining business activity implied sustaining consumption, which in turn required lowering the interest rates. This, inevitably, stimulated credit. Despite the public debts remaining relatively low in relation to GDP, the level of private debt has become increasingly worrisome: from 46% in 1979 to 98% in late 2007 in the US, from 20% to 80% of GDP in the UK.[38] Between 1975 and 2007, whereas the United States' GDP has been multiplied by 8.75, the private debt was multiplied by 20 and the public debt only grew threefold. The cumulative debt in 2007 had grown to a critical 350% of GDP.[39]

The increasing debt and the increasing complexity of the instruments intended to hide it—from SDRs to "subprimes" and agency debts, credit swaps, not to mention the selling off of gold reserves—have allowed the US economy to grow, keep consumption high and unemployment under control. President Clinton's "short term stimulus package," investing in high-tech and high value-added industries, managed to achieve successes at the expense of debt. To maintain the US edge, Clinton initiated a "Big Bang" deregulation of the financial market in the United States in 1996, closely followed by the UK and Japan.[40]

At the end of his mandate, when the now positive balance of payment could have been used to reduce the debt, Bill Clinton—only a few months from the end of his second term—left the strategic decisions to his successor.[41] George W. Bush, entering office on January 20, 2001, was elected on the promise of tax cuts—not the repayment of the public debt. The economic policy envisaged reducing the debt through decreased spending and budget cuts, in particular in the defense sector. Eventually, the September 11 attacks destroyed these plans.

It is not our role here to discuss the costs of wars or economic crisis but to emphasize how the costs of a protracted, decade-long and worldwide "Global War on Terror" (GWOT) have impacted the US economy. This is all the more vivid as, firstly the United States has assumed unilateral leadership in this endeavor, and secondly because, contrary to previous wars, GWOT was essentially funded through foreign borrowing.[42]

For the sake of this chapter, we will link the 2008 (subprime) and the 2010 (debt) crises, considering how the high amounts spent on the original bailouts exacerbated the more recent debt and liquidity crisis. In the Euro zone alone, the 2009–10 bailouts accounted for an increase of 14.5% GDP of the public debt.[43] The induced stall in the economy of industrialized countries has now reached geopolitical heights—so much so that, in fact, these may durably shape the global economy of the new century.

9.4   Geo-economic consequences for the twenty-first century

We will look into the rise of the "Southern" economies, the prospect for the "Northern" economies, the "default" and the "settlement" scenarios, and the prospects of the future decisive role of China in the global economy.

Firstly, the G20 and the economic instruments of the "Washington Consensus" have shown their limits. Today, the powerful and wealthy countries are the developing nations. Ironically, the "poor" countries are paying for the "rich." In 2010, the ratio of public debt to GDP was 80% in the ten "richest" countries of the G20; it was only 40% for the other half.[44]

Interest rates have undergone a race to the bottom; in some countries they have hit zero, and some economists have theorized so-called negative interest rates. The incredible rise of gold and precious metal prices, commodities and even food demonstrates the search for safer assets. Lower rates may reduce the service of the debt;[45] but they may provoke a flight of capital into the developing "real" economies. Most of the emerging or BRICS countries enjoy strong growth in the double digits. The prospects for the growth of their national consumer markets are sound.

Reducing public debt can only be achieved through economic growth and a positive balance of payments. The prospects for Europe, therefore, are not good. Indeed, productivity gains are more difficult to reach in the highly services-sector-oriented countries of the North than in the export-industry-focused countries of the South. The crisis therefore can only lead to the increase of free-trade measures and immigration.

Also, one must remember that while the public debt issue may be addressed, the repayment of the much larger private debt is really at the heart of the problem today. The inevitable rise in interest rates and, perhaps, inflation will deeply impact European societies. This may lead to a substantial decrease in real-term wages and domestic consumption.

Secondly, the economic fundamentals in the Northern countries—cumulating private and public debt—will not allow for a substantial repayment of the debt in the coming years. On the contrary, the slope is rising sharply: in 2010, the US debt represented 59% of GDP, the UK 80% and France 83.6%.[46] Even with increasing exports and profits, the European democracies will not be able to implement austerity policies—without losing the coming elections to demagogue politicians who will swiftly ruin the efforts of a mandate of rigor.[47]

In the past two centuries, 250 international and 68 national defaults have taken place, 126 of these in Latin America and 63 in Africa.[48] The issue at hand is not just limited to a few European countries. In order to avoid the dire consequences of a crash and a decade-long recovery, we will need to accept significant policy changes, perhaps political and structural ones. Further, in the medium term, international coordination and settlements will be required—in settings that may need to be created, or adapted. Indeed, neither the United Nations Security Council (UNSC), nor the IMF or the WTO, OECD or even the G7/G20/G77 have, so far, been able to take on this role.

Thirdly, the repayment of any substantial percentage of the debt may affect international trade, reducing the need for international cooperation and risking a return to protectionist or isolationist policies, in the USA or in developing countries. Only when trade channels are open, is it possible for creditors to hope to see a return on their investment.

Could the lack of liquidities affect international solidarity and development? Most Northern countries have committed themselves to various expenses, beginning with the 1% GDP foreign aid for achievement of the Millennium Development Goals (MDG). We believe that development investment from Northern countries will continue. It may, however, become more largely privatized, targeted and more self-interested.

The same can be said about environmental norms or carbon trading schemes. Some countries have gone so far as to turn their back on nuclear power, that is, cheap energy. In our view, it will not be possible for OECD countries to renounce their commitments. They may, however, apply increasing pressure on developing countries, particularly at the World Trade Organization (WTO) or in coming environmental negotiations, for the rapid generalization of these self-imposed measures and the establishment of stricter environmental norms on imports. It may be argued that such environmental norms will affect competitiveness in the industrial South more than in the post-industrial North. These may replace quotas and safety norms as the twenty-first century's next generation of Non-Tariff Barriers (NTB).

Fourthly, we turn to sovereignty. We have shown previously that states have recourse to solutions inaccessible to private financial actors. Some have resorted to regulation, nationalization and confiscation. Others have raised taxes and—even in the most recent bailouts—have in effect passed on public debt into private taxpayers' hands, mortgaging future economic growth and social welfare. Deflation is also an available tool, with grave national consequences.

A moratorium can be envisaged, or the rescheduling of the debt. Or even indirect agreements, involving for example land grabs, the increase of BRICS countries' foreign direct investment (FDI), or the development of the so-called Beijing Consensus. More likely, short term, we will witness substantial contracts and technology transfer in the form of arms purchases from the "former" industrialized countries to the Middle East and, increasingly, to Asia.[49]

Lastly, we cannot neglect the geopolitical shift toward Asia, tensions between creditor and debtor leading to potential friction and war. The specter of an economic and possibly an armed conflict between the "old" and the "new" economic powers may need to be addressed. While this would require a different study, we do not concur with Jacques Attali's views that the creditor systematically overtakes the debtor.

Indeed, surely there is a realization that instead of putting the United States in an inextricable situation, China has been supportive of the US Government, being committed to free trade and accepting a reevaluation of its currency exchange rate toward the dollar in 2011. China's participation in the US public debt has made it dependent on the US remaining solvent. This situation of interdependence is epitomized by the fact the US remains China's main investor and main market. We may be, therefore, looking more at a situation of co-dependency rather than a situation of competition. A default in the US, or even in Europe, may happen, but it must be managed—in the interest of both the creditors and the debtors.

Notes

1. Paul Bairoch (1997) *Victoire et déboires: Histoire économique et sociale du monde du XVIᵉ siècle à nos jours*, Paris: Gallimard.

2. John Clark (2003) *Worlds Apart: Civil Society and the Battle for Ethical Globalization*, New York: Earthscan.
3. John Christensen and Mark Hampton, OECD Economist Intelligence Unit. http://www.richard.murphy.dial.pipex.com/Fiscalparadise.pdf p. 21; http://www.taxjustice.net/cms/upload/pdf/Identifying_Tax_Havens_Jul_07.pdf [all websites last accessed April 1, 2012].
4. Jacques Attali (2010) *Tous ruinés dans dix ans? Dette publique: la dernière chance*, Paris: Fayard.
5. Joan Spero and Jeffrey Hart (1996) *The Politics of International Economic Relations*, London: Bedford/St Martin's.
6. Victor Davis Hanson (2005) *A War Like No Other: How the Athenians and Spartans Fought the Peloponnesian War*, New York: Random House.
7. Attali, *Tous ruinés*, p. 28.
8. Ibid., p. 32.
9. Ibid., p. 38.
10. Ibid., p. 40.
11. Ibid.
12. David Hume (1752) "Of Commerce," *Essays Moral, Political and Literary*, p. 40, http://presspubs.uchicago.edu/founders/documents/v1ch4s3.html.
13. Phil Davies (2007) "The Bank that Hamilton Built," *The Federal Reserve Bank*, September, http://www.minneapolisfed.org/publications_papers/pub_display.cfm?id=1141.
14. Jean-Marc Daniel and Corinne Lhaik (1997) "1797, quand la France était en faillite," *L'Express*, October 9.
15. Attali, *Tous ruinés*, p. 64.
16. Ibid., p. 65.
17. Ibid., p. 67.
18. Oreste Foppiani (1998) *La nascita dell'imperialismo Americano (1890–1898): L'impianto della politica di Potenza degli Stati Uniti d'America*, Rome: ESS.
19. Patrick Verley (1997) *L'échelle du Monde: Essai sur l'industrialisation de l'Occident*, Paris: Gallimard.
20. Attali, *Tous ruinés*, p. 67.
21. Alexandre Vautravers (1998) *L'impact de la technologie sur la conduite de la guerre*, DEA d'Histoire contemporaine, Université Lumière, Lyon 2.
22. Alexandre Gerschenkron (1962) *Economic Backwardness in Historical Perspective: A Book of Essays*, Cambridge, MA: Belknap Press.
23. John Maynard Keynes (1936) *The General Theory of Employment, Interest and Money*, London: Macmillan.
24. Attali, *Tous ruinés*, p. 72.
25. Ibid., p. 74.
26. Ibid., p. 77.
27. http://www.bis.org/about/arch_guide.pdf. Documents diplomatiques suisses (DODIS) database: http://db.dodis.ch/dodis;jsessionid=EC38EB26BA4F79065121 8AD58F54CE56?XE7lTUfUMvuyrondilT044GDbgZgesemqkvwyzpoVugSN7Dnz MV3HVksLDYYRZx0yhv.
28. Attali, *Tous ruinés*, pp. 77–8.
29. Ibid., p. 79.
30. Spero and Hart, *Politics of International Economic Relations*.
31. Whereas the original Military Assistance Program (MAP) specifically discouraged the purchase of US weaponry in NATO, in favor of European-designed and

produced systems, the United Kingdom purchased its first F-4 Phantom II in 1966, Germany purchased the McDonnell Douglas designed aircraft in 1968 and Japan ordered the same aircraft that same year. The three countries introduced a total of 181, 263 and 154 aircraft respectively. It can be argued that this case severely harmed these countries' national air and space industry, threatening to lead it into a situation of US dependency. http://en.wikipedia.org/wiki/McDonnell_Douglas_F-4_Phantom_II_non-U.S._operators.

32. Richard E. Caves, Jeffrey A. Frankel and Ronald W. Jones (2007) *World Trade and Payments*, Boston, MA: Pearson, p. 227.
33. Paul Bairoch (1970) *Diagnostic de l'évolution économique du Tiers-monde, 1900–1968*, Paris: Gauthier-Villars.
34. Attali, *Tous ruinés*, p. 85.
35. John Williamson (2009) *Understanding Special Drawing Rights (SDRs)*, Peterson Institute for International Economics, No. PB09-11, June, http://www.iie.com/publications/pb/pb09-11.pdf.
36. Spero and Hart, *Politics of International Economic Relations*.
37. Attali, *Tous ruinés*, p. 87.
38. Ibid., p. 88.
39. Ibid.
40. Spero and Hart, *Politics of International Economic Relations*.
41. Ibid.
42. Joseph E. Stiglitz and Linda J. Bilmes (2008) *The Three Trillion Dollar War: The True Cost of the Iraq Conflict*, New York: W. W. Norton & Company.
43. Attali, *Tous ruinés*, p. 94.
44. Ibid., p. 126.
45. Ibid., p. 126.
46. Ibid., p. 98.
47. Spero and Hart, *Politics of International Economic Relations*.
48. Attali, *Tous ruinés*, p. 119.
49. Paul Holtom, Mark Bromley, Pieter D. Wezeman and Siemon T. Wezeman (2012) *Trends in International Arms Transfers 2011*, Stockholm: SIPRI, http://books.sipri.org/index_html?c_category_id=65.

10
Conclusions and Outlook

Otto Hieronymi and Constantine A. Stephanou

The authors of the present volume share a strong concern about the seriousness of the debt issue and about the need for determined action and cooperation at the national and international levels. They are also aware of the high degree of uncertainty of future prospects. The broad range of themes addressed in the preceding chapters illustrates the complexity of the international debt situation. One of the principal objectives of this book is to show readers that there is a wide range of perspectives, opinions, theories, policy proposals and projections on the international debt issue. While there is convergence of views on many important points among the authors, no attempt has been made to seek consensus or agreement among them on a single set of conclusions and projections. Thus, the following paragraphs represent more of a selection than a summary or a hierarchy of the wealth of suggestions and conclusions that the reader can find in the preceding chapters.

- The number one priority is a new consensus, between political parties at the domestic level, within the European Union and among the leading Western countries that austerity as such will not create an adequate framework for debt reduction and fiscal discipline.
- Deficit and debt reduction must not be a cause or pretext for eliminating key social services. The lack of social concern and the growing marginalization of large segments of the population even during the boom phase was one of the most worrying aspects of the spread of "global finance." There is a high risk that the dramatic rise in unemployment will reduce the potential rate of growth and lead to a vicious downward cycle. This could dangerously undermine the political acceptance of competition, fiscal discipline and of the market economy itself.
- Confidence in the future and in the growth potential of the European and Western economies is an essential condition for solving the debt problem and for monetary stability. This is not an issue of market or government rhetoric or financial and fiscal engineering. The shared

conviction in the need and possibility to use the full resources of our economies and the commitment to cooperate of governments, business leaders, labor and taxpayers toward this common goal have been the mainsprings of growth and prosperity in the past. There is no valid alternative to such a conviction and commitment.

- There is a need for a new balance between the role of governments and of the scope of free markets in a liberal economic order. There is also a need to redefine the responsibilities of various levels of government: local, national, European and international. Trying to concentrate too much power at the European or international levels (including through ad hoc solutions like the "troika") at the expense of national legislative and executive decisions could achieve the opposite of the objective sought. It could lead to less, rather than more electoral support at the national level, and greater rather than less disaffection for the "European project" and for solidarity among the members of the Western Community.

- As this book is going to the press, there are continued signs of awareness of the need for further institutional and policy innovation and reforms. At the same time there is also skepticism among market participants about the effectiveness of the flow of new fiscal and financial rules. Trying to push toward a "European super state" or to give more power without accountability to organizations such as the IMF would create more problems than provide long-term solutions. Yet, the time is right for redefining a global framework for a stable monetary and financial system. The European Union and the Euro Area is too narrow for this to be sufficiently effective. The scope of the IMF or the G20 is too broad and unwieldy. As noted elsewhere in the book, it is the opportunity and the responsibility of the leading democracies and liberal market economies—the United States, Europe and Japan—to take the initiative and the leadership of an effective reform of the international monetary and financial system.

- The principal conclusion of this book is that the fiscal, financial, monetary, economic and social situation is sufficiently serious that there is no valid alternative to success. The search for adequate crisis management and for appropriate long-term reforms and institutional innovation needs systematic inputs from "experts"—economists, monetary and financial experts, business and labor leaders. Ultimately, however, success or failure will depend on the quality of political decisions and the ability or lack of willingness of elected political leaders to cooperate and to reconcile real or apparent conflicts of interests.

Appendix: The Information Crisis and the Need to Improve the Availability and the Use of Relevant Statistics

The international monetary and financial crisis has also been a major information crisis at both the national and international level. This was true for Stage I of the crisis (the "subprime crisis") and for Stage II (the "debt crisis").

Decisions are about the future—information is about the past. There is a broad agreement that the availability, the quality and the timeliness of qualitative and quantitative information have a major impact on the quality of the decisions of both private and public actors in the modern economy. Yet, the general disaffection following the outbreak of the financial crisis in 2007–8 for the so-called theory of rational expectations has to do with the (belated) dual recognition that (1) all information (or the most relevant information) is not available or correct, and (2) statistics from the past are far from being a perfect guide for the future, especially when it comes not only to projecting "trends" but predicting major "events" that disrupt trends.

The importance of this information and expectation issue has been dramatically demonstrated on two occasions since 2008: the suddenness and magnitude of the "subprime crisis" and the outbreak and brush-fire effect of the following "debt crisis."

The so-called information age or information society has been as much of a problem as an improvement when dealing with data relating to the complex economic structures of a globalized economy. As noted in Chapter 1, the great progress in hardware and software for collecting, storing, processing and distributing information that has occurred during the last 20 years has not prevented serious gaps in information or outright misinformation at the macro as well as at the micro level. Many claim, not without justification, that the "subprime crisis" was to a large extent an "information crisis" where the information problems were a combination of incompetence and of deliberate attempts to mislead markets and regulators. The Stage II debt crisis—with the outbreak of the "Greek debt crisis"—was a textbook example of negligence with respect to crucial information at all levels: government authorities, EU and ECB experts as well as leading international financial advisors and managers.

The "information crisis" has multiple aspects. The most common problems included: lack of availability of data, lack or insufficient comparability, insufficient diffusion or access, and the ignoring or misinterpretation by official and private observers and decision makers of the message coming from the data. There was, however, also: deliberate distortion or falsification, restricting access or diffusion by both private and official bodies to essential information that could have attenuated or even prevented some of the worst consequences of the crisis, as well as systematic disinformation of investors, of authorities and the general public at large. The most fundamental and most widespread "information breakdown" was the systematic ignoring of the storm warnings coming from the data—deliberately disregarding the "handwriting on the wall."

These problems have been recognized, although belatedly, by many people within national and international organizations, in the corporate world and in the research community. Since 2009–10 there have been notable efforts to improve the quality and the volume of the data relevant for the analysis of the debt situation at any given moment and of the trends and likely future developments. There has been a series of initiatives by organizations such as the IMF, the World Bank, the OECD, the BIS, the ECB, the European Commission as well as the national monetary and economic authorities, to speed up the availability of data and most importantly to better coordinate their availability. Further, the definition and use of tailor-made "warning packages" (such as the IMF "Fiscal Monitor") have increased.

Four major general lessons for the future should be mentioned here:

1. It is necessary to narrow the scope of "proprietary information," both for "business-sensitive" and "politically restricted" data.
2. There is a need for much closer and effective cooperation as well as competition and "redundancy" in data collection and diffusion.
3. Market transparency has to be enforced independently and much more systematically than in the past.
4. Finally, it is important to recognize that the prevailing confusion about what is available and to whom and on what conditions (subscribers, clients, government officials) represents a major source of future problems and has to be addressed as an urgent issue at the highest levels.

There remains much to be done on all four accounts. Some of the problems are technical, others are due to the unwillingness by both private and official actors to share information: "information is a key source of power" and tends to make the difference between success and failure, both for individuals and for organizations. It should be remembered, however, that discrimination in the access to essential information is contrary to the very nature of an open, liberal and competitive economic system. If there is no "level playing field" in terms of transparency and information the market economy cannot function properly. It is no exaggeration that recurring breakdowns in the access to relevant information could become a major economic and political threat to the very survival of "globalization" itself.

Bibliography

Ackerman, Frank and 101 Economists (2012) "Letter to Trade Ministers Re: Promoting Financial Stability in the Trans-Pacific Partnership Agreement," February 28, ase.tufts.edu.

Allen, Franklin and Douglas Gale (2000) "Financial Contagion," *Journal of Political Economy*, Vol. 108, pp. 1–33.

Allen, William and Richchild Moessner (2010) *Central Bank Co-operation and International Liquidity in the Financial Crisis of 2008–2009*, BIS Working Papers No. 310, Monetary and Economic Department, Bank for International Settlements, June.

Alloway, Tracy (2011) "A (Hard) Greek Restructuring by the Numbers," *Financial Times*, May 9.

Alloway, Tracy, Megan Murphy and David Oakley (2011) "Investors Count Costs to Banks of Greek Default," *Financial Times*, May 10.

Alogoskoufis, George (2012) *Greece's Sovereign Debt Crisis: Retrospect and Prospect*, Hellenic Observatory Papers on Greece and Southeast Europe, GreeSE Paper No. 54, London School of Economics and Political Science, January.

Amador, M. (2008) *Sovereign Debt and the Tragedy of the Commons*, Working Paper, Stanford University.

American Economic Association (1950, 1958) *Readings in the Theory of International Trade*, London: George Allen & Unwin, Ltd.

American Economic Association (1952, 1956) *Readings in Monetary Theory*, London: George Allen & Unwin, Ltd.

Ang, Andrew and Francis A. Longstaff (2011) *Systemic Sovereign Credit Risk: Lessons from the U.S. and Europe*, National Bureau of Economic Research Working Paper 16982, Cambridge, MA: NBER.

Angelatos, George-Marios and Jennifer La'O (2011) *Optimal Monetary Policy with Informational Frictions*, National Bureau of Economic Research Working Paper 17525, Cambridge, MA: NBER.

Angeloni, Chiara and Guntram B. Wolff (2012) *Are Banks Affected by their Holdings of Government Debt?* Bruegel Working Paper 2012/07, Brussels, March.

Angeloni, Ignazio and Jean Pisani-Ferry (2012) *The G20: Characters in Search of an Author*, Bruegel Working Paper 2012/04, Brussels, March.

Angelopoulos, Konstantinos, Sophia Dimeli, Apostolis Philippopoulos and Vanghelis Vassilatos (2010) *Rent-Seeking Competition from State Coffers in Greece: A Calibrated DSGE Model*, Working Papers No. 120, Bank of Greece.

Arndt, Swen W., Richard J. Sweeney and Thomas D. Willett (1985) (eds) *Exchange Rates, Trade and the U.S. Economy*, Washington, DC: American Enterprise Institute and Ballinger Publication.

Åslund, Anders (2010) *The Last Shall Be the First: The East European Financial Crisis*, Washington, DC: Peterson Institute for International Economics.

Attali, Jacques (2010) *Tous ruinés dans dix ans? Dette publique: la dernière chance*, Paris: Fayard.

Bairoch, Paul (1970) *Diagnostic de l'évolution économique du Tiers-monde, 1900–1968*, Paris: Gauthier-Villars.

Bairoch, Paul (1997) *Victoire et déboires: Histoire économique et sociale du monde du XVIᵉ siècle à nos jours*, Paris: Gallimard.

Bandulet, Bruno, Wilhelm Hankel, Bernd-Thomas Ramb, Karl Albrecht Schachtschneider, Udo Ulfkotte (2011) *Gebt uns unsere D-Mark zurück: Fünf Experten beantworten die wichtigsten Fragen zum kommenden Staatsbankrott*, Rottenburg: Gebundene Ausgabe, May.

Bank for International Settlements (2011) *81st Annual Report, 1 April 2010–11 March 2011*, Basel, June 26.

Bank for International Settlements (2012) "European Bank Funding and Deleveraging," *BIS Quarterly Review*, March 12.

Bank for International Settlements (2012) *82nd Annual Report, 2011–2012*, Basel, June.

Bank of Greece (2011) *Monetary Policy Report 2011–2012*, March.

Bank of Greece (2012) *Bulletin of Conjunctural Indicators*, No. 142, January–February.

Bank of Greece (2012) *Aggregated Balance Sheet of Credit Institutions*, February.

Bank of Greece (2012) *Governor's Annual Report*, April.

Bank of Greece (2012) *List of Credit Institutions Authorized in Greece*, April.

Bernanke, Ben S. (2000) *Essays on the Great Depression*, Princeton: Princeton University Press.

Bernanke, Ben (2012) "The Federal Reserve and the Financial Crisis Origins and Mission of the Federal Reserve," Lecture 1, George Washington University School of Business, Washington, DC, March 20.

Bhagwati, Jagdish (2000) *The Wind of Hundred Days: How Washington Mismanaged Globalization*, Cambridge, MA: MIT Press.

Bhagwati, Jagdish (2004) *In Defense of Globalization*, Oxford: Oxford University Press.

Biéler, André (1959, 2008) *La Pensée Economique et Sociale de Calvin*, Genève: Georg Editeur.

BIS Editorial Committee [Claudio Borio, Dietrich Domanski, Christian Upper, Stephen Cecchetti and Philip Turner] (2012) *International Banking and Financial Market Developments, BIS Quarterly Review*, Basel, March.

Bod, Péter Ákos (2010) "The IMF, the EU and the Sovereign Borrower: The Case of Hungary 2008–2010," *Theory, Methodology, Practice*, Miskolc University, Vol. 6, No. 2, pp. 3–9, http://tmp.gtk.uni-miskolc.hu/index.php?i=1009.

Bod, Péter Ákos (2010) *Hungary Turns to the International Monetary Fund in 2008—Anatomy of a Crisis*, Gazdasági Élet és Társadalom, WSUF, No. I–II.

Bod, Péter Ákos (2011) "On Business–Government Relations: The Hungarian Case," *Hungarian Review*, Vol. II, No. 5, pp. 30–40.

Boden, Jean (1576) *Les Six livres de la République*, translated by M. J. Tooley (1955), Oxford: Basil Blackwell, http://www.constitution.org/bodin/bodin_.htm.

Bombach, G., Netzband, K.-B., Ramser, H.-J. and Timmermann, M. (eds) *Der Keynesianismus III, Die geld- und beschäftigungs-theoretische Diskussion in Deutschland zur Zeit von Keynes*, Berlin, Heidelberg and New York: Springer-Verlag.

Boorman, Jack (2002) "Sovereign Debt Restructuring: Where Stands the Debate?" Speech by the Special Adviser to the Managing Director of the IMF, Conference cosponsored by the CATO Institute and *The Economist*, October 17.

Bordo, Michael D. and Barry Eichengreen (1993) (eds) *A Retrospective on the Bretton Woods System: Lessons for International Monetary Reform*, A National Bureau of Economic Research Project Report, Chicago: University of Chicago Press.

Bordo, Michael D., Agnieszka Markiewicz and Lars Jonung (2011) *A Fiscal Union for the Euro: Some Lessons from History*, National Bureau of Economic Research Working Paper 17380, Cambridge, MA: NBER.

Borio, Claudio (2008) *The Financial Turmoil of 2007–?: A Preliminary Assessment and Some Policy Considerations*, Bank for International Settlements (BIS) Working Paper No. 251, Basle, March.

Boudghene, Yassine, Matthaeus Buder, Zetta Dellidou, Christophe Galand, Violeta Iftinchi, Max Lienemeyer, Christos Malamataris and Danila Malvolti (2011) *State Aid Control in a Stability Programme Country: The Case of Greece*, Competition Policy Newsletter, No. 1, pp. 45–9.

Boughton, Mark (2009) "A New Bretton Woods?" *Finance and Development*, Vol. 46, No. 1, Washington, DC: IMF.

Bowels, Erskin and Allen Simpson (2011) *The National Commission on Fiscal Responsibility and Reform*, Washington, DC, January 31.

Bresciani-Turroni, Constantino (1937) *The Economics of Inflation: A Study of Currency Depreciation in Post-War Germany*, London: George Allen & Unwin, Ltd.

Brown, Brendan (1988) *Monetary Chaos in Europe: The End of an Era*, London: Routledge.

Brown, Brendan (2012) *Euro Crash: The Exit Route from Monetary Failure in Europe*, Basingstoke: Palgrave Macmillan.

Brzezinski, Zbigniew (2012) *Strategic Vision: America and the Crisis of Global Power*, New York: Basic Books.

Buchheit, Lee C. and Mitu Gulati (2010) *How to Restructure Greek Debt*, Working Paper, Duke Law Scholarship Repository, May.

Buchheit, Lee C. and Mitu Gulati (2011) *The Greek Debt—The Endgame Scenarios*, Working Paper, April.

Buiter, Willem and Ebrahim Rahbari (2010) "Is Sovereign Default 'Unnecessary, Undesirable and Unlikely' for all Advanced Economies?" *Citi Economics, Global Economics View*, Citigroup, September.

Burda, Michael and Charles Wyplosz (1993) *Macroeconomics: A European Text*, Oxford: Oxford University Press.

Butler, John (2012) *The Golden Revolution: How to Prepare for the Coming Global Gold Standard*, Hoboken, NJ: Wiley.

Caballero, Ricardo J. (2010) "Macroeconomics after the Crisis: Time to Deal with the Pretense- of-Knowledge Syndrome," *Journal of Economic Perspectives*, Vol. 24, No. 4, pp. 85–102.

Caballero, Ricardo J. and Arvind Krishnamurthy (2008) "Collective Risk Management in a Flight to Quality Episode," *Journal of Finance*, Vol. 63, No. 5, pp. 2195–230.

Calomiris, Charles W. (2008) "The Subprime Turmoil: What's Old, What's New, and What's Next," paper for Jackson Hole Symposium *Maintaining Stability in a Changing Financial System*, Federal Reserve Bank of Kansas City, August.

Cassidy, John (2009) *How Markets Fail: The Logic of Economic Calamities*, New York: Farrar, Straus & Giroux [London: Allen Lane, 2010].

Caves, Richard E., Jeffrey A. Frankel and Ronald W. Jones (2007) *World Trade and Payments*, Boston, MA: Pearson.

Cecchetti, Stephen (2011) "Fiscal Policy and its Implications for Monetary and Financial Stability," 10th BIS Annual Conference, Lucerne, June.

Cecchetti, Stephen G., Madhusudan S. Mohanty and Fabrizio Zampolli (2010) *The Future of Public Debt: Prospects and Implications*, BIS Working Papers, No. 300, Basel, March.

Cech, Zdenek and Anton Jevcak (2011) "International Reserves in the CEE8—Lessons from the Financial Crisis," *ECFIN Country Focus*, Vol. 8, No. 3, pp. 1–8.

Claessens, Stijn, Richard J. Herring and Dirk Schoenmaker (2010) *A Safer World Financial System: Improving the Resolution of Systemic Institutions*, Geneva Reports on the World Economy 12, Geneva: International Center for Monetary and Banking Studies (ICMB).

Clark, John (2003) *Worlds Apart: Civil Society and the Battle for Ethical Globalization*, New York: Earthscan.

Cline, William R. (1984) *International Debt: Systemic Risk and Policy Response*, Washington, DC: Institute for International Economics.

Coggan, Philip (2011) *Paper Promises: Money, Debt and the New World Order*, London: Allen Lane.

Committee on the Global Financial System (2011) *The Impact of Sovereign Credit Risk on Bank Funding Conditions*, No. 43, July, http://www.bis.org/publ/cgfs43.pdf.

Connell, Carol M. (2011) "Why Economists Disagree: Fritz Machlup's Use of Framing at the Bellagio Group Conferences," *PSL Quarterly Review*, Vol. 64, No. 257, pp. 143–66.

Constâncio, Vitor (2011) "Contagion and the European Debt Crisis," BIS central bankers' speeches, October 10.

Cooper, George (2008) *The Origin of Financial Crises: Central Banks, Credit Bubbles and the Efficient Market Fallacy*, New York: Vintage Books.

Corrales, Carmen Amalia (2010) "Toward a Cosmopolitan Ethic in Debt Restructuring," *Law and Contemporary Problems*, Vol. 73, No. 93, Duke University.

Council of the European Union (2011) *Statement by the Heads of State or Government of the Euro Area and EU Institutions*, Brussels, July 21.

Council of the European Union (2012) "Hungary: EUR 495.2 Million in Cohesion Fund Commitments Suspended," Brussels, March 13.

Csajbók, Attila, András Hudecz and Bálint Tamási (2010) *Foreign Currency Borrowing of Households in New EU Member States*, Occasional Paper No. 87, Magyar Nemzeti Bank (Hungarian National Bank), Budapest.

The Daily Bail (2012) "Wake Up America: The Real US Budget Problem: Defense and War Spending," in OZHOUSE.org.

Damrau, Dirk W. (1993) "The Market for Emerging Country Debt: Recent Trends and Outlook," Presentation at the Fifth Szirak Conference, Szirak Castle, Hungary, August.

Daniel, Jean-Marc and Corinne Lhaik (1997) "1797, quand la France était en faillite," *L'Express*, October 9.

Darvas, Zsolt (2012) *Real Effective Exchange Rates for 178 Countries: A New Database*, Bruegel Working Paper, Brussels, March.

Davies, Michael (2011) "The Rise of Sovereign Credit Risk: Implications for Financial Stability," *BIS Quarterly Review*, Basel, September.

Davies, Phil (2007) "The Bank that Hamilton Built," *The Federal Reserve Bank*, September, http://www.minneapolisfed.org/publications_papers/pub_display.cfm?id=1141.

De Meester, Bart (2010) "The Global Financial Crisis and Government Support for Banks: What Role for GATS?" *Journal of International Economic Law*, Vol. 13, No. 1 (March 25), pp. 27–63.

Deutsche Bundesbank (2004) *Monthly Report*, Frankfurt am Main, March.

Deutsche Bundesbank (2011) *Monthly Report*, Vol. 63, No. 10, Frankfurt am Main, October.

Deutsche Bundesbank (2011) *Financial Stability Review 2011*, Frankfurt am Main, November.

Deutsche Bundesbank (2011) "Vorstellung des Finanzstabilitätsberichts 2011 der Deutschen Bundesbank," Frankfurt am Main, November 10.

Deutsche Bundesbank (2012) *Monatsbericht, März 2012 64, Jahrgang Nr. 3*, Frankfurt am Main, March.

De Vries, Margaret Garritsen (1986) *The IMF in a Changing World, 1945–85*, Washington, DC: International Monetary Fund.

Dewatripont, Mathias, Rochet, Jean-Chalres and Jean Tirole (2010) *Balancing the Banks: Global Lessons from the Financial Crisis*, Princeton: Princeton University Press.

Dickerson, A. Mechele (2004) "A Politically Viable Approach to Sovereign Debt Restructuring," Scholarship Repository, *Emory Law Journal*, Vol. 53, pp. 997–1041.

Dodd–Frank Wall Street Reform and Consumer Protection Act, US Congress, HR 4173, January 5, 2010.

Dornbusch, Rudiger (1983) *Flexible Exchange Rates and Interdependence*, NBER Working Paper 1035, Cambridge, MA: National Bureau of Economic Research, Inc.

Dornbusch, Rudiger (1984) "Flexible Exchange Rates and Interdependence," in A. W. Hooke (ed.) *Exchange Regimes and Policy Interdependence*, Washington, DC: International Monetary Fund, pp. 3–30.

Draghi, Mario (2012) "Press Conference," Meeting of the Board of the European Central Bank, Barcelona, May 3.

Draghi, Mario (2012) "Introductory Statement," Hearing on the ESRB before the Committee on Economic and Monetary Affairs of the European Parliament, May 31.

Dyson, Kenneth and Kevin Featherstone (1999) *The Road to Maastricht: Negotiating Economic and Monetary Union*, Oxford: Oxford University Press.

The Economist (2010) "Orban out on a Limb: Hungary's New Prime Minister Takes on the World," August 5.

The Economist (2011) "Climbing Greenback Mountain," September 24–30.

Eichengreen, Barry (2004) *Capital Flows and Crises*, Cambridge, MA and London: MIT Press.

Eichengreen, Barry (2007) *The European Economy Since 1945: Coordinated Capitalism and Beyond*, Princeton and Oxford: Princeton University Press.

Eichengreen, Barry (2008) *Thirteen Questions about the Subprime Crisis*, paper for Conference of the Tobin Project *Toward a New Theory of Financial Regulation*, White Oak Conference and Residency Center, February.

Eichengreen, Barry (2011) *Exorbitant Privilege: The Rise and Fall of the Dollar and the Future of the International Monetary System*, New York and Oxford: Oxford University Press.

Eichengreen, Berry and Ricardo Hausmann (1999) *Exchange Rates and Financial Fragility*, National Bureau for Economic Research, Working Paper 7418, Cambridge, MA: NBER.

Eichengreen, Berry, Ricardo Hausmann and Ugo Panizza (2003) "The Mystery of Original Sin," Paper presented at the Inter-American Development Bank, August.

Eichengreen, Barry, Robert Feldmann, Jeffrey Liebman, Hagen von Jürgen and Charles Wyplosz (2011) *Public Debts: Nuts, Bolts and Worries*, Geneva Report on the World Economy, No. 13, Geneva: International Center for Monetary and Banking Studies, Centre for Economic Policy Research.

Euro Area (2012) "Euro Area Summit Statement," Brussels, June 29.

European Central Bank (n.d.) *The Monetary Policy of the ECB*.

European Central Bank (2001) *Structural Indicators for the EU Banking Sector*, December.

European Central Bank (2006) "Agreement with the Non-European Members on Stage 3 of ERM," Frankfurt am Main, March 16.

European Central Bank (2007) "The EU Arrangements for Financial Crisis Management," *ECB Monthly Bulletin*, February.

European Central Bank (2007) "Agreement with the Non-European Members on Stage 3 of ERM (Amending the Agreement of 16 March 2006)," Frankfurt am Main, December 14.

European Central Bank (2008) "Agreement with the Non-European Members on Stage 3 of ERM (Amending the Agreement of 16 March 2006)," Frankfurt am Main, December 8.

European Central Bank (2008) *The Incentive Structure of the "Originate and Distribute" Model*, Frankfurt am Main, December.

European Central Bank (2010) *Convergence Report*, Frankfurt am Main, May.

European Central Bank (2011) *Opinion of the European Central Bank of 4 November 2011 on Foreign Currency Mortgages and Residential Property Loan Agreement*.

European Central Bank (2012) *Euro Area and National MFI Interest Rates*, Frankfurt am Main, February.

European Central Bank (2012) *Monthly Bulletin*, Frankfurt am Main, March.

European Commission (2008) *European Union Public Finance*, 4th edn, Luxembourg.

European Commission (2011) *Convergence Report 2010*, Brussels.

European Commission (2011) *Green Paper on the Feasibility of Introducing Stability Bonds*, COM (2011) 818, November 23.

European Commission (2012) *Alert Mechanism Report*, COM (2012) 68 Final, Brussels, February 14.

European Commission (2012) *Scoreboard for the Surveillance of Macroeconomic Imbalances*, European Economy, Occasional Papers 92, Brussels, February.

European Commission (2012), *The Greek Loan Facility*, Directorate-General for Economic and Financial Affairs, Brussels, March.

European Commission (2012) *Convergence Programme of Hungary, 2012–2013*, Brussels, April.

European Commission (2012) "Commission Sets Out the Next Steps for Stability, Growth and Jobs," Press release, Brussels, May 30.

European Commission, COM (2011) 819 final, November 23, 2011.

European Commission, COM (2011) 821 final, November 23, 2011.

European Commission, Directorate-General for Economic and Financial Affairs (2010) *Economic Adjustment Programme for Greece*.

European Commission, Directorate-General for Economic and Financial Affairs (2010) *European Economic Forecast—Autumn 2010, Statistical Annex*.

European Commission, Directorate-General for Economic and Financial Affairs (2011) *The Economic Adjustment Program for Greece Third Review—Winter 2011*, Occasional Papers, Brussels.

European Community (1989) *Rapport sur l'Union économique et monétaire dans la Communauté européenne*, Brussels, 12 avril.

European Council (2012) *The European Council in 2011*, Luxembourg, January.

European Council (2012) *Towards a Genuine Economic and Monetary Union: Report by President of the European Council, Herman Van Rompuy*, Brussels, June 26.

European Council (2012) *Conclusions of the European Council, 28/29 June 2012*, EUCO 76/12, Brussels, June 29.

European Union (2004) *Implementation of the EU Commitment on Collective Action Clauses in Documentation of International Debt Issuance*, Economic and Financial Committee, Brussels, ECFIN/CEFCPE(2004)REP/50483 final, November 12.

European Union (2010) *Annual Accounts of the European Union, Financial Year 2010*, Brussels.

European Union (2010) "Consolidated Versions of the Treaty on European Union and the Treaty on the Functioning of the European Union, and the Charter of

Fundamental Rights of the European Union," *Official Journal of the European Union*, C83, Vol. 53, Brussels, March 30.

European Union (2012) "Treaty Establishing the European Stability Mechanism," Brussels.

European Union (2012) "Treaty on Stability, Coordination and Governance in the Economic and Monetary Union" ("Fiscal Pact"), Brussels.

Eurostat (2010) *Euroindicators, 2010.*

Eurostat (2012) *Central Government Debt,* http://epp.eurostat.ec.europa.eu/portal/page/portal/eurostat/home.

Farhi, Emmanuel, Gita Gopinath and Oleg Itskhoki (2011) "Fiscal Devaluations," http://www.economics.harvard.edu/faculty/gopinath/files/fiscal_devaluations.pdf, December 6.

Farrell, Henry and John Quiggin (2012) "Consensus, Dissensus and Economic Ideas: The Rise and Fall of Keynesianism During the Economic Crisis," http://www.henryfarrell.net/Keynes.pdf, March 9.

Financial Crisis Inquiry Commission (2011) *The Financial Crisis Inquiry Report: Final Report of the National Commission on the Causes of the Financial and Economic Crisis in the United States*, Washington, DC: US Government Printing Office, January.

Financial Stability Board (2011) *Shadow Banking: Strengthening Oversight and Regulation, Recommendations of the Financial Stability Board*, October, http://www.financialstabilityboard.org/publications/r_111027a.pdf.

Financial Times (2012) EU, IMF and Bank of Greece statistics, London, February 15.

Fischer, Stanley (2004, 2005) *IMF Essays from a Time in Crisis: The International Financial System, Stabilization, and Development*, Cambridge, MA and London: MIT Press, http://www.henryfarrell.net/Keynes.pdf

Fisher, Irving (1928, 2011) *The Money Illusion*, Mansfield Centre, CT: Martino Publishing.

Fisher, Irving (1932, 2009) *Booms & Depressions: Some First Principles*, Global Financial History Series, Pakthongchai, Thailand: ThaiSunset Publications.

Fisher, Irving (1933, 2010) *The Debt-Deflation Theory of Great Depressions*, Pakthongchai, Thailand: ThaiSunset Publications.

Fitch Ratings (2012) *Sovereign Rating Methodology,* http://www.fitchratings.com/jsp/

Foppiani, Oreste (1998) *La nascita dell'imperialismo Americano (1890–1898): L'impianto della politica di Potenza degli Stati Uniti d'America*, Roma: ESS.

G20 Leaders' Summit, Cannes (2011) "Final Communiqué," Cannes, November 3–4.

Gaddis, John Lewis (2011) *George F. Kennan: An American Life*, New York: Penguin Press.

Gardner, Richard N. (1956) *Sterling–Dollar Diplomacy: Anglo-American Collaboration in the Reconstruction of Multilateral Trade*, London: Oxford University Press.

Geanakoplos, John (2009) "The Leverage Cycle," Cowles Foundation Discussion Paper 1715, Yale University, June.

Gelpern, Anna (2003) "How Collective Action is Changing Sovereign Debt," *International Financial Law Review*, Vol. XXII, pp. 19–23.

Gereben, Áron, Ferenc Karvalits and Zalán Kocsis (2011) *Monetary Policy Challenges during the Crisis in a Small Open Dollarized Economy: The Case of Hungary*, BIS Papers No. 67.

German Council of Economic Experts (2011) "Assume Responsibility for Europe," First Chapter, Annual Report 2011/12, Wiesbaden.

Gerschenkron, Alexander (1962) *Economic Backwardness in Historical Perspective: A Book of Essays*, Cambridge, MA: Belknap Press.

Gianviti, Francois (2004) *Current Legal Aspects of Monetary Sovereignty*, Seminar Paper, Washington, DC: International Monetary Fund, http://www.imf.org/external/np/leg/sem/2004/cdmfl/eng/gianvi.pdf.

Giovanoli, Mario (2010) "The International Financial Architecture and its Reform after the Global Crisis," Mario Giovanoli and Diego Devos (eds) *International Monetary and Financial Law: The Global Crisis*, Oxford: Oxford University Press, pp. 3–39.

Giovanoli, Mario and Diego Devos (2010) *International Monetary and Financial Law: The Global Crisis*, Oxford: Oxford University Press.

Gold, Joseph (1978) *The Second Amendment of the Fund's Articles of Agreement*, Pamphlet Series No. 25, Washington, DC: International Monetary Fund.

González-Páramo, José Manuel (2011) "The Banking Sector towards the 'New Normal'—Some Considerations," BIS Central bankers' speeches, January.

Goodhart, Charles A. E. (2009) *The Regulatory Response to the Financial Crisis*, Cheltenham, UK and Northampton, MA: Edward Elgar.

Gortsos, Christos Vl. (2009) "Assessment of the Banking 'Rescue' Packages and 'Recovery' Plans of the Member States in the European Union," *Banking Rescue Measures in the EU Member States—Compilation of Briefing Papers*, Report, European Parliament, Policy Department, Economic and Scientific Policy, IP/A/ECON/RT/2008-29, pp. 9–46.

Gortsos, Christos Vl. (2011) "Basel III: The Reform of the Existing Regulatory Framework of the Basel Committee on Banking Supervision for Strengthening the Stability of the International Banking System," Werner Meng, Georg Ress and Torsten Stein (eds) *Europäische Integration und Gloablisierung: Festshrift zum 60-jährigen Bestehen des Europa-Instituts*, Schriften des Europa-Insituts der Universität des Saarlandes—Rechtswissenshaft, Band 84, Baden-Baden: Nomos Verlagsgesellschaft, pp. 167–84.

Gortsos, Christos Vl. (2011) *European Banking Law*, Notes for the postgraduate program of the Europa Institut, Universität des Saarlandes, http://www.ecefil.eu/Up1Files/monographs.

Gortsos, Christos Vl. (2011) *The European Banking Authority within the European System of Financial Supervision*, ECEFIL Working Paper Series No. 2011/1, http://www.ecefic.eu.

Gortsos, Christos (2011) Written Evidence in House of Lords: *The Future of Economic Governance in the EU*, European Union Committee, 12th Report of Session 2010–11, Vol. II: *Evidence*, EGE 6, March 24.

Graeber, David (2012) *Debt, the First 5000 Years*, New York: Melville House.

Greenspan, Alan (2007) *The Age of Turbulence: Adventures in a New World*, New York: Penguin Press.

Griffith-Jones, Stephany (1984) *International Finance and Latin America*, London: Croom Helm.

Gross, Daniel (2010) "Only Athens has the Power to Rescue Greece," *Financial Times*, April 15.

Group of Ten (1996) *The Resolution of Sovereign Liquidity Crises: Report to the Ministers and Governors Prepared under the Auspices of the Deputies*, May, http://www.bis.org/publ/gten03.pdf (the Rey Commission Report).

Group of Ten (2002) *Report of the Group of Ten Working Group on Contractual Clauses*, September 26, http://www.imf.org/external/np/g10/2002/cc.pdf.

Hall, Robert E. (2010) "Why Does the Economy Fall to Pieces after a Financial Crisis?" *Journal of Economic Perspectives*, Vol. 24, No. 4, pp. 3–20.

Hankel, Wilhelm, Wilhelm Nölling, Karl Albrecht Schachtschneider, Dieter Spethmann, Joachim Starbatty (2011) *Das Euro-Abenteuer geht zu Ende: Wie die Währungsunion unsere Lebensgrundlagen zerstört*, Rotenburg: Kopp.

Hanson, Victor Davis (2005) *A War Like No Other: How the Athenians and Spartans Fought the Peloponnesian War*, New York: Random House.

Hardouvelis, Gikas A. (2011) *The Greek Crisis, its Resolution and Implications for the EU and Beyond*, Vienna: Vienna Institute.

Hart, Oliver (1979) "Monopolistic Competition in a Large Economy with Differentiated Commodities," *Review of Economic Studies*, Vol. 66, pp. 1–30.

Hasse, Rolf H., Hermann Schneider and Klaus Weigelt (eds) (2005) *Lexikon Soziale Marktwirtschaft, Wirtschaftspolitik von A bis Z, 2., aktualisierte und erwiterte Auflage*, Paderborn, München, Wien and Zürich: Ferdinand Schöningh.

Hayek, Friedrich A. (1937, 1964) *Monetary Nationalism and International Stability*, New York: Augustus M. Kelley, Reprints of Economic Classics.

Hayek, Friedrich A. (1976, 1978, 1990) *Denationalisation of Money: The Argument Refined. An Analysis of the Theory and Practice of Concurrent Currencies*, London: Institute of Economic Affairs.

Heilperin, Michael A. (1968) *Aspects of the Pathology of Money*, London: Michael Joseph.

Hellenic Republic, Ministry of Finance (2012) "PSI Launch," Press release, February, http://www.minfin.gr/portal/en/resource/contentObject/id/7ad6442f-1777-4d02-80fb-91191c606664.

Hellenic Republic, Ministry of Finance (2012) Press release, April 25.

Hellenic Statistical Authority (2012) *Gross Domestic Product at Market Prices (Years 2000–2011)*.

Hieronymi, Otto (1973) *Economic Discrimination Against the United States in Western Europe, 1945–1958: Dollar Shortage and the Rise of Regionalism*, Genève: Librarie Droz.

Hieronymi, Otto (1980) (ed.) *The New Economic Nationalism*, London: Macmillan.

Hieronymi, Otto (1982) "In Search of a New Economics for the 1980s: The Need for a Return to Fixed Exchange Rates," Otto Hieronymi (ed.) *International Order: A View from Geneva*, Annals of International Studies, Institut Universitaire de Hautes Etudes Internationales, Geneva, Vol. 12, pp. 107–26.

Hieronymi, Otto (1995) "The Case for an 'Extended EMS': A New International Monetary Order to be Built by Europe, Japan and the United States," Miklos Szabo-Pelsöczy (ed.) *The Global Monetary System After the Fall of the Soviet Empire* (In Memoriam Robert Triffin, 1911–93, Sixth Conference of the Robert Triffin-Sziràk Foundation, Sziràk, 1993), Aldershot: Ashgate, pp. 57–67.

Hieronymi, Otto (1996) "International Capital Markets and the Financial Integration of the Transition Countries," Unpublished manuscript, Geneva.

Hieronymi, Otto (1996) "The International Financial Institutions and the Challenge of Transition and Reconstruction in the Former Communist Countries of Central and Eastern Europe," Miklos Szabo-Pelsöczy (ed.) *Fifty Years After Bretton Woods* (Sixth Conference of the Robert Triffin-Sziràk Foundation, Brussels, 1994), Aldershot: Ashgate, pp. 129–40.

Hieronymi, Otto (1998) "Agenda for a New Monetary Reform," *Futures*, Vol. 30, No. 8, pp. 769–81.

Hieronymi, Otto (2002) "Wilhelm Röpke, the Social Market Economy and Today's Domestic and International Order," Otto Hieronymi, Chiara Jasson and Alexandra Roversi (eds) *Colloque Wilhelm Röpke (1899–1966): The Relevance of His Teaching Today. Globalization and the Social Market Economy*, Geneva: HEI-Webster University, Cahiers HEI, Vol. 6, pp. 6–32.

Hieronymi, Otto (2005) "The 'Social Market Economy' and Globalisation: The Lessons from the European Model for Latin America," Emilio Fontela Montes and Joaquin Guzmàn Cueva (eds) *Brasil y la Economia Social de Mercado*, Cuadernos del Grupo de Alcantara, pp. 247–300.

Hieronymi, Otto (2009) (ed.) *Globalization and the Reform of the International Banking and Monetary System*, Basingstoke: Palgrave Macmillan.

Hieronymi, Otto (2009) "Rebuilding the International Monetary Order: The Responsibility of Europe, Japan and the United States," *Revista de Economia Mundial* (Madrid), No. 29, pp. 197–226, October.

Hieronymi, Ottó (2011) "The Economic and Social Policies of the Orbán Government—A View from Outside," *Hungarian Review*, Budapest, Vol. II, No. 3, pp. 40–60.

Hieronymi, Otto (2012) (ed.) *Renewing the Western Community: The Challenge for the US, Europe and Japan* (will be published in 2013).

Holmström, Bengt (2008) *The Panic of 2007: Maintaining Stability in a Changing Financial System*, Proceedings of the 2008 Jackson Hole Conference, Kansas City, MO: Federal Reserve Bank of Kansas City.

Holmström, Bengt and Jean Tirole (2011) *Inside and Outside Liquidity*, Cambridge, MA: MIT Press.

Holtom, Paul, Mark Bromley, Pieter D. Wezeman and Siemon T. Wezeman (2012) *Trends in International Arms Transfers 2011*, Stockholm: SIPRI, http://books.sipri.org/index_html?c_category_id=65.

Hooke, Angus W. (1984) (ed.) *Exchange Regimes and Policy Interdependence*, Washington, DC: International Monetary Fund.

Hördahl, Peter, Oreste Tristani and David Vestin (2004) *A Joint Econometric Model of Macroeconomic and Term Structure Dynamics*, European Central Bank, Working Paper Series No. 405, Frankfurt am Main, November.

http://epp.eurostat.ec.europa.eu/cache/ITY_PUBLIC/2-22102010-AP/EN/2-22102010-AP-EN.PDF.

http://www.bis.org/list/speeches/author_deepak+mohanty/index.htm.

http://www.bis.org/review/r110128a.pdf.

http://www.fitchratings.com/creditdesk/reports/report_frame.cfm?rpt_id=648978.

http://www.ieo.
imf.org/ieo/pages/IEOPreview.aspx?img=i6nZpr3iSlU%3D&mappingid=dRx2VaDG7EY%3D.

http://www.imf.org/external/np/pp/eng/2010/052710.pdf.

http://www.standardandpoors.com/ratings/articles/en/.

Hume, David (1752) "Of Commerce," *Essays Moral, Political and Literary*, http://presspubs.uchicago.edu/founders/documents/v1ch4s3.html.

IFO Institute (2011) "Bogenberg Declaration: Sixteen Theses on the Situation of the European Monetary Union," Munich, October 15.

International Monetary Fund (2002) *Collective Action Clauses in Sovereign Bond Contracts: Encouraging Greater Use*, IMF publication, prepared by the Policy Development and Review, International Capital Markets and Legal Departments, Washington, DC, June 6.

International Monetary Fund (2002) *The Design of Debt Restructuring Mechanism—Further Considerations*, Washington, DC: Legal and Policy Development and Review Departments, IMF, November 27.

International Monetary Fund (2003) "IMF Board Discusses Possible Features of a Sovereign Debt Restructuring Mechanism," *Public Information Notice* No. 03/06, Washington, DC: IMF, January 7.

International Monetary Fund (2003) *Collective Action Clauses: Recent Developments and Issues*, IMF publication, prepared by the International Capital Markets, Legal and Policy Development and Review Departments, Washington, DC, March 25.

International Monetary Fund (2003) "Report of the Managing Director to the International Monetary and Financial Committee on a Statutory Debt Restructuring Mechanism," Washington, DC: IMF, April 8.

International Monetary Fund (2003) "Communiqué of the International Monetary and Financial Committee of the Board of Governors of the International Monetary Fund," Washington, DC: IMF, April 12.

International Monetary Fund (2006) *Article IV of the Fund's Articles of Agreement: An Overview of the Legal Framework*, Washington, DC: IMF, June 28.

International Monetary Fund (2006) *Guidelines on Conditionality*, Decision No. 12864-(02/102), as amended by Decision No. 13812-(06/98), November 15.

International Monetary Fund (2010) *Central Banking Lessons from the Crisis*, Policy Paper, May 27, Washington, DC: IMF.

International Monetary Fund (2010) *G-20 Mutual Assessment Process—Alternative Policy Scenarios*, G-20 Toronto Summit, Toronto, Canada. Washington, DC: IMF, June 26–7.

International Monetary Fund (2011) *Annual Report on Exchange Arrangements and Exchange Restrictions 2010*, Washington, DC: IMF.

International Monetary Fund (2011) *Articles of Agreement*, Washington, DC: IMF.

International Monetary Fund (2011) *International Financial Statistics, Yearbook 2011*, Washington, DC: IMF.

International Monetary Fund (2011) *Japan Sustainability Report*, Washington, DC: IMF.

International Monetary Fund (2011) *Slowing Growth, Rising Risks*, World Economic Outlook, World Economic and Financial Surveys, Washington, DC: IMF, September.

International Monetary Fund (2012) *Balancing Fiscal Policy Risk*, Fiscal Monitor, World Economic and Financial Surveys, Washington, DC: IMF, April.

International Monetary Fund (2012) *Global Financial Stability Report: The Quest for Lasting Stability*, World Economic and Financial Surveys, Washington, DC: IMF, April.

International Monetary Fund (2012) *Growth Resuming, Dangers Remain*, World Economic Outlook, World Economic and Financial Surveys, Washington, DC: IMF, April.

International Monetary Fund, Country Report No. 12/57 (2012) *Greece: Request for Extended Arrangement Under the Extended Fund Facility—Staff Report; Staff Supplement*; Press Release on the Executive Board Discussion; and Statement by the Executive Director for Greece, Washington, DC: IMF, March 16.

International Monetary Fund, Independent Evaluation Office (2011) *IMF Performance in the Run-up to the Financial and Economic Crisis: IMF Surveillance in 2004–07*, Evaluation Report, Washington, DC: IMF.

Issing, Otmar (2004) "The New EU Member States: Convergence and Stability," EU Enlargement and Monetary Integration, Speech by Otmar Issing, Member of the Executive Board of the ECB, Third ECB Central Banking Conference, Frankfurt am Main, October 22.

Jacklin, Nancy P. (2010) "Addressing Collective-Action Problems in Securitized Debt," *Law and Contemporary Problems*, Vol. 73, pp. 173–91.

Kaletsky, Anatole (2009) "Economists are the Forgotten Guilty Men. Academics—and their Mad Theories—are to Blame for the Financial Crisis. They too Deserve to be Hauled into the Dock," *Financial Times*, London, June 2.

Kaminsky, Graciela L., Carmen M. Reinhart and Carlos A. Végh (2004) "When It Rains, It Pours: Procyclical Capital Flows and Policies," *NBER Macroeconomic Annual 2004*, ed. Mark Gertler and Kenneth S. Rogoff, Cambridge, MA: MIT Press, pp. 11–53.

Keynes, John Maynard (1920) *The Economic Consequences of the Peace*, New York: Harcourt, Brace and Howe.

Keynes, John Maynard (1922) *A Revision of the Treaty, Being a Sequel to the Economic Consequences of the Peace*, London: Macmillan and Co. Ltd.

Keynes, John Maynard (1936) *The General Theory of Employment, Interest and Money*, London: Macmillan.

Kiff, John and Paul Mills (2007) *Money for Nothing and Checks for Free: Recent Developments in U.S. Subprime Mortgage Markets*, IMF Working Paper, WP/07/188, Washington, DC: International Monetary Fund.

Kindleberger, Charles P. (1986) *The World in Depression 1929–1939*, rev. edn, Berkeley: University of California Press.

Koo, Richard C. (2009) *The Holy Grail of Macroeconomics: Lessons from Japan's Great Recession*, rev. and updated edn, Singapore: John Wiley & Sons (Asia).

Koo, Richard C. (2011) *The World in Balance Sheet Recession: Causes, Cure, and Politics*, Tokyo: Nomura Research Institute.

Krueger, Anne (2001) "International Financial Architecture for 2001: A New Approach to Sovereign Debt Restructuring," Address by the First Deputy Managing Director of the IMF, Washington, DC: American Enterprise Institute, November 21.

Krueger, Anne O. (2002) *A New Approach to Sovereign Debt Restructuring*, Washington, DC: International Monetary Fund, April.

Krugman, Paul (2010) "Give Me Your Tired, Your Poor, Your Hungary," *The New York Times*, August 4.

Krugman, Paul (2012) "Europe's Economic Suicide," *International Herald Tribune*, April 17.

Kunimune, Kozo (2004) *Overcoming Asia's Currency and Financial Crises: A Theoretical Investigation*, Occasional Papers Series, Chiba: Japan External Trade Organization.

Lamfalussy, Alexandre (2000) *Financial Markets in Emerging Markets: An Essay on Financial Globalization and Fragility*, New Haven and London: Yale University Press.

Lamfalussy, Alexandre (2009) "The Specificity of the Current Crisis," The Belgian Financial Forum and the Robert Triffin International Foundation, Brussels, April 30.

Lamfalussy, Alexandre (2011) "Keynote Speech," 10th BIS Annual Conference, Lucerne, June.

Lane, Philip R. (2010) *International Financial Integration and the External Positions of the Euro Area Countries*, OECD Economics Department, Working Papers No. 830, Paris.

Lastra, Rosa M. (2006) *Legal Foundations of International Monetary Stability*, Oxford and New York: Oxford University Press.

Lastra, Rosa M. (2011) *Cross-Border Bank Insolvency*, Oxford and New York: Oxford University Press.

Lastra, Rosa M. and Geoffrey Wood (2010) "The Crisis of 2007–2009: Nature, Causes and Reactions," *Journal of International Economic Law*, Vol. 13, No. 3 (September), pp. 531–50.

Lipinska, Anna (2008) *The Maastricht Convergence Criteria and Optimal Monetary Policy for the EMU Accession Countries*, European Central Bank, Working Paper Series No. 896, Frankfurt am Main, May.

Look, Chan Ho (2011) "Bank Insolvency Law in the United Kingdom," Rosa M. Lastra (ed.) *Cross-Border Bank Insolvency*, Oxford and New York: Oxford University Press, pp. 276–381.

Louis, Jean-Victor (2004) "Economic and Monetary Union: Law and Institutions," *CML Review*, Vol. 41, pp. 575–608.

Louis, Jean-Victor (2006) "The Review of the Stability and Growth Pact," *CML Review*, Vol. 43, pp. 85–106.

Louis, Jean-Victor (2010) "Guest Editorial: The No-Bailout and Rescue Packages," *CML Review*, Vol. 47, pp. 971–86.

Machlup, Fritz (1966, 2003) *International Monetary Economics*, London: Routledge.

Magnus, George (2012) "Allons enfants: The Euro Crisis and the French Elections," UBS Investment Research, *Economic Insights*, February 6.

Marsh, David (2009) *The Euro: The Politics of the New Global Currency*, New Haven, CT and London: Yale University Press.

Mauldin, John and Jonathan Tepper (2011) *Endgame: The End of the Debt Supercycle and How It Changes Everything*, Hoboken, NJ: John Wiley.

Meng, Werner, Georg Ress and Torsten Stein (2011) (eds) *Europäische Integration und Gloablisierung, Festshrift zum 60-jährigen Bestehen des Europa-Instituts*, Schriften des Europa-Insituts der Universität des Saarlandes, Rechtswissenshaft, Band 84, Baden-Baden: Nomos Verlagsgesellschaft.

Merler, Silvia and Jean Pisany-Ferry (2012) *Sudden Stops in the Euro Area*, Bruegel Policy Contribution, Issue 2012/06, Brussels, March.

MNB (Hungarian National Bank) (2008) *Letter of Intent*, http://english.mnb.hu/engine.aspx?page=mnben_stand-by_arrangement.

Mohanty, Deepak (2011) "Lessons for Monetary Policy from the Global Financial Crisis: An Emerging Market Perspective," Bank for International Settlements' central bankers' speeches, April.

Monti, Mario (1976) (ed.) *The New Inflation and Monetary Policy*, London: Macmillan.

Moreno, Ramon (2011) *Policymaking from a "Macroprudential" Perspective in Emerging Market Economies*, BIS Working Papers No. 336, Basel.

Münchau, Wolfgang (2011) "Muddling Through Will Not Work This Time," *Financial Times*, March 14.

Mundell, Robert (1980) "Monetary Nationalism and Floating Exchange Rates," Otto Hieronymi (ed.) *The New Economic Nationalism*, London: Macmillan, pp. 34–50.

Mundell, Robert (2006) "Acceptance of an Honorary Degree from the University of Bologna," Bologna, September 2.

Nafziger, E. Wayne (1993) *The Debt Crisis in Africa*, Baltimore, MD: Johns Hopkins University Press.

Nicholls, Anthony J. (1994) *Freedom with Responsibility: The Social Market Economy in Germany, 1918–1963*, Oxford: Clarendon Press.

Nierhaus, Wolfgang (2011) "Wirtschaftskonjunktur 2010: Prognose und Wirklichkeit," Ifo Schnelldienst 2/2011—64, Münich: Jahrgang.

Norberg, Johan (2009) *Financial Fiasco: How America's Infatuation with Home-Ownership and Easy Money Created the Economic Crisis*, Washington, DC: Cato Institute.

OECD (1988, 1989, 1990, 1991, 1992, 1993, 1994) *Economic Surveys: Japan*, Paris: OECD.

OECD (1999) *External Debt Statistics, Debt Stocks and Debt Service, 1987–1998*, Paris: OECD.

OECD (2002) *External Debt Statistics 2001–2002: The Debt of Developing Countries and Countries in Transition*, Paris: OECD.

OECD (2010) *Central Government Debt, Statistical Yearbook, 2000–2009*, Paris: OECD.

OECD (2012) *Fiscal Consolidation: How Much, How Fast and by What Means?* An Economic Outlook Report, OECD Economic Policy Papers No. 01, Paris, April.

Otte, Max (2011) *Stoppt das Euro-Desaster!* Berlin: Ullstein Streitschrift.

Padoa-Schioppa, Tommaso (1984) *Money, Economic Policy and Europe*, The European Perspective Series, Brussels: The Commission of the European Communities.

Padoa-Schioppa, Tommaso (1994) *The Road to Monetary Union in Europe: The Emperor, the Kings and the Genies*, Oxford: Oxford University Press.

Padoa-Schioppa, Tommaso (2004) *The Euro and Its Central Bank: Getting United after the Union*, Cambridge, MA: MIT Press.

Padoa-Schioppa, Tommaso (2010) *The Debt Crisis in the Euro Area: Interest and Passions*, Notre Europe Policy Brief No. 16.

Panetta, Fabio, Thomas Faeh, Giuseppe Grande, Corrinne Ho, Michael King, Aviram Levy, Federico M. Signoretti, Marco Taboga and Andrea Zaghini (2009) *An Assessment of Financial Sector Rescue Programmes*, BIS Papers No. 48, Monetary and Economic Department, Bank for International Settlements, July.

Paulson, Henry M. (2010) *On the Brink: Inside the Race to Stop the Collapse of the Global Financial System*, New York: Hachette.

Petrovic, Ana and Ralf Tutsh (2009) *National Rescue Measures in Response to the Current Financial Crisis*, ECB Legal Working Paper Series No. 8, July.

Pisani-Ferry, Jean, André Sapir and Guntram B. Wolff (2011) *An Evaluation of IMF Surveillance of the Euro Area*, Bruegel Blueprint Series XIV, Brussels: Bruegel.

Pisani-Ferry, Jean, André Sapir and Guntram B. Wolff (2012) *The Messy Rebuilding of Europe*, Bruegel Policy Brief, Issue 2012/01, Brussels, March.

Plickert, Von Philip (2008) *Wandlungen des Neoliberalismus*, Stuttgart: Lucius & Lucius.

Posner, Eric A. (2009) *The Perils of Global Legalism*, Chicago and London: University of Chicago Press.

Posner, Richard A. (2010) *The Crisis of Capitalist Democracy*, Cambridge, MA and London: Harvard University Press.

Praet, Peter (2012) "Monetary Policy at Crisis Times," Lecture, International Center for Monetary and Banking Studies, Geneva, European Central Bank, Directorate Communications, Press and Information Division, Frankfurt am Main, February 20.

Rajan, Raghuram G. (2010) *Fault Lines: How Hidden Fractures Still Threaten the World Economy*, Princeton: Princeton University Press.

Ràsonyi, Peter (2012) "Schamlose Libor-Manipulationen bei Barclays," *Neue Zürcher Zeitung*, June 28.

Reinhart, Carmen M. and M. Belen Sbrancia, with discussion comments by Ignazio Visco and Alan Taylor (2011) *The Liquidation of Government Debt*, BIS Working Papers, No. 363, Basel, November.

Reinhart, Carmen M. and Kenneth S. Rogoff (2009) *This Time is Different: Eight Centuries of Financial Folly*, Princeton and Oxford: Princeton University Press.

Reinhart, Carmen M. and Kenneth S. Rogoff (2010) "Growth in a Time of Debt," Draft, *American Economic Review*, Papers and Proceedings.

Reinhart, Carmen M. and Kenneth S. Rogoff (2011) *A Decade of Debt*, Washington, DC: Peterson Institute of International Economics.

Ritter, Gerhard A. (2006) *Der Preis des deutschen Einheit, die Wiedervereinigung und die Krise des Sozialstaates*, Munich: Verlag C. H. Beck.

Rochet, Jean-Charles and Xavier Vives (2004) "Coordination Failures and the Lender of Last Resort: Was Bagehot Right After All?" *Journal of the European Economic Association*, Vol. 2, No. 6, pp. 1116–47.

Rogoff, Kenneth and Jeromin Zettelmeyer (2002) "Bankruptcy Procedures for Sovereigns: A History of Ideas, 1976–2001," *IMF Staff Papers*, Vol. 49, No. 3, Washington, DC: International Monetary Fund.

Rogoff, Kenneth and Jeromin Zettelmeyer (2002) "Early Ideas on Sovereign Bankruptcy Reorganization: A Survey," *IMF Working Paper*, Washington, DC: Research Department, International Monetary Fund, March.

Rokas, Nikos K. and Christos Vl. Gortsos (2012) *Elements of Banking Law*, Athens: Nomiki Bibliothiki Group (in Greek).

Röpke, Wilhelm (1942) *International Economic Disintegration*, London: William Hodge.

Röpke, Wilhelm (1951) "Austerity," reprinted in Wilhelm Röpke (1962) *Wirrnis und Wahrheit*, Erlenbach-Zürich: Eugen Rentsch.

Röpke, Wilhelm (1963) *Economics of the Free Society*, Chicago: Henry Regnery.

Roubini, Nouriel, Arnab Das, Jennifer Kapila, James Mason, David Nowkowski, Elisa Parisi- and Christian Menegatti (2010) *A How-To Manual for Plan B: Options for Restructuring Greek Debt*, Roubini Global Economics.

Rudzio, Wolfgang (1983, 2006) *Das politische System der Bundsrepublik Deutschland, 7, aktualisierte und erweiterte Auflage*, VS Verlag für Sozialwissenschaften.

Ryan, Cillian (2011) "The Euro Crisis and Crisis Management: Big Lessons from a Small Island," *International Economics and Economic Policy*, Vol. 8, No. 1, pp. 31–43.

Sachverständigenrat zur Begutachtung der gesamtwirtschaftlichen Entwicklung (2011) *Chancen für einen stabilen Aufschwung*, Jaresgutachten 2010/2011, Wiesbaden.

Sakbani, Michael (1998) "The Euro on Schedule: Analysis of its European and International Implications," Miklós Szabó-Pelsőczi (ed.) *European Monetary Integration*, Avebury and the Robert Triffin Foundation, pp. 48–74.

Sakbani, Michael (2010) "The Global Economic Recession: Analysis; Evaluation and Implications of Policy Response and System Reforms Proposals," *Journal of Studies in Economics and Finance*, June.

Sakbani, Michael (2011) "The US Budget Impasse: Dogma v. Economic Sense," in michaelsakbani.blogspot.com, August 1.

Sarrazin, Thilo (2012) *Europa braucht den Euro nicht: Wie uns politisches Wunschdenken in die Krise geführt hat*, Frankfurt: DVA.

Savona, Paolo (2000) (ed.) *The New Architecture of the International Monetary System*, Boston, MA, Dordrecht and London: Kluwer Academic Publishers.

Schmid, Thomas (2011) "Theo Waigel gibt dem Euro noch weitere 400 Jahre," Interview with Theo Waigel, *Welt am Sonntag*, Hamburg, December 25.

Schumpeter, Joseph A. (1939) *Business Cycles: A Theoretical, Historical and Statistical Analysis of the Capitalist Process*, New York: McGraw-Hill Books [reprinted by Porcupine Books, 1982].

Schumpeter, Joseph A. (1950) *Capitalism, Socialism and Democracy*, 3rd edn, New York: Harper & Row.

Sibert, Anne (2011) *Debt Restructuring: Ramifications for the Euro Area*, Draft Briefing Note, IP/A/ECON/NT/2011-02, European Parliament, Committee on Economic and Monetary Affairs, Brussels, June.

Skidelsky, Robert (1992, 1994) *John Maynard Keynes: The Economist as Saviour, 1920–1937*, London: Macmillan.

Skidelsky, Robert (2000) *John Maynard Keynes: Fighting for Britain, 1937–1946*, London: Macmillan.

Skidelsky, Robert (2009, 2010) *Keynes: The Return of the Master*, London: Allen Lane [revised and updated edition published by Penguin Books).

Sohmen, Egon (1969) *Flexible Exchange Rates*, rev. edn, Chicago: University of Chicago Press.

Spero, Joan and Jeffrey Hart (1996) *The Politics of International Economic Relations*, London: Bedford/St Martin's.

Standard & Poor's (2010) *Credit Trends: Global Potential Fallen Angels*, September 10.

Stiglitz, Joseph E., José Antonio Ocampo, Shari Spiegel, Ricardo Ffrench-Davis and Deepak Nayyar (2006) *Stability with Growth: Macroeconomics, Liberalization, and Development*, The Initiative for Policy Dialogue Series, Oxford: Oxford University Press.

Stiglitz, Joseph E. and Linda J. Bilmes (2008) *The Three Trillion Dollar War: The True Cost of the Iraq Conflict*, New York: W. W. Norton & Company.

Summers, Larry (1997) "Testimony before the Senate Budget Committee," reported in *Financial Times*, October 22.

Than, Krisztina (2010) "Hungary Risks Markets' Goodwill with IMF/EU Failure," Reuters Analysis, July 23.

Taibbi, Matt (2010, 2011) *Griftopia: A Story of Bankers, Politicians and the Most Audacious Power Grab in American History*, New York: Speigel & Grau Trade Paperbacks.

Tirole, Jean (2002) *Financial Crises, Liquidity and the International Monetary System*, Princeton: Princeton University Press.

Tirole, Jean (2010) "Overcoming Adverse Selection: How Public Intervention Can Restore Market Functioning," Mimeo, Toulouse School of Economics.

Tirole, Jean (2010) "Lessons from the Crisis," Mathias Dewatripont, Jean-Chalres Rochet and Jean Tirole (eds) *Balancing the Banks: Global Lessons from the Financial Crisis*, Princeton and Oxford: Princeton University Press, pp. 10–77.

Tobin, James (1980) *Asset Accumulation and Economic Activity*, Chicago: University of Chicago Press.

Trezise, Philippe H. (1979) (ed.) *The European Monetary System: Its Promise and Prospects*, Washington, DC: Brookings Institution.

Triffin, Robert (1969) "The Thrust of History in International Monetary Reform," *Foreign Affairs*, http://www.foreignaffairs.com/issues/1969/47/3, Vol. 47, No. 3, April.

Unger, Roberto Mangabeira (2007) *Free Trade Reimagined; The World Division of Labor and the Method of Economics*, Princeton and Oxford: Princeton University Press.

US Congress, House Committee on Foreign Affairs, Hearing Before the Subcommittee on International Economic Policy and Trade (1989) *The International Debt Crisis: A Review of the Brady Plan*, Washington, DC, April 19.

Vallée, Shahin (2012) *The Internationalisation Path of the Renminbi*, Bruegel Working Paper 2012/05, Brussels, March.

Van Rompuy, Herman (2012) "The Discovery of Co-Responsibility: Europe in the Debt Crisis," Speech at the Humboldt University, Walter Hallstein Institute for European Constitutional Law, Berlin: European Council, February 6.

Van Rompuy, Herman (2012) *Towards a Genuine Economic and Monetary Union*, Report by the President of the European Council, EUCO 120/12, Brussels, June 26.

Vause, Nick, Goetz von Peter, Mathias Drehmann and Vladyslav Sushko (2012) "European Bank Funding and Deleveraging", *BIS Quarterly Review*, Basel, March.

Vautravers, Alexandre (1998) *L'impact de la technologie sur la conduit de la guerre*, DEA d'Histoire contemporaine, Université Lumière, Lyon 2.

Verley, Patrick (1997) *L'échelle du Monde, Essai sur l'industrialisation de l'Occident*, Paris: Gallimard.

Volcker, Paul and Toyoo Gyothen (1992) *Changing Fortunes: The World's Money and the Threat to American Leadership*, New York: Times Books.

Von Mises, Ludwig (1912, 1953) *The Theory of Money and Credit*, New Haven, CT: Yale University Press.

Wallerstein, Immanuel (1979) *The Capitalist World Economy*, New York: Cambridge University Press.

The Wall Street Journal (2012) "Greece Sets Austerity Plan: Leaders Approve Unpopular Cuts; Europe Wants Vote to Secure Another Bailout," February 10.

Wapshott, Nicholas (2011) *Keynes–Hayek: The Clash that Defined Modern Economics*, New York: W. W. Norton & Company.

Weisbrot, Mark (2010) "To Viktor Go the Spoils: How Hungary Blazes a Trail in Europe," *The Guardian*, August 9.

Williamson, John (1983) (ed.) *IMF Conditionality*, Washington, DC: Institute for International Economics.

Williamson, John (2009) *Understanding Special Drawing Rights (SDRs)*, Peterson Institute for International Economics, No. PB09-11, June, http://www.iie.com/publications/pb/pb09-11.pdf.

Wolf, Martin (2011) "Thinking through the Unthinkable," *Financial Times*, London, November 9.

Wolf, Martin (2012) "Banks are on a Euro Zone Knife-Edge," *Financial Times*, April 25.

World Bank (2012) *Global Development Finance: External Debt of Developing Countries*, Washington, DC: World Bank.

World Bank and International Monetary Fund (2010) *Quarterly External Debt Statistics Database*, Washington, DC: General Data Dissemination System (GDDS).

Wright, Mark L. J. (2011) *The Theory of Sovereign Debt*, Los Angeles: University of California Press.

Yoshikawa, Hiroshi (1999, 2001) *Japan's Lost Decade*, Tokyo: The International House of Japan.

Index

state-controlled economy, 33
state-owned economy, 33
Statutory Sovereign Debt Restructuring
  Mechanism, 159, 160
stepping-out guarantor (*see* guarantor)
stimulative measures, 74, 75
stimulus (*see* fiscal stimulus)
stock (index, indicator), 213
stock market boom-and-bust, 212
Stone, Richard, 65
"storage of value," 58
Strategic Defense Initiative, 232
stress test, 173–174
structural adjustment (*see* adjustment)
Structural adjustment program, 45, 136,
  232
subprime (*see* crisis)
subsidiarity, 62
Sudan, 231
Summers, Larry, 46, 47
supervision (banking, macro-prudential,
  micro-prudential), 118, 120, 145, 165,
  167
supervisory (measures, powers), 173–174
supply-side economics, 232
supranational authorities/institutions,
  124
surplus country, 25, 26, 27, 29, 30, 43
surveillance of budgetary positions (*see*
  budgetary surveillance)
surveillance of economic policies (*see*
  economic surveillance)
Sweden, 14, 16, 17, 101, 133, 143, 217,
  232
Swiss banking secrecy, 222
Swiss franc, 39, 52, 117, 118, 123
Switzerland, 14, 15, 16, 17, 27, 39,
  90n66, 116, 213, 222
systemic (crisis, risk), 1, 67, 84, 192,
  200, *see also* contagion

T
Taiwan, 232
tax (base, code, collection, compliance,
  cut, evasion, haven, measure, payer,
  rate), 5, 50, 73, 80, 97, 98, 99, 120,
  123, 127, 131, 154, 189, 197, 202,
  203, 204, 205, 207, 209, 222–223,
  233, 239, *see also* fiscal paradise
Taxation, 57, 96, 111, 190, 202, *see also*
  income tax

T-Bank, 177, 178
TEC (*see* Treaty on the European
  Community)
technology (diffusion, transfer), 34, 36,
  235
Templars, 228
terms-of-trade, 39
TEU (*see* Treaty on European Union)
TFEU (*see* Treaty on the Functioning of
  the European Union)
Thai, 232
Thatcherism, 77
Third World, 40, 231, 232
Tirole, Jean, 182n3, 197
"too much government," 83
too much market', 83
trade deficit (*see* deficit)
trade liberalization (*see* liberalisation/
  liberalization, integration)
trade protectionism (*see* protectionism)
transfer (issue, union), 32, 106
transfer of sovereignty, 59–60
transition country/economy/nation,
  110, 118
transmission mechanism, 19, 47
Treasury Bonds, 225
Treaty on European Union, 89n64,
  90n64, 134
Treaty on Stability, Coordination and
  Governance in the Economic and
  Monetary Union, 69, 149–151
Treaty on the European Community, 128
Treaty on the Functioning of the
  European Union, 90n64, 127, 171
Trichet, Jean-Claude, 190
Triffin, Robert, 30
trigger mechanism, 136
Troika, 103, 104, 131, 135, 136, 140,
  239
Turgot, 228
Turkey, 17, 104, 121, 126n17, 231
twin deficit/twin-deficit (*see* deficit)

U
U.S. (administration, balance of
  payments, dollar, economy,
  infrastructure, pension funds,
  universities), 9, 13, 22, 24–25, 26, 30,
  37, 39, 40, 46–47, 70, 73, 84, 95, 97,
  98, 100, 107, 121, 192, 213, 214, 220,
  232, 233

Printed and bound in the United States of America